Doing Business with

Ukraine

GLOBAL MARKET BRIEFINGS

Doing Business with Ukraine

THIRD EDITION

Consultant editor:
Dr Marat Terterov

Published in association with:
American Chamber of Commerce in Ukraine
and
Law Offices
BC Toms & Co

Publisher's note

Every possible effort has been made to ensure that the information contained in this book is accurate at the time of going to press, and the publishers and authors cannot accept responsibility for any errors or omissions, however caused. No responsibility for loss or damage occasioned to any person acting, or refraining from action, as a result of the material in this publication can be accepted by the editor, the publisher or any of the authors.

This third edition first published in Great Britain and the United States in 2005 by GMB Publishing.

120 Pentonville Road
London N1 9JN
United Kingdom
www.gmbpublishing.com

22883 Quicksilver Drive
Sterling VA 20166–2012
USA

ISBN 0 1–905050–00–3

British Library Cataloguing-in-Publication Data
A CIP record for this book is available from the British Library.

Typeset by Saxon Graphics Ltd, Derby
Printed and bound in Great Britain by Biddles Ltd., King's Lynn, Norfolk

Contents

PART FOUR: BUSINESS DEVELOPMENT: OPERATING AN ENTERPRISE

PART FIVE: AN INTRODUCTION TO DOING BUSINESS IN UKRAINE'S REGIONS

Foreword

HE Ihor Mitiukov, Ambassador of Ukraine

It gives me great pleasure, for many reasons, to write this foreword for the third edition of *Doing Business with Ukraine*. To begin with, Ukraine has not yet received the attention from abroad that it should have, and hopefully this book will help correct this. With 48 million inhabitants having a generally very high skill and educational level, the second largest territory in Europe and some of the richest agricultural land in the world, Ukraine should be a focus of investment interest. However, Ukraine has not yet caught the attention of the world's press, and there are too few foreign journalists assigned to Ukraine.

This is surprising, as Ukraine is now the 'tiger' of the European economy. In 2003, Ukraine had the fastest GDP growth in Europe at 9.4 per cent officially. (The real figure is probably much higher, and will continue to increase for this reason also as Ukraine moves to greater transparency in recording economic activity.) In 2004, the GDP figure will likely exceed 12 per cent. This rate of growth exceeds that of Ukraine's neighbours and, since 2000, has been comparable to that of China and India. Ukraine offers investors a location in Europe where manufacturing can be based at much lower cost than is possible in central or western Europe. Yet Ukraine is geographically close to western markets, with much of western Ukraine now bordering the enlarged European Union.

Economic growth in Ukraine is more broad-based, however, than just the increased manufacturing or the related development of raw materials. Every business, from the smallest retail shops to the largest privatized metallurgical industries, has for a decade become increasingly well organized, with greater reinvestment of profits each year. People forget how much had to be done upon Ukraine's independence in 1991 to create, essentially, not just a new democratic country, but also a new market economy, with a new method of organization for every business. During the 1990s, it was a challenge to stabilize an old economic system in disintegration while creating the basis for the new, market-based economy, with its own currency. The seeds of economic development sown then are now ripening.

This broad-based economic development is reflected in the retail sector, which grew at a rate of close to 20 per cent (officially) in 2003 and which should exceed this 20 per cent rate for 2004. Construction is another sector that is growing rapidly, and should continue to develop as Ukraine suffers from a shortage of housing compared to other Eastern European countries. For example, Kyiv now has a 20–40 per cent deficit in per capita housing space when compared to Bucharest, Prague, Budapest, Bratislava and Warsaw, which had more rapid growth in the 1990s. As per capita incomes in Ukraine increase, these disparities should narrow, although at current rates, it will take housing in Kyiv ten years to catch up with the per capita housing available in Prague, so there should be great opportunity for further building in Kyiv, as well as elsewhere in Ukraine, like Odesa, Dnipropetrovsk, Donetsk, Kharkiv and L'viv.

Ukraine has inspired this growth while maintaining fiscal responsibility. Ukraine's total state debt continues to decline as a percentage of GDP. As of August 2004, it was down to 27 per cent from 61 per cent in 1999. Ukraine's positive trade balance exceeded US$1 billion in 2003 and is expected to be over US$3 billion in 2004. The National Bank of Ukraine's net foreign exchange reserves have more than doubled so far in 2004, and Ukraine's Standard & Poor's (S&P) credit rating was recently increased to B+ and is expected to be increased further in the near future. These trends should lead to an increased valuation of the Ukrainian currency, which should make Ukraine an even more attractive market for foreign goods.

Thus, Ukraine should be increasingly a focus for foreign investment and trade, especially from Europe, and this book should be a useful guide for investors and others interested in doing business in Ukraine. On behalf of Ukraine, I wish to welcome you to our country.

List of Contributors

The **American Chamber of Commerce** in Ukraine (AmCham) is a non-governmental, non-profit business association based in Kyiv. AmCham serves two main purposes: first, to support Member Companies operating in Ukraine; second, to promote the entrance of new foreign investors into Ukraine. AmCham lobbies the Ukrainian government and its economic partners on matters of trade, investment and economic reform.

Today AmCham in Ukraine has over 370 Member organizations. Member companies represent a majority of the foreign direct investment in Ukraine. Due to the open nature of its Membership, AmCham represents the interests of the entire internationally oriented investment community operating in Ukraine, helping to ensure its success.

AmCham is funded entirely by membership dues, and has no political or economic ties or constraints. It is governed by a Board of Directors which is elected by its Members. AmCham has 16 committees, which provide Members with the opportunity to actively and directly participate in defining, developing, discussing and resolving issues affecting the operations of their businesses and organizations in Ukraine.

AmCham advocates free enterprise, and encourages reform aimed at the development of an equitable and transparent business environment in Ukraine. For more information about AmCham and its activities, please visit the AmCham website at www.amcham.ua.

BC Toms & Co is one of the largest and most prominent law firms in Ukraine. In 1991, it was the first Western law firm to establish an office in Ukraine, and its Kyiv office is ranked as one of the leading Ukrainian law firms by the European Legal 500, the principal European legal directory, and by Yuridicheskaya Practica (the leading Ukrainian law newspaper that conducts an annual survey of opinion of the leading companies and law firms in Ukraine on Ukrainian law firms).

The firm has a general corporate and litigation practice, and is particularly known for major transactions that it has handled in the real estate, construction, energy and financial sectors, among other areas. It has always had a leading tax planning department and has one of the most successful Ukrainian litigation practices. Its clients include major multinational companies and other investors in Ukraine, as well as leading global law firms.

BC Toms & Co was founded by **B C Toms**, who was previously a partner of a major multinational law firm, is a graduate of Yale Law School (JD, 1975; editor of the *Yale Law Journal*), and studied law at Magdalene College, Cambridge University (Law Tripos I, 1972–73). His undergraduate studies were at Washington and Lee University (BA, magna cum laude, 1971; Phi Beta Kappa) and the Institut d'Etudes Politiques de Paris (Soviet Studies 1969–70). Mr Toms, a principal founder of the British-Ukrainian Chamber of Commerce, is cited in Yuridicheskaya Practica as one of the leading lawyers in Ukraine.

The Firm is the principal author of *Doing Business with Ukraine*, as well as a forthcoming book, *The Law of Ukraine*, the first general treatise on the subject. Further information can be found on its website at www.bctoms.net or by contacting its Kyiv or London offices at the addresses cited in Appendix 1.

Taras Dumych is a corporate and real estate law specialist and graduate of the Lviv State University Law School (LLB, 1999), as well as the London Guildhall University Department of Law (LLM in International and Comparative Business Law, with Merit, 2002; Chevening Fellow). He is a member of the Bar of Ukraine, admitted in 1999.

Dmytro Korbut is a litigation and privatization specialist. He is a graduate of the Kyiv National University of Economics' International Economics and Law Department (LLB, 1997; LLM, 1998), as well as the Nottingham University Law School (LLM, 2002), and is a member of the Bar of Ukraine, admitted in 1998.

Svitlana Kheda is an employment law specialist admitted to the Bar of Ukraine in 1998 and a graduate of the Kyiv Taras Shevchenko University Law School (LLB, 1998; LLM, 1999).

Olga Prokopovych is an intellectual property specialist and a graduate of the Kyiv Taras Shevchenko University Law School (LLB, 1999; LLM, 2000), as well as the University of Missouri, St. Louis (MPPA, 2002; Muskie Fellow). She was admitted to the Bar of Ukraine in 2000.

Tina Radchenko is an energy law specialist and a graduate of the Donetsk State University (LLB, 2000). She is a member of the Bar of Ukraine.

Zoya Mylovanova is a tax law specialist, a member of the Bar of Ukraine, and a graduate of the Kyiv National Economic University (BA in Law, 2000; MA in Business Law, 2001), as well as the Northwestern University School of Law (LLM with honours, 2003; Muskie Fellow).

Igor Posypayko is a tax and leasing law specialist, a member of the Bar of Ukraine, and a graduate of the Kyiv Shevchenko University, Institute of International Relations (BA, 2001; MA in Law, 2002) and the University of Edinburgh (LLM with specialization in Tax Law, 2003; Chevening Fellow).

Institute for Reform: Advancing Economic Freedom. The Institute for Reform is Ukraine's leading non-governmental economic think tank. A national research and educational organization, we are dedicated to creating a free and open market in Ukraine. Since 1997, we have been working to foster dialogue at every level of government about the need for economic reform. Through our independent thought, leadership and outreach, we seek to lower taxes, keep government out of business, and bring transparency to regulatory processes. We support a fair marketplace where businesses of all sizes can compete equally. We believe an economy that is attractive to Western investors will bring new jobs and money to Ukraine.

The **International Finance Corporation** (IFC) is a member of the World Bank Group and is the world's largest multilateral investor in emerging markets. Since its founding in 1956, IFC has committed more than USD37 billion of its own funds and has arranged USD22 billion in syndications for 2,990 companies in 140 developing countries. IFC's worldwide committed portfolio as of FY03 was USD16.8 billion for its own account and USD6.6 billion held for participants in loan syndications. IFC finances private sector investments in emerging markets, mobilizes capital in the international financial markets, and provides technical assistance and advice to governments and businesses.

Ukraine became a member of IFC in 1994. It has five offices in Ukraine, with ninety local staff and an established technical assistance network. IFC is providing financing for investment projects with a USD238 million total cost, USD80 million of which are from IFC's own account. Priority areas are agribusiness, manufacturing and services, telecommunications and IT, and the financial sector.

In 2002, IFC launched the 'Ukraine Corporate Development Project' to promote the development of the private sector in Ukraine by introducing international best practices and advising enterprises, government agencies and educational institutions on corporate governance, financial management, and financing/investment strategies. To this end, IFC provides technical assistance to enterprises, educational institutions and government agencies. The aim of the project is to improve corporate culture, enhance company efficiency, and, as a result, create better conditions for investment in Ukraine.

Closed Joint-Stock Investment Company 'ITT-Invest' (CJSIC 'ITT-Invest') was founded in 1995 with the purpose of investment activities, transactions in security markets and asset management. In December 1995 the Ministry of Finance of Ukraine gave permission to CJSIC 'ITT-Invest' to perform activities related to the issue and turnover of securities, registered under No. 822 of 8 December 1995. Thus, the Company obtained the status of a securities trader and started its activities in the security market as a professional participant. CJSIC 'ITT-Invest' Mutual Fund was set up at the end of 1995 in compliance with the decision of the Meeting of Founders. In January 1996, the Company was authorized by the State Property Fund of Ukraine to perform commercial transactions with privatization papers and acquired the status of an investment company. In July 1996, the investment company established another Mutual Fund, 'ITT' CJSIC 'ITT-Invest', which is a branch of the Company. The investment company 'ITT-Invest' is managed by a team of highly educated and energetic specialists, who have worked fruitfully on the fund market of Ukraine since its creation. A team of skilled professionals in security transactions, privatization, shareholding of enterprises, and placing of new issues of securities composes the intellectual potential of the Company.

The Company is a member of the American Chamber of Commerce in Ukraine (AmCham), the OTC trading system (PFTS), the Ukrainian Association of Investment Business (UAIB), the

Ukrainian Stock Exchange (UFB), the Ukrainian Inter-bank Currency Exchange (UIBCE) and Kyiv International Stock Exchange (KISE). The Company is a shareholder of the National Depositary and Interregional Fund Union.

Within a short period of time 'ITT-Invest' has gained the reputation of a reliable professional partner in the securities market of Ukraine. 'ITT-Invest' Company performs direct management of more than 10 enterprises working in different branches of industry. At the present time 'ITT-Invest' has a stable position in the securities market and its name is on the list of Stock Exchanges, the Securities and Stock Market State Commission, and other trade and analytical institutions which are working in the securities market of Ukraine.

KPMG Ukraine has had a representation in Ukraine since 1992 and has been a wholly owned Ukrainian legal entity since 1997. Our predominantly Ukrainian staff number in excess of 100, with foreign national staff from the USA, the UK, the Netherlands and Albania. KPMG's objective in Ukraine is to use KPMG's global intellectual capital with the experience of Ukrainian professionals to assist leading Ukrainian companies and KPMG's multinational clients to achieve their business aims. The principal service lines of KPMG Ukraine include Assurance, Tax and Legal, Accounting, and Business Advisory Services. KPMG Ukraine's Tax and Legal professionals have experience in solving all types of business issues, but an overview of services includes: providing corporate and individual tax compliance services; reviewing and structuring transactions to reduce risk and enhance tax savings; representing clients in tax and legal proceedings; assisting foreign investors regarding formulating business strategies, setting up or acquiring companies, due diligence assignments, and documenting agreements; and providing legal opinions and advice and practical business approaches regarding Ukrainian corporate law, property law, banking, insurance and finance law, labour law, environmental law, and competition law.

David R Marples is professor of history at the University of Alberta, and the director of the Stasiuk Programme on Contemporary Ukraine, Canadian Institute of Ukrainian Studies. He is author of nine books, the most recent of which is *Motherland: Russia in the 20th Century* (Longman, 2002), and has been published very widely in scholarly journals. He is Vice-President of the Association for the Study of Nationalities (New York) and a member of the editorial boards of journals, *Slavic Review*, *Nationalities Papers*, *Eurasian Geography and Economics*, and the *Journal of Ukrainian Studies*. In 2003, he received the highest research award at the University of Alberta, the J Gordon Kaplan Award for Excellence in Research.

Miratech is an IT service and consulting corporation with the following businesses: software engineering services, BPO & IT enabled services, and software solutions. Software engineering services contain outsourcing, software team building, bespoke project development, and project management. BPO & IT enabled services are represented by data entry, IT site management, IT consulting, and legacy systems maintenance. Software solutions include computer telephony & call centres, ERP & CRM systems, system integration, and others. Miratech commits to deliver a high quality of service and is on the way to become a CMM Level 5 company; now its development centres are SW CMM Level 3 and ISO 9001:2000 certified. Serving clients worldwide, Miratech develops client support and has sales offices in EU and North American countries.

Dr Nikolay Royenko graduated from Moscow Phisiko-Technical Institute, Moscow, Russia in 1980. His specialty was Applied Mathematics. He also has a Ph.D in Computer Science (1984). He is President of Miratech Corporation, Kiev, Ukraine. In 2004 he was elected president of the association 'IT Ukraine'.

Munk, Andersen & Feilberg is a European business developer, specializing in the development and management of turnkey projects in Eastern Europe and the CIS. The company assists European production companies in implementing their internationalization strategies by providing legal and practical assistance. Munk, Andersen & Feilberg's mission is to make it simple, fast, and safe for production companies to enter emerging markets in Eastern Europe and the CIS, and to make it possible to utilize the opportunities for cost-efficient production. Major services offered are company registration, obtaining production approvals and permits, acquisition and renovation of industrial buildings, recruitment of key personnel, and coordination with local authorities.

Munk, Andersen & Feilberg has a branch office in Lviv, in Western Ukraine. Further information about the company, its services, and specific business possibilities in Eastern Europe can be found on www.mafcon.dk.

Raiffeisenbank Ukraine (RBUA) is a wholly-owned subsidiary of one of the largest banking groups in Central and Western Europe, Raiffeisen Austria, with more than 500 branches and more than 14,000 highly qualified employees. The central institution of the Group and one of the RBUA's shareholders, Raiffeisen Zentralbank Östereich Aktiengesellschaft (RZB-Austria), Vienna, initiated the implementation of a comprehensive Eastern-European Strategy during the 1980s. The first step was carried out in 1987, by establishing a subsidiary in Hungary (now Raiffeisenbank Rt.). Currently RZB-Austria operates subsidiary banks in Poland, Slovakia, Czech Republic, Russia, Croatia, Hungary, Bulgaria, Romania, Yugoslavia, Bosnia and Herzegovina, and Belorussia.

In 1994 RZB opened its representative office in Ukraine. In March 1998, the subsidiary bank, Raiffeisenbank Ukraine, was established. RBUA is a fully-licensed commercial bank with the right to offer to its corporate and individual clients a full range of banking products. At present, RBUA is in the top ten of Ukrainian banks in terms of assets, capital and loan portfolio.

At the time of writing, **Mykhaylo Kuzmin** was the Senior Risk Management Expert at Raiffeisenbank Ukraine.

Softjourn, Inc., a California-based company, is a network of IT services companies from Ukraine, whose areas of specialization include retail and distribution, health services, financial payment systems, image and data compression, billing systems, security and Web design. Softjourn is focused on moving companies as painlessly as possible to working with their own offshore teams by eliminating the typical difficulties associated with offshore: knowledge transfer, communications, vested interest and 'control' of a remote team. Through Softjourn's ATM.ua service, companies can have their own Virtual Operations Development Centers established in Ukraine.

Emmy B Gengler is in her eighth year working in Ukraine and has more than 15 years' experience in information technology solution development. In 2001, along with a partner, she started Softjourn, an IT services company focused on assisting companies in eliminating the distinction between in-house and offshore software development so that they can effectively take advantage of the cost savings associated with offshore. Ms Gengler has published papers on Ukraine and the development of its software exports market. She has also spoken at conferences in New York City, Washington DC and London on Ukraine and its potential. Ms Gengler was a three-term board member of the American Chamber of Commerce in Ukraine, including two years as Treasurer. For three years Ms Gengler also served as Chair of the IT committee of the chamber. Currently she is participating in the organizational committee responsible for coordinating Gartner Group's assessment of Ukraine and its software exports market.

Prior to founding Softjourn, Ms Gengler spent four years as President and CEO of a venture-backed IT and business consulting company based in Kyiv (Kiev), Ukraine. During her tenure, partnership agreements were signed with such companies as Oracle, Scala and Vimas Technologies (a Ukrainian software vendor). Implementation teams were established for Enterprise Resource Planning (ERP) systems in a very young IT consulting market. Prior to moving to Ukraine, Ms Gengler lived in Irkutsk, Russia, filling the role of project manager for a US independent software vendor (Arksys), which was developing a clearinghouse system for the Central Bank of Russia. The project included managing globally distributed software developers in Little Rock, Arkansas and in Irkutsk, Russia, coordinating hardware and cryptography issues with IBM, the systems integrators on the project, Kapti (a UK-based company), which provided the General Ledger application, and Andrews, which provided the VSAT solution.

She also has software development experience, as an employee and a consultant at such companies as Visa International, Johnson & Johnson, Pillsbury Corporation, Prudential Insurance and Bank One. Ms Gengler holds a Bachelor's degree in Management Information Systems from the University of Wisconsin and an MBA in International Business from the Monterey Institute of International Studies. She currently sits on the board of a non-profit organization in Northern California and is active on the Community Emergency Response Team (CERT) in Fremont, California.

TECHINVEST is a Ukrainian-registered technology-focused venture capital firm specializing in investments into and development of Ukrainian export-oriented high-tech companies and projects. TECHINVEST was formed in March 2004 as a result of the re-organization of AVentures Group. All corporate privileges, rights and liabilities in several Aventures' venture investments in export-oriented high-tech projects done during 2002–2004 were transferred to TECHINVEST. TECHINVEST serves as investor/co-investor in Ukrainian export-oriented technology companies and projects where its high-tech industry expertise and relationships can add significant value post-investment. TECHINVEST also provides the following services:

- business incubation of technology companies and technologies commercialization in international markets;
- international marketing, including building entry channels to international markets for Ukrainian technology companies;
- Ukrainian high-tech market research and analysis;
- investment management and consulting;
- fundraising for ventures investment funds/projects.

During September and November 2003, experts of AVentures/TECHINVEST jointly with Market-Visio (Gartner Group) conducted the first internationally recognized Research of the Ukrainian IT-export industry. Over 60 companies were interviewed during the research. All rights to the research (http://research.tech-invest.com.ua) of the Ukrainian export IT industry conducted jointly with Market-Visio belong to TECHINVEST as well.

In February 2003, AVentures/TECHINVEST initiated and provided funding for the establishment of the Ukrainian Software Consortium (USC). USC is a software development group with a wide range of competencies and strong experience in serving international businesses. In February 2004, USC opened its representative office in the USA, which is located in Menlo Park, Silicon Valley. This office was established as a joint venture between TECHINVEST and its US partner, IBA Ventures (www.ibaventures.com). The joint venture is focused on providing IT services, IT products and other innovative technologies to IT outsourcing and high-tech markets in the USA. TECHINVEST has formed a portfolio of selected innovative technologies. All of the selected technologies have strong potential for commercialization and solid IP rights. TECHINVEST has exclusivity agreements with the owners of the selected technologies for the commercialization of their technologies in international markets.

Currently TECHINVEST is setting up a USD50 million Ukrainian Technology Fund. Among the Fund's sponsors are the National Space Agency of Ukraine, National Academy of Sciences of Ukraine, and State Export-Import Bank of Ukraine. The Fund will seek to invest in high-tech innovation companies across a diversified spectrum of the high-tech sector in Ukraine. The Fund will focus on an expansion stage of development of dynamically growing IT and telecoms-related companies, as well as innovative technology companies of the transportation industry, that target local customers and that have potential to become market leaders.

For seven years, **Irina Strizhak** worked as a consultant and team leader on the International Finance Corporation's (IFC) technical assistance projects: the USAID-funded Small-Scale Privatization Project and the Unfinished Construction Privatization Project, and the Post-Privatization and Business Support Project and the Collective Farm Reorganization and Land Privatization Programme, funded by the British Know-How Fund. Strizhak has worked with all levels of government in Ukraine throughout the country. She has an MBA from the International Scientific-Technical University, and a BA in Agricultural Economy from the Ukrainian Agricultural Academy.

The Ukrainian Centre for Economic and Legal Analysis (UCELA) was established in Kiev in 2003. The Centre was formed to provide high-quality research and expertise on economic policy and business issues to both the public and private sectors in Ukraine. Key aspects of the Centre's expertise are as follows:

- Ukraine's accession to the European Union and to the World Trade Organization;
- economic, social and institutional reforms at national and regional levels;
- industrial restructuring and corporate governance;
- sectoral reviews ranging across primary, manufacturing, agriculture and service sectors of Ukraine;
- energy policies of Ukraine and FSU countries based on the best international practices and concepts.

UCELA comprises a dozen or so young economists with Western educational backgrounds who have in-depth experience of Ukraine's governmental bodies, of the emerging private sector and of international projects. The President of the Centre, **Sergiy Maslichenko**, has a PhD from Kiev National Economic University and carried out post-doctoral research at Oxford University in 2002/2003 as an FCO Chevening Scholar. From 1999 to 2002, he was an adviser to the Parliamentary Budget Committee and to the Deputy Prime Minister for Energy.

UCELA is well connected with a broad range of Ukrainian government bodies. Centre members are currently working with the Ministry of Economy and European Integration, the Ministry of Finance, the Ministry of Fuel and Energy, the State Committee on Statistics, the State Committee on Regulatory Policy and Entrepreneurship, the State Committee on the Stock Exchange and Financial Markets, and others. The Centre has worked with a number of international consulting firms.

The **US–Ukraine Foundation** is a not-for-profit, non-governmental organization established in 1991 to facilitate democratic development, encourage free market reform and enhance human rights in Ukraine. The Foundation creates and sustains channels of communication between the United States and Ukraine, in order to build peace and prosperity through an exchange of information. The Foundation is dedicated to strengthening the mutual objectives of both nations while advancing Ukraine as a cornerstone of regional stability and as a full partner in the community of nations. The Foundation is headquartered in Washington, DC and has six offices in Ukraine – in Kyiv, Cherkasy, Donetsk, Kharkiv, Kherson and Lviv. The Foundation's largest project in operation from 1997 to 2005 is the US–Ukraine Community Partnerships Project for Local Government Training and Education, a US Agency for International Development-funded programme.

Alica Henson brings several years' experience working with and in Ukraine. Having spent over two and a half years working in Ukraine for an economic reform NGO and the International Finance Corporation's Small-Scale Privatisation Project (funded by USAID) in the early 1990s, Henson then pursued an MSc in Development Studies at the University of London. She also worked as an East Europe and CIS analyst-editor at Oxford Analytica, a UK consulting firm which publishes economic and political analyses of emerging market regions. Henson joined the US–Ukraine Foundation's Community Partnerships Project for Local Government Training and Education in 1999 and is currently the Deputy Project Director in Ukraine. Alica Henson left the US–Ukraine Foundation during the summer of 2004 and is presently studying law in London. She can be contacted by email on Henson_RA@hotmail.com.

Since 1991, **Brad Bunt** has worked as Director of the Kilgore College Small Business Development Center in Longview, Texas. He has counselled hundreds of businesses on start-up, business planning and a host of small business related topics, earning him classification as a Certified Business Specialist from the Association of Small Business Development Centers. Bunt has also created the highly successful seminar series, 'Starting & Operating a Business in East Texas', which has instructed over 2,200 individuals on the complexities of starting a small business. In addition to his work in Texas for the Small Business Development Center network, he has travelled extensively in Ukraine, working with many cities on establishing Small Business Development Centers and on many economic development issues, having founded Ukraine's first SBDC in the city of Romny, Sumy Oblast. Brad has also owned and operated many small businesses and currently is the President/CEO of Rubicon Investments, Inc.

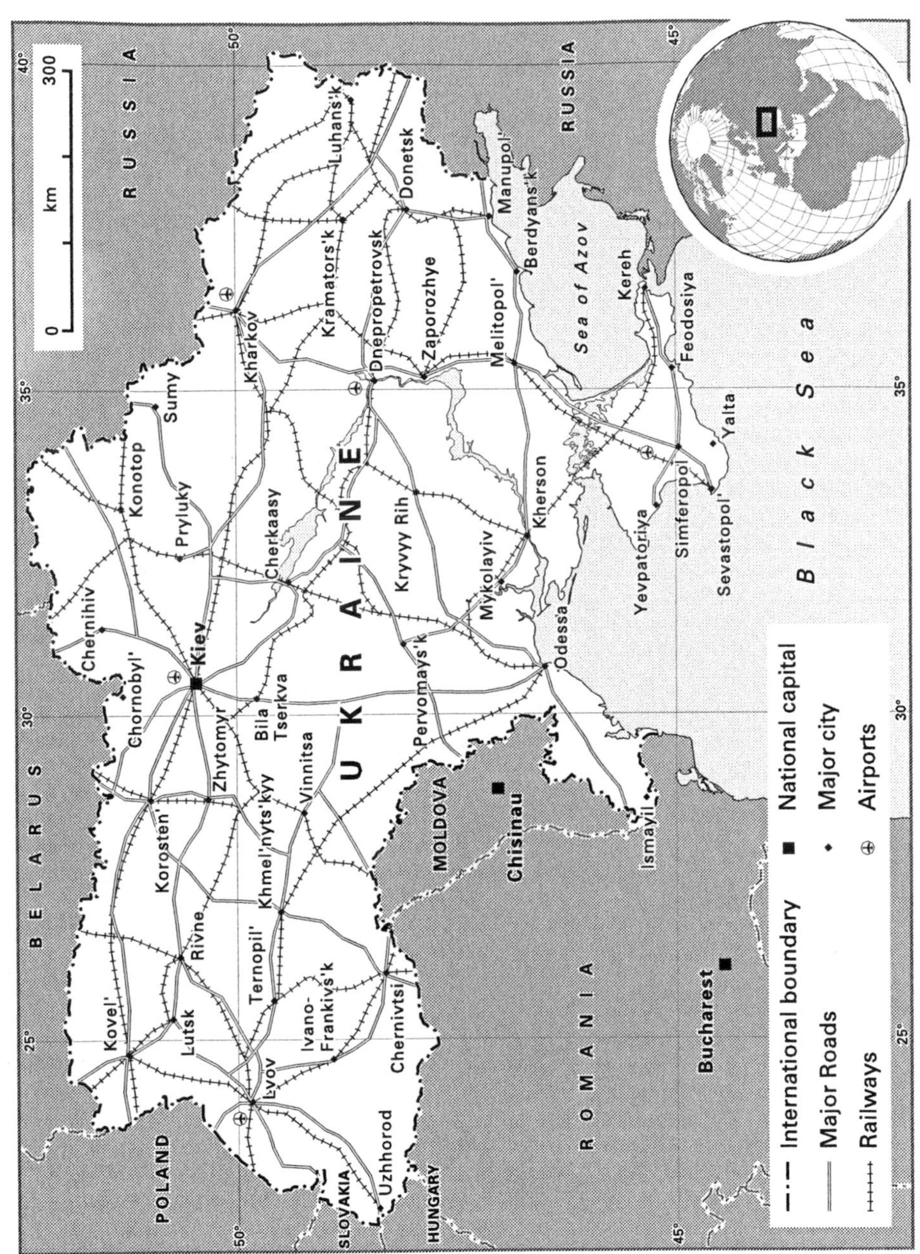

Map 1: Major rail and road networks in Ukraine

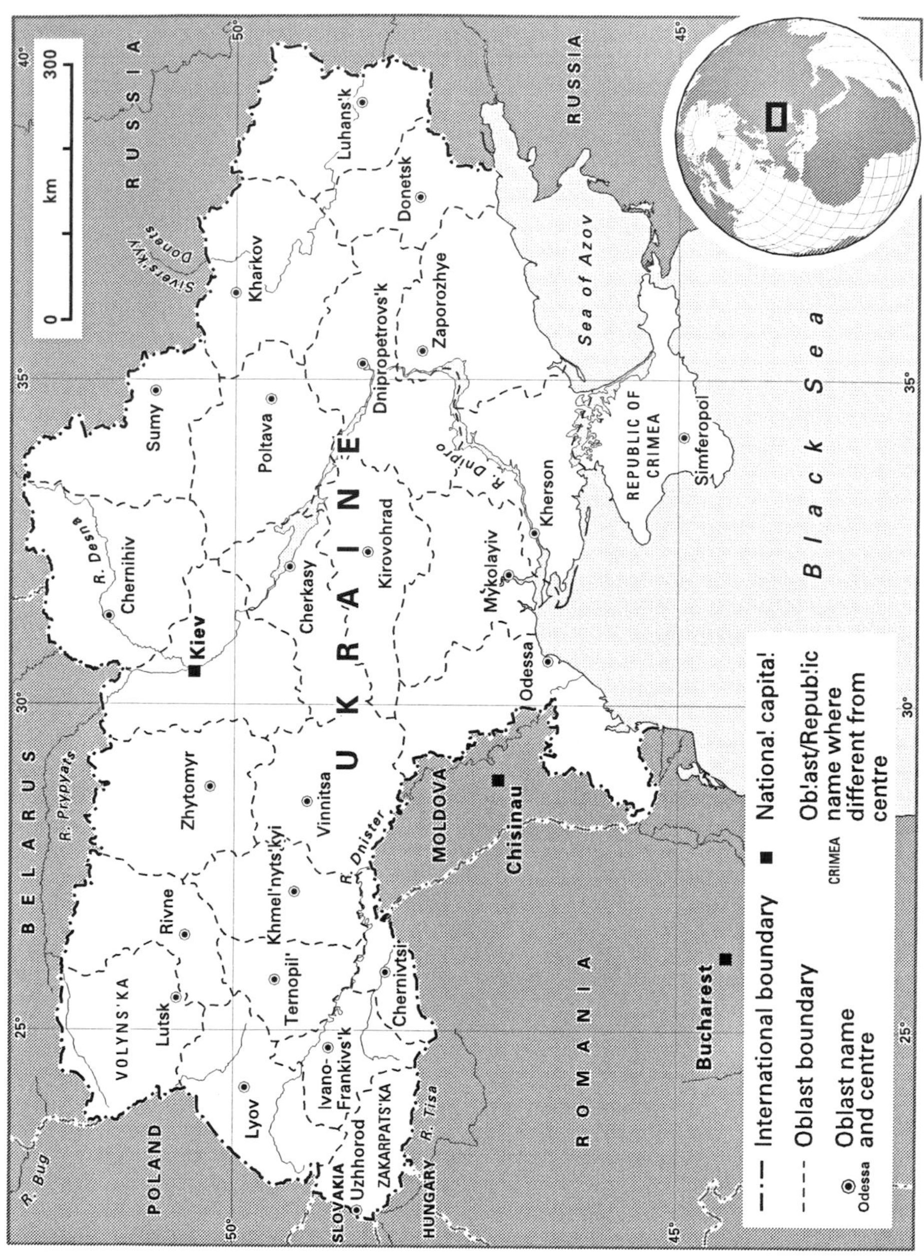

Map 2: National boundaries and neighbouring states

Map 3: Kiev and surrounding districts

Introduction

Dr Marat Terterov

The 13 years that Ukraine has spent as a sovereign state, independent of the Soviet Union, or for that matter of Poland, Austria-Hungary and other political powers that have stymied the country's autonomy, have been accompanied by a mixed experience of highs and lows within the context of the country's transition to a market economy and democratic society. Ukraine's statehood most certainly has deep traditions, tracing back to the reign of Volodymyr the Great and the emergence of Christianity in Kiev during the late 10th and early 11th centuries AD. Indeed, while city-states such as Kiev, Muscovy (Moscow) and Novgorod vied for supremacy as the dominant Slavic kingdom, a number of historians claim that the medieval Kievan Rus state (present-day Kiev, Ukraine's capital) is not only the forerunner of modern Ukraine, but is likewise the source of the Russian nation. However, it is in the shadows of its more illustrious Slavic sister-state, Russia, that Ukraine has dwelt for much of its national history – both under the regimes of the Russian Tsars of the 18th and 19th centuries, as well as Soviet Russia in the annals of more recent history. While the western regions of the country, with their administrative and cultural capital centred around the city of L'viv, have always been both independence-oriented and European in outlook, it is only since the collapse of the Soviet Union that an independent Ukraine appears to be consolidating its political identity outside of the Russian shadow.

It should be noted that there has already been a historic precedent of a modern, independent Ukrainian state existing prior to the one that emerged in August 1991, since the Ukrainian National Republic had been promulgated in L'viv shortly after the Bolshevik Revolution and functioned until the early 1920s, when it was incorporated into the newly formed USSR. The precedent of an independent Ukraine, and the never-ending intellectual and political dissidence that continued to operate in the country up until the introduction of President Gorbachev's reforms of the mid-1980s, ensured that the realization of Ukraine's independence was greeted with euphoria by various segments of the population. Furthermore, given Ukraine's vast diaspora communities in North America, Europe and other economically advanced regions, the re-emergence of Ukraine's independence in the early 1990s rapidly received the full backing of political endorsement in the West. Unlike the case of some former Soviet republics, the international community immediately recognized Ukraine's sovereignty, and a plethora of donor-funded technical assistance projects developed rapidly in order to assist the Ukrainian government in creating modern political and economic institutions commensurate with the rest of Europe.

However, while early optimism seemed to abound, instead of the expected pro-democracy and market economy gains, a typical post-Soviet political economy consolidated. As the central pillars of the Soviet state were formally disbanded, the national government in Ukraine found itself no longer able to perform its basic duties with regard to the population. Government services in many sectors – public works, utilities, health care, education, pensions, law and order, housing – either faded owing to dwindling resources or were, at best, supplied on an ad hoc basis. Corruption in the state bureaucracy rapidly accelerated and, as the state was no longer able to provide for a law-abiding society, organized crime became highly influential in business life in many profitable sectors. The state-led economy ground to a halt, since enterprise employees were no longer receiving their wages and in many cases were compelled literally to rob their own enterprises of their assets to ensure at least some form of primitive remuneration. Economic crisis fuelled hyperinflation, which could only be relieved by a proper standby credit facility from the international financial institutions. Furthermore, as Ukraine's unorthodox market capitalism expanded during the mid-1990s, the country's social and economic development was further undermined by some Ukrainian government officials amassing personal – billion dollar – fortunes by laundering public funds into their offshore bank accounts. Although the West continued to support an independent Ukraine throughout the decade, the country's appalling record, with corrupt officialdom, crony-capitalism and hesitation to pursue comprehensive economic reforms, made it difficult for Western policy-makers to legitimize further financial aid to Kiev. This situation had the effect of undermining the overall confidence in the country's increasingly fragile independence, and did little to create a suitable environment to attract much-needed foreign investment.

Whilst undoubtedly the 1990s have been testing times for policy-makers in Kiev, the question of Ukraine's sustained independence and the development of its consolidated role in an expansive Europe remains of great significance to the international political and business community. Policy-makers in London and Washington continue to view Ukraine as a strategic state from a geo-political angle, a south-western buffer to Russia where the ideals of a Western-style democracy and market economy need to develop inexorably in order to offset any lingering remains of the 'old regime'. For Brussels, a staunch proponent of a new pan-Europeanism, Ukraine is somewhere in the second, or perhaps third, tier of accession states, in line with a policy of promoting a broader Union of European states that may just be realized in our lifetimes. Although Ukraine's political economy of the 1990s is hardly compatible with the strategic vision held for Ukraine by either Brussels or the trans-Atlantic alliance, it is clear from the substantial levels of foreign aid still being channelled into Kiev that both are looking to continue supporting Ukraine's independence into the foreseeable future.

What bearing does this situation have for foreign businesses eyeing the Ukrainian market as a potential destination for their investment? There are two angles from which to consider this question. The first is from that of policy. Foreign investors with an interest in Ukraine should take comfort from the fact that the Ukrainian government is officially committed to working with them to improve the country's business climate and generally support the policy recommendations that it receives from its foreign donors. This is especially the case with regard to economic liberalization, which has been ongoing in Ukraine since the mid-1990s. To this effect, and as the reader will find by consulting the various chapters of this book, the Ukrainian government has achieved a great deal in the way of drafting a modern legal system which is – theoretically –sufficient to cater to foreign business practices. For much of the 1990s, the government of Ukraine has been committed to building a market-based economic system by pushing on with economic reform, including privatization, tight and well-managed fiscal and monetary policies, liberalization of trade restrictions, currency convertibility and rationalization and modernization of banking and finance. Furthermore, the government has sought to accord foreign investors various incentives, such as tax concessions, legal protection for their investment in the country and removal of any potentially restrictive business practices favouring domestic capital at the expense of foreign investment.

Although Ukraine's economy performed poorly for most of the 1990s, since 2000 the country has witnessed a vastly improved economic performance. In that year the economy grew by around 6 per cent of GDP and annual growth figures have continued to be impressive year after year (between 5 and 10 per cent of GDP annually from 2000 to 2003 inclusive). In a complete reversal to much of the previous decade, since 2000 Ukraine has seen the creation of an abundance of new jobs in various sectors of the economy, whilst wages and pensions arrears and monetary instability have become largely a thing of the past. Ukraine's initial economic recovery was widely associated with the premiership of Viktor Yushchenko, the former Central Bank governor, who was prime minister of the country from early 2000 until April 2001.[1] Yushchenko, around whom the hopes of many Ukrainian liberals and many pro-Ukraine Western policy-makers were harnessed, proved to be a dogged reformer, tightening economic management further, fighting corruption and generally creating the widespread impression that an efficient government had finally arrived in Ukraine. Furthermore, like at no other time during the previous decade, Ukraine's government under Yushchenko widely came to be seen as both pro-Western (although the country continued to maintain very close political and economic ties with Russia) and investor friendly (although to the chagrin of some of the country's oligarchs). Ukraine's successor governments have continued to ride the wave of economic growth which commenced in the country under the charismatic Yushchenko, as well as continuing to espouse investor-friendly policy rhetoric.

However, the fact that foreign investment levels in Ukraine have been amongst the lowest in Eastern Europe and the former Soviet Union is itself a reflection of the second angle from which to consider our original question, the level of practicality. While the government of Ukraine – as of November 2002 managed by Victor Yanukovich – has continued to promote the country to foreign investors, Ukraine's overall underdevelopment as an institutionally sound market economy has undermined the government's objectives. Although the levels of foreign direct investment (FDI)

[1] Although Yushchenko was prime minister of Ukraine through year 2000 and until April 2001, at the time of writing Leonid Kuchma remains president of Ukraine (Kuchma, the country's second president, has been in power since 1994). Ukraine's political system is largely a presidential – as opposed to a parliamentary – one and the president holds the dominant political power in the country. The prime minister is, in effect, the chief executive of the cabinet of ministers and reports to the president.

in Ukraine have been increasing since the economic recovery of 2000, during the first half of 2002 FDI in Ukraine was just USD126 per capita, compared to USD2,233 per capita in the Czech Republic and USD2,059 in Hungary. Ukraine's new, post-Soviet legal system may have been drafted by some of the finest foreign and domestic lawyers available, but laws can take generations to enter the psyche of the populace, whilst their enforcement has to be implemented by a strong, independent judicial arm of the state. Ukraine's judiciary can hardly be described as either strong or independent, leaving the legal regime to operate without any consistent culture of effective implementation. Wage levels in the state bureaucracy remain at near Third World levels, further undermining the capacity of government officials to enforce the law, or to punish offenders. Low wages in both the public and private sectors, and their incongruence to the cost of living in the official economy, has left the country largely devoid of a middle class, while the intelligentsia remains without any real political power. Ukraine's largely unaccountable business oligarchs, despite experiencing a sterner government under Yushchenko, continue to dominate both economic and political life. With the exception of some caveats, their businesses remain conducted in a protectionist and non-transparent manner, creating the impression of a highly uneven playing field for other would-be investors. The result is a cumbersome and judicially uncertain business climate, where foreign investment has been selective and pragmatic, as opposed to the largely investor-friendly business climate found in a good number of Eastern Europe's EU accession states.[2]

Foreign investors interested in Ukraine, however, should not be disheartened by some of the practical irregularities that arise in Ukraine's non-institutional business environment. While the country must surely be classified as an emerging, or an alternative, market from a foreign investment perspective, Ukraine is, for the most part, a highly stable country, with an underdeveloped, albeit rapidly growing, consumer market. Many sectors of Ukraine's economy should most definitely be seen as prospective from a foreign investment angle, and include some of the country's mainstay industries such as shipping, mining, agriculture and the food sector, metallurgy,

[2] Indeed, the most active foreign investors in Ukraine during recent years have been those coming from Russia. Russian investors in Ukraine, who see the country as their own 'backyard', have themselves often been (Russian) oligarchs and their financial-industrial groups are well acquainted with the type of business environment prevalent in Ukraine.

wood processing, aviation and industrial manufacturing. One should also add to the list of prospective sectors fast-growing industries such as telecommunications, information technology, computer software, tobacco, retailing and the consumer goods sector, and increasingly, tourism and leisure (particularly in the coastal towns of the Black Sea). While it is highly recommended that foreign investors take into consideration that the rules of the game for business in Ukraine, like in other emerging markets, may have their own cultural specifics, the country offers vast opportunities to foreign business. A highly practical geographic position between Russia, Turkey and the Eastern European EU accession states, inexpensive and high-quality human capital, a reasonable transport infrastructure, cheap energy and many abundant raw materials, and a pro-business government seeking to attract value added investment all reflect the clear opportunities that this country offers.

In this volume, now in its third edition, we have sought to bring together impressions of Ukrainian business from a great diversity of international and Ukrainian academics, lawyers, accountants, bankers, businessmen, consultants, research institutes and non-government organizations into one encompassing publication. Their efforts bring together no fewer than 43 separate chapters which comprise this volume, divided into five separate sections.

In Part One, we set out to give an overall background to Ukraine's business environment, where seven different authors discuss topics including political and economic overviews, perspectives on the country's foreign investment climate, banking and finance, privatization, corporate governance and small enterprises. In Part Two, we look at the different sectors of Ukraine's economy from a business opportunities perspective. In this section of the book, building on the previous edition of the publication, we take an in-depth look at some of Ukraine's traditional mainstay industries such as metallurgy, textiles and wood processing, as well as some of the more dynamic industries that have emerged in the country during the transition years of the past decade. The latter group particularly focuses on high-growth sectors such as mobile telecommunications, information technology and computer software. We also take an in-depth look at the legal regimes regulating Ukraine's energy sector, including oil, gas and electricity.

In Part Three we discuss the taxation and legal environment prevailing in the country, giving the reader a detailed overview of Ukrainian company registration and incorporation, banking and securities market law, as well as the taxation system. Part Four gives attention to other salient concepts relevant to Ukrainian business – both from a legal and operational perspective. From the former perspective our authors discuss the legal aspects to property transactions in Ukraine, dispute resolution, the labour code and intellectual property. From the latter perspective we have included special interest chapters on 'Ukraine specific' features of business culture that investors should be aware of when seeking to establish themselves in the country's marketplace, import and export procedures, and an overview of Ukraine as a new destination for international business. Finally, in Part Five, we again turn to a discussion of the emerging business opportunities that lie in the country beyond its capital city, Kiev – a look at the investment environment in Ukraine's regions. On top of the general discussions evaluating the country's regional investment climate, we also focus specific attention on seven regions of the country, some of which have rarely figured in publications of this type in the past. The book is finished off with a both rare and timely discussion on Ukraine's major domestic business conglomerates, which is the first time we have had the opportunity to incorporate such material into our publications on the countries of Eastern Europe and the former Soviet Union.

Marat Terterov
Oxford, England
January 2004

Part One

Background to the Market

1.1

Ukraine – A Country Profile

Dr David Marples, University of Alberta

Background

Ukraine became an independent state in two stages in 1991: first with a declaration of independence by its Supreme Soviet (parliament) on 24 August 1991, following the failure of the attempted coup in Moscow; and second, with a national referendum on 1 December 1991, which saw over 90 per cent of the electorate support the declaration. Simultaneously, the electorate backed the chairman of the Supreme Soviet, Leonid Kravchuk, a former Communist Party Secretary for Ideology, as the country's first president in a national election. Kravchuk won over 57 per cent of the vote on the first ballot. Initially, it was unclear whether the Russian Federation under Boris Yeltsin would accept Ukraine within the borders that had been established during and after the Second World War. However, on 8 December 1991, Kravchuk and Yeltsin, together with the leader of the Belarusian parliament, Stanislau Shushkevich, signed an agreement in the Brest region of Belarus to establish a loose federation, the Commonwealth of Independent States, thus signalling the end of the Soviet Union.

Twentieth Century history

The political history of Ukraine in the 20th century is often seen as tragic. Aspirations for independence manifested themselves early. In January 1918, following the 1917 revolution in Russia that led ultimately to the formation of a Bolshevik state, the Ukrainian Central Rada (parliament) declared independence from Russia. A protracted series of wars then followed, involving the weak government, Bolshevik forces, a White Army under General Anton Denikin, Anarchist troops under Nestor Makhno, and the German army, which permitted a short-lived 'Hetmanate' under Pavel Skoropadsky prior to the end of the First World War. The eventual Bolshevik victory ensured that Central and Eastern European territories became part of the Soviet Union that was formed in December 1922. However, following a Polish–Soviet war in 1919–20, the bulk of west Ukrainian territories were included in a Polish state, restored after more than a century by the Treaty of Riga. Smaller territories containing ethnic Ukrainians were included in neighbouring states: Transcarpathia was part of interwar Czechoslovakia; Bukovyna was annexed by Romania, along with Bessarabia, the last formerly part of the Russian Empire.

During the years of Lenin's New Economic Policy a relatively enlightened policy was adopted towards Soviet Ukraine, encapsulated by the phrase 'national in form, socialist in content'. The republic revived economically and made considerable progress in national and cultural development. The situation changed in the late 1920s, with Stalin's decision to introduce a programme of crash industrialization, accompanied by the collectivization of agriculture. The latter was carried out brutally in Ukraine. Once the farms were established, a grain procurement policy reminiscent of the civil war period saw all surplus grain taken from the farms. In 1933, when Ukrainian farms failed to meet state demands, supplementary products were also requisitioned by the authorities, and mass starvation ensued. Officially concealed for more than 50 years, the famine resulted in the deaths of at least 4 million rural residents in Ukraine and the Kuban region. Further devastation occurred with the Stalin Purges which reached a peak in 1937 and virtually eliminated the Ukrainian cultural elite, as well as national institutions.

In western Ukraine, Polish policy, though harsh and authoritarian, was more moderate, and allowed for the development of Ukrainian political life, both legal and illegal. Communism was prevalent in the 1920s, but in the 1930s, the Organization of Ukrainian Nationalists carried out a terrorist campaign against the Polish state. In September 1939, following the Nazi–Soviet Pact, the Red Army invaded and annexed western Ukrainian territories. The following summer, Stalin gave the Romanians an ultimatum to vacate Bessarabia and northern Bukovyna. The southern and northern parts of the former as well as northern Bukovyna were then incorporated into the Ukrainian SSR. The final component, Transcarpathia, was annexed by arrangement with Czechoslovakia in June 1945.

The Second World War had a devastating impact on Ukraine. Some 2.5 million Ukrainians served in the Red Army and the republic was occupied from the very start of the Soviet–German war in June 1941. Approximately one-quarter of the republican population was a casualty of conflicts, retribution, deportation, or fell victim to the later battles that took place between various forces, including Ukrainian and Polish guerrilla movements, and Soviet security troops. In the postwar period, Soviet policy saw the further development of heavy industry in the republic, especially coal mining, iron and steel, and the chemical industry. Agriculture, while still a mainstay for the Soviet economy, began to decline from the 1960s onwards. One consequence of rapid industrial development without due regard for safety was the Chernobyl nuclear disaster of April 1986, during an experiment to test safety equipment during a shutdown. The accident led to the direct and indirect deaths of approximately 3,000 people, contaminated a territory inhabited by 3.5 million Soviet citizens and contributed to the sentiment that the republic should determine its own national economic development without interference from the 'centre'.

Perestroika and Glasnost, the twin policies introduced by Soviet leader Mikhail Gorbachev, penetrated relatively slowly into Ukraine, a republic that was regarded as a nurturing point for Communist Party leaders. For a period of 16 years, the republic appeared compliant and loyal to the USSR under party leader Volodymyr Shcherbytsky. With his retirement in September 1989, political life in Ukraine changed rapidly, beginning with the formation of several important informal associations (later they were transformed into political parties), such as the Popular Movement for Perestroika (Rukh) and 'Zelenyi Svit' (Green World, a group devoted to ending nuclear power in Ukraine after the disaster at Chernobyl). Shcherbytsky's successor Volodymyr Ivashko elected to take up a post of deputy president of the USSR in Moscow, and Stanislav Hurenko, the new party leader, proved incapable of uniting either the Communists or the republic. Instead, focus centred on the Supreme Soviet, which declared sovereignty in July 1990. Though Communists dominated the body, they split into two factions: the rank and file under Hurenko and the parliamentary majority under Leonid Kravchuk. In August 1991, Kravchuk allied with democratic deputies in the decision to declare independence.

Independent Ukraine, 1991–99

The state that formed independent Ukraine had the same borders as Soviet Ukraine, but remained without a state currency for several years, and though a Constitution was under discussion from 1992, it was only approved in 1996. Subsequently, it has remained a source of dispute between president and legislature, with the executive gradually accumulating more powers. The country has 24 oblasts (provinces) and one autonomous republic (Crimea), and contains 415 cities, the largest of which are Kyiv, Dnipropetrovsk, Kharkiv, Donetsk and Odesa. The chief legislative branch of government is the parliament, or Verkhovna Rada, which has 450 members. Executive power is in the hands of the president, elected by a direct popular vote of those over the age of 18 every five years. The president relies on a Cabinet of Ministers, headed by a prime minister, whom he appoints personally.

The early years of independence proved extraordinarily difficult for Ukraine. Three major problems emerged. First, the new country suffered a sharp economic downturn, partly due to a reluctance to initiate radical changes to the economic structure and subsidized industry. It became heavily dependent upon the Russian Federation for imports of oil and gas at below-market prices, and its traditional coal industry had been devastated by a series of strikes that began in the summer of 1989. Second, and related to the first point, Russia took advantage of Ukraine's economic dependence to make a series of demands related to the future of the Black Sea Fleet, the status of the fleet's base, the city of Sevastopol, the status of Crimea itself ('given' to Ukraine by Russia in 1954), and the question of the fate of the Russian language in Ukraine. Third, Ukraine emerged from the Soviet era as one of four states to possess nuclear weapons. As part of its non-nuclear proliferation policy, the United States demanded that three states – Ukraine, Belarus and Kazakhstan – give up their weapons to Russia for dismantling. Belarus and Kazakhstan complied promptly, but Kravchuk, citing a threat from Russia, at first appeared reluctant to comply. The result was the casting of Ukraine as an 'international pariah' for a brief period, and the loss of potentially vital economic aid from the United States and Europe.

The situation changed in the summer of 1994, with Ukraine's second presidential election. After two ballots, Kravchuk, a native west Ukrainian, was narrowly defeated by Leonid Kuchma, the former manager of a weapons factory in Dnipropetrovsk, and one of Kravchuk's former prime ministers. Kuchma had campaigned on a platform of drawing Ukraine closer to Russia, but once in power he drew closer to the United States, which stepped up aid following Ukraine's removal of its nuclear weapons (completed in 1996) and Russia's involvement in a war in Chechnya. In 1994, Ukraine ratified the Strategic Arms Reduction Treaty and the Nuclear Nonproliferation Treaty and emerged from its isolation. Ukraine became the third-largest recipient of US aid by 1995–96. In 1997, Kuchma and Yeltsin signed a Treaty of Friendship and Cooperation, which resolved a number of issues, and permitted Russia to lease the port of Sevastopol for its portion of the Black Sea Fleet for a period of 20 years. Kuchma, like Kravchuk, faced a recalcitrant parliament in which Communists and Socialists made up a majority of deputies. In the parliamentary elections of 1998, Communists again won a plurality of seats under their leader Petro Symonenko.

Ukraine since 1999

Failure to implement radical reforms signified that Ukraine continued to struggle economically, despite substantial foreign aid. Nevertheless, entering the 1999 presidential election, Kuchma received perhaps unexpected support from voters in western Ukraine, traditionally a region that would like to see Ukraine move away from Russia and towards Europe. The reason was west Ukrainians' fear that the country might elect Communist leader Symonenko as the new president. In the event, Kuchma comfortably won a run-off against Symonenko and embarked on a second term of office that, he anticipated, would see Ukraine finally turn the corner and attain political and economic stability. There were some promising signs, such as the appointment of former chairman of the National Bank of Ukraine, Viktor Yushchenko, as the new prime minister. Yushchenko, pro-Western with an American wife, offered hope that Ukraine would restructure its industry, end subsidies to bankrupt firms and reduce the corrupt practices among new business elites known as 'oligarchs'.

However, the government had become increasingly corrupt and its proclaimed 'multi-vectored' foreign policy has failed to take root. Ukraine had remained only an associate member of the CIS, a body that appeared increasingly defunct by the late 1990s. On the other hand, the European Union rejected Ukraine's bid for associate status on the grounds that the country failed to meet European standards in a number of areas. The 1999 election had also demonstrated the 'regionalization' of Ukraine between an east and south more oriented towards Russia, and which contained the centres of heavy industry; and the agricultural west with a strong nationalist element. Kyiv, the capital, embodied elements of both camps. Ukraine under Kuchma also became increasingly authoritarian. The media especially was muzzled.

Matters came to a head in mid-September 2000 with the disappearance of a journalist, Georgy Gongadze, editor of the Internet newspaper *Ukrains'ka Pravda*. Two months later, the journalist's headless body was discovered in the Tarashcha woods near Kyiv. Kuchma's personal bodyguard, Mykola Melnychenko, subsequently defected to the West carrying tapes he made of conversations between President Kuchma and his security chiefs, on which the Ukrainian leader urged them to remove Gongadze. After several international examinations, the tapes are now believed to be genuine. They also indicate the president's apparent willingness to sell military technology to the then Iraqi leader Saddam Hussein, and specifically Kolchuha aircraft-detection systems, which prompted the US administration to withhold indefinitely some USD55 million in aid. By the spring of 2001, a series of protests against Kuchma in light of the Gongadze tapes undercut his popular support and seemed close to bringing about his resignation. However, the president's control over the military, the police, and security forces limited the damage, and several prominent journalists have died in mysterious circumstances in more recent years.

In April 2001, Kuchma dismissed Yushchenko and appointed a personal ally, Anatoly Kinakh, in his place. In March 2002, Yushchenko exacted some revenge in the new parliamentary elections when his faction 'Our Ukraine' received over twice the popular vote (23.5 per cent to 11.9 per cent) of the president's own faction 'For a United Ukraine', and a relatively poor 20 per cent for the Communists. The dramatic results were negated by political intrigues that manipulated the electoral system whereby half the parliamentary seats had to be decided based on party lists on the basis of proportional representation, and the other half by one-seat constituencies. For a United Ukraine picked up an additional 66 seats through the latter process and then, with the aid of the government, pressured another 18 deputies to join its ranks, and through further alliances gained a narrow majority of support. Our Ukraine, the Tymoshenko Bloc (led by former deputy prime minister Yulia Tymoshenko, an avowed enemy of Kuchma), and the Socialist Party (led by Oleksander Moroz) issued protests at what they saw as electoral manipulations and the bribery of officials. The leader of For a United Ukraine, Volodymyr Lytvyn, was then controversially appointed the Speaker of the Parliament.

A bitter conflict has raged since the elections between the 'democratic opposition' and the government. The key players on the government side, in addition to Kuchma, are as follows: Viktor Medvedchuk, Kuchma's chief of staff, Evhen Marchuk, the new National Security Adviser, and Viktor Yanukovych, who replaced Kinakh as prime minister in November 2002. Yanukovych is the former leader of the important Donetsk oblast. Together this group has worked to solidify Kuchma's authority, often on the grounds that he remains the best of the available alternatives. However, his mandate as president ends in 2004, so that unless the Constitution is amended, the president must step down. The democratic forces, who would likely stand behind Yushchenko as their candidate for president, have fought strongly against potential constitutional amendments, which have posited, among other things, reducing the size of the parliament and establishing an upper house (somewhat similar to the situation in the more repressive neighbour to the north, Belarus).

Paradoxically during a period of internecine strife, the country appears to have begun economic recovery. The GDP rose a remarkable 14 per cent in 2001, and continues to hover between an annual growth rate of 5 and 9 per cent. The turnaround appears to be the result of increased Russian investment rather than from the West or the Far East. Moreover, in the summer of 2003, Kuchma signed an agreement with the leaders of Russia, Belarus and Kazakhstan on forming a common economic space (in many ways a rewriting of the CIS), an unexpected move given Ukraine's avowed pro-European orientation. The European option, given Kuchma's personal dilemmas, may be a distant dream. On 1 October 2003, a new visa regime began with Poland, with its official entry into the EU. Though Ukrainians at present receive visas to Poland free of payment, it remains to be seen how Ukraine will be affected economically by the loss of one of its chief trading partners to the European community.

Lastly, the country that was devastated by the Chernobyl disaster has not achieved satisfactory standards of living, health care, or workers' protection. Death rates exceed considerably the birth rates, with the resulting decline of population from 52.5 million at the time of independence to 48.4 million in 2002. Industrial accidents, especially in the coal mines, are very common. Diseases such as tuberculosis and even cholera, and increasingly HIV, are prevalent. About a quarter of the population lives below an officially designated poverty line of USD33 per month, and there is great regional diversity between the relatively affluent areas, most notably the major cities (Kyiv and the east), and the relatively poor west, and poverty-stricken Tatar villages in the Crimea and parts of Transcarpathia. Ukraine thus presents a very mixed picture 12 years after independence: the potential seems unlimited but the achievements to date have been disappointingly few.

1.2

Political and Economic Overview

Mykhaylo Kuzmin, Raiffeisenbank Ukraine

Politics of change

The political landscape in Ukraine is currently determined by the forthcoming presidential election in October 2004. The autumn is normally the time when social tension takes place, thereby setting the political agenda for the entire following year. Autumn 2003 was relatively quiet, devoid of strikes and political scandals. Presidential political technologists (or spin doctors, as they are referred to in the West) initially came to Ukraine from Russia. They generated large-scale 'events' (see below) proactively with wonderful consistency to divert public attention away from typical social problems.

The first of these events was a series of parliamentary debates over Constitutional amendments seeking to transform the political system from president-parliamentary to parliament-presidential. The second was the agreement signed by the presidents of four countries (Russia, Ukraine, Belarus, Kazakhstan) to form a single economic union (the so-called Common Economic Area, or CEA) with a supranational managing committee. Third was the border conflict between Ukraine and Russia near Tuzla-spit (Crimea). The last, also referred to as 'the Crimean incident', was too obvious a decoy, and expensive for both parties. However, PR (public relations, which in the post-Soviet countries has a negative connotation as marketing something unfair) is costly at all levels, and especially at such a political level. However, few politicians consider the main proposals under the CEA seriously. All the signatories to the CEA have signed similar documents during the past decade, but no concrete actions have followed. Manipulating the Constitution is a more serious matter, even for PR, as the pro-president parliamentary majority does not have an eligible number of votes.

In any case, all of these tricks and manoeuvres have a single clear motive: transmission of power from the current President Kuchma to his successor. However, since the pro-president political parties and their leaders have only slight support from the population, democratic leader Viktor Yushchenko is the most likely candidate to be elected the next president of Ukraine. According to opinion polls regularly conducted by Razumkov's Center, 25.2 per cent of voters will vote for him (17.8 per cent for the current PM V. Yanukovich and 10.1 per cent for communist leader P. Symonenko). His slogan – European choice and market reforms with the priority of national interest, in contrast to the private interest of oligarchic clans – is seen as a threat from the present economic elite who have obtained benefits from close ties with Ukraine's nucleus of political power.

During his second term in office, President Kuchma has concentrated power entirely in his own hands. This can be confirmed by briefly recalling the parliamentary elections of 2002. The opposition parties, namely, Our Ukraine (obtained 103 seats in Parliament), the Communists (60), and the Socialist Party (20) and the Yulia Tymoshenko Bloc (18), won the most votes amongst individual parties and were thereby elected to parliament. However, the pro-president bloc, For a United Ukraine, was able to mobilize the majority of independent candidates and thereby collect the necessary 50 per cent of seats (225) to manipulate parliament. The pro-presidential forces have no chance of winning fairly contested presidential elections in 2004 and they are therefore predominantly occupied with finding some ingenious means of self-preservation and prolonging their power. About a year ago the president declared his intention to carry out constitutional reform. However, it appears that the underlying objective of this move was to change the rules of the game without changing the team. In our view, the aim was to turn the next president (ie possibly Yushchenko) into a dummy – a ceremonial doll – rather than maintain the position of the president at the centre of political power. After 12 years of independence, Ukraine has yet to show any hint of developing a balance between power centres: strong president, strong parliament and strong government.

Today Ukraine's president exercises virtually unlimited power. According to Viktor Yushchenko (against whom the constitutional reforms were primarily directed), it may be acceptable for transition countries such as Ukraine, whilst at the very beginning of the transition process, to exercise a fairly centralized concentration of political power, thereby stabilizing the system in the face of anarchic and centrifugal forces. However, as the transition to a democratic, open society gathers pace, excessive power vested in the presidency becomes an obstacle to development. Yushchenko adds that such an imbalance in political power should be eradicated by relinquishing some of the presidential responsibilities to the Cabinet, and not to parliament as is currently proposed.

The Cabinet is presently managed by Viktor Yanukovich, leader of the party, Regions of Ukraine, and representative of the powerful Donetsk oligarchic group. When President Kuchma (who originates from Denpropetrovsk) nominated Yanukovich to the post of Prime Minister, he set control of economic and financial flows as one of his main goals. Another key figure is Viktor Medvedchuk (the leader of the social democrats, representative of the Kyiv business group), who steers the Presidential Administration and controls both access to the first person in the country as well as the mass media channels (the lack of an independent media is one of the major elements responsible for the weakness of the opposition). However, understanding both Medvedchuk's ambitions to play the lead role in Ukrainian politics and economics and the level of power wielded by the post of Head of the Presidential Administration, Kuchma has balanced him with a competitor – Yanukovich – as Prime Minister. Thus Kuchma has effectively created a stable and controlled political structure: a pro-presidential majority in parliament which is able to pass the necessary legislation, the easily shifted Prime Minister Yanukovich, and his competitor Medvedchuk, a strategist who is too preoccupied with public relations. The president has also appointed loyal individuals to key posts in the National Bank, the armed forces and the security structures, whilst leaving the opposition highly fragmented.

Indeed, while the opposition initially declared that they would propose a single candidate for the presidency, the ensuing 'constitutional reforms' effectively split their unity. In terms of the opposition parties, the Communists are most effective in playing their role in a 'new-old world'. They are the 'eternal' opponents to the authorities and effectively exploit the social nostalgia of the population by reminiscing about the long-gone economic and social stability experienced by Ukraine during the last generation of the Soviet Union. The Socialists (led by Olexandr Moroz) view the establishment of a parliamentary republic in Ukraine as their main goal. Yulia Tymoshenko, the leader of an autonomous opposition block and former vice-Prime Minister in the Government of Yushchenko, holds an electorate which is highly similar to that of Viktor Yushchenko. One could therefore assume that there is much scope for a political alliance between these two popular figures in Ukrainian politics. However, a union between the two is not seen as strategically convenient for Yushchenko given the intensive discrediting that Tymoshenko has suffered in the mass media. Although a union between the two has not at this stage emerged, if Yushchenko does succeed in becoming president, we foresee that Tymoshenko is likely to play a similar role in the new Cabinet as she did when Yushchenko was Prime Minister in 2000. One may recall that at that time she stopped grey, virtual schemes in the energy sector and made many enemies amongst the oligarchic clans. The record of the two working together is generally good, and they did succeed in significantly reducing the degree of non-financial (barter) transactions which were dominant in the Ukrainian domestic economy.

Foreign policy

Following the recently much discussed tape and Kolchuga scandals, Ukraine's foreign affairs changed its orientation from pro-European to 'multi-vectoral' and, finally, to pro-Russian. Appealing to Russia for support during these difficult political circumstances brought dividends for Russian business, which was able to obtain access to Ukraine's assets and infrastructure. In particular, Ukraine's interests have been undermined in negotiations on common usage of the gas pipeline and the Odesa–Brody oil pipeline in favour of the Russian energy lobby. By signing a four-party agreement with Russia, Belarus and Kazakhstan on a Euro-Asian customs union (the so-called Common Economic Area), Ukraine has in effect taken steps to move the country away from the World Trade Organization (WTO) and the European Union (EU). However, the agreement had also had a positive effect as it has split the parliamentary groups and the Cabinet, and speeded up negotiations with the EU.

The government plans to finish its preparation for accession to the WTO in 2004. Ukraine's dialogue with the EU continues to be bogged down by Kyiv's desire to obtain a policy statement from Brussels that would recognize its prospects for membership. However, Brussels is not ready to produce such a statement and it is also widely believed that the EU does not wish to provoke Russia regarding Ukraine, which such a statement might do. The EU is also dissatisfied with Ukraine's multi-vector attitudes. In short, the EU supports *gradual* integration of the social and economic structures between the enlarged Union and Ukraine. In our opinion, Ukraine should take a more patient position on EU integration and make greater efforts on its way to economic, legislative and democratic convergence with Europe. We believe that it may take up to 15 years for Ukraine to be genuinely considered a full member.

The way to the European Union passes through democratization not only in Ukraine, but also in Russia, which still sees Ukraine as its constituent. For instance, the Tuzla border incident reflects the archetypical pattern of the political unconscious of Russian and Ukrainian leaders. They still believe they have the right to manipulate people's opinions for the sake of a higher goal. In other words, the goal justifies the means. No one knows exactly what the higher goal is, but preservation of imperial–patrimonial relations is assumed.

Macroeconomic overview

In 2003 the Ukrainian economy demonstrated a high pace of growth. Real GDP increased by 5.3 per cent year-on-year for eight months of 2003. The main contribution to economic growth was provided by construction (25 per cent growth), the manufacturing industry (16.5 per cent), wholesale and retail trade (11 per cent) and transport (10.1 per cent). This year's huge industrial growth at 14.6 per cent was partly compensated by a decline in agriculture (24.6 per cent y/y drop), owing to a bad grain harvest (estimated at 55–60 per cent of the previous year).

Economic growth has brought higher wages and disposable income, greatly boosting domestic demand and consumption. In turn, the economy was stimulated by the expansion of domestic consumption for both the private and public sectors. The former leads to growing retail trade turnover, which increased by 17.1 per cent in real terms. This growth is explained by a three year growth in the wages and cash income of households (by 23 per cent and 20 per cent on average). Looking ahead, we recognize the risk of inflation in the first half of 2004, owing to problems in the agricultural sector this year. Currently, inflation made up 3.3 per cent ytd over 9 months, but wholesale prices on grains increased twofold compared to 2002, and this will lead to higher prices on the food market. The government will be not able to subsidize bakery plants to keep bread prices steady. We expect an increase in bread prices by 30–50 per cent this autumn. Since food makes up two-thirds of the consumption basket, and 2004 is the year of presidential elections, typically accompanied by additional spending and populist measures, and pressure on producer prices owing to more expensive inputs (basically, energy and labour), we forecast inflation of consumer prices at 7.7 per cent in 2003 and 9.2 per cent in 2004.

In 2003, the export of goods grew at a rate of 25.6 per cent, but imports increased by 27.2 per cent. Exports were stimulated by external demand on a new growing business cycle. The leading export area is metallurgy (which increased by 31 per cent). The main destinations of metallurgy goods were the countries of Asia (45.5 per cent of total), CIS and Africa. The increase in the import of goods was provided by consumer demand (including for durable goods like cars) and investment goods. Investments in fixed capital increased by 26 per cent, which gives a good perspective on further growth. Currently, heavy industry has obsolete fixed assets which depreciated by 70–80 per cent, but has free capacity at 15 per cent of the total. Corporations try to renovate their assets, because of growing competition on the external and domestic markets. We foresee that both exports and imports will grow further in 2004, keeping in mind the worldwide economic recovery and the expansion of trade. We expect that the total trade surplus will slowly deteriorate from USD2 billion in 2003 to USD0.95 billion in 2004, but that the current account balance will still be positive (2.4 per cent of GDP), providing optimism that stability of the hryvnia will prevail.

Despite the uncertainty connected with the presidential elections, foreign direct investments (FDI) peaked during 2003. In the first half of 2003 the net inflows of FDI reached USD736 million (USD698 million for the whole of the previous year). Some analysts, however, suggest that a large share of FDI is made up of reinvestment of capital owned by local businessmen, who accumulated their capital in offshore zones through grey schemes. Ukraine is likely to be an even more attractive market for investment during 2004, as many international ratings agencies have upgraded the country's sovereign debt rating. Fitch upgraded Ukraine from B to B+ in June, Standard & Poor's revised its outlook on the sovereign rating from B stable to positive, and Moody's put Ukraine on the watch list and it is likely that it will upgrade the outlook in January to positive (now B2 stable). The agencies justified their ratings on the basis of two major factors: reduced debt-servicing pressures and robust economic growth. Concerning the first factor, Standard & Poor's notes the strong expansion of international reserves and the fact that the country could cover its debt obligations. The agency took into account the successful Eurobond float (USD800 million) and hails the generally positive international position of the country. In terms of the second factor, Standard & Poor's sees good economic growth driven by exports and expects 3–4 per cent growth over the next couple of years, even if structural reforms are slow.

The monetary policy is currently adequate to the growing demand (M3 grew by 42 per cent in 2002 and by 27.5 per cent in the period to September 2003), but is lagging in controlling inflation. 2004, as the year of presidential elections, will bring an additional surplus of cash to the market, with pressure on the currency and prices. Strict and unfair government regulations in the agricultural sector, together with bad weather conditions this year, led to price hikes which will increase consumer prices next year.

Two important laws should have come into force on 1 January 2004: a new Tax Code and a Law on Mortgages. The Tax Code, which reduces the average tax burden, will put into force a flat 13 per cent income tax instead of a progressive tax of 10–40 per cent, VAT at 17 per cent in place of the current 20 per cent, and 25 per cent corporate profit tax, compared to 30 per cent. The tax cut will lead to a reduction in budget receipts by UAH4–5 billion, if many tax benefits and exemptions remain. Hopes are high that the Tax Code will further stimulate Ukraine's economy. With the adoption of the Law on Mortgages conditions are created for introducing practical mechanisms for raising the liquidity of mortgage credit operations through securitization, ensured by collateral packages. The clause of the Law on Mortgages on agricultural land comes into effect on 1 January 2005.

The financial sector functions adequately, in proportion to the prevailing levels of economic growth. Loans to the economy grew at a rate of 56 per cent p.a. Credits to households have expanded even faster – at 118 per cent p.a. In January 2004 the Law on Mortgages should have come in force, which will additionally stimulate retail banking and individual consumption. Expected inflation will lead to growth of interest rates both in local (owing to growth in the expectation of inflation) and foreign (owing to expected growth of LIBOR rates after the Fed and the European Central Bank (ECB) start to increase base rates) currencies. High rates of growth, together with inflation, will lead to higher MM rates, which increased in 2003 in comparison with 2002. The foreign exchange (FX) market will be relatively stable for the main trading currency, USD. For 2004 the state budget assumes an FX rate of UAH/USD5.42 as the yearly average, but we foresee less devaluation, assuming NBU holds the 50 per cent norm of obligatory FCY sales and intervenes in the FX market as usual. The euro FX market will fluctuate with 10 per cent p.a. volatility

Table 1.2.1 Basic macroeconomic indicators

Macroeconomic indicators	1999	2000	2001	2002	2003E	2004F
Nominal GDP, USD bn	25.0	31.3	38.5	41.4	46.1	53.0
GDP, % yoy	–0.2	5.9	9.2	4.8	6.3	7.6
Industry, % yoy	4	13.2	14.2	7.0	14.5	11.4
Agriculture, % yoy	–6.9	9.8	10.2	1.9	–9.1	8.9
Capital investments, % yoy	0.4	14.4	20.8	8.9	20.4	15.2
CPI, % Dec/Dec	19.2	25.8	6.1	–0.6	7.7	9.2
PPI, % Dec/Dec	15.7	20.8	0.9	5.7	8.1	7.3
Consolidated budget balance, % GDP	–1.5	–0.67	–0.3	–0.74	2.2	–0.7
Unemployment rate, % yoy	4.3	4.2	3.7	3.8	3.6	3.8
Export, $ mn	16,332	19,278	21,086	23,351	28,817	34,394
Import, $ mn	15,327	17,947	20,473	21,494	26,802	33,452
Trade balance, $ mn	1,095	1,331	613	1,857	2,014	943
Current account	932	1,237	1,402	3,173	3,606	2,861
FDI net, $ mn	489	594	769	698	1,336	1,175
NBU reserves, yoy, $ mn	1,094	1,505	3,089	4,417	6,550	7,650
Import cover, weeks	3.7	4.4	7.8	10.7	14.5	15.6
External debt, $ mn	13.5	11.9	12.1	12.7	13.6	13.1
Debt service ratio, % Export	16.1	14.5	14.6	12	10.4	8.1
FX rate UAH per USD, yoy	5.216	5.435	5.299	5.333	5.336	5.353

Sources: National Statistics, NBU; E, F – RBUA expectation and forecast

according to the volatility of the EUR/USD rate. The expected range of fluctuation in EUR/USD is 1.05–1.20 as the yearly average, hence the EUR/UAH rate should be in the range 5.6–6.4.

Summary and outlook

The run-up to Ukraine's presidential elections has started and is already stimulating instability both in parliament and in society. President Kuchma has sought to amend the Constitution in order to redistribute power away from the next president, to parliament. For the amendments to be passed, a yes vote must be obtained from 300 MPs and we consider that the debates over this issue will constitute the main source of instability in 2004. On the foreign policy front, we have already noted that Ukraine has been moving closer to Russia and somewhat further away from the EU and WTO blocs, and this multivectoral approach to foreign politics may lead to tense domestic relations between various social groups.

Viktor Yushchenko remains the front-runner to succeed Mr Kuchma and still may be presented as a possible presidential candidate by three opposition parties (Our Ukraine, the Socialists, and the Yulia Tymoshenko Bloc). In the event that this takes place, it is possible that he could obtain the 38 per cent of the vote, which would allow him to become president after the first round of voting. Yushchenko's main rivals for the presidency, current Prime Minister Yanukovich, the Communist Symonenko, and National Bank Governor Tyhypko, have less chance of being elected (18 per cent, 10 per cent and 3 per cent respectively). It is likely that economic reform will be accelerated after the election, but weak administrative capacity and general resistance to reform by the current business élite will create serious constraints.

Like the run for the presidential race, the Ukrainian economy is also speeding up. Real GDP growth is expected to reach 6.5 per cent in 2003 and, taking into account growing external and domestic demand, 7.6 per cent in 2004. Improving international standing, growing foreign trade with positive balance, high foreign reserve cover of imports and increased inflow of FDI collectively provide grounds for stability of the hryvnia against the US dollar. However, growth in the price of food after a poor grain harvest in 2003, pressure from producer price inflation and extension of cash circulation in the year of the presidential election make inflation the main risk factor to further hryvnia stability and fast economic development.

1.3

The New Legal Framework

Bate C Toms, Dmytro Korbut and Olga Prokopovych, BC Toms & Co

For the more than 13 years of its independence during the process of transition, market transformation and constant political and legal reform, Ukraine has, despite the occasional steps backwards, made extraordinary progress towards an independent Western-style democracy. Ukraine increasingly shares common values with the rest of Europe, while developing a democratically-based Western-style legal system. The result is uniquely Ukrainian, unlike in many of the other former Soviet Union republics that have more or less followed the Russian model, or even returned to quasi-Soviet-style governance. Despite this progress, there are still significant difficulties and numerous legal traps for the unwary in Ukraine that remain to be resolved.

It should be borne in mind that the Ukrainian legal system is based on centuries of common political and legal tradition with the rest of Europe. As an independent state and as a part of various empires (such as those of Austro-Hungary and Russia), Ukraine developed within a common European cultural, political and economic context. Going back to medieval times, Ukraine, then known as 'Kyiv Rus', was one of the most important nations of Europe, having its own language and legal system, with strong ties to France, Hungary, Scandinavia and what was later to become the Moscow state. Today, Ukraine can be viewed as returning to its true roots.

Foundation of the legal framework

The Ukrainian legal framework is primarily based on the Constitution of Ukraine (the 'Constitution') adopted by the Ukrainian Parliament (known by its Ukrainian name as the 'Verkhovna Rada') on 28 June

1996. As a document written in the Western European tradition, it laid a firm foundation for the subsequent democratic transformation of the state and complete overhaul of the legal system. The Constitution provides that it shall be the supreme law of the land, directly applicable to all legal relations governed by Ukrainian law.

Human rights and economic freedoms

The Constitution provides for the protection of the human rights (in their widest meaning, including political, social and economic rights) of the citizens of Ukraine and other individuals residing permanently or temporarily in Ukraine. Among other things, the Constitution guarantees that foreign nationals in Ukraine shall have the same rights as the citizens of Ukraine, with the exception of certain political rights, such as to be able to vote and to be elected to government or to enter the civil service. It also, for the first time in more than 70 years, officially recognizes the existence of private property and guarantees its protection. The Constitution establishes the right of all individuals to engage freely in entrepreneurial activity and expressly prohibits any arbitrary state interference into the activities of individuals or legal entities.

Ukraine is also a member of the Council of Europe and has joined the European Convention on Human Rights, submitting itself to the jurisdiction of the European Court of Human Rights in Strasbourg. This allows for an additional well-developed mechanism of human rights protection to be used by those whose rights and freedoms are violated. A number of cases have been brought against Ukraine before the European Court of Human Rights as the final and highest institution of justice for such cases. For example, a number of cases have raised issues on the inadequate protection of human rights in prisons, which has led to a reform of the Ukrainian penitentiary system.

The governmental structure and the separation of powers

Under the Constitution, Ukraine is an independent, democratic and social state consisting of 24 administrative regions (called 'oblasts' in Ukrainian), the cities of Kyiv and Sevastopol and the Autonomous Republic of Crimea. It provides that the official state language is Ukrainian, which must be used for all official documentation, although in certain regions state bodies may use the language of the dominant ethnic minority along with Ukrainian.

State power in Ukraine is divided among three branches: legislative (Verkhovna Rada of Ukraine – the Parliament), executive (the Cabinet of Ministers of Ukraine being the highest executive authority) and judicial (the courts of general jurisdiction, including specialized courts, culminating in the Supreme Court of Ukraine, and the Constitutional Court of

Ukraine). The delimitation of powers between the Cabinet of Ministers and the Parliament, and the basis for their effective co-operation, is still being worked out, and in the past year, Ukraine witnessed a number of *ad hoc* agreements in this area. Further developments can be expected as the parties in power try to push previously initiated constitutional/ political reform. As a result of these reforms, the political system in Ukraine may shift from being a presidential republic towards becoming a parliamentary republic, where the Parliament will have more authority to form the Cabinet of Ministers or even elect the President of the country. At the moment, several reform plans are being reviewed by the Parliament.

Under the Constitution, the judiciary is based on the 'European' model, with the Constitutional Court being separated from the rest of the judiciary (courts of general jurisdiction). The Constitutional Court has the sole authority to render official interpretations of the Constitution. It is also authorized to examine laws for their compliance with the Constitution.

In their turn, the courts of general jurisdiction, including the commercial and other specialized courts, form a single system, with the Supreme Court of Ukraine being the highest judicial body. The judiciary continues to undergo a major overhaul connected with a general streamlining of the judicial structure. All of the specialized courts, like the commercial courts that handle disputes involving companies and entrepreneurs, have now been brought within the system of the courts of general jurisdiction as branches. Further judicial reform is under way to provide for the establishment of courts of administrative jurisdiction.

The President of Ukraine stands apart from this structure. His role is perceived to be that of the guarantor of the Constitution and an intermediary between the branches of government. He is the Commander-in-Chief of the Armed Forces of Ukraine, and has the right to submit bills to Parliament and nominate the Prime Minister and the other ministers, subject to parliamentary approval. Since the adoption of the Constitution, the presidency of Ukraine has, in practice, developed into a powerful institution capable of shaping both the internal and external policies of the state. Recently proposed constitutional amendments are aimed at transforming the position of President by taking away many powers and giving them to Parliament and the government, but there is still uncertainty whether such proposals will be adopted before Presidential elections in October 2004.

Sources of applicable law

Ukraine is a civil law country and, as such, recognizes statutory law as the main source of law. Secondary legislation, for example decrees and resolutions of the President of Ukraine, resolutions and regulations of the Cabinet of Ministers of Ukraine and legal acts of the various ministries and other state bodies may be issued only within their respective competence as set forth by the Constitution and the laws. International agreements of Ukraine duly ratified by the Parliament of Ukraine also constitute national legislation and have priority over all other laws (statutes) but not over the Constitution.

Although theoretically judicial decisions are not formally recognized as a source of law, they tend to play an important role in the interpretation of statutory provisions. Resolutions and Explanations of the Supreme Court of Ukraine are commonly followed by the lower courts, while the rulings of the Constitutional Court of Ukraine serve as the official interpretation of the Constitution. In fact, in view of the many problems arising from gaps in the developing Ukrainian legal system, the Supreme Court has taken an activist role, effectively, to fill in gaps until the legislature can act.

An interesting development is the provision in the new Civil Code (which became effective from 1 January 2004) for 'business practices' to be a source of law. Certain forms of such 'soft law' already apply in Ukraine. For example, the use of INCOTERMS in trade contracts between Ukrainian and foreign persons was mandated by a Decree of the President of Ukraine as early as 1994.

Legal reform

The transformation of Ukrainian law, including the regulatory environment for business, towards principles commonly accepted in the West began after the proclamation of Ukrainian independence in 1991. This legal reform accelerated after the adoption of the Constitution of Ukraine in 1996, beginning with an overhaul of the taxation system. Presently, Ukraine is completing a period sometimes referred to as the 'code revolution', with the new Criminal, Budgetary and Land Codes adopted in 2001, the Customs and Family Codes adopted in 2002 and the Civil, Commercial and Penitentiary Codes adopted in 2003, which all together came into force simultaneously on 1 January 2004. The Civil Procedure Code adopted in 2004 is supposed to enter into force on 1 January 2005, provided that the Administrative Procedure Code, which has not yet been adopted, enters into force at the same time. The new Labour Code, substantial changes to the Subsoil Code and other major changes to the current legislation are also underway.

Many of the recent developments of Ukrainian law can be attributed to the efforts of the Ukrainian government to make Ukraine eligible for membership in the WTO (World Trade Organization) as well as the European Union. This intention was initially declared in the

Resolution of the Ukrainian Parliament of 2 July 1993 'On the Main Principles of Ukrainian Foreign Policy' and has since been repeated on many occasions.

Pursuant to Article 51 of the Treaty on Partnership and Co-operation between Ukraine and the European Community and their Member States of 14 June 1994, Ukraine undertook an obligation gradually to harmonize its legislation with the laws of the European Union, one of the prerequisites for future integration of Ukraine into the European Union. Particular attention in this respect has been given to the following areas: customs regulations, company law, securities regulation, banking, tax and accounting, intellectual property, financial services, technical rules and standards, competition law and consumer protection. As discussed below, significant progress has been made in many of these areas in recent years, including, in particular, in intellectual property protection and the prevention of money laundering, as well as the legal regulation of the circulation of electronic documents and electronic digital signature of such documents.

The remaining discussion reviews in greater detail some of more significant developments of legal regulation in areas that are of particular importance for business activity and foreign investment in Ukraine. Many of the areas are also dealt with in greater depth in the other chapters on specific topics, as indicated.

Civil law and commercial transactions

Commercial transactions had been regulated by the old 1963 Civil Code that was originally designed to govern business transactions for a centralized Soviet economy based on state ownership of the property. Not surprisingly, over the past 10 years, a considerable part of this Civil Code became effectively inoperative. Instead, transactions in the emerging market economy were increasingly regulated by new statutes specially covering legal areas, for example, the Laws 'On Pledge' dated 2 October 1992, the Law 'On Mortgage' dated 18 November 2003 and the Law 'On Property' dated 7 February 1991. However, this patchwork regulation often resulted in conflicts of legal rules and confusion as to the applicable law, so a new code project was initiated.

On 1 January 2004, after eight years of redrafting, the new Civil Code and Commercial Code became effective. The new Civil Code is largely based on the Dutch and German civil law traditions and can fairly be viewed as one of the greatest accomplishments of Ukrainian lawmakers. Among other novelties, this Code provides for the unlimited legal capacity of legal entities (they no longer have to enumerate their powers in the corporate charters) and, in general, liberalizes the legal regulation of commercial transactions. However, there are still many discrepancies between new Civil and Commercial Codes and holes in their coverage that need to be resolved in the immediate future.

The trend towards liberalizing the general business environment is also reflected in the simplified procedure for the state registration of businesses. According to the new Law 'On State Registration of Legal Entities and Individual Entrepreneurs' adopted in May 2003 and which became effective on 1 July 2004, this registration should be handled by the state registrar of the district executive administration of the relevant local self-government body within three business days. Information from the registry of legal entities and individual entrepreneurs, including on authorized signatories and limitations on their authority, has been made, for the first time, publicly available.

Regulation of cross-border transactions

The Law of Ukraine 'On Foreign Economic Activity' of 16 April 1991 paved the way for a free market to replace the state control over cross-border trade, which used to be within the exclusive competence of the central Soviet authorities in Moscow. Since then, state control and regulation have been steadily reduced. Today, there remain only a few official limitations on the free flow of international trade with Ukraine, including the following requirements:

- licensing and other requirements for the import or export of certain goods into and out of Ukraine;
- state registration of certain types of foreign contracts, mainly those for barter arrangements or transactions involving the importation of goods that are subject to licensing, quotas or antidumping proceedings;
- a special regime for the export of certain goods of a military or dual-purpose character;
- currency exchange controls, including requiring that Ukrainian sellers be paid for exports of goods within 90 days of the export (similarly, in an import transaction, goods must be imported by the buyer within 90 days from the date of any prepayment), unless an extension is granted by the National Bank of Ukraine (NBU) in an individual licence.

It should be noted that transfers of hard currency from Ukraine are still closely monitored by the state authorities and are limited to certain justifiable transactions. Care must therefore be taken for a particular transaction to ensure that any necessary cross-border transfer of funds will be allowed. There is an even more important trend in Ukrainian legislation and government towards enhancing the fight against money laundering in accordance with the international obligations of Ukraine and the recommendations of the Financial Action Task Force (FATF). The progress of the Ukrainian government in this area was recognized when those foreign countries that had imposed financial sanctions against Ukraine according to the FATF recommendations in 2002 subsequently cancelled these sanctions.

Ukraine also took a serious step towards creation of a legal framework for effective functioning of e-commerce when the Laws 'On Electronic Documents and Electronic Exchange of Documents' and 'On Electronic Digital Signature' were adopted by the Ukrainian Parliament on 22 May 2003. According to these Laws, electronic documents became equal to those on paper and can be used as evidence in courts.

As a practical matter, complex procedural rules and the requirements of various authorities, including for certification and sanitation control, may make certain cross-border trade transactions excessively burdensome compared to what one would typically expect in the West. The long waited admission of Ukraine to the World Trade Organization (WTO) should lead to further development of foreign trade, as well as liberalization of Ukraine's trade policies.

Foreign investment regime

Soon after independence, the Ukrainian Parliament decided that the best way to attract foreign investment would be to grant special tax privileges to foreign investors. The 1992 Law 'On Foreign Investment' and the 1993 Decree of the Cabinet of Ministers created a special regime of tax holidays for significant investments. These tax holidays were abolished in 1997, and there is little prospect of their being brought back. It is thought that the tax holidays contributed little to attracting investment, lost revenues needed for the state and unfairly favoured foreign over local businesses. However, termination of these previously granted tax holidays, on reliance of which several large Western investments were made, resulted in some controversy and litigation.

In the future, there may be incentives for investments in specific economic sectors and particular locations that are deemed to need special assistance. Thus, a number of special economic zones have been created in which significant tax privileges exist for any investors. However, the government's principal announced intention is to attract foreign investors by developing a legal framework that meets international standards. It is thought that most investors seek not so much tax incentives as a stable legal regime in which their legitimate rights and expectations will be adequately protected.

In order to promote faith in the rule of law, the court system has been transformed. It functions increasingly well to protect legal rights. Western parties can now expect to be able to take Ukrainian individuals and entities to court where necessary and, where justified, to win and have their judgments readily enforced against the defendant's assets. A number of Western investors have had success in such litigation against private Ukrainian entities as well as against the state.

Land law

Traditionally, issues over land ownership and the legal regulation of transactions involving land have been controversial. Ukraine is claimed to have over 30 per cent of the world's black soil resources, and there are those who have argued that this agricultural asset should remain in state ownership. However, the Ukrainian Constitution expressly permits private ownership of land, and gradually 'collective' ownership of land is being transformed into private ownership. The new Land Code, adopted by the Parliament on 27 October 2001, provides for the private instead of collective ownership of land, including agricultural land, and liberalizes the purchase and sale of all land, subject to certain restrictions. Foreign legal entities and individuals now have the right to own land under the buildings that belong to them. The Land Code has, however, a significant drafting problem, that impairs the land ownership rights of Ukrainian companies with foreign investment. This problem has been partially cured by the legislative amendments in 2003, but further changes are needed to resolve the problem entirely.

Criminal law reform

The old Soviet Criminal Code, adopted in 1961, in its implementation fell far short of recognizing the human rights values of a modern Western society. It differentiated between crimes against the state and communal property, which received harsher punishment than many types of homicide and crimes against the property of individuals. Enforcement of the old Code was overly harsh and repressive, as manifested in the widespread use of imprisonment even for relatively insignificant crimes (eg petty theft).

The new Criminal Code, adopted on 5 April 2001, which entered into force on 1 September 2001, has proved to be a considerable improvement. The new Code has increased the protection of the individual and private property. On the other hand, punishment for some economic crimes has become more lenient. For example, the threshold for a case of tax evasion to be considered criminal has increased substantially to around USD11,603, and such a major increase is also attributed to the changes in tax legislation. Some of the typical Soviet-era crimes simply have ceased to exist, such as speculation (defined as the reselling of goods at higher prices, which was sometimes used to prosecute any kind of entrepreneurial activity) and transactions in hard currency.

The new Code has also taken account of new technological and political developments. Such crimes as terrorism, trafficking in people and forgery of bankcards are specifically addressed.

There is also a new Penitentiary Code of Ukraine adopted on 11 July 2003, which came into force on 1 January 2004. This Code implements new principles for the penitentiary system aimed at the controlled correction of criminals being more consistent with human rights' values.

Banking regulation and system of taxation

One of the real successes of the legal and regulatory reform has been the laws governing the banking sector. The importance of the banking sector for the economic and social stability of the country became widely understood after the hyperinflation and the bad loan crises of the early 1990s. In the ensuing years, the National Bank of Ukraine has taken an increasingly rigorous stand in its banking supervision, effectively adhering to the guidelines set by the Basle Committee.

Presently, Ukrainian banking law follows the European practice of permitting 'universal' banks. Banks are set aside from other financial institutions as being the only bodies authorized to accept deposits and open bank accounts for customers. In 2001, the Law 'On Payment Systems and Electronic Funds Transfer' officially introduced the use of electronic documents and electronic (digital) signatures on banking documents. Work is also under way to develop a feasible mechanism for guaranteeing the bank deposits of individuals, as a means of encouraging private savings and boosting the banking sector.

Special importance is being attached to a radical overhaul of fiscal regulation. It is widely perceived that a more economically justified and equitable system of taxation, with lower rates and more consistent application, should contribute to the continuation of the economic growth that began in 1999. A large step forward was taken when a number of new tax laws and significant legislative amendments came into force on 1 January 2003, including: the Law 'On Personal Income Tax' providing for a uniform flat tax rate of 13 per cent, the Laws 'On Private Pensions Provision' and 'On Mandatory State Pension Insurance' providing for substantial pension reform, and the amendments to the 'Profits Tax Law' decreasing the tax rate on corporate profits to 25 per cent. In addition, some of the major amendments to the Law 'On Value Added Tax', including decreasing the VAT rate to 17 per cent, which were adopted by Parliament in 2003 but vetoed by the President, are expected to be reintroduced to Parliament and may be adopted in the future.

Some remaining problems

Despite the apparent successes in a number of key areas of legal regulation, there still remain a number of unresolved problems. To begin with, the Civil Code and the Commercial Code of Ukraine contradict each other in some important areas of regulation. The implementation of these codes is likely to result in numerous controversies between businesses and controlling state bodies, which will need to be addressed by the courts.

There has been rapid economic growth in Ukraine since 1999, and especially over the past three years, with official GDP growth of about 10 per cent and actual GDP increases estimated at more than 20 per cent per year as well as an increase of over 40 per cent in foreign investments.

Ukraine is now one of the fastest growing economies in Europe. However, challenges remain. There is still a significant shadow economy in Ukraine. In order to attract further investment, Ukraine will also need to ensure better corporate governance, transparency of joint stock companies and protection of shareholders' rights as well as strict respect for democratic principles.

Conclusion

It is difficult not to overemphasize the enormity of the task faced by Ukraine in 1991, when it had to develop a new legal system to respond to its move both to independence and to a market economy. While problems remain in the details, enormous progress has been made. The legal system now functions much like those in the West. At the same time, it is essential for an investor in any transaction to seek advice from legal counsel and accountants with in-depth Ukrainian experience and expertise. There are numerous examples of companies trying to operate on the basis of expectations and experience developed elsewhere, in particular in Russia, running into serious difficulties in Ukraine. Despite some similarities, the Ukrainian legal system has been developing independently for more than a decade and is now unique.

1.4

Ukrainian Investment Perspectives: Credibility and Stability Are Key

Jorge Zukoski, President, American Chamber of Commerce in Ukraine

Overview

Recently the international business community has been watching Ukraine closely as the political environment, which will have a major influence over the country and its investment climate over the next several years, takes shape. As Ukraine finds itself once again at a crossroads, international investors are looking intently for the signs and movements that will trigger their ability to start to invest heavily for the future. The questions many investors are asking include things such as: Is Ukraine really committed to European integration and taking the difficult decisions that are necessary to fulfil that goal? Will Ukraine push forward and become a member of the World Trade Organization and enjoy the benefits that membership in this global marketplace provides? How will Ukraine structure the Common Economic Area agreements? Will the current leadership of Ukraine ensure that democratic and free elections take place that will bring additional political stability to the country? How will Ukraine utilize its indigenous and imported energy resources, addressing issues such as generation, distribution, exploration and transportation? How will Ukraine handle privatization of Ukrainian State assets? Will these privatizations involve the international investment community or be limited to a privileged few? These and many other issues are in the forefront of investors' minds as they plan their future strategic development regarding Ukraine.

On a very positive note, statistical results for the year 2003 confirm that the basic macro economic indices match if not exceed forecasted ones. The preliminary assessment of GDP growth issued at the beginning of 2003 amounted to a cautious 4.1 per cent and now the official figure provided by the State Statistics Committee for the first half of 2003 is 5.1 per cent growth as compared to the same quarter of 2002. This correlates with the optimistic scenario for development of the Ukrainian economy, and provides attractive figures that grab the attention of prospective investors.

For over 12 years, the American Chamber of Commerce in Ukraine has been encouraging cooperation between foreign investors and local companies, government, central and local authorities on matters of trade, investment and economic reform. We are constantly collecting information from our Members as well as our partners in the Ukrainian government and the international donor and diplomatic community, which has resulted in our ability to generate what we believe to be a realistic and comprehensive overview of the economic situation in Ukraine following the first half of 2003, incorporating some reasonable forecasts regarding foreign direct investment in the future.

Industry

The fastest rates of growth were observed in the manufacturing industry making up almost 75 per cent of the total industrial production in Ukraine – 12.8 per cent (7.6 per cent in 2002), mining industry – 2.4 per cent (0.6 per cent in 2002), production and distribution of electricity, gas and water – 11.5 per cent (1.1 per cent in 2002). The growth of consumer purchasing power and the import substitution effect resulted in a substantial growth of consumer goods production oriented towards internal markets. Among the growing industries, machine building leads the way with 26.6 per cent growth, production of wood and wooden articles 22.2 per cent, and the cellulose and paper industry and printing production 16.1 per cent. Considerable growth as compared with the same period of 2002 was also observed in the chemical and petrochemical industries (13.3 per cent) as well as in metallurgy and metal processing (12.5 per cent). For the first time since Ukrainian independence light industry demonstrated 0.7 per cent growth as compared to January–May 2002. The mining of coal and peat is still declining, posting a 5.4 per cent slide along with oil processing, losing 2.1 per cent. All Ukrainian regions have posted positive growth figures in industrial development except for the Khmelnitska and Poltavska regions where the decline amounted to 1.5 and 2.0 per cent respectively.

Agriculture

Production of agricultural goods in the first half of 2003 in all categories declined by 6 per cent as compared to the same period of 2002. The overall volume of sales of agricultural goods receded by 1 per cent owing to shrinking volumes of sales in crops (18 per cent). The sale of cereal crops in the first half of 2003 diminished by 33.9 per cent as compared to the same period in 2002. For this reason the actual GDP sank by 5.6 per cent in July 2003 as compared to July 2002. Nevertheless, the government analysts have expressed no apprehensions as to this fact and still forecast GDP growth of 4.7–6 per cent in 2003.

Budget and investments

The actual revenues into the State Budget between January and June 2003, against the same period of 2002, grew by 15.5 per cent (the State Budget grew 17.8 per cent correspondingly). A substantial part of it was made up of revenues from privatization of communal and state property – UAH1,029.7 million (UAH967.8 million directed to the General Fund), which is three times more than in the first half of 2002.

Foreign trade

Beginning in the middle of the year, the situation on the external global market also saw improvement, which translated into better export numbers. According to the statistics published by the State Committee for Statistics at the beginning of August 2003, the surplus of Ukraine's foreign trade in commodities January through June was estimated at USD444.6 million (USD478.5 million in the first half of 2002). The ratio of coverage of imports by exports in the first six months of 2003 was 1.05 (1.06 in the same period of 2002). The overall volume of foreign trade in commodities over the period under review grew by 27.9 per cent from the same period last year to USD20.175 billion. Exports totalled USD10.310 billion (a 26.9 per cent rise) and imports USD9.865 billion (a 29 per cent rise).

Ukraine traded with 195 countries in the first half of 2003. The overall volume of foreign trade in commodities over the period under review grew by 27.9 per cent from the same period last year to USD20.175 billion. Exports totalled USD10.310 billion (a 26.9 per cent rise) and imports USD9.865 billion (a 29 per cent rise). The largest volume of exports fell on Russia – 17.9 per cent of the total volume, Italy – 5.9 per cent, Germany – 5.7 per cent, China – 4.6 per cent,

Poland 3.8 per cent, Turkey – 3.6 per cent, Hungary – 3.3 per cent, and the US – 2.4 per cent. The largest imports to Ukraine came from Russia – 38.5 per cent, Turkmenistan – 9.3 per cent, Germany – 9.2 per cent, Poland – 3.4 per cent, Italy – 2.7 per cent, the UK, France and Kazakhstan – 2.3 per cent each.

Direct foreign investment

Market analysts unanimously consider foreign direct investment (FDI) as an essential condition for sustained economic growth. In a survey conducted in 2002, Sigma Bleyzer, a Member of the American Chamber of Commerce, estimated the needs of the Ukrainian economy to be USD40 billion in FDI over the next decade if Ukraine is to maintain a significant level of sustainable growth. According to the most recent figures provided by the State Statistics Committee, the FDI in the first half of 2002 reached USD126 per capita, which is the highest since 1991, with only USD78 in 2000 and USD89 in 2001. Nevertheless, this is still a long way to go compared with the Czech Republic and Hungary, whose FDI per capita in 2000 was USD2,233 and USD2,059 respectively.

FDI dynamics

The largest volume of FDI took place in 1998, when foreign investors contributed USD757 million. In 1999, investment dropped by almost 50 per cent. This drastic decline in FDI occurred because of the 1998 economic crisis and an increase in perceived political risk owing to the Ukrainian presidential election in 1999. Until 1999, the average rate of investment approached the average rate for the CIS and Russia. Today Ukraine lags significantly behind Russia. Despite the fact that JP Morgan considered Ukraine one of the most attractive countries for foreign investors (57.1 per cent return on bonds in 2001), net FDI declined by 10.5 per cent. In 2002 foreign direct investments into Ukraine reached USD780 million, a definite step forward owing to the adoption of several important taxation laws allowing more investment into construction, banking and transport rather than only trade and services.

The forms of investment also have changed over the years. While 47.5 per cent of all FDI constituted monetary investments in 1999, their share increased by 10.3 per cent in 2000 and by 8.7 per cent in 2001, reaching 66.5 per cent of all foreign investments. The share of investment in the form of property, plant and equipment varies slightly, although this form of investment comprises (on average) 30 per cent of FDI. Investments in securities steadily declined during the past three years, from 14.9 per cent in 1999 to 0.9 per cent in 2001. Unfortunately, no annual figures on investment from changes in 2002 are available yet.

Recently Standard & Poor's upgraded Ukraine's Eurobond rating from 'negative' (under-weight) to 'stable' (market-weight), which is expected to attract even more investment into Ukraine. This achievement is mostly due to positive changes in legislation conforming to international requirements as well as government promotion of Zones for Free Economic Trade and Priority Areas. Thus the first half of 2003 was marked with USD581.8 million in FDI injected into the Ukrainian economy, according to the State Statistics Committee. At the same time non-residents withdrew USD123.2 million from Ukraine in the first six months of 2003; thus the withdrawal rate was 21.2 per cent. As was reported, the direct foreign investments made in Ukraine in the first quarter of 2003 rose by 18.3 per cent (USD252.8 million) from the same period last year. The Economics Ministry projected this year's direct foreign investment growth in the 2003 national budget at USD750 million.

Main obstacles for FDI flow

FDI is a universal and key source of long-term development for the economy. Separate surveys carried out by international organizations and AmCham Member Sigma Bleyzer identified the following main difficulties impeding additional foreign investments:

- instability and excessiveness of government regulations;
- ambiguity of the legal system;
- uncertainty in the economic environment;
- corruption;
- high tax burden;
- problems in establishing clear ownership conditions;
- depressed disposable income level;
- difficulty negotiating with government authorities;
- lack of physical infrastructure;
- volatility of the political environment.

These factors have led to government intervention and to conflicts with the private sector. The absence of a system for investment insurance, as well as the monopolization of the economy and restrictions for land transactions, also affects the level of foreign investment. A study conducted by the International Private Capital Task Force (IPCTF) developed a range of recommendations for attracting foreign capital to Ukraine, including the creation of a favourable investment climate, improvement of Ukraine's image in world financial markets and development of a system that could attract foreign entrepreneurs and renew foreign investors' confidence in Ukraine. The Task Force specified the following key 'policy actions' that affect the business climate in Ukraine and generate foreign investments:

- liberalization and deregulation of business activities;
- stability and predictability of the legal environment;
- corporate and public governance;
- liberalization of foreign trade and international capital movements;
- financial sector development;
- corruption level;
- political risk;
- country promotion and image;
- targeted investment incentives.

If action were to be carried out in all mentioned areas, Ukraine could expect FDI to increase to over USD3.5 billion per year within 10 to 15 years. Furthermore, the first three 'policy actions' were identified as those that most significantly affect the investment environment. Improvements in these areas alone could propel FDI to USD2.5 billion per year by 2005.

The rate of investment withdrawal should decrease in the second half of 2003, provided that the Ukrainian legislators pursue new positive amendments to the taxation and privatization legislation. The long-awaited Tax Code is being adopted on a step-by-step basis which is anticipated to facilitate the adoption of politically sensitive issues. Many of the proposed changes to the taxation legislation are designed to help bring businesses from the 'shadows' and establish a larger, more predictable tax base. The latest achievement for tax legislators and their supporters was the reduction of personal income taxes, starting from 1 January 2004, and approved by parliament. Still, this measure could become effective only provided there are accompanying cuts in the social funds taxes that employers have to pay. Moreover, the much-needed reduction of VAT from 20 per cent as well as its proper implementation regarding refunds to exporters is still a hot issue among parliamentarians and a primary issue stifling additional FDI into Ukraine.

Another important issue that foreign investors would like to see addressed is privatization, a major challenge to foreign businessmen seeking opportunities of investing into Ukraine. Privatization during the period of January–July 2003 earned Ukraine UAH1.322 billion which was 18.3 per cent up on the budgeted revenue expectations. The government is pushing a new long-term National Privatization Programme for 2003–08 which it is hoped will stimulate investment. The Programme is to create a nationwide inventory of public property, establish registers of enterprises of all forms of ownership and design mechanisms for effective tenders and allocation of returns. The architects of the reform envisage that, unlike in the past, 25 per cent of the privatization revenues will be allocated for restoration of capital assets of property to be privatized. All the activities of the Programme are aimed at reaching a balance between preserving strategic assets and offering attractive high-quality opportunities to prospective investors.

1.5

The Framework for Foreign Direct Investments in Ukraine

Vladimir Piddubniy, Investment Company ITT

Introduction

During the past several years, one can safely say that Ukraine has achieved macroeconomic stabilization. The government's economic reforms have been key in improving the country's investment climate, which in turn has led to the growth of foreign direct investment. Ukraine's GDP grew by almost 6 per cent in 2000 and 9 per cent in 2001. The National Bank of Ukraine was forecasting growth of GDP by around 5 per cent in 2003. Ukraine's GDP growth in the first half of 2003 had already reached 7.5 per cent. Over the past few years, Ukraine has taken significant steps to liberalize its markets, reduce regulation, eliminate most licensing requirements, eliminate most restrictions on foreign exchange, and transform the agricultural sector from state-run farms to private agriculture.

Legislative framework

The major piece of legislation governing foreign investment in Ukraine is the Law on the Regime of Foreign Investment (25 April 1996). The document contains the following major statements:

- protection against changes in legislation (foreign investor is guaranteed protection for 10 years in the event that Ukraine foreign investment legislation is changed);
- protection against nationalization;

- guarantee of compensation and reimbursement of losses suffered as a result of improper or negligent actions of state authorities or their representatives;
- guarantee in the event of termination of investment activity (right to remit revenues and withdraw investment from Ukraine);
- guarantee for repatriation of profit.

There are exceptions in the law. For example, foreigners are prohibited from participating in the manufacture of weapons or alcoholic spirits. Until recently, the law provided certain investment incentives, including VAT and duty exemptions on property, and tax exemptions, but on 17 February 2000 the Law of Ukraine 'On Removal of Discrimination in Taxation of Business Entities Founded With the Participation of Domestic Property and Funding' was adopted. The Law cancels privileges granted to joint ventures by Ukrainian legislation and has retroactive force. Joint ventures (JVs) have sued and a court has noted inconsistencies in the law.

On 9 January 2002 another Law of Ukraine 'On Amending Certain Laws to Avoid Tax Evasion by Enterprises Founded with the Participation of Foreign Investors' was passed; it cancelled all government and court decisions providing for certain privileges to JVs (it also has retroactive force). A 29 January 2002 Constitutional Court decision and a 14 May 2002 State Tax Administration letter caused the two Laws to come into force and confirmed that tax privileges for joint ventures with foreign participation had been cancelled by the introduction of appropriate amendments to several laws (eg the 1996 Law 'On Foreign Investment Regime').

At the same time President of Ukraine Leonid Kuchma signed the Decree 'On the Introduction of an Amendment to the Decree of the President of Ukraine of 7 July 2003 # 580'.

The document amends the Decree of the President of Ukraine of 7 July 2003 'On Additional Measures Aimed at Attracting Foreign Investments into Ukraine's Economy', giving item 2 of article 1 of the Decree the following wording:

2) in accordance with the established procedure take actions to set up by 1 January 2004 a joint stock company 'Agency on Foreign Investments', the main tasks of which are:

to promote attraction of foreign investments, formation of a positive investment image of Ukraine and its regions;

to provide economic and legal consultations on possibilities of the introduction of foreign investments into the economy of Ukraine;

to search for potential investors for domestic business entities;

to assist foreign investors in their cooperation with bodies of the executive power, bodies of local self-government;

to follow investment projects, promote protection of investments' rights;

to work out proposals aimed at encouraging investment activity, in particular taking into consideration the experience of other states in the sphere of attraction of foreign investments and the elimination of barriers which have a negative impact on the investment climate in Ukraine;

to organize training of specialists in the sphere of investment activity;

to publish information and analytical materials on the social and economic development and investment possibilities of Ukraine and its regions.

The above-mentioned 'Agency on Foreign Investments', therefore, is expected to become an organization responsible for the consolidation of the efforts of the central and local authorities in attracting foreign investment to Ukraine.

Investment attractiveness of regions

A recent study compiled by the Kyiv-based think tank, the Institute of Reform, rated Ukraine's regions in terms of their investment appeal. It assigned scores in the areas of economic development, market and financial infrastructure, human resources development and the cooperation of business and local authorities. Kyiv topped the ranking in 2003 for the third consecutive year, with the city's total score twice that of the nearest runner-up.

The city has drawn USD1.3 billion in foreign capital since independence, one-third of the USD3.9 billion in foreign capital that Ukraine has attracted in the past decade. Kyiv is followed on the list by Ukraine's industrial regions. Dnipropetrovsk oblast took second place, despite the relatively poor development of its small businesses and the country's highest crime rate. Ukraine's most heavily industrialized and densely populated area, Donetsk oblast, was placed third in the overall ranking, followed by Kharkiv and Zaporizhya oblasts.

Its high level of entrepreneurial activity and business-friendly authorities pulled Lviv oblast into the sixth spot on the list. Odessa oblast and Crimea were ranked seventh and eighth respectively.

The survey suggested that reducing the number of bureaucrats may be key to improving regions' investment climate. Ukraine's two regions with the lowest investment appeal in the ranking, Kirovohrad and Zhytomyr oblasts, had the highest ratio of government officials per 1,000 residents. Institute of Reform data shows that the city of Kyiv and six of Ukraine's 25 regions have accounted for 75 per cent of all the foreign investment brought to the country over the past 10 years.

FDI statistics

According to the State Statistics Committee of Ukraine, the foreign direct investments coming into Ukraine (during the first half of 2003) totalled USD52.4 million (a 10 per cent decrease versus the same period a year ago). USD4.194 billion was attracted as of 1 October 2001, including USD702.9 million from the United States (16.8 per cent), USD400.3 million (9.5 per cent) from Cyprus, USD367.3 million (8.8 per cent) from the Netherlands, USD363.1 million from Great Britain (8.7 per cent), USD292.9 million from Russia, and USD265 million (6.3 per cent) from Germany. The largest investments have been attracted to the food industry and for refining agricultural products (USD817.8 million), trade (USD589.1 million), financial activities (USD336.3 million), transport (USD294.8 million), chemical and petrochemical industries (USD224.5 million), coke production and oil refining (USD167.2 million), and metallurgy (USD164.2 million). As of 1 October 2001, 7,928 Ukrainian enterprises were granted investments. The enterprises located in Kyiv and six regions (the Kyiv, Donetsk, Zaporizhya, Odesa, Dnipropetrovsk and Lviv regions) received the largest investments.

By origin of the investment, as of 1 July 2003, the United States, which had made investments valued at USD997.6 million, led, with 16.5 per cent of all investment, followed by Cyprus with 10.5 per cent, the United Kingdom (9.4 per cent), Virgin Islands (8.0 per cent) and the Netherlands (6.8 per cent) (see Table 1.5.1).

The Ukrainian government has suggested that Ukraine needs around USD40 billion in order to fully restructure the country's economy. Almost all industries in Ukraine require investments: metallurgy – USD7 billion, the automobile manufacturing industry – USD8.5 billion, transport industry – USD3.7 billion, chemistry and oil industry – USD3.3 billion. However, during the past 10 years, Ukraine has received only a fraction of what was expected. Annual FDI inflow was increasing during the first years of independence but has remained at the USD500 million mark for the past five years. To compare, during the same time period, Poland has received investments of approximately USD39.0 billion during 1990–99 from foreign states, including

Table 1.5.1 Foreign direct investment by countries of origin

Countries	1 January 2003		1 July 2003	
	Mn USD	% of total	Mn USD	% of total
Total	**5,339.0**	**100.0**	**6,037.5**	**100.0**
Including:				
USA	898.0	16.8	997.6	16.5
Cyprus	602.6	11.3	631.1	10.5
UK	510.5	9.6	564.7	9.4
Virgin Islands	398.8	7.5	481.4	8.0
Netherlands	337.0	6.3	410.7	6.8
Germany	322.6	6.0	359.7	6.0
Russia	312.1	5.8	342.9	5.7
Switzerland	272.7	5.1	300.1	5.0
Austria	210.9	3.9	243.3	4.0
Korea, Republic	170.5	3.2	172.1	2.9
Other countries	1,303.3	24.5	1,533.9	25.2

Source: Ministry of Statistics of Ukraine

USD5.2 billion of United States investments (data from the Polish Embassy in Ukraine). According to statistics, foreign investment in Ukraine was just USD70 per capita over 10 years, the second-lowest figure among 15 former Soviet republics, after Belarus.

The United States remains the number one foreign investor in Ukraine, with companies such as Coca-Cola, PepsiCo and Philip Morris among the largest contributors. However, the board of directors of the European Bank of Reconstruction and Development (EBRD) has recently proclaimed that the Bank is going to raise investment inflow to Ukraine, continuing the support of private companies with national and foreign capital. The EBRD's comments suggest that the volumes of the Bank's future investments in Ukraine will be connected with the establishment of an improved investment climate, including steps taken to foster a stable tax regime, well-regulated law, and an independent judiciary for the settlement of commercial disputes. During the past nine years the EBRD has committed to investing EUR1.4 billion in 57 projects. The Bank is the largest and most diversified investor in Ukraine.

Special economic zones and priority development territories

There are 11 special economic zones (SEZs) and nine priority development territories (PDTs) in operation, offering tax and import duty exemptions and other benefits to encourage investment and production of goods for export, and reportedly covering some 10 per cent of Ukrainian territory. They differ by tax concessions granted to business entities that choose to operate in the zones. SEZs generally mandate privileges for 10 to 30 years (depending on the investment).

Analysis of the SEZs' performance has shown that for the period 1999–2001, Ukrainian SEZs and PDTs attracted almost USD680 million in investments, far below the initial projections of USD2 billion. The enterprises in SEZs and PDTs produced goods with an estimated total value of UAH7.1 billion, of which USD400 million were for export. State statistics show the creation of 92,000 jobs by enterprises in SEZs and PDTs. The tax exemptions amounted to UAH1 billion, but over three years such enterprises paid about UAH600 million to central and local budgets, and about UAH260 million to different specialized funds.

Conclusion

Despite the fact that Ukraine's investment climate is still maturing, many national as well as foreign companies are successfully doing business in Ukraine. The more successful amongst them have adopted their business strategy to a changeable economic environment and have become familiar with having to forecast business and other risks which arise from time to time whilst engaged in the practice of business in the country.

Main sources used: State Statistics Committee of Ukraine; Business Information Services for NIS.

1.6

Privatization in Ukraine

Bate C Toms and Dmytro Korbut,
BC Toms & Co

In 1991, the year of Ukraine's independence, one of the declared priorities for the country was the privatization of state property. The main objective of this privatization process, as professed in the 1992 Law of Ukraine 'On the Privatization of State Property', the framework legislation on privatization in Ukraine, was to improve the social and economic efficiency of the use of state property and to attract funds for the reconstruction of Ukraine's economy. Privatization is now an important part of the Ukrainian government's domestic policy, as well as one of the significant sources of income for the state.

History

The process of privatization of state property may be divided into three types:

- privatization of land and assets in the agricultural industry;
- privatization of housing;
- privatization of state-owned industrial and other non-agricultural property (excluding housing).

While the agricultural privatization process has been markedly slow in its development, the other two types have gone much further and produced better results.

Since the agricultural and housing types of privatization have been mostly reserved for Ukrainian citizens, this chapter will focus on the privatization of industrial and other non-agricultural property (hereinafter 'industrial privatization'). This industrial privatization has moved through three stages and is now approaching the end of its final stage, as follows:

1. *Initial stage (1992–94).* During this period, privatization was typically carried out through the leasing and subsequent purchase of the property of state companies by the management and employees of these companies.

2. *Mass privatization stage (1995–97).* This stage began in 1995 when all Ukrainian citizens received the right to obtain privatization certificates, a special type of security that could be exchanged for shares of state companies sold in special privatization certificate tenders conducted by certificate auction centres. Another type of security used in these privatizations was the compensatory certificate issued to cover the losses incurred by the holders of deposits in the State Savings Bank during the period of hyperinflation from 1991 to 1995. Most of these privatization and other certificates were used by the end of 1997, although some tenders using these certificates took place up until 2000. Parallel to these certificate privatizations, thousands of small state-owned firms and other state properties were sold through auctions for cash to private owners.

3. *Large-scale cash privatization stage (approx. 1997–present).* Unlike the two preceding stages, the main emphasis during this third stage is to raise substantial revenue for the state. As a rule, during these larger privatizations, shares in medium and large companies are privatized by sale for cash in blocks at tenders or as individual shares at stock exchanges. One of the characteristic features of the current privatization process is the sale of shares of strategic and monopolistic companies, for example natural monopolies like the mining and metallurgy industrial giants Ukrrudprom and Kryvorizhstal and the energy distribution companies like Kievoblenergo.

According to the Chairman of the State Property Fund, which is responsible for the privatization process in Ukraine, during the second half of this last stage the aim will be to complete the privatization of state property, developing massive strategic private ownership and ensuring that the transformation to a market economy is irreversible, as well as to provide for the market adaptation of the governmental sector of the economy. Thus, both the processes of privatization and the transformation of the state monopoly regulation system will be synchronized. The main tasks will be to sell all shares remaining under the control of the state in open joint stock companies as well as 'individual privatization' of the majority of the monopolistic and especially important and competitive state-owned enterprises. The combination of these two actions should result in reduction of the state-owned share of Ukrainian economy to 8 to 10 per cent in total.

The general perception is that the financial state and management of the privatized companies have improved. In certain branches of the economy, such as the food industry or metallurgy, most privatized companies appear to have enjoyed strong economic growth. However, in the view of many economic commentators, privatization in Ukraine has not yet achieved most of its declared goals.

On the one hand, privatization has not created a broad class of property owners, as the majority of the shares in privatized state companies, especially the most valuable ones, were accumulated by a few powerful corporate groups or by the existing senior managers of these companies. On the other hand, the first two stages of industrial privatization demonstrated that privatization by itself does not automatically guarantee any improvement in the management of the companies or the property involved, or result in any genuine restructuring of the economy beyond the change in ownership. All too often, controlling shares were accumulated by a company's existing directors, who continued to apply Soviet-style management techniques. In addition, non-cash privatizations often failed to involve sources for the funding needed for the modernization of the privatized companies and their future growth.

Privatization process

The privatization process is primarily regulated by the Laws of Ukraine and legal acts of the State Property Fund. The basic Laws governing the process are 'On the Privatization of State Property' (the 'Privatization Law'), 'On the Privatization Securities' and 'On the Privatization of Small-Sized State Companies (Small Privatization)' all adopted in 1992. These Laws regulate the overall legal framework and determine what can be privatized, who can be parties to the privatization process and what privatization procedures apply.

The Privatization Law identifies the following three groups of state-owned property that are subject to privatization: (1) shares in the capital of business companies and other entities; (2) unfinished constructions and mothballed developments; and (3) certain individual items of property or 'integrated property complexes' (defined as being a group of assets sufficient to conduct a separate business activity) of state-owned companies. This law also effectively excludes from privatization state property that is defined as being of 'national importance' (the principal examples of such property are listed in Table 1.6.1). Based on these criteria, a list of particular companies and property that are excluded from privatization has been adopted and, from time to time, is modified by the Parliament of Ukraine (the Verhovna Rada).

Table 1.6.1 Selected property that cannot be privatized owing to its 'national importance'

Assets of enterprises that ensure the issuance and storage of banknotes, coins and securities
Radio and television transmission centres
State radio and television channels
Educational, sport and scientific establishments funded by the state
Assets of enterprises producing and repairing arms used by the Ukrainian army
Assets of aviation industry enterprises
Roads outside a company's premises
Railroads and enterprises producing locomotives and railcars
Metros and other electric transport in cities
Assets ensuring the operation of the united energy system and the dispatch of electricity as well as the operation of high voltage networks
Atomic electro-power stations, combined heat and power plants, and hydro-electro power stations using dams that ensure water supply and hydro-melioration
Oil and gas underground storage facilities and major pipelines
Assets of enterprises producing spirits, wine and hard liquor

The Privatization Law establishes few restrictions on who can be the purchasers of state property in a privatization. It prohibits from participation in privatizations only: (1) legal entities more than 25 per cent owned by the state; (2) state government bodies; and (3) employees of state privatization bodies.

The State Programme of Privatization adopted by Ukraine sets forth the main objectives and terms of privatization for each specified Programme period. The privatization programme is meant to be reviewed and approved by the Parliament in co-ordination with the annual state budgets for the relevant period, and remains effective until a new programme is approved. Currently, the State Programme of Privatization for 2000–02 adopted in May 2000 (the '2000–02 Programme') still remains in force, since the Draft Law on the State Programme of Privatization for 2003–08, submitted for consideration by Parliament, was rejected in June 2003. A newly-developed Draft Law on the State Programme of Privatization, revised to apply for the period of 2004–06, was re-submitted to Parliament in March 2004, however, the process for its consideration is likely to be slow until after the Ukrainian Presidential elections.

Ukrainian law does not provide for any express restrictions on the participation of foreign persons or entities in privatization. However, there are some statutory limitations on the foreign ownership of, or investment in, the capital of certain entities that may effectively limit foreign involvement, as described in Table 1.6.2. In principle, pursuant to the Partnership and Co-operation Agreement between Ukraine and the European Community, the application of many of these limitations to EU-based companies is to be eliminated. There is also a formal requirement of approval by the Cabinet of Ministers of Ukraine for the privatization of monopolistic or strategic state-owned enterprises, as well as for the involvement of foreign investment pursuant to the international agreements of Ukraine.

The draft Programme of Privatization for 2004–06, which was submitted to the Parliament in March 2004, proposes to prohibit the participation of certain legal entities in the privatization of especially important state-owned enterprises or joint stock companies, if, in each case, the State Property Fund of Ukraine is not able to identify all of the persons controlling such legal entity based on the information submitted with the application for participation in the privatization. It can be expected that the government will pay more attention to the reputation of investors and the origin of funds used in privatizations in future, especially for the privatization of major industrial enterprises.

The State Property Fund of Ukraine

The main state body responsible for the development and implementation of the state privatization policy is the State Property Fund of Ukraine (SPF), established in 1992 by the Parliament pursuant to the Privatization Law and the 'Temporary Regulation on the State Property Fund of Ukraine' approved by the Resolution of Parliament of 7 July 1992, No. 2558 (the 'Temporary Regulation').

The SPF is created by Article 7 of the Privatization Law as an independent state body that is subordinated to, and reports to the Parliament. However, in 1998 the Constitutional Court ruled that this provision subordinating the SPF to Parliament was unconstitutional. The status of the SPF was to be clarified in the proposed law on the SPF, the draft of which was submitted to Parliament in June 2003 but rejected in September 2003. The principal debate surrounding this

Table 1.6.2 Foreign investment in Ukrainian companies

Foreign investment in Ukrainian companies is limited to 30% for the following types of Ukrainian companies:

- publishing houses;
- organizations distributing publications;
- information agencies;
- broadcasting companies and television and radio organizations.

draft law focused on whether to subordinate the SPF to the Cabinet of Ministers (the principal state executive body).

The scope of the SPF's authority is currently spelt out in Article 7 of the Privatization Law and the Temporary Regulation, as well as in other relevant decisions by the President and the Cabinet of Ministers of Ukraine. Among other powers, the SPF is given the authority to perform the following functions:

- sell state-owned property in the course of privatization, including the property of liquidated enterprises and uncompleted construction projects;
- take actions to engage foreign investors in the privatization process;
- develop and submit to the Cabinet of Ministers drafts of national privatization programmes, and organize and control their implementation;
- change the organizational and legal form of state-owned enterprises in the course of their privatization by transforming them into open joint stock companies (to facilitate share sales);
- exercise the authority of the owner of the shares of state-owned joint stock companies, which were not sold in the course of a privatization, and bear the commercial risks connected with such shares;
- approve plans for the privatization of state-owned property;
- conclude agreements with intermediaries regarding the organization of the privatization process and the sale of state property;
- act as a lessor of state-owned property;
- participate in the development and conclusion of international agreements on property and the use of state-owned property;
- represent, in Ukraine and abroad, the state's interests in state-owned shares, as well as the interests of state enterprises, organizations and institutions etc, and
- exercise control functions over state-owned shares in joint stock companies that were not sold in the course of a privatization, including by electing individuals representing the government to the management boards of such companies.

Privatization methods and procedures

The methods and procedures for privatization differ depending on the entities or other property to be privatized, as listed in a Privatization Programme. In the 2000–02 Programme, which remains in force pending adoption of the Draft new Programme for 2004–06, the entities or property to be privatized are grouped by type (eg strategic and monopolistic companies, unfinished construction, etc) and the number of persons employed at these state companies.

The Privatization Programme is implemented by the Cabinet of Ministers and the SPF. They typically begin by creating a privatization commission for each company being privatized, and the commission prepares the actual privatization plan covering all aspects of the privatization process to be implemented. Under the Privatization Law, the impetus for a privatization may come from the SPF, or it may be in response to an application from any foreign or domestic prospective buyer (which may include employees of the company to be privatized).

In the past, many privatizations took place through so-called 'non-commercial' tenders, when the winner was the person that, for the fixed price stated for each such tender, proposed the best investment and operational terms. Presently, the bidders in such tenders also propose the price. At these tenders, the winner not only pays for the acquired shares, but also undertakes to make certain investments and accepts other obligations. The Draft new Programme for 2004–06 proposes to prohibit privatization based on competing investment and operational terms and limit it only to competition based on the best price.

Currently, priority is generally being given to 'commercial' tenders for the larger privatizations, where the winner is determined solely on the basis of written sealed submissions by the potential purchasers quoting a price, with the best price winning. The SPF can also impose special qualifying conditions for bidders willing to take part in the privatization of monopolistic or strategic state-owned enterprises. If there is only one bidder qualified for a tender, a special 'independent evaluation procedure' can be arranged to determine the 'commercial' price of the property being privatized.

In addition to non-commercial and commercial tenders, the two principal methods of privatization, the Privatization Law also permits auctions, buyouts and sales through stock exchanges and OTCs (over-the-counter markets).

The privatization procedure depends on the type of property to be privatized. Privatization procedures for monopolistic or strategic state-owned enterprises may include the following stages: preparation of the state-owned enterprises for privatization, establishment of a state-owned open JSC, valuation of the object of privatization, development of special conditions for the purchase and sale agreement, determining the winner of a commercial tender and monitoring fulfilment of the buyer's obligations under the purchase and sale agreement.

The sale of state property in a privatization is documented by a notarized purchase and sale agreement with the SPF. The agreement ordinarily provides for additional obligations to be imposed on the buyer, usually for defined periods of time, which may include:

- criteria for the reconstruction of the facilities;
- an obligation not to decrease the number of jobs;
- preservation of the production of certain products;
- preservation of a certain social infrastructure;
- making subsequent investments of certain amounts;
- performance of 'mobilization tasks' (measures designed to restructure the company quickly in case of a threat of war, etc).

Restrictions may be placed on any subsequent sale of property acquired in a privatization, if such sale occurs before any such privatization obligations are performed or expire.

According to Article 27 of the Privatization Law, the purchase and sale agreement may be terminated (including by rescission) or declared invalid by a court in the event that one of the parties fails to perform its privatization obligations in a timely manner. Although, as a matter of legal theory, arguments can be made against the use of this provision on invalidity, it is in practice used to reverse privatizations even where the obligation stated in the purchase and sale agreement can only be performed by the company and not directly by the one or more shareholders who bought their shares in the company's privatization. In such cases, it is essential for the acquiring shareholders to have effective control over the management from the outset.

An additional basis for termination of the purchase and sale agreement can be found in Article 29 of the Privatization Law, which states that 'a violation of the privatization procedure established by law or of the purchaser's rights shall be a basis for declaring a purchase and sale agreement to be invalid' by which such property was acquired. This provision may apply, for example, where one of the applicants for shares was denied the right to participate in a tender in violation of the privatization procedure. Article 29 also provides for a variety of penalties that apply in the event of contractual non-performance in a privatization.

Ordinarily, purchase and sale agreements concluded in the privatization process provide for payment by the purchaser shortly after the agreement is executed. Article 29 of the Privatization Law contains an important limitation that prevents any extensions of the time for payment and inhibits conditional sales as well. It provides that failure to pay for any privatized property within 60 days from the moment when the purchase and sale agreement was concluded or registered results in annulment of the sale and in fines on the purchaser.

In the privatization of six electricity distribution companies in 2001, this meant that bidders could not make payments into an escrow account and make their bids conditional on due diligence problems being resolved before payment would be irrevocably released to the SPF. The result was that because the resolution of the due diligence problems was expected to take over 60 days and the SPF refused to extend the deadlines for the execution of the purchase and sale agreements, the bids in the tender may have been consequently reduced.

Privatization in 2003 and beyond

The 2000–02 Programme

The plan for the present privatization process in Ukraine continues to be governed by the 2000–02 Programme adopted on 18 May 2000. In many respects, this Programme marked the advent of a new era in the state's privatization policies compared with the previous privatization programmes. The 2000–02 Programme introduced such measures as privatization conducted exclusively by cash sales, individualized approaches for each of the companies subject to privatization and significantly increased information transparency during the privatization process. The implementation of these measures could be further facilitated by the involvement of professional advisers to restructure companies before they are offered for sale, and by the employment of a competitive mechanism for sales.

The main emphasis of the 2000–02 Programme is the privatization of a number of significant strategic and monopolistic companies, including certain 'natural' monopolies such as the electricity distribution and telecommunication companies (the so-called 'Group G' state property). This is thought to be the most attractive property to sell in order to raise substantial revenue for the state. The Programme introduced a number of special provisions aimed at increasing the efficiency of such sales. A key notion for such procedures is to provide that the so-called 'industrial investors' (companies meeting certain qualifying criteria, including with respect to production and management experience) shall be the sole bidders allowed to participate in privatizations in certain areas considered attractive to foreign investors, such as the fuel and energy sector, metallurgy, the petrochemical industry, radio electronics, airlines and machine building.

This approach is designed not only to maximize the income from these privatizations, but more importantly, to ensure the long-term stability of companies that have a key role in the national economy. While there has been some criticism of the very restrictive criteria applied in some tenders for qualifying industrial investors to bid, it appears highly likely that similar principles will be retained for the near future.

The privatization of Group G companies must be conducted through sales of blocks of shares of these open joint stock companies at commercial tenders. The usual condition for such privatizations is that the sale of the controlling block of shares (being at least 50 per cent plus one share) must be to a single buyer. If the controlling block of shares is instead retained by the state, the investor may still be granted the right, at its request, to manage all or part of the state-owned block of shares, depending on the tender's terms.

One of the important preconditions for the sale of shares in monopolistic companies as well as many of the larger state companies is for the bidder to obtain prior approval for its acquisition from the Antimonopoly Committee of Ukraine. Even if this is not a precondition, it is highly advisable for the bidder to verify whether it requires such approval under Ukrainian competition law, as the approval process may take some time. In certain regulated sectors, such as electricity, bidders must also be approved in advance by the relevant state regulator for their industry.

As previously mentioned above, the draft State Programme of Privatization for 2004–06, accompanied by a group of proposed amendments to the privatization laws in force, was submitted to Parliament in March 2004. This new draft Programme should set forth new strategies and approaches to further improve the privatization process by taking into account previous experience. The aim of this new Programme will be to accomplish privatization of state property, decreasing the state-owned share of the Ukrainian economy to 8 to 10 per cent in total. It should provide for privatizing the majority of the monopolistic and particularly competitive state-owned enterprises. A priority of the new Programme should also be to raise the level of trust of potential buyers in the privatization process through increased openness and transparency for all related procedures.

The new draft State Programme of Privatization for 2004–06 contains many new or improved elements for the privatization process, such as encouraging sales through stock exchanges and OTCs, assisting in the development of a stock market, and expediting the sale of all shares in open joint stock companies in which the state currently owns less than 50 per cent. This draft Programme sets forth in much greater detail the procedure for preparation of state-owned enterprises for privatization and improves the methods for selling joint stock companies.

However, the most substantial and controversial novelty in this draft Programme is the implementation of such improvements to the privatization of the most important state-owned enterprises and joint stock companies, including by allowing the State Property Fund to modify the conditions under which corporate bidders can take part in privatization tenders. This means that the choice of specific methods of privatization, conditions of purchase and sale agreements, the price of the assets being sold and other important details could be determined depending on the qualifications of buyers and subject to the effective functioning of the company after privatization, in contrast to the pure market mechanisms of open tenders. The draft Programme also provides that the government of Ukraine may only, under certain specific, limited conditions, decide that especially important state-owned companies can remain under state control. It attempts to ensure that such decisions by the government will be public and transparent, providing for improved access to information to support the privatization process.

Privatization in the energy sector

Privatization tenders for the sale of six electricity distribution companies were successfully held in April 2001. Despite the uncertainty over the future of the government of Ukrainian Prime Minister Viktor Yushchenko at that time and the insufficient preparation of the companies for privatization (eg lack of clear title to certain key assets, land use rights, required operational approvals and other appropriate documentation), the shares of all six companies were sold to strategic investors, and the prices for two of these companies were significantly higher than some had predicted. Two companies were purchased by the US firm AES Washington Holdings BV, and four by the Slovakian enterprise Vychodoslovenske Energeticke Zavody. Ukraine received approximately USD160 millions from these sales. This privatization was also the first occasion when the SPF involved a sophisticated Western bank, Credit Suisse First Boston (CSFB), as its principal adviser. CSFB effectively lobbied for the regulatory framework for the operation of electricity distribution companies to be made acceptable for potential bidders, for example on matters such as the setting of electricity prices. Based on this experience, the SPF plans to sell the remaining 12 state-owned electricity distribution companies.

The success of future privatizations in the energy sector may depend, in part, on how the Ukrainian government resolves the problem of the huge debts of the state companies being privatized. For the first six electricity distribution companies privatized in 2001, these debts were restructured over five years with no payments within the first two years and no interest or penalties on the delayed payments. This approach might not work for some of the 12 companies to be privatized in the next stage, which have accumulated substantially larger debts. According to preliminary information in the press, the total debt of 9 of these 12 companies exceeds one billion US dollars. This debt significantly exceeds the minimum price that is expected to be required for bids for these 12 companies, which should be approximately USD375 million.

The schedule for the next major privatization in the energy sector is not yet clear. In the past three years it has been continuously postponed as the government was not sure of attracting major Western multinational energy companies as strategic investors. Hopefully, any delays will be used to prepare the companies better for privatization, including resolving issues on land ownership and use rights, operational approvals and other problems that often come up in the due diligence of state companies. Documenting land ownership rights to replace land use rights based on the new Land Code (which entered into force on 1 January 2002) can effectively provide an additional guarantee of value for purchasers.

After all of the electricity distribution companies have been privatized, it is anticipated that privatization of the state electricity generation companies will follow. In 2001, there were several attempts by powerful Ukrainian corporate groups to take control of these electricity generators by acquiring and enforcing their large debts. This process is commonly known as 'hidden privatization'. Several debts were enforced on this basis and recoveries were made against the assets of these state companies, effectively allowing the assets to be acquired to satisfy debts at a small fraction of their true market value. This potentially dangerous trend was halted by the Ukrainian Parliament imposing a moratorium on such recoveries, including through bankruptcy proceedings, against the assets of companies that are 25 per cent or more state-owned.

Telecommunications – the privatization of Ukrtelecom

One of the next major privatizations in Ukraine should be of Ukrtelecom, the national telecommunications operator of Ukraine. The adoption of the special Law 'On the Peculiarities for the Privatization of the Open JSC Ukrtelecom' of 13 July 2000 (the 'Ukrtelecom Law') establishes the basis for this sale. The Ukrtelecom Law provides that 50 per cent plus one share of Ukrtelecom shall be retained by the state, while at least 25 per cent plus one share must be sold off to a single qualifying industrial investor in an open tender.

According to Article 17 of the Ukrtelecom Law, 30 per cent of the proceeds received from the privatization must be transferred by the SPF to Ukrtelecom after it is privatized as a subsidy for the development of its telecommunications network and for the purchase of modern equipment. The capital fund of the privatized company should accordingly be increased by the issuance of additional shares, which will be added to the remaining state-owned shares and thereby reduce the investor's percentage shareholding. The net effect of these transactions on the percentage shareholdings in Ukrtelecom is as yet unclear, and it is likely that the law on this reinvestment will be amended. However, the winning investor should, in any case, also have the right to acquire contractually the right to manage up to half of the shares that are expected to be retained by the state. This, in turn, should allow the investor to exercise effective control over the company for the term of the share management contract.

To qualify as a bidder, the investor must be a telecommunications operator (or a consortium including a telecommunications operator) having at least five years of operational experience and must satisfy certain documentation requirements. Normally bidders are also required to make a cash deposit of, or to provide a bank guarantee for, about 10 per cent of the minimum required bid amount. Bidders may not be registered in 'offshore' (ie tax haven) jurisdictions. We understand that, as for the privatization of the electricity generators, bids will be placed in a glass box by the bidders at the tender, with the bids then being immediately opened to reveal the winner – a literally transparent procedure. The winning bidder must then enter into a formal purchase and sale agreement for the purchase of the shares, and pay in cash within 30 days after the execution of the purchase and sale agreement.

The Ukrtelecom Law also expressly requires that the company continue rendering telecommunication services to those persons who are presently benefiting from certain tariff privileges, irrespective of when the state actually pays the planned compensation to the company to make up for the subsidy in these artificially low tariffs. In addition, the conditions of the tender and the qualification requirements for the investors must be determined by the Privatization Commission and approved by the Cabinet of Ministers. An audit by an international accounting firm of Ukrtelecom's accounts for the year preceding the tender will also need to be completed.

It is currently estimated that the 42.86 per cent block of Ukrtelecom shares will be offered for sale in 2005, but, as in previous years, this may be postponed. Conditions for this privatization, approved by the Order of the SPF in July 2004, provide that qualified bidders can participate in the sale if they are not registered in offshore countries and if the SPF can properly determine the persons of whom such bidders are under control. It will be prohibited to pay for Ukrtelecom shares with funds obtained from illegal or hidden sources.

Conclusion

The experience of recent privatizations in Ukraine shows that the Ukrainian authorities are prepared to offer for privatization, companies that occupy leading positions in the Ukrainian economy. However, recent practices of the SPF to limit competition from outside of Ukraine in the privatization of such huge enterprises like Kryvorizhstal, which is one of the 30 largest metallurgical plants in the world, have raised some doubts with respect to transparency and the degree to which an 'equal playing field' is being created by the privatization process. In June 2004, one Ukrainian bidder, the Investment Metallurgy Union, controlled by powerful Ukrainian business groups, purchased 93.02 per cent of the state-owned shares of Kryvorizhstal for UAH4,260 million, thereby setting the record for the largest sale in the history of Ukrainian privatization. Nevertheless, this sale is more widely discussed because the discriminatory qualifying conditions for other bidders made it impossible for such reputable potential bidders like US Steel, LNM and Russian 'Severstal' to participate in the privatization, despite some press reports that they were prepared to offer a significantly higher price.

Nevertheless, it appears that many Ukrainian state assets will continue to be sold at a substantial discount to the prices that would be paid for similar assets in Western, or even Central Europe. This is resulting in many unique business opportunities in Ukraine, such as existed 10 years ago in Central Europe, when countries like the Czech Republic and Poland privatized their state assets. While the proposed privatization of Ukrtelecom and the remaining electricity distributors and generators have attracted the most attention, in fact a wide variety of businesses are to be privatized in the near future, including in the metallurgy, machine-building and chemical industries. Initial information on the companies offered for privatization can be obtained from the SPF's website at www.spfu.gov.ua.

1.7

The Ukrainian Banking System

Mykhaylo Kuzmin, Raiffeisenbank, Ukraine

Introduction

The Ukrainian banking system has two tiers: the National Bank of Ukraine and commercial banks of various forms of ownership, including the state-owned Export-Import Bank and a specialized commercial Savings Bank. The evolution of the national banking system in Ukraine started in March 1991, after the adoption of the Law of Ukraine 'On Banks and Banking' by the Ukrainian parliament (Verhovna Rada).

The National Bank of Ukraine serves as the country's central bank pursuing a uniform state monetary policy to ensure, stability of the national currency.

Commercial banks are joint stock companies or limited liability companies with both legal and natural persons as shareholders. The banks act in accordance with the Constitution of Ukraine, the Laws of Ukraine 'On the National Bank of Ukraine', 'On Banks and Banking', the Civil Code, the Ukrainian legislation on joint stock companies and other economic entities, as well as with the normative regulations of the National Bank of Ukraine and their Statutes.

The range of commercial banks' activities includes: attracting deposits of enterprises, institutions and households, crediting of economic entities and households, investments in securities, maintenance of accounts, cash and settlement servicing of the economy, foreign exchange operations, depository and custodian service, and other services. Banking operations are subject to licensing by the National Bank.

National Bank of Ukraine

According to Article 99 of the Constitution of Ukraine, adopted in 1996, the main function of the country's central bank is to ensure the stability of the national currency, the hryvnia. To carry out its main function, the National Bank must foster the stability of the banking system and, within its competence, price stability.

According to the Law of Ukraine 'On the National Bank of Ukraine', the National Bank is the central bank of Ukraine, a specific central body of the state administration, its issuing centre which pursues common state policy in money circulation and credit; it coordinates the functioning of the banking system in general and determines the exchange rate of the national currency against foreign currencies. The National Bank determines the kind of banknotes, their denomination, their distinctive features and their protection system. It ensures the accumulation and custody of gold and currency reserves and the conduct of transactions with them and the banking metals. The National Bank determines the discount rate and other interest rates; it gives permission for commercial banks' registration and licenses banking business; and determines the standard of emergency funds for commercial banks and other financial and credit institutions.

The highest management body of the National Bank is the Council of the National Bank of Ukraine. The governing body of the National Bank is the Board of the National Bank of Ukraine. The Council of the National Bank consists of 14 people. (The president of Ukraine appoints seven members of the Council, including the governor, and the other seven are appointed by parliament.) According to Article 100 of the Constitution of Ukraine, the Council of the National Bank shall develop the general principles of monetary policy and monitor its implementation.

The Governor of the National Bank shall be appointed, subject to submission by the president of Ukraine, by the majority of the constitutional complement of the Verkhovna Rada of Ukraine for a period of five years.

The National Bank of Ukraine represents the interests of Ukraine in relations with other countries' central banks, international banks, and other financial and credit institutions, on behalf of Ukraine. The National Bank of Ukraine is entitled to a legislative initiative.

The National Bank of Ukraine is accountable to the president of Ukraine and to the Verkhovna Rada of Ukraine within the limits of its constitutional power.

History

On 20 March 1991, the resolution of the Verkhovna Rada of the Ukrainian SSR entitled 'On Procedure of Enactment of the Law of Ukrainian SSR "On Banks and Banking Activity"' was adopted, pursuant to which this law took effect on 1 May 1991.

The National Bank of Ukraine was resolved to be created on the basis of the Ukrainian Republican Bank of the State Bank of the USSR.

Article 7 of the Resolution of the National Bank of Ukraine directed that, no later than 1 November 1991, a procedure should be established for issuing licences to bankers' establishments, authorizing them to fulfil transactions in foreign currency within the Ukrainian SSR and abroad, and to reconsider all the issued licences authorizing the fulfilment of these transactions, as well as to implement re-registration of all the banks, their affiliates, and other credit establishments located on the territory of Ukraine.

On 7 October 1991, the Statute of the National Bank of Ukraine (NBU) was approved by a resolution of the Presidium of the Verkhovna Rada of Ukraine. The NBU was acknowledged as a state establishment accountable to the Verkhovna Rada of Ukraine.

In December 1991, the Verkhovna Rada passed a resolution on the ratification of the name and characteristic attributes of the monetary unit of Ukraine, the hryvnia. At the beginning of 1992 the first Ukrainian bank with foreign interest was registered, and by the beginning of February 22 commercial banks had already been opened, direct correspondent relations had been arranged with many foreign banks, and the NBU's computer centre had been created with a view to providing interbank settlements.

In June 1992, the formation of the Stabilization Fund for the Ukrainian National Currency began. In July 1992, a single settlement cash centre of the NBU was created with the transition to settlements with the CIS member states via correspondent accounts opened by the NBU. In August 1992, the Currency Exchange of the NBU was created. In September 1992, Ukraine joined the International Monetary Fund and the World Bank, and in October of the same year it joined the European Bank for Reconstruction and Development. In November 1992, Ukraine left the 'rouble zone'.

In 1996, the new national currency, the hryvnia (UAH), was issued. During the first two years of its circulation the NBU paid great attention to its stability, maintaining a tough monetary policy and intervening in the foreign exchange market to stabilize the hryvnia exchange rate when the US dollar was high.

The rise and development of Ukraine's banking system has proceeded in extremely adverse conditions. The most important of these include: the destruction of resources with respect to Ukrainian banks as part of a central, Russia-based system in 1990–91; the economic crisis, which manifested itself in a massive, powerful depression of production; the decline of gross domestic product (to 38 per cent of the 1989 level); the keen decrease in citizens' incomes; and continued inflation (which reached its peak at 10,260 per cent p.a. in 1993). The tax pressure of 1994 also negatively affected banks. Another factor that affected the banking sector was the public's attitude towards banks. These factors accompanied the transition process in Ukraine's economy for several years. However, in spite of these difficulties, Ukraine's banking system has proceeded step by step in its evolution towards the stabilization of its role in the society and economy.

Development of the banking system is closely connected with the names of NBU's governors, Vadym Hetman (1992) and Viktor Yushchenko (1993–2000). In the period of transition from an administrative-command to a market-oriented economy, they defined the monetary policy of Ukraine, created new instruments of the monetary market, conducted experiments, and advocated rigid monetary decisions in parliament.

Owing to NBU's strict control of banks and limitations on risky operations or instruments, its fast reaction to changing circumstances allowed the Russian financial crisis of 1998 to be overcome without heavy losses and bankruptcies for the financial system and the economy. After 1998 the banks won the trust of the Ukrainian people.

Current trend

The development of the banking system over the past three years gives reason for optimism. During 2000–02 the capital of the banking system increased 2.3-fold from UAH4.5 billion to UAH10.1 billion. Retail deposits increased 4.4-fold, from UAH4.3 billion to UAH19.1 billion. Credits to enterprises increased 3.4-fold, including a rise in long-term credits – 4.5-fold. To improve the resources, the National Bank of Ukraine mandated the norms of obligatory reserves for deposits in the banking system: from 16 per cent to 0 per cent for long-term deposits and to 2 per cent for short-term deposits in local currency (LCY). In the past three years (when NBU was headed by Volodymyr Stelmakh) several instruments have been introduced by NBU to maintain banks' liquidity. Among these are, first, REPO-crediting for the maintenance of immediate liquidity by using the government's bonds, then short-term bank refinancing for a period to nine months; it was also Mr Stelmakh who introduced the scheme of long-term credit for the economy through long-term bank refinancing for investment projects. For that period the refinancing rate decreased from 30 per cent to 8 per cent.

Owing to the reduced *refi* rate and to a decrease in the norms of obligatory reserves for deposits, some positive results followed:

- On the money market both interest rates and their volatility declined.
- Banks increased the deposit activity first of all of individuals: deposits grew at an average annual rate of 64 per cent. At the same time deposit rates declined: from 21.4 per cent (2001) to 6.7 per cent (June 2003).
- Owing to getting resources more cheaply, credit rates declined from 43.3 per cent to 19.4 per cent, which stimulated economic growth.
- Inflation declined steadily from its peak in 2000 of 25.8 per cent to the deflationary result of 2002 (0.6 per cent).

When he came to NBU in December 2002, Governor Sergiy Tyhypko made some changes to NBU's strategic directions in development. Tyhypko overturned the policy of the central bank of the country for further liberalization, and started a programme to make the banking sector more reliable and transparent. The new priority of the banking system must be stimulation of economic growth with the maintenance of stability of the local currency, prices and banking activity. This was announced by the new head of the NBU in presenting his *'Complex programme of the development of the banking system in Ukraine for 2003–05'*. Among the main goals are: reducing credit interest rates, expanding the terms of credit, including the retail sector, and strengthening the banking system. Tyhypko thinks that to achieve these goals a higher capitalization of banks must be achieved, as well as an increase in the level of corporate management and internal audit in banks, a strengthening of the role and quality of external audit, the introduction of an effective system of risk management, etc. The main measures aimed at liberalizing the market will include easing the requirements involving the submission of documents by banks seeking to participate in transactions, broadening individuals' opportunities to transfer funds abroad, and simplification of the procedures regulating trading sessions. An absolutely new instrument was also introduced by the central bank – starting operations with forward and futures contracts. Thus, since 2003, futures and forward contracts can be bought abroad by plenipotentiaries and among the very first plans of the NBU is the introduction of a local system of forward and futures operations. The latter is the signal for the development of the stock market with further implementation of the main financial instruments.

Banks

According to the data available as of 1 July 2003, 179 commercial banks were registered in Ukraine. Twenty of these have a foreign capital share (seven banks have 100 per cent foreign capital). One hundred and fifty-five banks are actually functioning in Ukraine with a total authorized capital of UAH6.5 billion (USD1.2 billion) or UAH42 million (USD7.9 million) per bank on average. Two banks (Savings Bank and Export-Import Bank) are owned by the state.

The Ukrainian banking system has been developing intensively over the past four years, following the default of 1998. Its general level is not appropriate considering economic output and the demand for banking services. In fact, banking assets, which grew by 34 per cent to UAH67.8 billion in 2002, account for only 32 per cent of GDP. In CEE countries this share is 72 per cent (see Table 1.7.1).

The Ukrainian banking system shows a high level of capital and a concentration of banking operations. Thus, more than half of the assets, loan portfolio and liabilities (54.4, 54.3 and 57.1 per cent respectively) are held by the top 10 banks, as is 41 per cent of securities investments and 38.4 per cent of total banking capital. More than half of corporate deposits and two-thirds of individuals' assets are attracted by the top 10. It is evidence of a non-developed banking market when only banks with a good market history (Prominvestbank, Privatbank, Aval, Ukrsotsbank), with good (state or foreign capital) support (Savings Bank, Ukreximbank, Raiffeisenbank Ukraine), or which are well known owing to investments in marketing policy (Nadra, Ukrsibbank, FUIB), can show stable and transparent development.

There are seven banks with 100 per cent foreign capital function in Ukraine: Raiffeisenbank Ukraine (Austria), Citibank (USA), Credit-Lyonnais (France), Alfa-Bank (Russia), HVB Ukraine (Germany), ING Bank Ukraine (Netherlands) and Pekao Bank (Poland).

The foreign banks became more active participants on the market, 'importing' to Ukraine Western standards, products, and style of business. Most of them have their own specific market segment (mainly comprising Ukrainian representatives of the main clients of the 'mother bank'). For instance, Raiffeisenbank Ukraine is the only

Table 1.7.1 Banks' activity as share of GDP

	Assets	Loans	Deposits
Ukraine 2002	32%	22%	27%
CEE5* 2001	72%	36%	46%

*CEE5 countries: Czech Republic, Hungary, Slovenia, Slovak, Poland

foreign bank that does banking for individuals, and one of a few that lend to Ukrainian corporations, competing with Ukrainian banks for market share. The market share of banks with 100 per cent foreign capital in corporate lending increased from 6.5 per cent in 2001 to 8.1 per cent in 2002.

On the deposit market, foreign banks are not so active and 'well known'. They deal basically in the corporate deposit segment (market share 5.6 per cent); however, their retail activity has begun to increase recently, and their market share reached 0.9 per cent on 1 June 2003 (0.6 per cent in 2002).

Retail banking – a promising sector

Competition in the corporate loans market pushes banks to search for new sources of banking activity. For this reason, many of them turned their attention to the retail market. The expanded banking retail credit policy became the new engine of asset distribution. The growth of corporate loans is slower than that of individual lending (45 per cent growth in corporate loans, 134 per cent growth in householders' lending on 2002 data).

The liabilities side of banking activities shows a similar tendency. The continuing growth of individuals' deposits takes the prize (28 per cent growth in corporate deposits versus 70 per cent in household deposits in 2002). In 2002 the total volume of household deposits exceeded corporate deposits.

Retail banking is now a growing market, owing to reforms in the banking sector. NBU cancelled the restriction on lending to individuals in foreign currencies, and therefore simplified the lending process for individuals. Thus, since March 2003 the lending procedure has become more convenient and attractive for the population, foreign loans have become more accessible, and people will be able to get not only consumer credit but also other types of loans (car and mortgage loans, etc). The banks tested the principles of mortgage lending in advance of the Law 'On Mortgages' which should have come into force in January 2004; however, Parliament put a moratorium on land trading until 2010. There are also some new laws ready to be signed by the president. Thus, Laws 'On Mortgage Lending and Factoring Operations with Mortgage Liabilities' and 'On Finance-Credit Mechanisms of Residential Construction' stipulate the main operating conditions for the new market: mortgage lending, conditions for using mortgage securities, the requirements on construction companies and banks. The laws regulate the requirements for participating in the mortgage market. In particular, construction companies working with mortgages should have three years of construction experience according to their accounts, and also the possibility of undertaking construction in several places. The special requirements for banks are: they must have five years' experience and have NBU permission to back operations with the assets and securities of individuals. Financial institutions are allowed to attract resources for mortgage lending from different sources at the same time, by issuing new loans when old ones are redeemed, and by issuing mortgage-backed securities. The laws create the opportunity for banks to take part in such future markets.

1.8

Corporate Governance

IFC, Ukraine Corporate Development Project

As a result of Ukraine's process of mass privatization started in 1992, more than 36,000 joint stock companies and more than 17 million shareholders have emerged. The transformation of state-owned enterprises into private property called for a new management approach by companies, placing an emphasis on management training, enhancement of investment opportunities, risk management and a balance of interest for all parties to corporate relations. The issue of improving corporate governance in Ukraine became particularly urgent in the wake of transition from certificate to cash-based privatization. The appearance of real owners has subsequently brought demands for guarantees of stability and profitability of their investment, transparency of company operations and protection of their rights.

The overall investment climate in Ukraine may be regarded as risky and corporate governance at a moderate level, combined with inadequate legislation, inefficient courts and a nascent stock market. These factors discourage investors from investing in Ukrainian business. Lately, however, both the government and stock market authorities have been taking steps to improve corporate governance in Ukraine, including the adoption of the Ukraine Corporate Governance Principles in December 2003, and the coming into force of the new commercial and civil codes on 1 January 2004. Legal reform and a gradual change of enterprise directors' mindsets should provide the security needed to improve the attractiveness of Ukrainian companies and to encourage the adoption of international corporate governance standards.

A brief description of the ownership structure

Of the 36,000 joint stock companies that exist in Ukraine, approximately 23,000 are 'closed joint stock companies'.[1] A smaller number of open joint stock companies reflects the general tendency of market activity. At present, approximately 250 joint stock companies are traded on the Ukrainian stock market, while only 14 are traded on foreign stock exchanges. The Securities and Stock Market State Commission (SSMSC) considers the development of a liquid, reliable and transparent capital market to be a top priority for Ukraine. Figures from the SSMSC obtained in 2002 indicate some growth in the market, with the registration of more than 2,000 share issues, and more than 100 bond issues. One of the key reasons for such a spur of activity on the stock market is the adoption of a number of changes to regulatory acts and an overall increase in the level of sophistication of market participants and authorities. As well, stock market participants are increasingly looking outside of Ukraine for investment and capital, and as such as are recognizing the importance of corporate governance to potential investors.

The level of awareness of shareholders is a critical issue facing many joint stock companies. During mass privatization, when shares were purchased with privatization certificates, all Ukrainian citizens were eligible to obtain a share of the state property. As a result, a large class of minority shareholders was formed. Some joint stock companies are owned by thousands of shareholders. Unfortunately, these minority owners take little or no interest in corporate governance, do not get involved in company management or make any attempts to stand up for their rights. Many wish to sell their shares but owing to low market demand they are confined to the role of mere observers. A separate group within the class of minority shareholders is made up of employee shareholders, whose rights are often violated by large external shareholders and by management, the latter often being both an employer and a majority shareholder.

Despite low market demand, a process of ownership consolidation has been under way in Ukraine since the late 1990s. Minority shareholders are being replaced by majority shareholders, including legal entities and individuals who have accumulated substantial or controlling blocks of shares. As they become shareholders, real investors try to institute reforms and introduce principles of good

[1] Closed joint stock companies are those in which shares are distributed exclusively among the founders and these registered shares may not be traded on a stock exchange. In open joint stock companies, shares, both registered and bearer, are distributed by way of open subscription and may be traded on a stock exchange.

governance. They are not, however, always successful in their effort, often facing resistance from the older, traditional directors, and it is often impossible to replace old management owing to the lack of properly trained professionals in Ukraine.[2] In addition, the ownership of large blocks of corporate shares by many managers also hampers reform.

The state remains one of the largest and most powerful shareholders, with a stake in more than 2,000 joint stock companies. It retains control of strategic companies and those operating in sectors of national security interest. The state retains temporary control of other non-strategic holdings that will eventually be sold. Many of these companies offer excellent investment opportunities, but their full privatization is slowed by lack of investor interest. Moreover, the state does not manage its assets effectively and many state-controlled companies experience problems that require additional capital injections, without which they may face serious financial difficulties. Analysis has shown that companies with the worst financial and economic performance levels are those in which the state holds a more than 75 per cent controlling interest. Interestingly, companies in which state bodies hold less than 25 per cent are also poor performers. The state appears to show little interest in these companies, but is unwilling to relinquish its shares. The result is the impediment of company development through non-corporate methods such as abusing its authority as a regulator. Low corporate efficiency may also be partly attributed to the state's lack of funds to preserve its stake in the charter capital and its opposition to additional share issuances, in spite of the desire of the new co-owners to invest in the company.

Institutional investors play a lesser role in the development of the Ukrainian stock market. Many investment funds and investment companies were created during privatization in order to pool and invest funds from small investors. The adoption of the new Law 'On Joint Investment Institutions (Co-Op Share and Corporate Funds)' set off a process of transformation of investment funds into co-op shares and corporate funds. As privatization nears completion, many investment companies and mutual funds are being liquidated as a result of having accomplished their missions. Banks and insurance companies are at the early stages of becoming active market players but still have not significantly contributed to the process of the introduction of good corporate governance practices in Ukraine. Moreover,

[2] The topic of corporate governance was not included in Ukrainian university curricula until 2000. With the assistance of the IFC's Ukraine Corporate Governance Project (1999–2002), approximately 30 post-secondary education institutions have now included corporate governance into their course programmes.

they do not usually control large blocks of shares and do not get involved in company management.

A review of the legal framework for corporate governance

Ukraine is one of the few countries in the former USSR that does not have specific legislation regulating activities by joint stock companies, although the need for new legislation is widely recognized and publicly debated. Currently, these joint stock companies are governed by the Law of Ukraine 'On Companies' adopted in 1991. Despite numerous changes and addenda, the law fails to meet market needs and cannot be applied effectively. Only 26 articles of the law are dedicated to activities by joint stock companies, including one article referencing the supervisory board, one for the audit committee, and two articles on the management board. The law neither provides for any means of protecting minority shareholders, such as cumulative voting or tag-along rights, nor allows shareholders to monitor activities by the management board. Numerous loopholes in the law make it possible for managers to violate shareholder rights while formally acting within the law. Current legislation makes it impossible to build a transparent and sound governance structure based on internal control and accountability. Many issues that are not properly regulated by legal acts are addressed within company by-laws. Given the low level of awareness and a poor understanding of corporate governance, however, such regulation is rarely administered in an acceptable manner and often contradicts international best practices. Under such circumstances, the adoption of a specific law on joint stock companies is extremely important for Ukraine. Such legislation is considered by many observers, both domestic and international, as being critical to bringing Ukraine closer to international corporate standards. Despite such an evident need, the Parliament of Ukraine has been unable to pass a new law. A new draft is expected before parliament by the end of 2003.

Pursuant to the Law 'On State Regulation of the Stock Market in Ukraine', the SSMSC monitors observance of investor rights by issuers and professional market players. Within the scope of its power, and despite imperfect legislation, the SSMSC keeps a record of cases comprising the practice of corporate law, participates in law-making and develops regulations with an aim to introduce international standards of corporate governance. In an effort to meet the market's needs, the SSMSC drafts and approves documents designed to eliminate deficiencies and loopholes in the law. In 2002, it assisted in the development of more than 50 laws and legal acts, and issued a large number of rules and regulations to guide business activity. Aware of the inadequacy and inefficiency of stock market regulation through existing legislation and individual company by-laws, the SSMSC has actively promoted the draft Law 'On Joint Stock Companies' and continues to take steps to educate market players about its importance.

Violations of corporate governance

The stock market in Ukraine is prone to violations owing to imperfect legislation, limited shareholder awareness, a general lack of information about corporate governance and poor corporate culture.

Typical violations of shareholder rights occur at the point of calling the annual general meeting of shareholders, and at the actual holding of the meeting:

- Shareholders are not allowed to call a general shareholders' meeting if the management board has refused to do so at their request; they have no access to the register to send out meeting notices; the registrar refuses to inform shareholders about upcoming meetings; shareholders have no funds by which to call a meeting.
- The proxy certification procedure is not adequately regulated. As a result, numerous violations are committed and the legitimacy of meetings and resolutions is often challenged.
- There is no standard procedure for determining the quorum of a meeting, and whether it should be determined only once or maintained throughout the meeting. As a result, meetings are sometimes undermined.
- Documents related to the meeting agenda are not always provided. Typically, such documents are either not completed or not provided at the request of shareholders concerned.
- Voting is conducted without the necessary quorum or on motions that are not set in the meeting agenda.
- Registration is denied to shareholders or shareholder nominees participating in the meeting.

Share dilution by means of an additional share issuance and tampering with the shareholder registry are widespread. Despite a series of preventive measures taken by the SSMSC, 'pocket' registrars that undermine investor confidence in the system of share registration still do exist. Other types of investor right violations include:[3]

[3] According to the Ukrainian Association of Investment Business, www.uaib.com.ua.

- *Lack of shareholder participation in the process of making decisions to convey company assets to another company and inability to monitor large transactions.* Current legislation neither provides a definition of large and conflict-of-interest transactions nor stipulates liability for executing them. This greatly increases the risk of management selling off company assets at below fair market value without the approval of the general meeting or the supervisory board.
- *Incomplete disclosure of information to shareholders and potential investors.* Minority shareholders and non-shareholders have virtually no access to information about the company. The requirement by law to publicize the annual report is not enforced since the law does not prescribe any liability for non-compliance. Investors holding large stakes do not always have access to accurate, relevant and consistent information.
- *Investors are prevented from serving on the supervisory board.* In many companies, the supervisory board performs only formal duties. In practice, investors buying a significant stake, but not a majority holding, are often prevented from participating in supervisory board meetings or from electing their representative to sit on the board. If the new law on joint stock companies is passed, it is expected that the concept of cumulative voting will be introduced, thus giving minority shareholders representation on the supervisory board.

Enforcement

Inadequate legislation makes it difficult for the court system to respond promptly or effectively to violations in corporate governance. The analysis of court practice indicates that judges lack the proper qualifications and do not fully understand the fundamental issues of corporate governance. The result is that often cases are determined in an inconsistent manner, and the enforcement of the law is weak. Furthermore, risk of corruption and bribery in legal proceedings is still high. Stock market players have little confidence in the court system and prefer to settle disputes out of court. Recently, however, owing to the efforts of a number of technical assistance projects, various institutions in Ukraine have started offering training for judges and organizing round tables for judges, stock market players, and scholars to discuss problems in corporate governance. In turn, courts are beginning to take measures to make summaries of court decisions passed in corporate disputes to introduce uniform guidelines for applying legislation.

As in-court dispute resolution loses favour, the SSMSC as a regulator assumes greater responsibility for efficient control and prevention of violations, and issuers, shareholders and other market players increasingly appeal to the Commission for protection. As an example of improvement, last year, the Commission investigated 177 claims with regard to violations on the securities market. In the previous year only 60 were investigated.

Self-regulating organizations (SROs) – associations of professional market players – are very active in the prevention of illegal activities. SROs have their own charters and codes of practice and also perform compliance monitoring. Unfortunately, Ukraine currently has no organizations similar to the Institute of Directors or an Institute of Corporate Secretaries, and to date, the Ukrainian Association of Shareholder Rights Protection and the Ukrainian Union of Shareholders both maintain a low profile and do not fully perform their functions.

New trends in the development of corporate governance

Lately, the government has been paying a great deal of attention to the development of corporate governance within individual companies in Ukraine. The importance of corporate governance was stressed in the Presidential Decree of 21 March 2002, 'On Measures to Improve Corporate Governance in Joint Stock Companies', which reaffirmed the need to improve the legal framework for corporate governance in joint stock companies and identified the main directions of policy development, including shareholder protection, improvement of information disclosure practices, a clear distribution of responsibilities among governing bodies and the introduction of sound principles of corporate governance. The Decree is the first document to stress the need to develop and introduce national principles of corporate governance in Ukraine. Pursuant to the Decree, the SSMSC was responsible for conducting this work.

As part of its work to encourage Ukrainian joint stock companies to bring their management practices in line with internationally accepted principles of corporate governance, the SSMSC chairs the Special Task Force on Corporate Governance and the Protection of Shareholder Rights (Task Force), which is also involved in work related to the national principles mentioned above.

The Task Force was formed in 1998, in accordance with the Memorandum between the governments of Ukraine and the United States. Its mission is to steer activities by international and Ukrainian experts towards creating a transparent and competitive capital market in Ukraine. The Task Force, currently chaired by the SSMSC, is composed of government agencies, stock market players, legal firms, educational institutions, stakeholders and international organizations, including the IFC.

In response to the Presidential Decree of 21 March 2002, the process of drafting the Ukrainian Corporate Governance Principles, that was started in late 2002, was completed with the adoption of the document by the SSMSC on 11 December 2003. In April 2003, the draft Principles were approved by the Task Force and by the SSMSC. The Ukrainian Principles, based on the universally accepted Organization of Economic Cooperation and Development (OECD) principles, are designed to improve corporate culture, step up investment processes and increase investor confidence in Ukraine. A series of public discussions of the Draft Principles were held through the latter half of 2003, the final version being submitted in autumn 2003. With the process of discussion and the adoption of the Principles, signs are beginning to show of increased interest in improving governance among Ukrainian corporations; a number of high-profile companies are already preparing their own internal governance codes modelled on the Ukrainian Corporate Governance principles.

The adoption of the Civil and Business Codes, which came into force on 1 January 2004, indicates progress in the development of legislation in Ukraine. Despite discrepancies between the codes and a number of conflicting provisions, their adoption is viewed by stock market players as an important step forward in addressing matters currently unregulated by existing legislation. It is anticipated that the new codes will contribute to further improvement of corporate legislation and will prepare the legal groundwork needed to bring into force a new joint stock company law.

Overall, the state of corporate governance in Ukraine is still a challenge for business, but the country's experience to date is not altogether different from that of other transition economies that went through a similar privatization process. As described above, the legislative and enforcement environments are less than perfect, and significant psychological changes on the part of Ukrainian managers are still needed. Nevertheless, positive developments have been seen, particularly with the adoption of the Ukrainian Corporate Governance Principles and the implementation of changes to the civil and business codes. As the market becomes increasingly sophisticated and the investment needs of Ukrainian companies grow, it is anticipated that this trend will continue.

Biography

The International Finance Corporation (IFC) is a member of the World Bank Group and is headquartered in Washington, DC. It shares the primary objective of all World Bank Group institutions: to improve the quality of the lives of people in its developing member countries.

Established in 1956, IFC is the largest multilateral source of loan and equity financing for private sector projects in the developing world. It promotes sustainable private sector development primarily by:

- financing private sector projects located in the developing world;
- helping private companies in the developing world mobilize financing in international financial markets;
- providing advice and technical assistance to businesses and governments.

IFC offers a full array of financial products and services to companies in its developing member countries:

- long-term loans in major currencies, at fixed or variable rates;
- equity investments;
- quasi-equity instruments (subordinated loans, preferred stock, income notes);
- guarantees and standby financing;
- risk management (intermediation of currency and interest rate swaps, provision of hedging facilities).

IFC's Private Enterprise Partnership provides technical assistance to the private sector in the former Soviet Union with the goal of building successful businesses. The Partnership focuses on three key areas where it can add maximum value:

- promoting direct investment with emphasis on foreign direct investment;
- supporting the growth of small and medium-sized enterprises (SMEs);
- improving the business enabling environment.

IFC has been providing technical assistance to Ukraine since 1992, beginning with privatization initiatives in the retail and agricultural sectors, as well as privatization of large enterprises and unfinished construction sites. IFC also developed local consulting companies to provide enterprise-level business support to SMEs and worked to develop the legal framework for the financial leasing sector growth. As of today, IFC supports four initiatives in Ukraine: Agribusiness Development Program, Corporate Governance Project, SME Survey, SME Toolkit.

1.9

Business Enabling Environment for SMEs in Ukraine

IFC Ukraine

Since Ukraine's independence, small and medium enterprises (SMEs) have taken on an increasingly important responsibility in creating employment opportunities, developing competition and encouraging economic growth in the country. Despite that, methods for assuring equal treatment, compliance, and predictability of administrative and regulatory procedures applicable to private enterprise are still in development.

The SME sector, which has existed in Ukraine for just over a decade, plays a vital role in established market economies. In Europe, SMEs employ three-quarters of the labour force and account for about two-thirds of the GDP of the European Union.[1] In Ukraine, accurate figures for the SME sector simply do not exist, as the sector has not been separately defined by official statistics yet. It is not possible to obtain a figure of any exactitude on the number of SMEs in the country, let alone verifiable estimates for the share of the labour force working in small and medium-sized enterprises, or their share of the country's GDP.[2]

In 1996, under its Business Development Project, IFC began to conduct annual surveys of the SME sector in Ukraine, to analyse the state of the business enabling environment for these firms. The surveys have been effective in promoting policy reform on private

---

[1] The Resource Center for Small Business (http://docs.rcsme.ru/rus/RC/Statistics/).

[2] The State Statistics Committee keeps records on private entrepreneurs as well as small enterprises, defined as legal entities with up to 50 employees. Experts estimate that small firms (fewer than 50 employees) accounted for 82 per cent of all enterprises in the country in 2002.

sector development issues, and have been used as a tool to monitor the progress of various reforms and changes in the business environment.[3]

The recent 2003 IFC study of the business enabling environment had as its goal a clear and factual representation of the issues that face Ukrainian entrepreneurs in starting and developing their business. In this sense, it is not an exhaustive examination of, or an attempt to catalogue, all the issues related to business development and regulation of private sector activity in Ukraine. Rather, the purpose is to allow the government, non-governmental organizations (NGOs) and international organizations to understand the policy decisions that are most strongly influencing the growth of small business in Ukraine, as these policy decisions are seen by entrepreneurs.

Data of the State Statistics Committee on the number of firms registering yearly in Ukraine confirms the findings of the latest IFC study on the decreasing of businesses starting operations. Figure 1.9.1 shows a substantial drop in the number of small firms registering in Ukraine per year, over the past six years.

Without entering the debate on exact figures, it is nevertheless well understood that the growth of small enterprises should be further encouraged and assisted, if Ukraine is to join the ranks of developed nations with modern economic systems. Perhaps a beginning can be made by defining the sector officially, and providing clear and updated information on its most important indicators. This would encourage more effective policy development by allowing the government to monitor and evaluate its own policies towards the private sector.

The issues of focus for the latest IFC study include the availability of competitive external financing, the system of taxation, and a number of regulatory processes: state inspections of enterprises, import and export operations, obtaining permits for business activities, certification, licensing and business registration. In considering the extent to

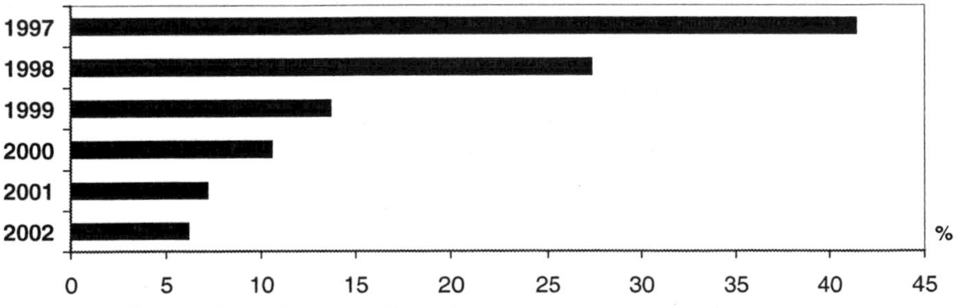

Source: Ukraine State Statistics Committee

Figure 1.9.1 Newly registered small firms in Ukraine, 1997–2002

[3] IFC Private Enterprise Partnership (www.ifc.org/pep).

which administrative and regulatory processes, as well as the method of their implementation, create so-called 'barriers to business', the intent is to display the effect of government policies on entrepreneurs, as a starting point for constructive dialogue between the public and private sector. Figure 1.9.2 shows the main barriers to business development cited by firms' managers.

Many of the general improvements in the Ukrainian business environment seen between 2000 and 2001 have suffered setbacks in 2002. In particular, firm assessment of difficulties raised by political instability, anti-competitive practices, corruption, and unwarranted state interference in business activities have each increased by 10 or more percentage points year-on-year. While assessments of the majority of other business environment issues have also deteriorated, this change has been less significant (see Table 1.9.1).

Firms rate the system of taxation as the main barrier to business activities, with 70 per cent citing taxation as an obstacle to growth and development. Ukrainian firms see the key difficulties of taxation as: high tax rates, unstable tax legislation and the overall number of taxes, each of which was cited as a barrier by more than three-quarters of all surveyed companies. On the other hand, survey results show that the simplified tax has significantly decreased the barriers involved in taxation for small firms, which rate all aspects of the tax system as less of a burden than their larger counterparts. Over half of surveyed firms

Table 1.9.1 Comparison of barriers to business development, 2001–02 (ranked by % of respondents citing the issue as a major or significant obstacle in 2002)

Issue	2002 %	2001 %
Tax rates and tax administration	70	70
Unstable legislation	69	63
Cost of energy resources	65	65
Unfair competition	56	45
Insufficient purchasing power	56	59
Political instability	51	40
Corruption	51	39
Inflation, unstable exchange rate	48	45
Regulatory environment	43	38
Obtaining external financing	41	42
Interference of local authorities in business activities	40	23
Interference of central government authorities in business activities	35	19
Infrastructure development	29	25
Criminal pressure	26	13

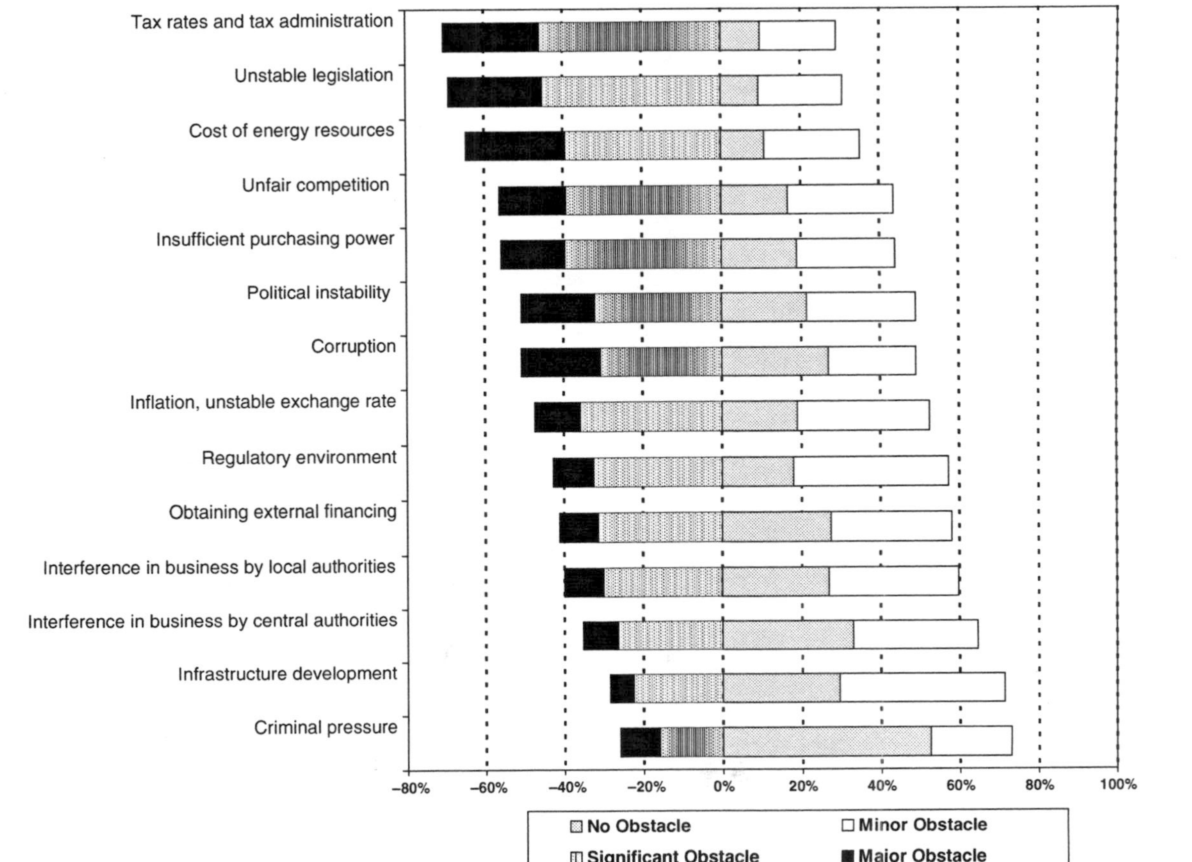

Figure 1.9.2 Perceptions of main barriers to business development in Ukraine, 2002 (ranked by % of firms citing the procedure as a significant or major barrier)

cited frequent changes to legislation, anti-competitive practices of other firms, political instability and corruption as serious barriers to business activities.

Ukrainian enterprises have rated criminal pressure as last on the list of possible barriers to their operations. These results coincide with the previous survey findings: firms have consistently rated criminal pressure as the least serious barrier to operations and growth over the past three years.

While most enterprises are relatively satisfied with the work of the central authorities, Ukrainian enterprises remain much more critical of their local business climate. Less than a third of firms believe that the actions of local authorities do not impede business operations. A quarter of firms consider the business environment in their city as conducive to investment and growth, while under one in five believe that local authorities strive to create equal opportunities for entrepreneurs. Overall, SMEs are less satisfied with their local business environment than are large enterprises.

External financing options are limited for Ukrainian firms, and bank financing is rare. Only 17 per cent of surveyed firms obtained a bank loan in 2002. Loans for a period of three years or more account for less than 5 per cent of all loans obtained by surveyed firms in 2002. Moreover, nearly one in two firms with a need for external financing did not apply to a bank, with half of these enterprises citing high interest rates or prohibitive collateral requirements as the key reasons for not having turned to a bank to meet investment needs.

The regulatory climate in Ukraine was cited as a barrier to business development by 43 per cent of surveyed firms, which is an increase from the result of 38 per cent obtained in 2001, and presents a return to levels seen in 2000.

Regulatory climate in focus

In order to assess which specific regulatory issues are most acute for entrepreneurs, surveyed firms were asked to rate each regulatory procedure separately, based on the level of difficulty that it presents for their company's operations. A total of six regulatory procedures were covered by the survey. Figure 1.9.3 presents survey findings.

Inspections were cited as the most significant regulatory barrier to business, with 48 per cent of firms considering the procedures to cause major or significant barriers to operations. In 2002, the typical surveyed firm was inspected a total of 14 times. Firms report that the total duration of all inspections averaged 17 working days in 2002. Customs procedures, which presented problems for 38 per cent of firms involved in foreign trade, were ranked second in order of difficulty.

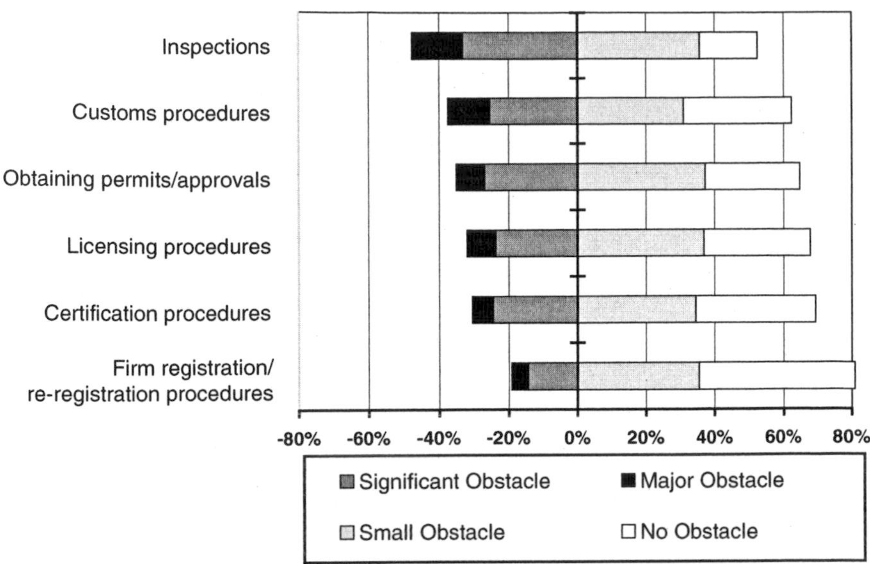

Figure 1.9.3 Specific regulatory and administrative issues as barriers to business development in Ukraine

Obtaining permits, meanwhile, was cited as a barrier to operations by just over a third of all firms. Survey findings show that the share of firms obtaining permits in Ukraine, including obligatory permits to start operations, has been declining over the past three years. At the same time, firms report that the difficulty of receiving each of the most commonly issued permits for business operations increased significantly between 2001 and 2002.

Table 1.9.2 shows that the negative trend seen in firms' attitudes towards the overall business environment in Ukraine does not affect the appraisal of specific regulatory procedures. When each regulatory

Table 1.9.2 Regulatory barriers to business development, 2001–02 (% of firms citing each procedure as a major or significant obstacle)

Issue	2002 %	2001 %
Inspections	48	46
Customs procedures	38	46
Obtaining permits/approvals	35	41
Licensing procedures	32	35
Certification procedures	30	40
Firm registration/re-registration procedures	19	21

issue is considered separately, firms' opinion has shown improvement over the past three years. The single exception is inspection procedures, which surveyed companies have consistently rated with increasing severity.

When these results are analysed by size of enterprise, it is clear that in 2002 large firms were relatively more severe in their assessment of procedures which are rated to be the most difficult overall, such as inspections and customs. SMEs, on the other hand, tended to have more difficulty with registration, permits, certification and licensing (see Table 1.9.3).

Regulatory 'time tax'

An estimate of time tax refers to the amount of time that firms' management spends dealing with state officials and completing the requirements of regulatory agencies. While it is clear that such procedures are vital for the protection of the health and safety of company employees as well as the public at large, the time that enterprises spend completing such procedures obviously takes resources away from their typical business activities. It is therefore expected that a regulatory time tax should be as low as possible, and in this sense, time tax estimates allow an appraisal of the efficiency of government officials in carrying out regulatory procedures. They also point towards the clarity, stability and predictability of the regulatory base – the fewer changes to regulations, the less management time spent gathering information and advice on how to comply with official requirements.

In 2002, enterprise managers estimated that the average share of their time spent on regulatory matters was 14 per cent, which is lower than the 16 per cent cited in 2001. This tax remains under 20 per cent for firms operating in all cities of Ukraine, with the exception of Khmelnytsky (see Figure 1.9.4). In 2002, as had been the case in 2001,

Table 1.9.3 Regulatory barriers to business development by firm size in 2002 (% of firms citing each procedure as a major or significant obstacle)

Issue	Firm size 2002 Small	Medium	Large
Inspections	46	47	57
Customs procedures	37	34	41
Obtaining permits/approvals	36	34	33
Licensing procedures	32	34	29
Certification procedures	32	32	25
Firm registration/re-registration procedures	21	18	13

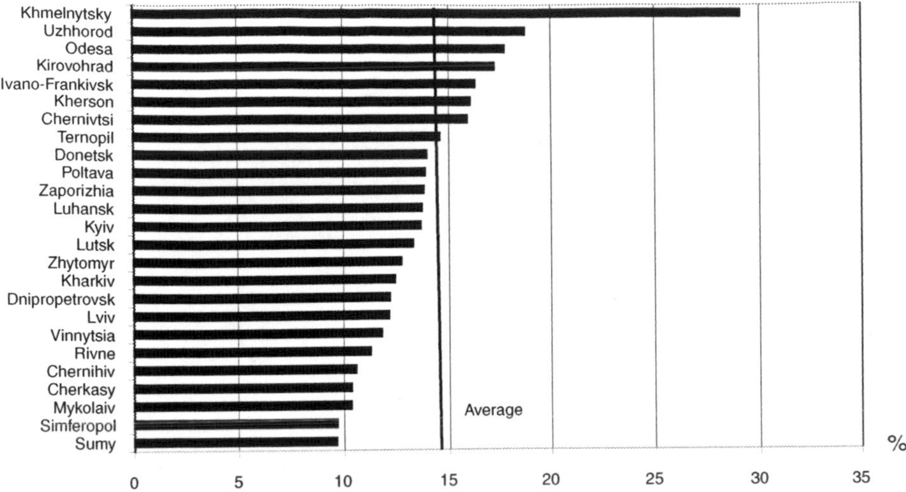

Figure 1.9.4 Enterprise manager time tax: regional variations in 2002 (% of firm time spent on regulatory matters)

Uzhhorod, Odesa, Kirovohrad and Kherson remained amongst the most 'taxed' cities across Ukraine. Meanwhile, results show that the time that firms are asked to allot to regulatory questions is similar for all sizes of business and remains level across most industries.

Unofficial payments

Close to a quarter of surveyed firms stated that unofficial payments are likely to be required of the average Ukrainian company when completing each of the regulatory procedures covered in this report. The single exception is obtaining permits and approvals, a procedure for which fully 40 per cent of firms claimed that the typical Ukrainian enterprise is likely to pay unofficially (see Table 1.9.4).[4]

Conclusions

Study results over the past three years show that a number of issues in the overall business environment are becoming increasingly acute

[4] Firms stating that the average company usually pays only the 'official fee' to complete a given regulatory procedure ranged from 24 per cent for customs to 57 per cent for registration. A significant portion of firms, between 15 per cent for permits and 50 per cent for customs, had difficulty in answering this question.

Table 1.9.4 The unofficial cost of regulatory procedures (% of firms citing unofficial costs as likely required for a typical enterprise to complete each regulatory procedure)

Procedure	Small	Medium	Large	**Average**
Obtaining permits and approvals	42	38	33	**40**
Customs procedures	26	28	31	**27**
Registration procedures	28	26	18	**26**
Licensing procedures	27	26	23	**26**
Certification procedures	24	23	23	**24**

for firms in Ukraine, such as political instability, corruption, anti-competitive practices and official interference in business activities. Firms' assessment of regulatory procedures which they must complete in order to conduct business activities, however, is softening. In some sense this disparity in result can be attributed to a change of focus on the part of companies – firms are beginning to see issues that directly affect their day-to-day profits as more of a difficulty. At the same time, it should be noted that the legislative basis for certain regulatory procedures is also slowly being clarified.[5]

Nevertheless, firms continue to experience difficulties with the regulatory environment, with 43 per cent of surveyed companies citing the regulatory climate in Ukraine as a barrier to their operations. Moreover, each of the specific procedures covered in this report remains problematic for a significant portion of Ukrainian companies. It should also be underlined that, despite the legislative progress mentioned above, many regulatory processes continue to operate outside of a clear legislative framework, and lack the benefit of unifying legislation to define their goals, procedures, terms and conditions, or all of the agencies involved in the process.

Most regulatory procedures also have in common other important deficiencies, including a lack of clarity in regulations that do exist and a lack of availability of information to allow entrepreneurs to become familiar with a regulatory process and its requirements. The requirements prescribed in normative acts are often either incomplete or so general as to be open to a number of interpretations. Even in cases where clear information exists, it often remains inaccessible for entrepreneurs. Between 10 and 50 per cent of entrepreneurs claim that

[5] This process began with the adoption of the Law on Licensing in 2000. Encompassing legislation was passed in 2001 on certification and standardization procedures, although the technical specifications needed to enforce the legislation are yet to be adopted. In January 2004, the Law on Registration will come into effect.

they had difficulty in obtaining information necessary to complete the regulatory procedures covered in this report, depending on the procedure. In many cases, results show that the lack of access to information directly increases the costs and timeframes required for a firm to complete procedures. This also creates the conditions for rent-seeking behaviour on the part of state officials allowed to 'monopolize' access to information. Given this situation, survey findings document that it is the *practice of implementation* of procedures lacking transparency, and open to a number of interpretations, that is problematic, rather than the intent of the procedures themselves.

1.10

Privatization of Small Enterprises in Ukraine

Irina Strizhak

The privatization process in Ukraine differs fundamentally from the same process in countries with well-developed market economies. This is largely due to the fact that privatization of state-owned enterprises in Ukraine must be built upon the existing economic system. Economic dynamics, such as forms of ownership and manufacturing relations, increase. There has been a significant level of redistribution of material, financial, labour and other resources of the country, and changes in the ways in which resources are distributed and utilized. Ukraine's legal framework is also in the process of change and renewal. All of these changes are connected to larger and more complicated sets of problems. If the privatization is held on a greater scale and in a relatively short period of time, it is likely to have negative implications on the sphere of manufacturing, financial, social, labour, and other economic sectors and conditions. To describe the entire process of privatization is lengthy and requires considerable detail; therefore, I would prefer to focus on one of its many aspects – privatization of small enterprises, the so-called 'small privatization'.

Economic, organizational and legal foundations of small business privatization

The most important prerequisite for the transition of a socialist economy to a market economy, as learnt through the experiences of many 'post-Soviet territories', is the process of privatizing state properties. In the privatization programme adopted in 1992, the Ukrainian government stated its intention to create 'forms and proportions, characteristic for the market economy through an extended process of property change and privatization, which will last 3 to 5 years'. At that time, it was projected that the share of state property would decrease from 100 per cent to 25–30 per cent.

The privatization process also requires the resolution of a number of political, economic and social problems. One of the main political issues in Ukraine was the creation of a wide spectrum of private entrepreneurs, who maintain private property and who can become the foundation and support for the nascent social and economic system. The following were the economic challenges:

- creation of economically independent manufacturers (private entrepreneurs, economic entities, associations, and other necessary entities of the modern market economy);
- creation of an economic environment that will promote effective functioning of remaining entities owned by the state;
- creation of a mechanism to pay down the state debt with revenues collected from the sale of state-owned property.

Small privatization in Ukraine requires a strong legal foundation, which includes state laws as well as local normative acts. On the state level the foundation of the legal system consisted of five main laws:

- state privatization programme;
- Law of Ukraine 'On Privatization of the Property of the State-Owned Enterprises';
- Law of Ukraine 'On Privatization of Small-Sized State Enterprises';
- Law of Ukraine 'On Documentation on Privatization';
- Law of Ukraine 'On Renting of the State Properties'.

Ukraine's Verkhovna Rada (the Supreme Council) was confirming[1] annually the State Programme of Privatization and presenting it for review to the Cabinet of Ministers of Ukraine. The programme defines the main goals, priorities, logistical concerns, conditions, and organizational tasks necessary for privatizing state-owned entities under this programme. It also establishes a number of entities that need to be privatized, such as defining which property belongs to the state and to the Autonomous Republic of Crimea.

Small enterprises such as retail stores, retail services and food establishments are critical to the establishment and function of the market infrastructure. These types of establishments were subject to privatization early, and thus paved the way for the privatization process, the beginning of radical reforms in Ukraine, which was the very first step on the way to a modern market economy.

---

[1] Since the process of privatization continues today, the privatization programme is confirmed annually.

In contrast to the privatization of large enterprises, which requires significant efforts without immediately visible results, the sudden existence of small private enterprises created a more immediate demand for consumer goods and services. Owing to the simplicity and relative promptness of their sale, the existence of small private enterprises became an integral part of Ukraine's transition to an effective market economy.

Mechanisms and methods of small business privatization

The first step on the way to small business privatization is a clear delimitation of the sphere of municipal and state property and the subsequent commercialization of enterprises. In Ukraine, there appeared a need to eliminate the wholesale economy through which goods were distributed to the retail trade. On the municipal level, deputies were adopting special resolutions that would make all small business entities (enterprises of the retail trade, services and food establishments) declare themselves independent legal municipal entities, making them responsible for their own problems of supply, transportation, contract signings, financing etc.

Previously established networks for the wholesale trade were eliminated as legal entities were reorganized into intermediary entities without the right to interfere in the activities of independent retail trade. By introducing competition between the suppliers of goods for the retail trade, the government laid the ground for the privatization of small stores and shops.

Regretfully, the process of commercialization of small enterprises in many cities of eastern and southern Ukraine was fictitious, ie the enterprises were not broken down into small components (eg, one enterprise could include up to 100 stores). At the same time, in the western and central regions of Ukraine, each enterprise was registered as a separate legal entity.

The aforementioned situation was directly linked to the political situation at the time and the support of the privatization process on the part of the municipal governments in different regions of Ukraine. For example, owing to a complicated political situation in the Autonomous Republic of Crimea, not a single enterprise was actually privatized until 1995.

For example, the small enterprise figures included such 'enterprises' as school cafeterias,[2] public bathrooms, glass recycling centres,

---

[2] In accordance with the Law of Ukraine, these enterprises fell under the category of social services and therefore were not to be privatized.

etc. In addition, there were lists of small enterprise entities, approved by the Verkhovna Rada deputies, as the 'entities not to be privatized', and these actions were argued as 'protection of socially valuable entities'. The number of enterprises of such a kind changed constantly, either decreasing or increasing. Over time, political support for the privatization process grew. The number of small enterprises appearing on the list of those 'not to be privatized' dwindled. The UPF put in order information on statistical data, which it received from the regions, and by the end of 1996 it was estimated that about 60,000 small businesses were to be privatized.

According to the adopted State Privatization Programme, the following were the methods of privatization of enterprises in so-called group 'A':[3]

- buyout of the enterprise by its employees;[4]
- commercial and non-commercial tenders;
- auction.

Despite the fact that holding open auctions, has proved to be the fastest, most honest, least corrupt and most profitable privatization process in the world, employee buyout of the enterprise became the most favoured method of privatization in Ukraine, owing to the rather narrow framework of the national legislature.

In practice, implementation of the Programme got off to a slow start. The first auction[5] involving small enterprise privatization was held in L'viv (20 February 1993), only a year after the Programme was adopted.

In accordance with Ukraine's legislature, the buyers of state property fall into the following categories:

- citizens of Ukraine, foreign nationals and stateless persons;
- legal entities registered in Ukraine;
- legal entities of other countries.

Buyers of state property could not be the agencies of the federal government, employees of UPF and its regional affiliates, or legal entities that own more than 25 per cent of state property. The following privatization methods existed:

---

[3] In accordance with the Law of Ukraine, group 'A' includes entities of small privatization.

[4] Rental of state enterprises by the employees with the possible option of buying it out also falls under the group 'A' method.

[5] The auction was selling 17 enterprises and the right to rent for five years; nearly 200 bids were submitted; the budget received nearly 1 billion karbovanets in revenues (nearly USD 400,000 according to the current exchange rate).

- privatized property certificates;
- compensation certificates;
- housing checks;
- land bonds.

Every citizen of the country had the right to participate in the privatization of state enterprises using the aforementioned privatization certificates.

In the process of small business privatization, municipal governments were governed by the following principles:

- Preserve the nature of the activities of privatized enterprises that manufacture or sell consumer goods for five years after privatization.
- No fewer than three bidders should participate in the auction.
- Favourable conditions for employees wishing to buy the enterprise (for example, 30 per cent discount, payment by instalments).
- Wide use of selling leases for 5–10 years with the right to subsequent purchase (this method worked well in cases where several enterprises were located in one building; if the building were to be sold, multiple owners would have to agree among themselves, which would complicate and encumber the process).

Scale and chronology of small business privatization

From the very beginning of the privatization process, the sale of state property was complicated and slow. This could be explained by a number of negative factors characteristic of the transition period from a command economy to a market economy:

- political contradictions and inconsistencies in realizing market reform;
- insufficient methodological and systematic preparation of employees of privatizing agencies;
- political interference in the privatization process;
- efforts to exclude from privatization some of the most attractive and lucrative enterprises, which represented ministerial, local, and in some cases, personal interest for the heads of the enterprises, by some branch ministries and municipal agencies etc.

It is crucial to note that the existing legislation was changed and additions were made, that is to say, the rules of the game were ever-shifting.

Despite the impediments, Ukraine purposefully stayed its course in the creation of a market economy, based on the equal functioning of all forms of property. During the three years since the Privatization Programme and its supporting laws were adopted, more than 35 per cent of small enterprises have been privatized.

It should be noted, however, that the level of privatization in the various regions of Ukraine differs significantly. Among the large cities and oblast centres, the following were the leaders in privatization: Cherkasy – 85 per cent, Mariupol – 80 per cent, Kmelnytsky – 80 per cent, Uzhhorod – 75 per cent, Luhansk – 70 per cent.

The reason for such a varied picture resulted from the clearly expressed will on the part of the municipal governments to complete the transfer of small enterprises to private hands. Also attributable are the high levels of professional training of employees of municipal privatization agencies, for example, Kyiv – 25 per cent, Poltava – 20 per cent, Kirovohrad – 10 per cent, Donetsk – 5 per cent, ARC[6] – 0 per cent.

Prior to the Supreme Council's imposition of a moratorium[7] on the privatization process, Ukraine's process unfolded at a steady pace and scale. The last quarter before the moratorium was imposed brought the volume of privatization to a level equal to the levels of the past two years. In other words, deceleration of the process after the moratorium was significant. It is clear that without the moratorium, the number of privatized entities by the end of 1994 would have reached 'a critical mass',[8] even given the contradictory and incomplete legal framework in place at that time.

In 1995, a Presidential Decree 'On Measures to Accelerate the Process of Small Business Privatization' abolished the moratorium. According to the Decree, 1995 was to be the year for the transfer of small enterprises to be completed. However, owing to a number of other impediments, the privatization process of small enterprises was stretched out for several years:

- The State Privatization Programme for 1995 was not confirmed by parliament.
- Legislative acts, which would amend some contradictions between the existing legislature and the Presidential Decree in the mechanism of privatization of state-owned entities, were not adopted.

---

[6] Autonomous Republic of Crimea.

[7] In accordance with the Law of Ukraine, state-owned entities could not be privatized before they had been officially listed among the enterprises to be privatized.

[8] It is customary to consider the 'critical mass' to be 75 per cent or more.

- There was a half-hour delay in the publication of the official and confirmed list[9] of enterprises to be privatized in 1995.

In 1998, UPF announced the end of small enterprise privatization. By that time, some 49,500 small enterprises had been privatized, amounting to approximately 83 per cent of the total. Overall, the privatization process of small enterprises continued for almost eight years until 2000, when the number reached approximately 59,000 (99 per cent).

In May 1999, the circulation of privatization certificates[10] was terminated. With the end of certificate privatization, this form of selling securities as a certificate auction was rendered obsolete. In addition, privileged sale of stocks using certificates was no longer practised. From that time on, one could talk with confidence about an entirely new form of privatization with monetary tenders only.

The privatization process continues today. The practice of privatizing state-owned enterprises by means of selling stocks of open joint stock companies is spreading rapidly. In the context of current economic conditions, this form of privatization is the most effective.

The national privatization programme for the years 2003–08 has been developed and envisions the improvement and institutionalization of the privatization process. The new political goal of economic reforms in Ukraine has been set – completion of privatization as a system of reforms of the transitional period.

The main aim of privatization in 2003–08 is to increase the level of social and economic efficiency of production by means of widespread privatization.

The mechanisms of implementation stipulated by the Programme create market barriers for the shadow economy and artificial devaluation of state property, as well as transfer of ownership of state property according to non-privatization procedures. Quite often, creditors were paid with highly liquid state assets.

Currently, the State Privatization Programme is an innovative document. The outcome of set goals will do much to define the future of Ukraine for the next 10 years.

---

[9] In accordance with the Law of Ukraine, state-owned enterprises could not be privatized until they were officially indicated in the lists of entities to be privatized.

[10] In the privatization process of small enterprises, property certificates were mainly used by the employees of the enterprise.

Problems and shortfalls of small enterprise privatization

Overall, the programme of privatization of small enterprises in Ukraine has been successful thus far, if it is evaluated on the basis of achieving the goals that were set. A new and quite vast social stratum of private entrepreneurs has been created, and the state's share of ownership in small enterprises property has decreased to 1 per cent, in sharp contrast to privatization revenues which in some years amounted to 5–7 per cent of the state budget. Finally, owing to the privatization of small enterprises, a civilized market environment has been established and has instilled the necessary conditions for the further realization of reforms in Ukraine.

Results of the privatization process in different industries vary, as well as the timeframe of the process itself. However, it is important to emphasize that in Ukraine privatization became the only block of microeconomic reforms which was conducted reasonably dynamically. Today we can say without exaggeration that a new layer of property owners and entrepreneurs has been established and the personal interests of these individuals are closely related to the development of production, the resolution of social issues, and the improvement of the well-being of employees. An economic analysis of the operations of privatized small businesses shows that the majority of them have experienced a dynamic increase in the volume of production. The development of the non-governmental sector became the main boost to the economic growth of Ukraine beginning in 2000. In comparison, the production volume of privatized enterprises is more than 2.5 times the production volume of state and communal enterprises.

Despite the success achieved, the overall pace of small enterprise privatization has been slower than expected. A number of factors have contributed to this. One notable reason is the fact that many cities and districts joined the programme far too late and very often were privatizing the enterprises designated as those 'not to be privatized'. Little attention was paid to privatization of such entities as residential buildings and related entities, which belonged to various organizations.

Another deterrent was the absence of government guarantees. Some managers feared that the absence of such guarantees would prevent enterprises from retaining their particular specializations, and would likewise have negative consequences such as reductions in goods or consumer services provided. The resulting disappearance of some enterprises, which occurred occasionally, became one of the most significant losses of small enterprise privatization.

On the other hand, there were arguments in favour of giving the new owners the right to change the speciality of the enterprise as they wished, as such freedom could make enterprises more attractive to potential investors. Therefore, closure of certain enterprises was a testament to the fact that the market mechanism was beginning to function, which is one of the main goals of privatization.

The experience of small enterprise privatization in Ukraine shows many problems and shortfalls but signifies that useful lessons can be drawn from Ukraine's experience.

Part Two

Market Potential

2.1

The Metallurgy and Machine-Building Industry in Ukraine

Munk, Andersen & Feilberg

Introduction

During the time of the Soviet Union, Ukraine was one of the largest metal-producing and metal-processing republics. Ukraine's prospected resources of iron ore are 20 per cent (59.4 million tons in 2002) of the prospected iron resources in the world.

Metallurgy is the leading Ukrainian export. It consists of approximately 70 companies and generates approximately 40 per cent of hard currency incomes – approximately EUR7,800 million in 2002 (Figure 2.1.1).

Ferrous metals

The most important metal resource in Ukraine is steel. The volumes of steel produced in Ukraine are 3.7 per cent of the total world production. According to International Iron and Steel Institute (IISI) (www.worldsteel.org), Ukraine ranks seventh after China, Japan, the US, Russia, South Korea and Germany.

After the successful year 2000 for the world metallurgy industry, 2001 and 2002 were characterized by a lack of balance between demand and supply. Ukrainian metallurgy imports have been facing many antidumping investigations followed by a constant decrease of quotas in the US, the EU, Canada, Mexico, Malaysia, Thailand, China, the Czech Republic and Russia.

Paradoxically, all these prohibitive sanctions brought positive results for the industry. A favourable situation on the world markets,

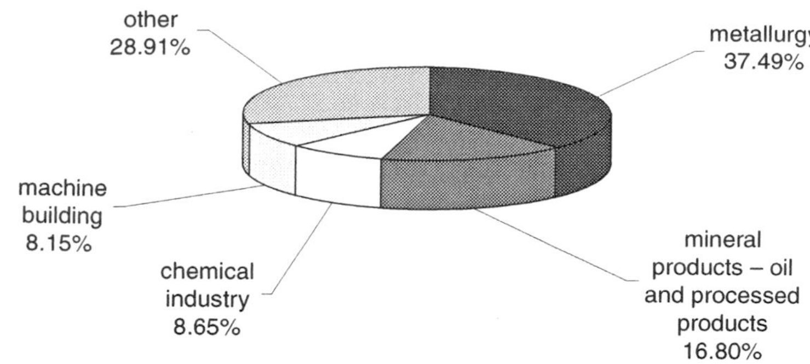

Structure of Ukrainian metallurgy industry, 2001–02

Ferrous metallurgy products	Tons ('000)	Non-ferrous metallurgy products	Tons ('000)
Hot rolled steel sheets	8,000	Primary aluminium	110
Cold rolled steel sheets	2,000	Spongy titanium	6
Finished rolled metal	26,400	Nickel	3
Crude steel	34,542	Mercury	0.1
Cast iron	27,600	Secondary lead	0.1
Steel pipes	1,527	Secondary zinc	0.05
Stainless steel	600	Uranium dioxide	0.1
Ferroalloys	1,400		

Figure 2.1.1 Ukrainian export structure, % (1st quarter of 2003)

starting from the second half of 2002, stimulated Ukrainian exports of ferrous metals measured both quantitatively and in cash. Export contracts have been concluded in a situation when demand is exceeding supply.

As one of the results, the local market has faced a deficit since producers preferred mostly to export – 85.9 per cent of ferrous metal production is export oriented – especially when taking into account the fact that export prices are higher than local ones (Figure 2.1.2).

For instance, local market demand for a company such as OJSC 'Zaporizhstal' (founded 1933; number of employees – 20,000; turnover – UAH3.2 billion; www.zaporizhstal.com) is quite small compared to its total production output. However, the biggest local consumer of 'Zaporizhstal' is the pipe industry and the second is machine building.

The competitive advantage of Ukraine on the world steel markets is mostly provided by comparatively low prices and by constant growth of semi-finished production in export structure – up by 1 million tons in 2002.

Conversely, exporters with dipper processing are facing trade barriers. For example, at the beginning of 2003 Russia introduced a 24.3 per cent antidumping duty on galvanized sheets supplied mostly

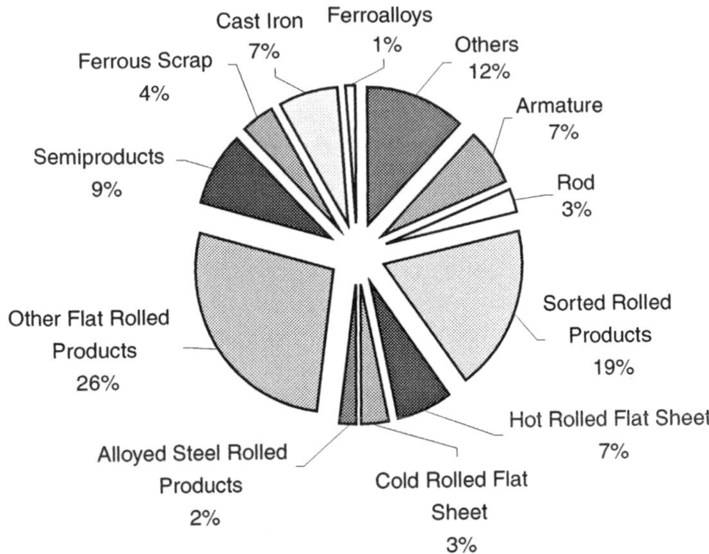

Figure 2.1.2 Structure of Ukrainian ferrous metal export, 2002

by the Ilyich Iron and Steel Works of Mariupol (www.ilyich.com.ua) with sales volumes reaching 120,000 tons annually.

A very positive tendency in Ukrainian metallurgy in 2002 was a diversification of export markets. Thus, the large metallurgical combines are exporting to more than 100 counties. After Russian oil companies decreased their imports, pipe export outside the CIS (to the EU, the Middle East, South-East Asia) more than doubled compared to 2001.

Economical growth in Asia and the Middle East compensated Ukrainian metallurgy losses on other markets, first of all the US. For now, almost 60 per cent of metal exports go to Asia and the Middle East markets.

Export regimes

The Ukrainian Ministry for the Economy redistributes quotas to local exporters and grants them licences. The Ukrainian Ministry of Foreign Affairs sets indicative prices, a minimum price, for exported ferrous metal in order to prevent possible money laundering in offshore zones.

Metal products which have been processed, even in a very simple way, are not subject to quotas, can be freely exported and are not subject to indicative prices.

Local ferrous metals supply

In 2003 the deficit of local supply diminished slightly. However, producers and consumers simply cannot agree with each other. Owing to constantly growing costs, producers have to increase comparatively low prices. On the other hand, consumers believe that domestic metal is too expensive already and in some cases it is even cheaper to import.

Earlier, the local Ukrainian market was satisfied by cheap carbon steels. Starting from 2002, there has been increasing demand for sophisticated high-alloy steels such as high-temperature steel, stainless steel and tool steel. The dynamics of this increase show a clear tendency for the Ukrainian machine-building industry increasingly to demand expensive and quality metals, especially sectors that produce high-tech products.

The machine-building industry

Today there are 2,000 medium-sized and large machine-building companies and specialized scientific organizations in Ukraine. The machine-building industry includes up to 60 sectors and sub-sectors and has 1.6 million employees.

The metal-processing and machine-building industry is also a leader of the Ukrainian economy, with 12.2 per cent of industrial output in 2002. Machine-building exports generated EUR2,800 million in 2002, which constitutes 14.6 per cent of total exports. Simultaneously, in 2002 Ukraine imported EUR4 billion worth of machines and equipment.

Generally, the biggest obstacle for growth in the sector is low purchasing power, especially in the agricultural sector, and a lack of credit facilities for investments in production facilities.

As a legacy from the past, almost all Ukrainian metal-extracting or metal-producing companies are integrated and without specialization. This means that, within the same organization, they start with concentrated iron ore as input and finish up with rolled metal in billets or pipes as output.

The machine-building industry is also integrated and without specialization. Specialization in processing and in competencies is a new phenomenon in Ukraine and a part of the ongoing adaptation to the market economy.

In 2000, the industry experienced a growth in production for the first time in 10 years (Figure 2.1.4).

The electro-technical industry is growing compared to the other sectors. The products include turbines, generators, electric motors, transformers, heavy flanges and other metal works for power

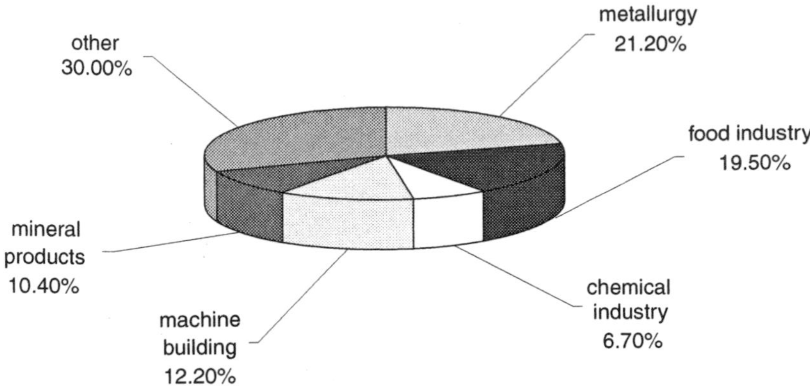

Figure 2.1.3 Industrial output of Ukraine, 2002, %

stations. The industry has a big export potential, though mostly to CIS countries.

Heavy machine building as a branch is also growing in importance. The products include ships, spacecraft, aircraft, locomotives, railway trucks, etc.

All metal-extracting companies are located in the eastern part of the country near the raw material resources. The large integrated metal-processing companies are also located in the east. Some of the largest and best known are the automobile concerns – ZAZ and KrAZ, the power industry supplier – Zaporiztransformer, the railway industry suppliers – Kriukovo Trucks Works, Donetsk Locomotive Works, Luhansk Locomotive Works, and the chemical industry supplier – Poltavakhimmash.

Before 1991, the military complex, nuclear power stations, and the space and aircraft industries accounted for up to 80 per cent of total

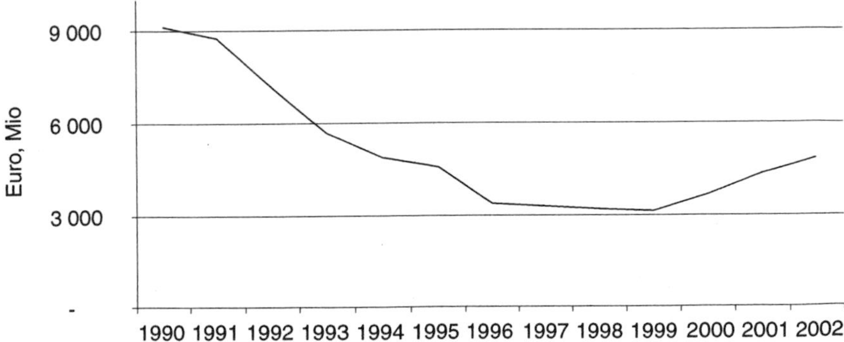

Figure 2.1.4 Production volumes in metal processing and machine building industry

production in the metal-processing sector. Today this figure is down to 10 per cent.

Some of the companies representing the military-industrial complex today are Malyshev Tank Plant (tanks), Yuzhmash (components of rockets and spaceships), Motor Sich (aircraft engines) and Turboatom (equipment and machines for nuclear stations).

Shipbuilding

Ukraine is among the 10 main shipbuilding countries. The industry consists of 59 companies and different institutions, including 11 shipyards, and employs up to 60,000 personnel. The shipyards build vessels of deadweight up to 180,000 tons.

The year 2002 was one of the most successful years for the industry – production growth reached 23 per cent and sales amounted up to EUR222 million. During this year 43 ships worth EUR120 million were delivered to customers. Of these, 38 were exported. The biggest growth is shown by OJSC 'Damen shipyard Ocean' at Mykolaiv. In 2002 the company produced 11 ships worth EUR23 million.

Automobile industry

The automobile industry is facing a period of growth. Market trends indicate that Ukraine is turning into a genuine car state.

The main Ukrainian car producer CJSC 'Zaporijja automobile building plant' made approximately 24,000 vehicles in 2002. Lutsk automobile plant produced approximately 13,000 Russian VAZ, UAZ and Korean KIA cars. In 2002 the Czech producer Skoda assembled approximately 2,000 cars at Zakarpattia Special Economic Zone. There is an ongoing project on the assembly of Audi and Volkswagen vehicles as well.

In 2003 'AutoKraz', located at Kremenchyh, planned to increase their production by 90 per cent to 2,500 cars. This plant is specialized in the production of dump-trucks, side-loading trucks, timber lorries, army vehicles etc. Recently 'AutoKraz' opened its own assembly line in Vietnam.

Machine building in western Ukraine

Before 1991, large machine-building companies were established close to the available resources, ie in the eastern part of the country, while the small and medium-sized metal-processing and machine-building companies were situated in the western part of the country. Their size, flexibility, and proximity to Western Europe are now one of their main advantages.

As opposed to other regions, western Ukraine does not have a unique specialization in certain products, but has companies representing all production techniques and needs.

In 2002, the output from the metal-processing and machine-building companies in western Ukraine amounted to EUR160 million and they employed about 110,000 people. The output constituted 15 per cent of the regional GDP. Metal-processing and machine-building companies are clustered geographically around L'viv and the other oblast centres such as Ivano-Frankivsk, Lutsk and Chernivtsi. The plants are in a tolerable state, with workshops and specialized equipment, although some are idle. The standard equipment is much depreciated and dates from the mid-1980s or in some cases from the late 1950s. Only a few companies have digitally controlled equipment. Present equipment is mostly universal, which affects the efficiency of production of big batches, and power consuming.

The financial state of 100 per cent Ukrainian-owned companies is poor. They have high debts and lack working capital. As a consequence, many companies are unable to finance materials for order processing and usually ask for pre-payment for 40–50 per cent of the total contract sum. To be engaged in such a pre-payment arrangement is, from experience, very risky and should be avoided. One way to bypass this situation is to buy the raw material through a registered representative in Ukraine. In this case the foreign customer will also be the owner and supplier of the raw material and the plant's creditors can therefore have no claims on it.

Company profiles

The following short company profiles give an impression of the level and qualifications available in existing companies:

- *Novo-Rozdilskiy experimental plant 'Karpaty'.* The company has facilities to carry out metal structure testing (x-rays, ultrasonic testing etc). Presently, the company is taking orders from Dima in Italy, Mano in Germany, Budapest Chemical Plant in Hungary, and some Danish companies. At present, the company is producing special containers for export to Western Europe. Usually, the orders do not exceed 20 pcs per month.
- *Chervonograd Ferroconcreate Plant.* The plant has during recent years specialized in the construction of special containers for Western European producers. The company exports primarily to Techmo in France. List price FCA is around EUR0.8–0.85 per kg.

Furthermore, the company has an extensive and growing export of flanges and rings for pipelines to Poland.

- *L'viv experimental mechanical plant.* The company's core activity is production of non-standard equipment for the oil and gas industry. The present capacity utilization is only 10 per cent. The company has started to produce orders for Delim in the Netherlands and Burmeister in Germany on complex technological constructions.
- *Plant of technological equipment 'Electron'.* The company specializes in frames and module constructions, containers, and packing machines for the food industry. The company's main foreign client is the German Fueller GmbH. At present the company has a capacity utilization of 40 per cent.
- *Ternopil Combine Plant.* The company produces sugar-beet harvesters. Its total capacity is 4,000 pcs per year but produced approximately 240 pcs last year. A contractor produces the engines; all other parts are produced in the company. Besides harvesters, the company produces spare parts for agricultural machinery, special tooling, hardened gear, refractory powdering, implements for self-propelled tractors etc. Its main clients are Russian agricultural companies but German companies are placing small orders.
- *LAZ Tools* plant is a subsidiary of the L'viv bus plant. It specializes in implements and tools for the mother company. In recent years, the plant has used its competencies to produce press forms, cast forms, and stamp forms for export. Strong technological features of the company are thermal processing and hard powdering. Capacity utilization is about 95 per cent. Its main clients are Webasto from Germany and the French company Techmo.
- The *'Conveyor'* company specializes in production of conveyors for industrial needs. It has 560 employees. Since the domestic market for the company's products has disappeared, the company has changed to fulfil small orders for Western companies, such as Mannesmann Dematik, Germany (conveyor details, metal constructions), Transystem, Poland (metal constructions), Nepol, Czech Republic (agricultural implements).
- *L'viv milling benches plant.* The company's main specialization is milling-, turning-, and drilling-benches and multi-spindle processing centres. The company has refocused on production of agricultural equipment, especially cultivators for the domestic market. The company still produces benches for Russia, Iran and South Africa. Ninety per cent of total production is exported, but capacity utilization is at about 10 per cent.

Foreign involvement in the metal sector

The metal-processing sector and machine-building industry in western Ukraine has experienced growing interest from foreign investors. Since 1995 foreign companies have invested EUR16 million in the sector, of which EUR5.7 million was invested in 2000. Since 1995, foreign companies have created several thousand jobs in western Ukraine. The largest and best-known foreign investments in the area are the Ball Bearing Plant in Lutsk oblast and Webasto-Electron in L'viv oblast. Metal-processing companies with 100 per cent foreign ownership have created only a little more than 800 jobs in western Ukraine, but as most foreign companies are not investing but outsourcing, several thousand jobs have been created indirectly at local companies.

OJSC Lutsk Bearing Plant (LBP) (http://lbp.com.ua), a SKF Group company (www.skf.com), specializes in manufacturing taper roller and needle roller bearings. Modern equipment enables the production of up to 6 million bearings per year. The company employs around 1,000 people.

Webasto-Electron specializes in the production of heaters and coolers for trucks, cars, vans, etc. The company started in 1996 as a joint venture with 80 per cent German ownership (www.webasto.com) and 20 per cent local ownership. The company today employs 41 people.

Supply and cost of raw materials

The best cost-based argument for placing orders in Ukraine is not just the difference in salaries between Western Europe and Ukraine but the cost difference on raw material. Raw material constitutes the largest part of the direct cost in metal processing and machine building, and after minimal processing the material can be exported to EU countries without limiting quotas.

Raw material costs constitute about 35–50 per cent of all direct costs. The local prices in Ukraine are uniform but dependent on the type of steel, its shape, and characteristics. On average, Ukrainian wholesale prices for steel are 25–35 per cent lower than wholesale prices in Poland. For ribbed rods, rolled steel, hot or cold rolled steel sheets, seamed pipes etc prices range from EUR0.23 per kg to EUR0.40 per kg. Ukrainian wholesale operators are either metallurgy companies or their trading companies.

There are numerous wholesalers in every oblast, which supply the local machine-building plants and other metal-processing companies. There are around 20 small metal wholesalers in western Ukraine – the largest are IMVO, UVTK and Hightech.

IMVO in L'viv supplies 800 companies in western Ukraine. Monthly turnover is 3,000 tons. Its export share is 60 per cent. Besides metal trading, the company is involved in simple metal processing and project management in more complex metal-processing operations.

Owing to the present economic situation, domestic prices are sometimes higher than export prices because suppliers prefer to export at a lower price than sell to local companies with a high risk of default or late payment. Another reason is the difference in volumes, which makes it possible to give a higher discount on the export markets.

Ukrainian standards and conformity to the DIN standards

Ukrainian metal-processing companies operate to the GOST standard. GOST is an abbreviation for State Standards. Although the logical bases for the European DIN standard and the GOST are very similar, it is not always possible to find the exact correspondence. When comparing standards for steel, sheets, pipes, armature and small hardware the standards are very similar. But when talking about rolled profile products and similar products, there might be essential differences, which again can affect performance and accomplishment. These can be ramp angles, hole positions and dimension, strength limits, the degree of warping etc. As a consequence, the foreign company will initially have to adapt its processing methods to the input material. All the GOST are well described and technical adaptation has been shown not to be an obstacle for processing. It is in any case recommended to check conformity with standards before placing orders. Conformity can be checked at the local Standard and Metrology Institution or at a specialized consulting company.

It is expected that Ukrainian producers will start to deliver according to DIN standards. But as long as they are facing strict export restrictions from the EU and the US, they do not yet have an economic incentive.

Quality assurance systems and principles of certification

It is not common for a Ukrainian metal-processing or machine-building company to be certified according to ISO 9000 standards as recognized by European companies. However, a number of export-oriented companies are certified according to the ISO 9000 standards, or are implementing a total quality management (TQM) system. In particular, those companies with products facing high quality requirements are certified. An example is the Armature Plant in Ivano-Frankivsk. The company specializes in the production of nuclear power station heat exchangers, oil pipeline valves and latches, and chemically resistant flanges. Its products are not only exported to the other CIS countries but also to Germany and Austria. As more and more local companies become aware of the importance of being certified, the numbers of certified companies are growing. Although the ISO system is a tool for control of the processing procedures and not for quality, it gives an indication of the company's degree of professionalism and its approach towards international competition.

Almost all companies producing ferrous metal in its rough form, especially rolled products and pipes, are fully or partially certified according to ISO 9000, since they are all export oriented.

Companies oriented towards the domestic market or towards the CIS prefer the cheaper certification of Ukrainian certifying agencies. Usually, these agencies only certify a part of the production or single welders but very seldom the total production. Although not recognized by Western European producers, it is generally considered that companies certified according to local standards can provide products of sufficient quality and reliability, ie the local Ukrainian standards are on the same quality level as the ISO system.

The Tuev-Nord agency or Lloyds has certified most of high-quality welding facilities located at shipyards. These shipbuilding companies are certified according to the European welding standard EM 729. All ISO-certifying agencies are located in Kyiv. The best known are Veritas (www.dnv.ru) and the Ukrainian Association of Quality (www.quality.kiev.ua).

Labour costs and qualifications

Labour costs are one of the biggest constituents of direct costs and are generally around 10–20 per cent. A welder in Ukraine, of third category, is usually paid around net EUR100 a month. Including taxes, social charges etc, the total monthly labour costs per month are some EUR150. Very often, Ukrainian direct workers are employed under a strict piecework contract, which changes the actual expenditures. For comparison, a Polish welder of third category has a net salary of approximately EUR570 a month. Even though it can be argued that efficiency is higher in Poland than in Ukraine, the salary difference is still very significant.

The labour cost for the local manager is, as a minimum, double that for a manual worker, ie EUR200.

Another factor, which is very difficult to measure but extremely important, is the local workers' work attitude, the attitude towards private ownership, and the general attitude towards foreign involvement in the economy. In contrast to eastern Ukraine, the people and institutions in western Ukraine are oriented towards Western Europe and are pro-Western. In many aspects Poland and western Ukraine are culturally alike; this is probably why many EU companies find it easier to work in western Ukraine than in other regions. The necessary management methodology is to give very specific and precise tasks to everyone and to develop a very strict system of control – initiative is not a local tradition.

Since independence, the educational system in Ukraine has been undergoing restructuring in order to meet the demands of a market economy. The system is still very centralized, has too much capacity and is mostly financed – or underfinanced – by the state.

There are a number of specialized educational institutions preparing specialists for metal processing and machine building in Ukraine. The sector-specific educational system has four levels.

In western Ukraine, around 12,000 students graduate every year from specialized educational institutions of the second level and approximately 10,000 from establishments of the third and fourth levels, specializing in metal processing and machine building. The demand for qualified personnel in the branch is growing. Nevertheless, the level of unemployment in the industry is still high, keeping a downward pressure on salaries. A large number of graduates re-qualify or take lower qualified jobs.

Despite the excess supply of various specialists to the metal-processing and machine-building industry, it is still very difficult to find and attract local marketing specialists and qualified top-level managers.

Technology

Modern technologies are rarely used in Ukraine. It is difficult to find laser-cutting equipment, refractory powdering technologies etc. Sophisticated technologies are almost only used in the space and aircraft industries, machine building for power stations, and in some branches of the military industry, especially for tanks. These industries try to keep pace with the latest R&D and have their own know-how, which is valued by some very specific foreign customers. The world-renowned space programme Sea Launch, in which Ukraine participates with its rockets, its AN-70 and AN-160 aircraft and the Malyshev Plant's tanks, which are mostly bought by Asian and African countries, is clear evidence of the attractiveness of the these products in the world market.

Still, the main asset of Ukrainian machine building for foreign customers is the possibility of carrying out simple, power-consuming operations such as welding, mechanical machining etc at large and capacious metal construction firms. The work of Ukrainian ship welders from Mykolaiv is in high demand from Western companies. There are many foreign orders at vat, boiler and cistern-producing plants.

There are large assembly facilities in Ukraine, which allow the assembly of trucks, cars and agriculture combines at low cost for both internal and external markets. Besides, assembly operations in Ukraine allow the bypassing of numerous import customs duties, which the state imposes on importers to protect domestic producers. For example, Daewoo prefers to import the components of its cars to Ukraine and assemble them in Illichivsk and Zaporijja. The advantages are obvious: the company saves on more effective transportation and cheaper assembly operations, and bypasses custom duties. This results in very competitive car prices on the Ukrainian market.

In general, the technology in Ukrainian metal processing can be broken into four categories:

- metal machining without metal dust (metal bending, cutting etc);
- metal machining with metal dust (machining at turning benches, drilling, grinding etc);
- surface treatment (galvanizing, anti-corrosion coating etc);
- joining (welding, riveting, assembly operations etc).

All of the above technologies, except surface treatment, are willingly ordered by foreign customers from Ukrainian metal-processing companies. In general, the labour force in Ukraine has sufficient skills, and the equipment used in Ukraine for operations like these is almost the same as in the West.

Surface treatment operations, such as galvanizing, painting, hot zinc coating, etc, are not usually ordered in western Ukraine, because of coating. The exception is high-quality plastic coating, which is popular with foreign clients. At docks and shipyards there are modern painting systems, bought abroad, which provide high quality painting. The foreign clients of shipyards usually order the whole spectrum of services, including painting, and are satisfied with its quality.

2.2

The Textile Sector in Ukraine

Munk, Andersen & Feilberg

Introduction

The Ukrainian textile sector is a very old sector with long traditions. More than 50 per cent of the Soviet textile industry was located in Ukraine and western Ukraine was one of the biggest textile centres in the Union. Nowadays, western Ukraine's favourable geographic location, proximity to the European markets, short distances to the borders of several EU-accession countries, a relatively good transport infrastructure and low cost structures create a unique competitive advantage for the industry.

Rough estimation shows that the number of foreign operators working just in L'viv oblast reaches 100 companies. Western companies are utilizing the low cost structures and are raising their profit margin in Western Europe – Ukraine still does not have a profitable domestic market. Calculation shows that under similar conditions, production cost in Ukraine is approximately 50 per cent lower than in Poland – an important benchmark when evaluating investment success. As a rule of thumb, a European company can save EUR400,000 a year by relocating 100 sewing operators from Poland to western Ukraine.

According to statistics, the textile sector in Ukraine employs 200,000 people. Of these, there are approximately 70,000 employees who officially work in the textile sector of western Ukraine. The correct figures are very likely higher. A large number of vocational schools, colleges and universities ensure a qualified educational background for the employees, which in combination with Western management practice has proven to be an important factor in reaching an acceptable level of efficiency.

The textile sector in Ukraine

Components of the textile sector

The textile sector consists of the following sub-sectors:

- fabric manufacturing – knitted, woven, and non-woven fabric;
- dyeing of fabric;
- sewing – production of sewn garments/clothes (suits, dresses, shirts, blouses, trousers, coats, jackets, work-wear), linen, notions etc;
- knitwear production – tricot, hosiery and knitted garments (knitting and sewing of hosiery, sewing of T-shirts, knitted jackets, underwear etc).

The sector after 1991 – post-communist history

The disintegration of the Soviet Union and the collapse of the centralized economy significantly affected the Ukrainian textile sector. Most of the companies were cut off from their usual trade partners. Purchasing power fell, the companies were unable to introduce market-based management principles and the industry was facing pressure from the import of goods of better quality. A large part of the sector was unable to adapt to the new situation and stood idle or was producing with a very low utilization of capacity. To summarize, the main reasons for the recession in the industry after 1991 were:

- collapse of distribution system – for input materials as well as for markets;
- diminishing purchasing power;
- lack of modern production facilities;
- lack of qualified managers and qualifications needed to adapt to the market principles;
- a competitive situation.

The share of light industry (including production of fabric, clothes and shoes) is currently just around 0.8 per cent of total production. However, starting from 1998–99 the industry demonstrated a slow recovery, experiencing a snowball effect in the following years. In 2002 the increase in textile and apparel production was 12 per cent compared to 2001 (13.8 per cent in 2001 compared to 2000), which was mostly caused by growing interest from Western European companies which placed subcontracting orders with local Ukrainian companies from the mid-1990s. As such, the textile industry is one of the fastest-growing sectors in the Ukrainian economy.

The devastating crisis in the country and in the textile industry in particular has led to a situation where the companies have readily available production capacity and very low cost structures, but at the same time insufficient management skills, depreciated technology and therefore low efficiency. By bringing in new technology and management skills, Western European companies can significantly raise productivity and utilize the low cost structures in an optimal way. Most of the enterprises that are actually active already have some kind of cooperation with foreign investors. They are still not utilizing their full capacity, but are constantly improving their performance.

The central and western parts of Ukraine have traditionally been the most important textile centres in the country. For illustration, a regional breakdown of textile production is shown in Table 2.2.1. Respectively, Kyiv and L'viv are still the main areas of textile production.

The present structure of the textile sector in western Ukraine

There are more than 300 officially registered textile enterprises in western Ukraine. The majority of these textile companies are sewing

Table 2.2.1 Textile production breakdown by regions of Ukraine, 2001

Oblast	Production output, €m 2001	Share of total production, % 2001
Western Ukraine	**70.4**	**26.52**
Chernivtsi	7.4	2.77
Ivano-Frankivsk	15.6	5.86
Lviv	22.4	8.44
Rivne	2.7	1.02
Ternopil	6.4	2.41
Transcarpathia	13.2	4.98
Volyn	2.8	1.04
Central Ukraine	**46.5**	**17.51**
Eastern Ukraine	**34.6**	**13.03**
South Ukraine	**19.2**	**7.22**
North Ukraine	**94.9**	**35.73**
Ukraine	**265.5**	**100.00**

factories and knitwear producers. These two sub-sectors constitute some 97 per cent of the total textile sector in western Ukraine (see Figure 2.2.1). Only a few factories are involved in fabric manufacturing and dyeing.

Sewing

According to statistics, there are 1,128 sewing companies in Ukraine, of which 300 have more than 100 workers. Approximately 225 sewing companies are working in western Ukraine. These are mainly located in Chernivtsi oblast (about 30 per cent) and Transcarpathia oblast (about 25 per cent). The lowest number of functioning enterprises is located in Volyn oblast. However, the size of companies in Chernivtsi and Transcarpathia oblasts is comparatively smaller than those located in L'viv oblast, and the biggest share of sewn garments is produced in L'viv oblast. The companies in the L'viv area are larger and have larger production volumes than the companies in Chernivtsi and Transcarpathia oblasts. The activity of sewing factories can generally be grouped as follows: sewing factories subcontracting with foreign partners, sewing factories producing state orders, sewing factories producing garments for the Ukrainian market, and sewing factories producing garments for export.

Sewing factories subcontracting with foreign partners
The vast majority of Ukrainian sewing factories are subcontracting with foreign companies or their local production units, producing 70–95 per cent of Ukrainian sewing production. Total dependence of the sewing industry on foreign orders is so great that sewing production in Ukraine in 2002 compared to 2001 decreased by 3.6 per cent because of

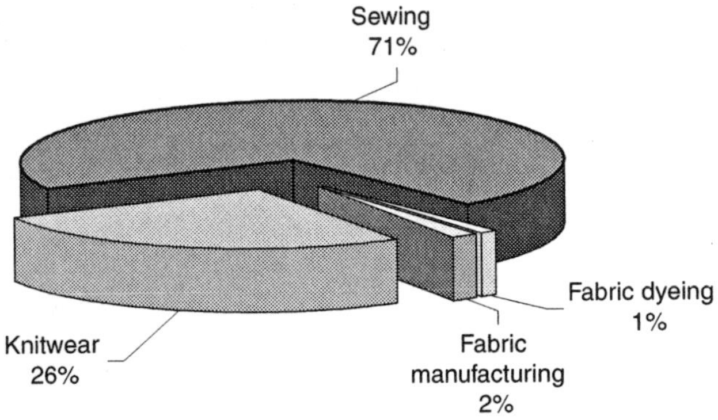

Figure 2.2.1 Distribution of textile companies by oblasts in western Ukraine

a decrease of subcontracting orders from US, French and German companies.

For most of the local sewing companies, subcontracting is the only way to survive. Furthermore, subcontracting in Ukraine usually includes a paid upgrade of technology and management. As a result, most of the factories are able to produce all types of sewn products and master all techniques.

Medium-sized and large Western companies that are not satisfied with the efficiency and price level of Ukrainian subcontractors may decide to set up their own production in Ukraine. In this case the subcontracting scheme remains the same, but the foreign company controls management, financial flows, level of margin, and efficiency.

Sewing factories producing state orders
State orders mainly comprise military clothes of different types. Owing to decreasing volumes of orders and the poor financial situation of the state, this kind of production scheme is diminishing.

Sewing factories producing garments for the Ukrainian market
According to the specialists, 60–70 per cent of the domestic market in Ukraine consists of goods brought to Ukraine illegally (primarily from Turkey and Poland). The rest of the market is split between legal import and local production. Ukrainian producers have been put out of the market by private 'shuttles', which avoid paying VAT and other taxes through illegal import. The difference in prices for legitimate companies caused by VAT makes competition practically impossible.

However, during 2000–02 Ukrainian companies won back part of the market (up to 30–50 per cent in some commodity groups). These factories are carrying out their own product design, supply of materials, production, marketing and sales.

Sewing factories producing garments for export
Owing to high entry barriers and poor development of the marketing function, export of own products is still a rare event for Ukrainian enterprises.

There are still fewer successful, ie profitable, sewing factories than unprofitable factories. Most sewing factories have very low capacity utilization and low capability of renewing production equipment. However, there is a positive trend in this respect as well – more and more sewing factories are strengthening their financial position.

Fabric manufacturing

Previously, ie before 1991, Ukrainian factories supplied the industry with all types of fabric, including woven, knitted and non-woven fabric.

The main supplier of raw material was Uzbekistan. Yarn of different types, which is a raw material for the sector, is virtually not produced in Ukraine. Moreover, the supply of cotton and wool yarn into Ukraine from other countries has decreased and chemical thread is not produced in Ukraine at all.

Currently, there are only a few fabric manufacturers in western Ukraine; the most famous is Texterno in Ternopil (during recent years Texterno has controlled about 70 per cent of the domestic production). Most of the enterprises either stand idle or work with a capacity utilization of 10–20 per cent. Knitted fabric is partly being produced by specialized fabric manufacturers and partly by knitwear producers having a full cycle of production. However, the capacities of Ukrainian knitwear producers are quite obsolete compared to Western European producers.

The quality of the Ukrainian fabric is low compared to imported products. Even the low price of local fabric does not make it popular. The fabric sold in Ukraine is mainly of Italian, Chinese, Polish or Russian origin.

In 2002, the Danish company Sunds Velour started fabric production and dyeing in the town of Sokal, not far from L'viv. However, the fabric produced so far is not sold on the local market.

Fabric dyeing

There are 11 companies specializing in fabric dyeing in western Ukraine. Even though there are dyeing capacities, in general the equipment of these enterprises is quite obsolete and mostly not utilized. There is simply no demand for fabric dyeing, since most of the Ukrainian sewing factories are subcontracted by foreign companies, and only use fabric of EU origin.

The Ukrainian market for textiles and clothing

The total Ukrainian clothes market is estimated to be at least EUR1.2 billion, including second-hand clothing (Figure 2.2.2). Low-income consumers with a monthly income less than EUR120 constitute about 80 per cent of the market. The Ukrainian market for knitted and sewn garments is quite fragmented and mostly consists of smuggled low-priced products. However, a slight upward trend in prices should be noted during recent years.

Second-hand clothing is an important part of the Ukrainian market. In 2001, this market amounted to 60,000 tons or EUR60–70 million. According to prognosis, in 2002 the market was expected to grow 10–20 per cent, and thus reach EUR80 million. Eighty per cent of imports of second-hand clothing are from Western Europe.

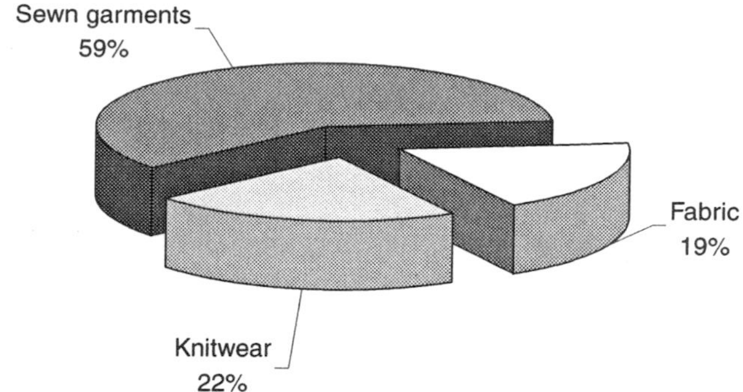

Figure 2.2.2 Breakdown of textile sales in Ukraine

Most sales at the market are made via bazaar vendors (approximately 80 per cent of the total sales), the producers' own shops, and small intermediate companies. Wholesale market and legal distribution channels are not developed yet. The biggest and most popular textile bazaars are located in four oblast centres – Chernivtsi, Khmelnytsky, Odessa and Kharkiv.

The factories – both official enterprises and illegal private workshops – located in the cities near the 'bazaar centres' are utilizing most of their capacity producing textile products for sale in the bazaar. Demand and therefore competition for qualified labour force in these regions is very high. Currently, more and more local production is replacing imports from Turkey and China.

The small workshops are very viable because of their flexibility, 'free-of-taxes' activity and the attractiveness of high salaries to sewers. Small workshops (10–20 sewing operators) do not require large investments and big premises. Sometimes they are even located in private apartments, basements etc. The salary level is considerably higher than at official enterprises. Some companies create their own marketing and sales function, and sell some 10–30 per cent of production at the local market. The sales are mostly organized via own shops and regional sales representatives. There are also some solely Ukraine-oriented producers, who produce garments of high quality and comparatively low price, but the number of these is quite low.

Exports, imports, and EU quotas

The textile industry currently enjoys a trade surplus. Exports in 2002 amounted to about EUR20 million, and imports were about EUR9 million. A growth trend appeared in the sector in 1999 and is still continuing (with a small reduction in exports in 2002). The region's proximity to the Russian market accounts for the dominance of trade with Russia. Trade with Western Europe has also continued to grow considerably each year since the country's independence. A favourable geographic location, short distances to the borders of several EU-accession countries and the availability of low-cost transportation allow western Ukraine to compete successfully for access to many international markets.

In order to protect its own domestic markets, in 1993 the EU established quotas on imports of some categories of Ukrainian textile products. The Ukrainian Ministry of Economics redistributed quotas to local exporters by granting them export licences. Since then, Ukraine has concluded several international treaties and bilateral agreements with the EU. These agreements helped open the EU market to Ukrainian textile companies.

On 12 January 2001 the Ukrainian government decreased import duties on textile goods to the maximum rates set by the EU in the World Trade Organization (WTO). In response, the EU lifted all quotas on imports of textile and clothing products from Ukraine on 26 March 2001.

Surveillance (licensing without quotas) is still maintained for the time being for a certain number of textile products such as shirts, coats, pullovers and cotton fabrics.

'EU rates' indicates that the maximum rates to be applied by Ukraine are the rates bound by the EU in the WTO. EU bound rates (2004) for yarns and fibres are generally 4 per cent, for fabrics generally 8 per cent, for carpets generally 8 per cent, and for clothing and made-ups they are generally 12 per cent. In some cases the bound rates are below these general rates.

Sewn garments

Owing to the predominance of the subcontracting scheme in textile production, the volume of exports of sewn products from Ukraine substantially exceeds the value of imports. This trend was formed and settled at the end of 1990s. As shown, up to 95 per cent of sewn garments are produced under subcontracting conditions. Although the total export value in 2002 has increased by 8.4 per cent compared to 2001, it is still expected to grow in the years to come.

Table 2.2.2 Maximum import duty rates

Product types	2000	2001	2002	2003	2004
Yarns and fibres	–	EU rates	EU rates	EU rates	EU rates
Fabrics	–	EU rates	EU rates	EU rates	EU rates
Clothing and made-ups	13%	EU rates	EU rates	EU rates	EU rates
Carpets	17%	12%	10%	EU rates	EU rates

The proportion of export by regions has not changed significantly over recent years. In 2002, the biggest importer of Ukrainian apparel was Germany with 46 per cent of export value (Figure 2.2.3). Export to the USA and France constitutes 11 per cent and 9 per cent respectively. Among the most stable partners of Ukraine are the UK, Italy, Denmark, Hungary and the Netherlands.

The geography of imports of sewn garments has changed compared with the situation in 2001 in Ukraine. The main imports were from China (25 per cent) in 2002 (Figure 2.2.4). The shares of Polish and Turkish products are 10 per cent respectively, Italian – 9 per cent, German – 7 per cent. The most stable partners in this area are companies from Russia, the USA, Belgium, the UK, France, Hungary and the Netherlands. It is worth mentioning that a large share of imports (according to experts, up to 90 per cent) is illegal; smuggled goods mostly come from Turkey, China, Vietnam and Poland. These figures obviously do not appear in the official statistics.

Knitwear

According to the State Statistics Committee of Ukraine, knitwear exports increased by about 11.5 per cent during the first six months of 2002 compared with the analogous period in 2001. Ukraine's largest partners with respect to knitwear exports (Figure 2.2.5) are Germany (29 per cent), Poland (20.33 per cent), Hungary (14.42 per cent), Denmark (10.93 per cent) and Italy (7.26 per cent).

Based on official statistics, the import of knitwear goods dramatically increased by about 56 per cent during the first six months of 2002. The growth of imports can be explained only by the fact that illegal importing has become harder. Therefore goods previously imported unofficially now enter Ukraine legally. The main importers are Germany (18.38 per cent), China (12.98 per cent), Poland (12.56 per cent) and Denmark (11.62 per cent).

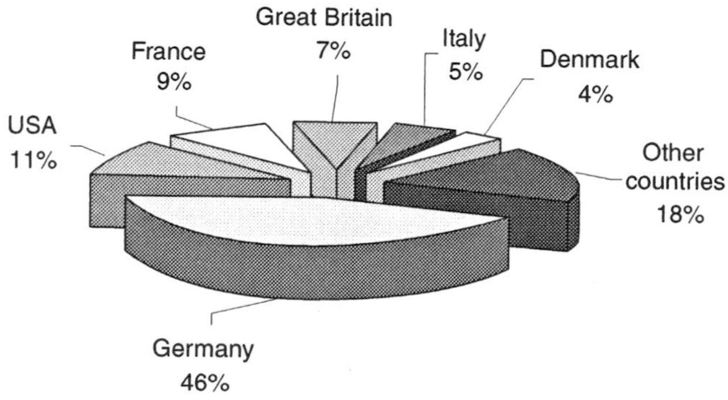

Figure 2.2.3 Regional breakdown of export of sewn garments in 2002

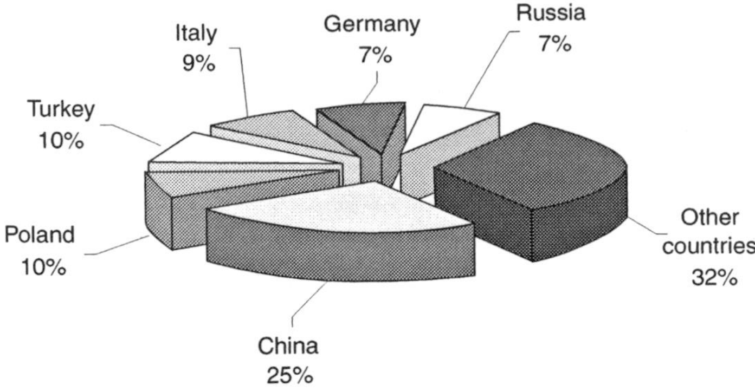

Figure 2.2.4 Regional breakdown of import of sewn garments in 2002

Employment and salary level

According to the official statistics there are approximately 70,000 employees in the textile sector in western Ukraine. It is estimated that approximately 50,000 people in western Ukraine work unofficially in the textile sector, producing mostly for bazaars.

Today, it is estimated that in the city of L'viv there is a lack of approximately 500 sewers caused by a growing demand from new factories (especially foreign).

The low salary level is the single most important factor and cost-based argument for foreign investors working in the Ukrainian textile

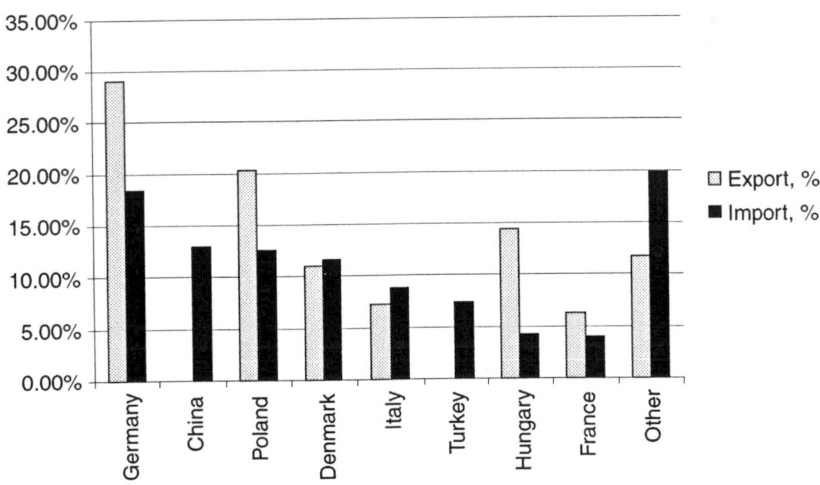

Figure 2.2.5 Knitwear export and import breakdown by countries in 2002

sector. Calculation shows that under similar conditions, the production cost in Ukraine is approximately 50 per cent lower than in Poland.

Ukraine has a net salary level of EUR0.42 per hour or EUR104 gross per month. Salary levels within western Ukraine are, however, not uniform and depend on the following criteria:

- *Size of the city where the factory is located.* The level of salary is higher at the factories located in bigger cities.
- *Ownership of the factory.* The companies with foreign ownership usually offer higher salaries. This is not only because of the their 'foreign' status, when employees expect them to pay more than Ukrainian factories, but mostly due to higher efficiency than at local companies.
- *Regional location.* The regions with a higher concentration of textile factories are characterized by comparatively higher salary levels owing to higher professional levels and keen competition in the labour force. Therefore, the salary level in L'viv, Chernivtsi and Khmelnytsky oblasts is slightly higher than in Volyn and Transcarpathia oblasts.

The difference in salary of a sewing operator starts from EUR34 gross per month at a Ukrainian company located in a village/small town and peaks at EUR104 gross per month and more at EU production units operating in big cities in western Ukraine.

The upward trend in salaries has been accompanied and stimulated by a general increase in labour efficiency and a growing demand for employees in the sector (Figure 2.2.6). The experience of EU textile producers in western Ukraine proves that efficiency could be raised very quickly by introducing new management principles and modern technology.

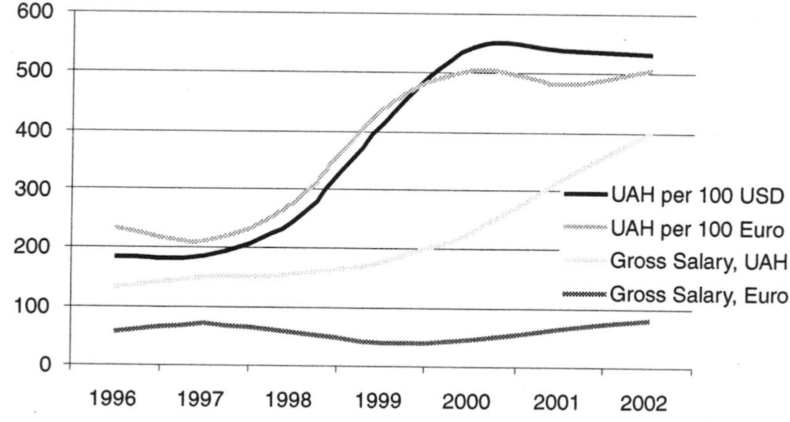

Figure 2.2.6 Tendencies in labour costs in western Ukraine

2.3

The Wood-Processing Industry in Ukraine

Munk, Andersen & Feilberg

Introduction

Ukraine was one of the largest wood-processing sectors in the former Soviet Union. Raw materials, production facilities, traditions, educational institutions and the necessary human resource base are all existent and concentrated in Ukraine.

After an immense drop in the 1990s, the wood-processing sector revived and is one of the fastest-growing sectors in Ukraine. This is not only a result of high and rising exports of processed wooden products to Europe and the CIS, but also a result of a growing domestic market for furniture and other wooden products.

Wood processing

According to official statistics, there were 3,653 wood-processing and furniture companies operating in Ukraine as of 2001. Unofficial estimates set the real number of operating units to at least twice as many. Many newly established small and medium-sized companies are not officially registered or do not declare wood processing as their main activity. The wood-processing companies are mostly concentrated in western Ukraine.

After the breakdown of the system, most of the integrated companies collapsed economically as they failed to adjust to the new market conditions. The existing companies from the old system are still underutilizing their capacity. Estimates state that the average capacity utilization in Ukraine is around 45 per cent. For example, plywood production dropped by 35 per cent from 1990 to 2002. Sawn timber volume dropped 75 per cent in the same period.

In 2002 Ukraine processed only 1.9 million m^3 of sawn timber and produced 103.4 m^3 of plywood compared with 1990 when the output was 7.4 million m^3 of sawn timber and 169,000 m^3 of plywood (Figure 2.3.1). The development in the furniture industry has been just as devastating in the period from 1990 to 2002. However, production of plywood and boards is recovering after its lowest output level in the mid-1990s. Official production data for sawn timber are not so optimistic and illustrate the stagnation of timber production. But one fact should be taken into consideration – unofficial felling and sawing of logs is very widespread in Ukraine. Therefore, the growing production of wooden products is not threatened by the stagnation of sawn timber production presented in official data. By now, there is no shortage of timber on the domestic market.

There are 13 companies in Ukraine today that produce chipboard, 14 companies that produce plywood, two companies that produce fibre board and only one company that produces MDF (Medium Density Fibreboard). This company is called 'NOVA' and it was established at the end of 2000 in Ternopil' in western Ukraine.

For plywood production Ukrainian factories use birch, alder and beech. For fibre and chipboard production they use low quality timber from different kinds of trees (pine, spruce, fir, alder, ash tree, beech, hornbeam etc). Fibreboard is scarcely produced in Ukraine. Only two companies manufacture this product, 'FUNPLIT' (Kyiv) and 'UNIPLIT' (Vygoda, Ivano-Frankivsk region). In 2001 the production volume of fibre board amounted to 19,930 thousand m^2, which is 20 per cent higher than in 2000.

Producers within the supply chain for furniture are experiencing tremendous growth in production. In 2002 the growth in production of chipboard was 45 per cent and for plywood production 29 per cent. This development is mainly due to rising exports but also the internal market for these products is growing.

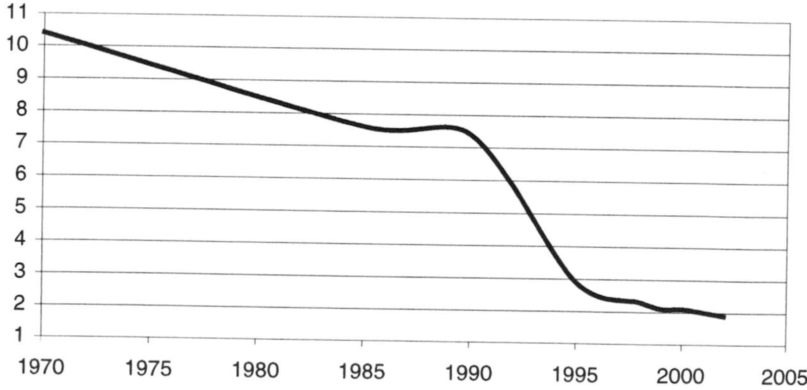

Figure 2.3.1 Dynamics in the production of sawn timber, 1970–2002, million m^3

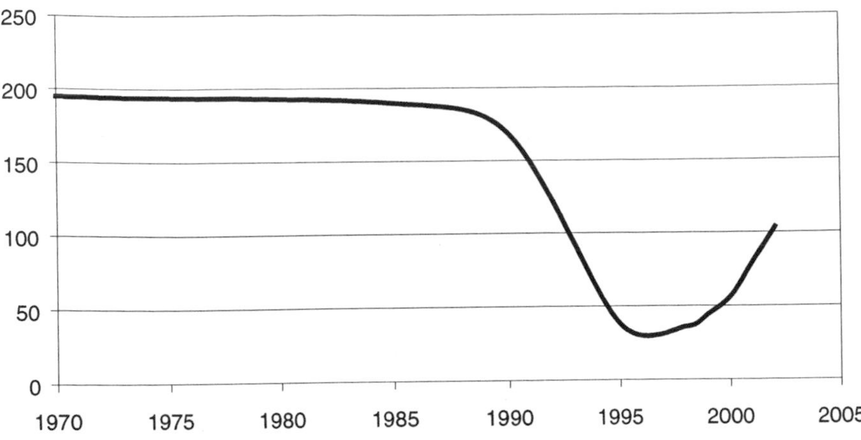

Figure 2.3.2 Dynamics in the production of plywood, 1970–2002, thou. m^3

According to the State Committee of Statistics (www.ukrstat.gov.ua), in 2001 Ukraine produced:

- 8,850,000 m^3 of laminated chipboard;
- 378,750 m^3 of non-laminated chipboard;
- 79,900 m^3 of plywood.

According to state statistics, veneer is produced by 39 enterprises. Eighteen of them produce planed veneer, 21 produce rotary cut veneer. Around 60 per cent of these companies are wood-processing integrated factories for whom veneer is not the only product. Usually veneer is produced out of beech, oak and birch, more rarely out of ash, maple, alder and wild cherry. The actual production of veneer is difficult to determine since most Ukrainian plywood factories produce veneer for their own internal production purposes.

There are a lot of companies from different European countries that buy veneer from Ukrainian enterprises. Those countries are Germany, Italy, Spain, Turkey, Austria and the Netherlands. In 2002 Ukraine exported veneer worth of EUR7.58 million and in the first six months of 2003 it was EUR5.2 million.

The forest fund and supply of raw materials

The forest fund plays an important role in the Ukrainian economy. Ukraine covers an area of 603,700 sq km and the total area of forestry is 107,820 sq km, or 15.8 per cent of the territory, with an estimated stock of timber of 1,700 million m^3. Because of the different climatic conditions in the country the large forests are all situated in the western and northern parts of the country (Figure 2.3.3), ie in Transcarpathia, Ivano-Frankivsk, Rivne, Zhytomir and Volyn oblasts (regions). The forest fund in these oblasts constitutes some 30–50 per cent of the territory. In contrast to this, forests are scarce in the steppe regions, in the east, such as Dnipropretrovsk, Kherson, Mykolaiv and Zaporizhzhia. In these oblasts the forest fund constitutes only 2–4 per cent of the territory. For some sorts of wood, especially the more rare types of hardwood, the eastern part of the country can be of interest, even though the total stocks of timber in these areas are quite small.

In 2001 the annual growth constituted 42,577 ha of lumber with annual cutting of only 23,200 ha (or 54 per cent). Such a disproportion is caused by low demand for middle and low quality lumber. High quality lumber is often imported, mainly from Russia and Belorussia.

Specific soil and climatic conditions for forestry in western Ukraine have pre-conditioned a specific composition of forest. The most common coniferous species are pine (3,209,000 ha) and spruce (706,900 ha). The most common deciduous species are oak (2,330,000 ha), beech (706,800 ha), hornbeam, birch and alder (Figure 2.3.4). Western Ukrainian forests are also rich in species such as maple, cherry and pear, especially of interest for the furniture industry.

The forest fund in Ukraine is in state ownership. The State Committee of Forest Economy of Ukraine manages more than 70 per cent of the forest fund while the remaining part is managed by other state organizations such as the Ministry of Defence, municipalities, health resorts and educational institutions. Twenty per cent of the forest fund is managed by Collective Agricultural Enterprises (CAEs). In all oblasts of Ukraine there are so called 'Derzhlisgosp', or executive state agencies, which are responsible for forest protection, felling, and basic processing. Ukrainian

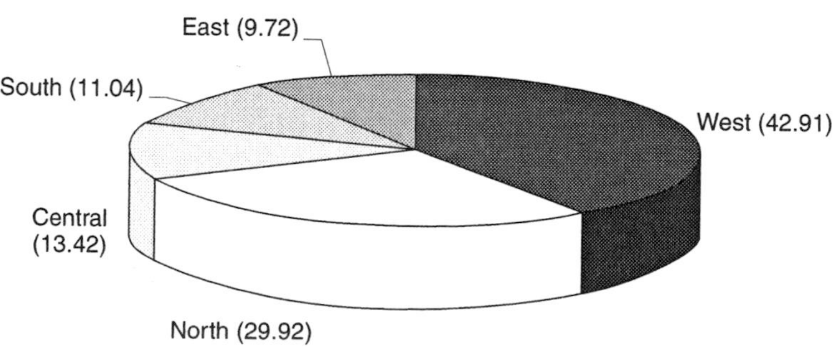

Figure 2.3.3 Distribution of forest areas among Ukrainian regions, 2002, thou. km^2

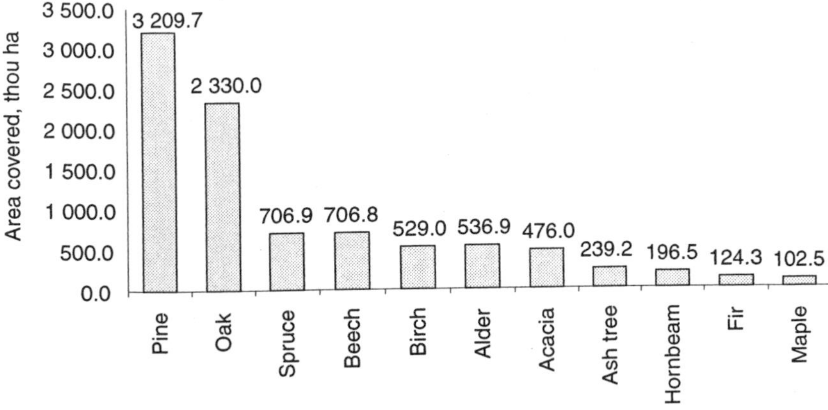

Figure 2.3.4 Area covered with major species of wood in Ukraine, 2002, thou. ha

forest management and maintenance is not certified according to FSC or PEFC requirements.

Ukrainian law does not allow for private persons or private legal entities to own forest in Ukraine and the commercial exploitation of the forest fund is administered through a licence system. One must therefore purchase timber from already licensed companies, local or foreign, or try to receive a licence for felling. Usually, companies will find a local supplier because the local licence system is not very transparent for new players on the market. Most wood in Ukraine is bought from Derzhlisgosps, which sell round timber.

Labour costs and qualifications

Besides the cost of raw materials, labour cost is one of the biggest constituents of direct costs. As of July 2003, an average net salary in the wood-processing industry is UAH435 (EUR72.5) per month. For comparison, a Polish direct worker of third category has a net salary of approximately EUR450 a month, or about six times higher than a Ukrainian worker of the same category.

Figure 2.3.5 gives a good indication of the trends in salary level in western Ukraine. The salary-level data presented in Figure 2.3.5 is given by the Ministry of Labour and Social Policy (www.mlsp.gov.ua) and represents official data declared in companies' reports.

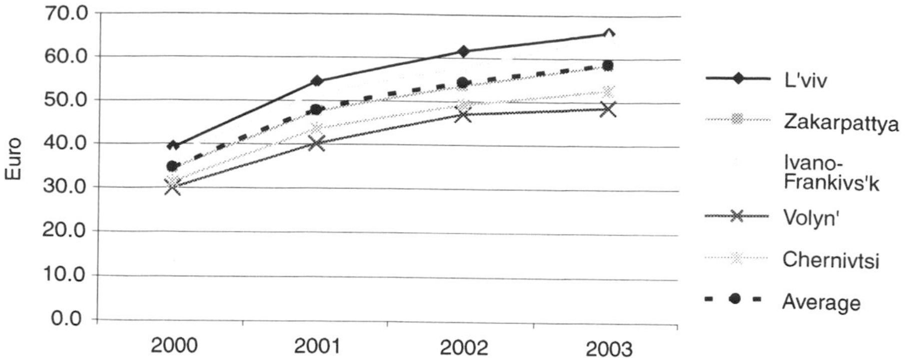

Figure 2.3.5 Tendencies in labour costs in western Ukraine

Wood-processing technology in Ukraine

Modern technologies are not very often used in the Ukrainian wood-processing industry. Since the majority of companies were previously state owned, most equipment used in production processes is outdated or obsolete. In general, all companies in the industry can be divided into three groups:

1. Previously state-owned companies, without new owners (obsolete machines, 10–15 years old, with no or very low percentage (5–10 per cent) of new equipment used).
2. Previously state-owned companies with new owners (usually bought by local investors, they buy new or used foreign equipment, which then constitutes 40–60 per cent of all machinery in the factory. The rest of the equipment is the remaining old machinery (5–10 years old), which is still in fairly good condition).
3. Joint ventures, foreign companies or successful local companies (90–95 per cent of all equipment is brand new and was installed only 2–3 years ago). These companies use imported equipment, which is often identical to the equipment used by European wood-processing and furniture companies. Equipment is mostly imported from Finland, Germany, Italy, or the Czech Republic.

Of 3,653 companies operating in the wood-processing and furniture industry in Ukraine, around 50–55 per cent belong to the first group, 35–40 per cent to the second group and only 10 per cent to the third group of the above classification.

In general, the technology in Ukrainian wood processing can be broken into four stages:

1. basic wood processing (log sawing, plank sawing, production of different blanks etc);
2. medium wood processing (cutting veneer, planing veneer, parquet production etc);
3. intermediate wooden-product production (plywood, chipboard, fibreboard, MDF, glue-banded details production etc);
4. furniture production (cutting details from natural wood, chipboard, polishing and varnishing, assembling furniture etc).

The fact that more than half the wood-processing companies were integrated in the past basically enables most companies to be self-supportive and able to execute all four stages within one enterprise. Since most factories have 50–70 per cent of their production facilities standing idle, those companies are no longer able to perform a full production cycle.

Technological schemes and production methods in most stages of wood processing are the same as those used in Europe. This is due to the fact that a lot of companies have imported equipment. Rotary-cut veneer, planed veneer and plywood production is mostly done using RAUTE machine lines (Finland). Even if Ukrainian machines are different they are constructed using the same principle used in imported machines.

In the wood-processing sector the following brand equipment is used: Steinmann, Holzma, Hyster (Germany), RAUTE (Finland), Cremona, Rojek (Czech Republic), Fiac, Balestrini (Italy) etc.

One of the peculiarities of the Ukrainian wood-processing industry is that most companies do not have modern and good-quality drying facilities. Only recently have some companies been able to install modern drying cameras. On the other hand, there are large drying facilities still existing at the big previously state-owned companies. As a rule, these cameras are energy consuming and cannot always provide appropriate humidity of the wood (8 per cent). In spite of this, many Ukrainian furniture and wood-processing factories give wood for drying to those companies. This way most companies can get their wood dried almost anytime, but it will not always be high quality drying.

In chipboard and fibreboard production mostly old production lines and equipment are used. The average depreciation rate of this equipment could sometimes reach 70–80 per cent.

Furniture production is the sector wherein the stock of machinery and other equipment is most modernized. Most factories try to renew their equipment as soon as they have money for it. As a consequence, around 50–60 per cent of the equipment in most furniture factories in Ukraine is not more than 4–6 years old. Some of the furniture producers have acquired and adapted so-called 'processing centres'. Such a centre replaces about 10 different machines and can process whole wood as well as boards. It enables the company to immediately readjust its entire production from one type of product to another. Some of these companies successfully manufacture Euro-beams and Euro-shields, which can be used further in furniture production or exported.

We conclude that the main asset of the Ukrainian wood-processing industry in terms of technology is the possibility of processing wood for almost every kind of further use. Ukrainian factories are able to carry out simple processing operations (wood sawing, blanks sawing, veneer cutting) as well as rather complicated processes in terms of technology and energy-consuming operations (drying wood, gluing plywood, chipboard production and lamination, MDF production). Also, almost every furniture factory would have at least 5 or 10 (big factories 20–45) different machines to process wood of different shapes and density to produce furniture details.

In other words, Ukrainian factories are capable of producing exactly the same products as can be produced in Western Europe, but with a number of drawbacks, the major ones being:

- low automation of the production process (high labour force involvement);
- insufficient availability of modern drying facilities (wood humidity is not always appropriate);
- average depreciation level of equipment is 50–60 per cent (lowers the productivity);
- low capacity utilization – 40–45 per cent on average.

Import–export of wood products

Prices for many wood products on the domestic Ukrainian market are significantly lower than international prices. This disparity boosts exports of wood products and export volumes rise from year to year. In 2002 Ukraine exported raw materials worth EUR289.6 million but imported only EUR81.9 million worth. The only imported products that are competitive in Ukraine are boards. The main export destination countries are Germany, Italy, Poland, Hungary, Turkey and Spain. Imports come, basically, from Russia, Poland, Hungary, Belorussia and Slovakia. Estimates show that exports of wooden products from Ukraine will continue growing.

There are neither quotas nor licences required for import–export of wood products. According to Customs Tariff of Ukraine, wood and wooden products are subject to import duty with rates from 0–5 per cent.

Table 2.3.1 Wood products import–export data for first half of 2003, million €

	Lumber	Saw timber	Veneer	Plywood	Chipboard	Fibre board
Export	39.65	92.10	5.16	10.49	5.46	0.72
Import	3.01	0.50	0.18	1.03	11.56	5.06

There are no customs duties for wooden products upon export to other countries.

How to utilize local resources

There is enormous potential and many possibilities for business development in Ukraine, but there are also enormous challenges for the Western company. Ukraine is still a transition economy, which is based on different traditions and a different logic from the West. The following statements and advice have proven to be essential to avoid basic mistakes when entering the Ukrainian market:

- The foreign company should insist on contributing management, knowledge of project coordination, and standard operational procedures – traditionally a weak point in Ukrainian companies.
- The foreign company should invest much energy and resources in identifying the most reliable cooperation partners, especially concerning suppliers of raw material.
- The foreign company should prepare in advance very detailed and clear technical product specifications, taking into consideration the differences in quality standards.
- The foreign company must give clear instructions on the sequencing in processing, ie technological instructions.
- It is recommended that foreign companies should turn to experienced consulting/law companies to choose the optimal scheme of investment/cooperation with local companies.
- The foreign company should order a cost breakdown from the local partner (it is recommended that this should be demanded from the Ukrainian company, in order to see if the company charges the cost elements fairly, especially overheads).

The most used form of cooperation between an EU company and a local company is a joint venture. The Western partners bring in new machinery, management and sometimes capital, while the local partner brings in building, some machinery, and a market position in the area. However, more and more foreign companies prefer to establish 100 per cent owned production units in order to avoid future disagreements with the local partners on company development and profit distribution. Another form of cooperation is the traditional outsourcing of tasks, where the foreign company places specific orders at a local company. Since the foreign company in these cases will not have any structured influence on the local management and often will have to upgrade the local company, it runs the risk that a third foreign company takes over the local plant after upgrading – a reality seen several times in western Ukraine.

Foreign companies usually limit orders to simple operations where companies have an intensive use of material, labour and energy. From experience, these tasks can successfully be outsourced to local Ukrainian companies.

2.4

Telecommunications Sector Overview

Serhiy Loboyko, President and CEO, TECHINVEST

In the course of the past four years, telecommunications has been one of the fastest-growing industries of Ukraine's economy. In 2003, telecom revenues grew 24 per cent to USD2.48 billion. As the industry outperformed the rest of the economy, the share of telecommunications services in GDP increased from 3.6 per cent in 2000 to 4.7 per cent in 2003 (see Figure 2.4.1).

Data transfer and mobile communications continued to be the most dynamic segments of telecommunications in terms of revenue growth in 2003 (see Figure 2.4.2), with revenues generated by data transfer services expanding 1.8 times and revenues from mobile communications growing by 43 per cent. Although growing rapidly, data transfer services still constitute only a small share of telecom revenues (the share increased from 1.8 per cent in 1999 to 4.9 per cent in 2003).

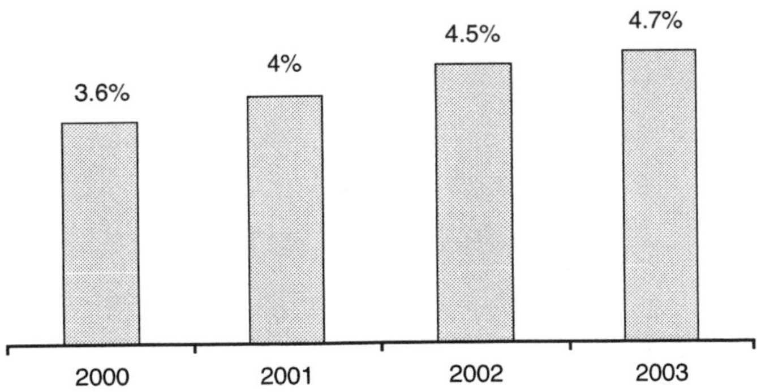

Source: State Statistics Committee, TECHINVEST

Figure 2.4.1 Telecommunications revenue as % of GDP, 2000–2003

The impending privatization of Ukrtelecom in 2004 continues to attract foreign financial and strategic investors to the Ukrainian telecommunications market. Especially strong interest in Ukraine's telecommunications market has been shown by Russian investors. Such leading Russian telecommunications market players as 'Alpha Group', AFK 'Systema', and 'Svyazinvest' have indicated strong interest in expanding their market presence in Ukraine. Among Western investors, Turkcell and Telenor expressed their interest in the privatization of Ukrtelecom.

Fixed-line telephony

Highlights

- Over 11 million fixed-line subscribers – a penetration rate of 23 per cent.
- State-owned incumbent Ukrtelecom continued to be a dominant player on the Ukrainian telecommunications market, enjoying a nearly 60 per cent market share.
- The government's regulatory strengthening in order to boost Ukrtelecom's value before its privatization deters competitive local exchange carriers' (CLECs') activity. Gradual deregulation is expected in 2004–05 after the incumbent is privatized.
- In the long run, the fixed-line voice market is likely to face a threat of cannibalization by mobile service providers and is not expected to develop to the current Western penetration levels.

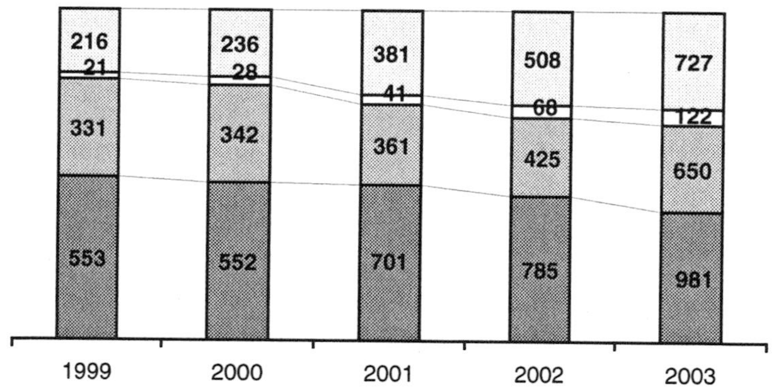

Source: State Statistics Committee, TECHINVEST

Figure 2.4.2 Telecommunications revenue growth vs. nominal GDP ($), 2000–2003

- At the end of 2003, fixed-line penetration in Ukraine amounted to 23 subscribers per 100 inhabitants (see Figure 2.4.3).

During 2003, the implementation of the fixed-line communications network modernization and expansion continued on the basis of the fibre-optic cable lines. As a result, the share of digital communication lines reached 71 per cent at the end of 2003. During the same period, Ukrtelecom continued to construct an international fibre-optic cable line between the countries of Eastern and Western Europe under the TEL/TET project.

Ukrtelecom continued to be a dominant player on the Ukrainian telecommunications market, enjoying a nearly 60 per cent market share. The national telecommunications giant and its fully owned subsidiary Utel own the majority of the network infrastructure and process most of the long distance and international traffic.

Today, Ukrtelecom is the largest provider of the fixed-line voice services (local loop and long-distance) and the largest data carrier. The company employs over 120,000 people and operates four international gateways, 18 analogue and 26 digital long distance exchanges. It services over 9 million customers, which amounts to 80 per cent of all customers in the country.

The government started the process of restructuring the telecommunications sector in 1993 when it separated telecommunication services (Ukrtelecom) from the main postal entity (Ukrposhta). Within the Ukrtelecom structure, each region had its own local telephone company, and a separate company, Utel, provided long-distance telephone services. Utel was privatized at an early stage, when AT&T, Deutsche Telekom and KPN Telecom all bought stakes, with Ukrtelecom retaining 51 per cent.

The government intended to privatize Ukrtelecom in 2001–2002. However, due to the unfavourable market conditions, the tender was

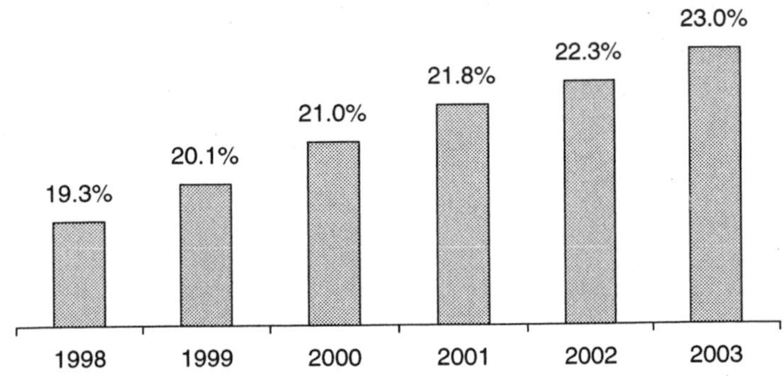

Source: ITU, Ukrtelecom

Figure 2.4.3 Fixed-line penetration, 1998–2003

postponed until 2004. This year, the government plans to sell 42.86 per cent of Ukrtelecom shares. As a result, the government will retain its controlling stake (50 per cent plus one share) in the company. The rest (7.14 per cent) of the shares have been already sold to Ukrtelecom employees under preferential terms. In the course of pre-privatization restructuring, the company has consolidated its 27 regional entities and is improving its personnel structure. In 2002, Ukrtelecom acquired the minority stakes in Utel from the foreign investors. The other significant asset, a 51 per cent share in UMC, Ukraine's largest mobile operator in terms of revenue, has been sold to the Russian MTS in order to support the government's privatization revenues.

In 2003, private operators continued to further consolidate their position as regional alternative providers of fixed-line telephony. They were primarily targeting corporate customers and succeeded in winning the market from Ukrtelecom by offering premium quality services. The largest private operators in Ukraine are Farlep, Optima Telecom, Golden Telecom and Krymtel. Today, these companies offer a full spectrum of services and are expanding their operations throughout the country.

Farlep and Optima Telecom are both owned by private Ukrainian investors. Golden Telecom is a full subsidiary of Golden Telecom Inc (NASDAQ: GLDN). Golden Telecom also holds a GSM 1800 licence and provides mobile communications services in Kiev and Odessa. Overall, the company has invested USD62 million in its operations in Ukraine.

In 2003, fixed-line operators commissioned 803,000 numbers, whereas mobile operators activated 2.7 million numbers. The larger part of numbers introduced by Ukrtelecom was not allocated to new customers but was used to substitute analogue numbers. It is expected that in 2004 the rate of growth of mobile communications will continue to exceed the rate of growth of fixed-line telephony.

It is anticipated that several new players, such as 'Confidential Telecommunications', 'Digital Global Telecommunications' (DGTel) and 'Silver Telecom', will enter the fixed-line communications market in 2004. Apart form these newcomers, such well-established companies as mobile operator 'Kyivstar' and satellite communications services provider 'UkrSat', have also announced their intentions to start providing fixed-line telephony services. We believe that the imminent entrance of these new players will lead to market consolidation during 2004.

Trends

To sustain Ukrtelecom's competitive position, the government has *de facto* discontinued issuing long-distance and international licences to private operators pending the privatization of Ukrtelecom.

Ukrtelecom's privatization is considered the single most significant source of strategic uncertainty for private operators, which deters large-scale investment projects and entry of new CLECs.

Softening of the government's regulatory position and gradual deregulation of the market are expected to take place after privatization, making the market attractive for CLECs. Upon privatization, Ukrtelecom's strategic investor is expected to improve the company's competitive position in the most lucrative segments by taking advantage of its economies of scale.

Significant growth in demand for data services is expected in the next few years. Therefore, the fixed data services projects have a good potential to create value.

In the mean time, mobile service providers are capturing an increasingly significant share of consumer voice expenditures. In the long run, the fixed-line voice market is not expected to reach levels of penetration comparable to those of Western markets and is likely to face a threat of cannibalization by mobile service providers.

Mobile telephony

Highlights

- High degree of market concentration – UMC and Kyivstar service 98 per cent of subscribers.
- Prepaid customers account for over 70 per cent of net subscriber additions. Market average, average revenue per user (ARPU) fell from USD84 in 1999 to UDS22 in 2003.
- During 1999–2001, the mobile communications market in Ukraine experienced an impressive annual subscriber growth of 170–190 per cent. Although the subscriber growth rate was slowing down, in 2002 it was still impressive at 68 per cent; in 2003 it reached 75 per cent, and the market amounted to 6.5 million subscribers – a penetration rate of 14 per cent of the population (see Figure 2.4.4).

Two operators – UMC and Kyivstar GSM – continue to dominate the mobile services market, accounting for over 98 per cent of all subscribers (see Figure 2.4.5). However, their dominance was challenged by JEANS, the first virtual operator in the country, which was launched by UMC. Very low tariffs introduced by JEANS made it very popular, and it started to compete successfully with the other leading operators, even diverting subscribers from its mother company UMC. The other three operators – Golden Telecom, WellCom and DCC – do not influence the competitive landscape significantly and enjoy only small subscriber additions.

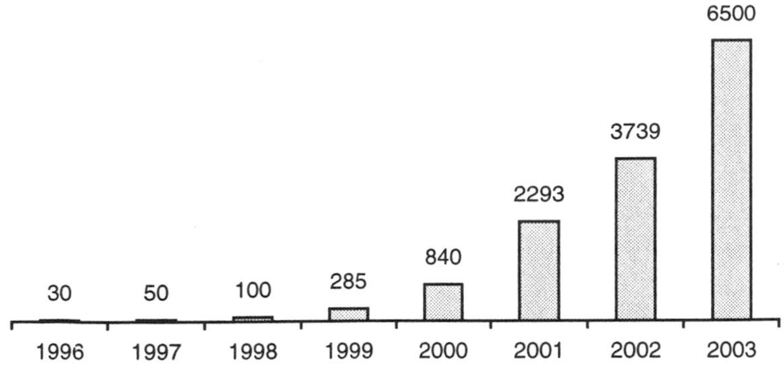

Source: State Statistics Committee, TECHINVEST

Figure 2.4.4 Number of mobile subscribers, 1996–2003, '000

Taking advantage of the duopoly situation, the large players so far have not engaged in strong price competition, which allowed them to sustain profitability but had a negative impact on subscriber growth (see Figure 2.4.6).

But the Ukrainian mobile market continued to attract foreign mobile operators. One of such operators, Turkcell, a leading GSM-operator in Turkey, announced its intention to enter the market by acquiring a 51 per cent stake in DCC for USD50 million. DCC plans to build a GSM network that will cover 80 per cent of Ukraine's territory within the next two years.

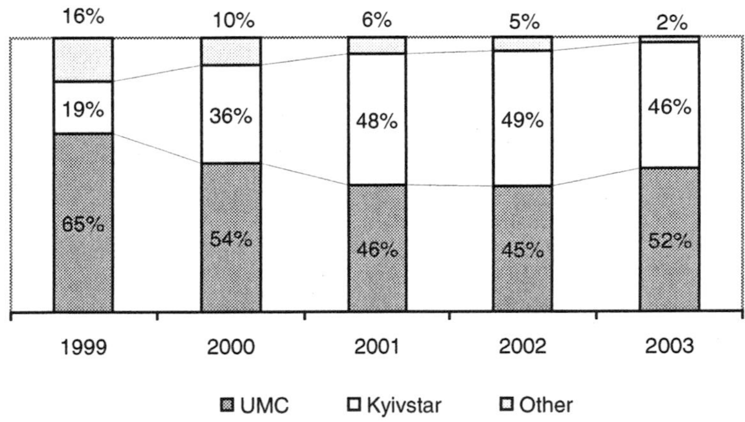

Source: TECHINVEST

Figure 2.4.5 Market share of two largest operators (increases over time)

Table 2.4.1 Operator profiles

Operator	Network	Launch date	2001	2002	2003	Change	Pre-paid
UMC	GSM-900/1800	1993	1,045	1,700	3,400	100%	70%
Kievstar	GSM-900/1800	1997	1,100	1,850	3,000	62%	75%
Golden Telecom	GSM-1800	1996	45	42	41	–2%	n/a
URS	GSM-900/1800	1998	33	37	40	–8%	n/a
DCC	D-ARMS	1996	70	110	85	–22%	n/a

Another mobile operator, WellCom, also declared its plans to develop a nationwide GSM network that will enable it to compete with Kyivstar and UMC. However, it is doubtful whether DCC and WELLCOM will be able to marshal the required resources to build the nationwide network, which are estimated at USD400 milllion.

Along with the lack of competition, low per capita income in Ukraine is seen as the main constraint for market development. The ARPU decreased from USD84 in 1999 to USD22 in 2003 (see Figure 2.4.7). The overall share of prepaid subscribers in the customer base has reached 75 per cent for Kievstar GSM and 70 per cent for UMC.

In 2003, leading mobile operators were actively campaigning for the cancellation of the paid incoming calls, which were introduced under the amendment to the Law 'On Communications' adopted by Verhovna Rada (Ukrainian Parliament) in February that year. However, all the mobile operators were obliged to stop charging for the incoming calls starting from 19 September. Although the amendment to the Law 'On Communications' was cancelled soon after that, Ukrainian mobile operators are expected to retain the 'calling party pays' (CPP) arrangement.

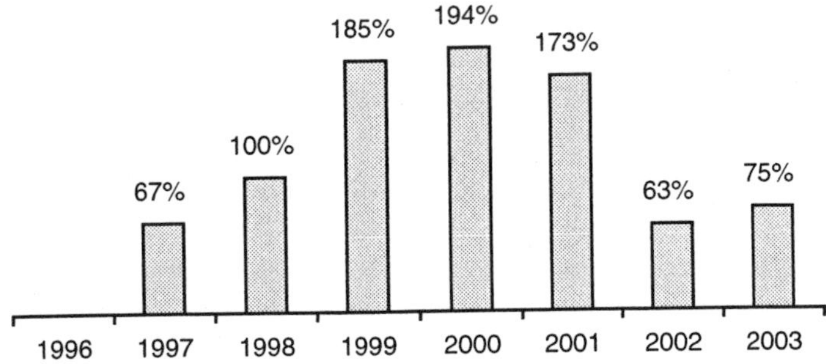

Source: TECHINVEST

Figure 2.4.6 Growth of mobile subscriber base, 1997–2003

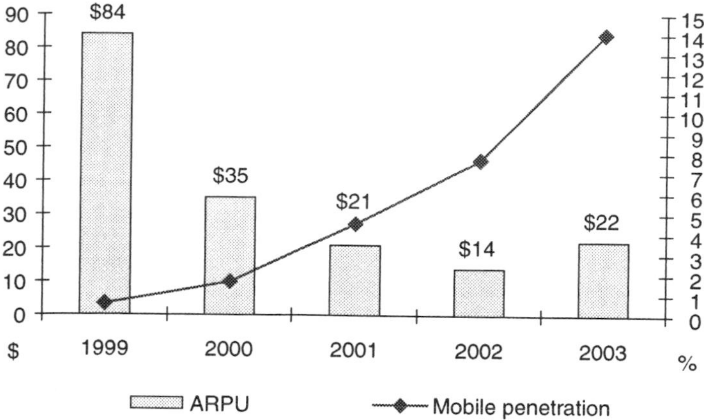

Source: State Statistics Committee, TECHINVEST

Figure 2.4.7 Mobile penetration and ARPU, 1999–2003

Trends

With ARPU falling drastically, in the future operators are expected to reduce subscriber growth targets and to concentrate primarily on improving profitability. With WAP, GPRS and MMS in place, yet undiscovered by most subscribers, value added services are likely to account for a larger share of operators' revenues.

In the next three years, we expect ARPU to stabilize a little above the USD20–25 level. Subscriber growth is likely to decrease gradually as the market starts to saturate in 2005–06 at 17–20 per cent penetration levels.

The government has not yet announced the 3G licence tender; however, both UMC and Kyivstar GSM, as well as Ukrtelecom, have expressed interest in participating.

Internet

Highlights

- 3.9 million Internet users in 2003 – penetration of 8 per cent.
- Annual returns of the data transfer sector increased 1.8 times in 2003 and reached about USD120 million.
- Although the market is still fragmented (300 Internet service providers (ISPs)), the leaders are beginning to emerge. Economies of scale will be the major driver for consolidation.

- Most ISPs are heavily dependent on Ukrtelecom for network access. Ukrtelecom's privatization is expected to lead to the strengthening of its ISP business, which in turn will encourage further consolidation among private players.
- In 1998–2003, the number of regular users grew at a rate of about 50 per cent annually.
- Dial-up remains the prevalent type of connection, with virtually all residential users and up to 80 per cent of corporate users using dial-up connection.
- Over 80 per cent of Internet users in Ukraine are located in the seven largest cities. Kyiv alone accounts for about 30 per cent of users.

During 2003, the ISP market in Ukraine continued to undergo gradual consolidation, with several integrated telecom operators emerging as dominant players. Such players were able to substantially reduce Internet access tariffs due to cross-subsidies from other services provided by them. As a result, nearly 80 per cent of all the Internet users are serviced by the 10 largest ISPs, although overall there were about 300 ISPs operating in the country. The largest ISPs were Ukrtelecom, Optima Telecom, IP Telecom, Lucky Net, UkrNet and Adamant.

In 2003, annual returns of the data transfer sector increased 1.8 times and reached about USD120 million. However, the share of the data transfer services did not exceed 5 per cent of the total revenues of the telecom sector.

During 2003, the number of hosts in the national segment of the network increased by 24 per cent and amounted to 88,200. Over the same period, the number of websites grew by 4 per cent and reached 28,800. At the end of 2003, the capacity of the external channels of Ukrtelecom, through which flows the main part of Internet traffic, amounted to 700 Mbps.

In 2003, the leading participants of the Internet market made a decision to build a nationwide network of Internet traffic exchange to be based on Ukrtelecom infrastructure. In February 2004, approbation of this network was carried out in eight regions of Ukraine. At the first stage of its operation, the network throughput capacity will amount to 34 Mbps.

At present, Ukraine has the UA-IX nationwide network of traffic exchange, which was built in 2001 by the members of Ukraine's Internet Association. Currently, the network has more than 60 participants. This network has the main and backup points of Internet traffic exchange. It is estimated that over 80 per cent of Ukrainian Internet traffic exchange takes place via the network.

In 2003, the Wi-Fi technology came to Ukraine, and the first Wi-Fi access points or hot spots were activated in Kyiv. At present, the existing hot spots operate using Sisco equipment of 802.11b standard. The majority of these hot spots are located in company offices. It is expected that by the end of 2004 the number of hot spots in Kyiv will amount to 150–200. As a result, the emerging Wi-Fi technology will start challenging traditional wireless networks, which are ubiquitous but offer Internet access at slower speeds.

At present, the major impediment to the development of Wi-Fi technology in Ukraine is the requirement for a licence to use the required radio frequency. Since there is a shortage of radio frequencies currently available for allocation to Wi-Fi Service Providers, it is not easy to obtain a licence from the authorities. Furthermore, the amount of payment for such a licence frequently exceeds the cost of the Wi-Fi equipment. If new regulations on the allocation of radio frequencies are enacted in 2004, the Wi-Fi market in Ukraine can be expected to grow quickly.

Trends

The number of Internet users is likely to grow by 40–50 per cent annually in the next three years. Slightly lower growth rates of ISPs' revenues are expected still largely to outperform the rest of fixed-line services.

Large ISPs enjoy considerable scale economies in international traffic expenses and POP usage. The net profit margin of a large ISP can be up to 15 per cent larger than that of an otherwise comparable small provider. During 2001–2003, Ukrtelecom started developing its ISP services by introducing dial-up and DSL access. Although its current market share in the end-user ISP segment does not exceed 15 per cent, the company is putting pressure on private ISPs by competitive pricing and regional expansion. In order to sustain their competitive position, large ISPs are very likely to make efforts to grow through mergers and acquisitions (M&A). Several large ISPs such as UkrNet have already started doing so.

2.5

Ten Years of Mobile Telecommunications in Ukraine

UMC

With the break-up of the USSR and Ukraine's acquisition of the long-awaited independence, the country needed to develop its own system of telecommunications. There was not a single international telephone exchange in the country and all the phone calls were continuing to be routed via Russia. The basic network, as well as the public use network, was analogue, and there was no mention at all of the Internet or mobile communications, which were thriving abroad. The Ministry of Communications initiated work on three types of telecommunications, in which the country lagged behind the most: international communications, mobile communications and data transfer. The meagre finances of the young country, especially in foreign currencies (the only fax machine in the Ministry was donated by a foreign negotiating partner), led to a decision to attract Western capital. Consequently, three joint ventures: 'Utel' (international communications), UMC (mobile communications) and 'Infocom' (data transmission and Internet) were established as a result of cooperation between Ukraine and Western investors.

The Ukrainian–German–Danish–Dutch joint venture UMC was registered 11 November 1992 by the Pechersky District Administration of the city of Kyiv, after which the company was granted a licence for mobile communications and frequencies. The newly established mobile communications operator made the first shipment of the telephone exchange and of six base stations into Ukraine. They were manufactured by Nokia (Finland) for the NMT-450i network, which was to be established in Kyiv.

The development of the market in mobile communications started on 1 July 1993, when the first phone call in the UMC network buzzed. History preserved the name of the first Ukrainian subscriber: it was the first president of independent Ukraine, Mr Leonid Kravchuk. As a matter of fact, Ukraine was one of the first countries of the CIS to develop mobile communications. As of July 1993, mobile phone networks in the CIS existed only in Russia and Uzbekistan (with only one base station, though).

NMT was chosen for Ukraine because it was cheap and because the network developed quickly. By the end of the year, 2,800 people or 0.01 per cent of Ukraine's population had become subscribers of UMC.

By the end of 1995, 12 regional centres of the country were covered by mobile communications; the number of UMC subscribers reached 14,000 people. Mobile communication became an integral part of the image of a 'new' Ukrainian. The time came when the ears of businessmen grew overheated and 'folded down' because of talking, and their phone bills often reached $2–3,000.

Four more events that subsequently affected the market for mobile communications passed barely noticed. The creation of Bankomsvyaz (consequently Golden Telecom) in 1993, Kyivstar in 1994, Digital Cellular Communications (DCC) in 1995 in Donetsk and Ukrayinski Radiosystemy (WellCOM) in Kyiv were among those events.

At the time when UMC started its operations in 1993, digital standard GSM-900 already existed in Europe, providing subscribers with better quality and more confidentiality. But there were two obstacles: first, the reluctance of the military to give away the 900 MHz frequencies, caused by lack of finances for their conversion; and second, the lack of a base digital network in Ukraine. By 1996, thanks to Ukrtelecom's efforts, the problem of a digital network was partially resolved and it was decided to make the final conversion with the funds of the companies claiming these frequencies. In 1996, after four years of UMC's successful activity, other carriers appeared in the market, seeing its good prospects. 'Digital Cellular Communications' was the first to start operating in April 1996 in Donetsk in the digital cellular communication standard D-AMPS.

The Golden Telecom company set up its digital standard GSM-1800 cellular mobile communications network in Kyiv and Boryspil in December of the same year. In addition, the Quallcom company (USA) with the Ukrainian side instituted the joint venture 'Telesystemy Ukrainy' for the development of wireless communications in the CDMA standard 800 MHz frequency band. There were 30,000 subscribers in Ukraine by the end of 1996.

The National Committee for Communications announced in the winter of 1997 a tender for the 900 MHz frequency band. There were three winners: UMC, Kyivstar and Ukrainsky Radiosystemy.

Yet before the GSM network started functioning, one more event that was symbolic for the market occurred. For the first time in Ukraine, UMC, having entered into a contract with the 'Moscovskaya Sotovaya Svyaz' carrier, initiated automatic roaming with Russia in the NMT-450i standard, as well as with Switzerland in the GSM-900 standard via the company Swisscom.

After the moratorium expired, the first in Ukraine to launch the GSM-900 network on 17 September 1997 in Kyiv and on 17 December in Odessa was UMC.

The Global Star satellite mobile communications provider, the company Elsacom-Ukraine, was created in November 1997.

The Kyivstar company entered the market under the trademark Bridge on 9 December 1997.

The year 1997 thus resulted in four operators functioning with 60,000 subscribers and the charges for mobile communications gradually nearing the charges for paging communications.

The mobile communications market of Ukraine marked its first five years on 1 July 1998. In August the financial crisis that practically 'killed' the cellular market in Russia reached Ukraine. The Ukrainian market for mobile communications did not suffer any particular losses because it was little developed. Mobile phones were still used by a relatively small number of well-off people, who were not seriously affected by the financial difficulties. The last player, Ukrayinski Radiosystemy (URS), under the trademark of WellCOM, entered the Kyiv market in October. The company made its contribution to the overall reduction in prices: the URS charges were generally 10 per cent lower than the average charges in the market.

The short text message service (SMS) was launched into the services market in 1998, but the SMS boom did not start until five years later. Satellite mobile communications too were developing more actively in 1998: Golden Telecom entered into a contract for roaming services with Iridium (commercial operations have never started), and Elsacom-Ukraine made the first test call in the Global Star system.

From 1 March 1999 prepaid services under the SIM-SIM trademark were brought into the market by its leader, UMC. Kyivstar entered the market with its prepaid services in September, having presented two packages: Ace and Base. Only WellCOM, of all the GSM operators, did not launch prepaid services, having introduced instead the WellCOM Class package without a subscription fee. Mobile communications charges were significantly reduced.

Telesystemy Ukrainy left the mobile communications market in 1999 after not being able to enter it, and in the summer of 1999 the South Korean Daewoo started going bankrupt and rumours about a possible sale of the corporation's 49 per cent stake in Ukrainsky Radiosystemy spread around the market.

Verkhovna Rada (the parliament) adopted the resolution in March 'On the Prevention of Crisis in the Publicly Owned Part of the Communications Industry', providing for the buying back of the UMC foreign participants' share by the state.

The year 1999 did not pass without new technologies. UMC joined the World Wide Web of the Internet in the summer. The company has two Web sites: the corporate www.umc.com.ua and the one for prepaid mobile communications services at www.sim-sim.com.

In December UMC started rendering mobile communications services to its clients in the Kyiv subway. UMC continued to develop the regional wireless network, having covered that year 200 towns and villages and 7,500 automobile roads. In addition, the company was the first in the market to operate a control centre for the GSM and NMT networks, enabling it to control their functioning and to remove defects on time.

There were about 300,000 mobile communications subscribers in the country by the end of the year, 186,000 of them enjoying the services of UMC.

Charges per second were introduced by all mobile operators for all subscribers in 2002.

In June, UMC launched international roaming services for SIM-SIM clients.

Also in June, UMC and Aval bank announced the launching of m-banking by the end of the year. Kyivstar and Privatbank presented StarCard at the end of July. VABank and WellCOM announced an analogous project, but the bank later decided to carry it out autonomously, working with all the operators.

In June–July subscribers got access to the Internet from mobile phones: UMC and Kyiv Star made a commercial launch of WAP services for term-contract subscribers. In November UMC and then Kyivstar extended WAP access to the Internet to the clients of their prepaid services.

Golden Telecom started mobile cellular communications services in Odessa at the end of summer 2002.

Daewoo finally made a formal announcement about its intention to leave the WellCOM project at the beginning of summer 2002. Its replacement by new owners was to take place by the end of the year. Taking into account the serious fight for subscribers, URS gave up competing in 2000.

The prepaid services, having started their victorious march in 1999, shot up in 2000. Economic growth finally started in the country, bringing with it an increase in income for its people. The combination of these factors led to an explosive growth in the number of clients, though a more quantitative than qualitative one.

The number of users of wireless communications grew 190 per cent to 816,000 in one year.

The networks of the GSM-900 carriers in large cities were not prepared for such numbers of new users and couldn't cope with the traffic. Temporary lack of signal was a typical problem of the end of

2000. In October, UMC acquired a licence for GSM-1800, and Kyiv Star also applied for this frequency band.

In 2000 the mobile communications market acquired the features which are characteristic of it today: there are two leaders of the market – UMC and Kyivstar, and two companies, Golden Telecom and WellCOM, that have filled the niche of urban area operators (Figure 2.5.1). DCC has positioned itself in the centre: having a regional network of its own, it has not (because of the difference in standards) been able to compete strongly with the leaders.

Internal corporate conflict among shareholders arose in Golden Telecom in February 2001 and the company abandoned the race for subscribers as a result. In general, events unfolded during the year as follows. UMC and subsequently Kyivstar introduced the GSM-1800 standard in Kyiv in February, improving the quality of communication. UMC passed strategic benchmark of 500,000 users in the same month.

Also in February, MPs Boris Bespaliy and Volodymyr Bondarenko produced a draft law providing for the cancellation of charges for incoming calls from telephones of any type. The mobile carriers sustained the initiative under the condition that the state introduced the European mechanism of payments between them and traditional telephone operators.

Starting in April, all the operators started charging for calls by the second, beginning with the first second.

In September, the Pan Telecom company started offering the mobile satellite communication service of the Thuraya system under the trademark Thuraya Ukraine. UMC, Golden Telecom and WellCOM signed roaming contracts with Thuraya (Kyivstar would join them in 2002).

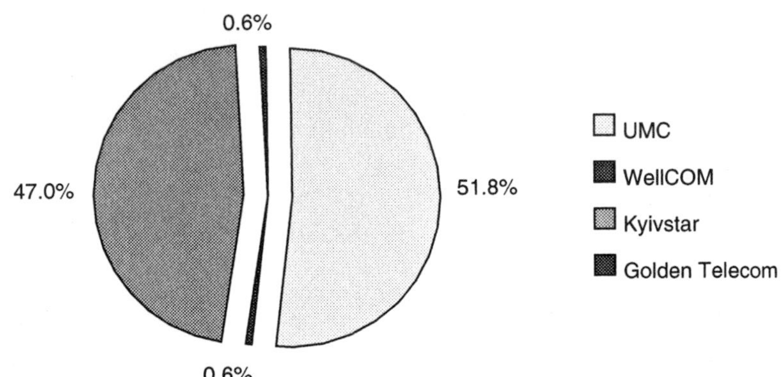

Source: www.mforum.ru

Figure 2.5.1 GSM operators in Ukraine – Market share as of 31 December 2003

Kyiv Star got the status of a national operator with the launch of the GSM-900 network in Chernivtsy in September, having covered all the regional centres of Ukraine.

The subscribers' base continued to grow at an impressive rate in 2001. It grew 172 per cent in a year and its penetration rate reached 4.4 per cent of the population of Ukraine. Some 2.2 million people used wireless communications by the end of the year. The market started acquiring the first features of a market of scale.

The year 2001 twice became a remarkable year for UMC as the company celebrated half a million subscribers in February and in December it became a 'millionaire'.

The year 2002 became a year of settlement of conflicts, redivision of property in the mobile communications market, and of the new price policy.

The conflict in Golden Telecom calmed down after the replacement of the Director General and the sale by the Ukrainian stakeholders of their share to the Russian holding company Golden Telecom Inc, controlled by 'Alpha' Group.

Kyivstar became involved in the re-allocation of the shares of its equity among the company's stakeholders in July. After a number of transactions by the company's majority stakeholder, Norwegian Telenor, the shares were finally distributed between Telenor (54.2 per cent), Storm (40.1 per cent) and Omega (5.69 per cent).

It was UMC's turn in November to get its strategic investor. The largest Russian wireless operator, the company Mobylniye Telesystemy, announced the acquisition of a 75.7 per cent stake of the Ukrainian operator at $194.2 million from Ukrtelecom (25 per cent at $84.2 million), from Deutsche Telecom and from KPN (16.3 per cent from each at $55 million). In July 2003 MTS signed contracts for the acquisition of the remaining 16.3 per cent stake from TDC and became the 100 per cent owner of UMC.

The new large-scale division of the market ended in 2002, when Daewoo agreed to sell its stake in WellCOM to the Ukrainian shareholders, related to the Privat Group.

The changes in the price policy of the operators went on from July to November. UMC was the first, having introduced six plans with free minutes for subscribers with contracts. The company made its price policy transparent to the maximum degree. The new charges were introduced in July for users of the prepaid service SIM-SIM. In addition, with the new prices, UMC introduced the new services UMC-Family and SIM-SIM Family, enabling users to talk with the holders of the numbers of their choice at a lower price. Changes in pricing continued with the launch of the 'Osoblyviy' ('Special') plan, where the cost of the minutes of a call reduced with their number. WellCOM took over this initiative, having launched three plans in July, each including free minutes and different costs, depending on the time of the day and the distance of a call. Golden Telecom introduced the plan 'Vygidny' ('Advantageous'), providing for the reduction of the cost of a call depending on its duration. Kyivstar joined this general reform of price plans in October, offering the subscribers on contract three packages based on the same principle of proportionate reduction of charges per minute, with free minutes included. The last to go into the market with the new plans was DCC, presenting three plans in December with free minutes and the possibility for a client to use the remaining minutes next month.

There were some changes in the roles of the players in the market. DCC announced its intention to convert before 2010 to the GSM-1800 standard, abandoning D-AMPS. It applied to Derzhcomzvyazok (National Communications Committee) for the necessary licence. The company submitted one more application for a frequency band to the Committee, this time for 900MHz bandwidth.

The number of Golden Telecom clients started dwindling, beginning in the summer of that year, and closer to the end of the year the company said that it would freeze territorial development of its cellular network. Novacell also left the market, not having changed its status of a potential participant. The stakeholders of the company initiated liquidation processes, the final decision to liquidate being taken in the following February.

Among the other novelties that occurred in the market in 2002, the introduction of bi-directional roaming for users of SIM-SIM in June might be remembered, together with the abrupt limitation of the terms of validity of prepaid services vouchers for the prepaid service Ace & Base by Kyivstar in March and the launch of the SMS service in September.

In February, UMC started providing its key clients with Internet access, supported by GPRS technology. As the service was being tested, it was provided to subscribers free of charge.

In general, the rate of growth of the client base in 2002 slowed down somewhat in comparison with 2000–01. The number of users of wireless communications increased in one year by 64 per cent to 3.6 million. The market started gradually becoming saturated.

The year 2003 started with the Verkhovna Rada overruling the president's veto in February. Yet in March Mr Leonid Kuchma legalized the cancellation, starting in autumn, of charges for incoming calls. The operators introduced charge-free incoming calls (CPP – Calling Party Pays principle) on 19 September 2003, in accordance with the amendments to the Law 'On Communications'.

In July 2003, Mobile TeleSystems (or MTS) completed transactions on acquiring 100 per cent of UMC. MTS is the largest mobile phone operator in Russia in terms of both subscribers and revenues. In

September 2003 the company provided services to over 13 million customers in Russia, Belarus and the Ukraine and had a Russian national market share of approximately 37 per cent.

Market leaders were also developing their regional networks. UMC announced its contract with French Alcatel for supplies of equipment, as did Kyiv Star with Swedish Ericsson. The leaders got ready for expansion into the regions to strengthen their positions before a third national operator emerged.

There were two participants in the market who claimed that role. DCC acquired the Astelit company in February, which had the licence for GSM-1800. An analogous proposal to the owners of WellCOM did not end with a deal, and DCC started looking for other ways to access GSM-900. URS, in their turn, announced their readiness to become the third national operator.

UMC together with its parent company MTS launched a new service, the virtual operator JEANS: a new prepaid service with low charges and a bright youthful image. JEANS had won the Ukrainian market after one month of operation and became the third-largest operator in Ukraine: its clients numbered over 100,000.

The most significant technological event of 2003 was the beginning of the high-speed data transmission service GPRS and of multimedia messages (MMS). The operators tested both technologies, which were considered transitional to the mobile telephone communications of the third generation. At the end of 2003 Kyivstar made a commercial launch of GPRS, and UMC launched MMS and GPRS. The milestone of the first 10 years of mobile cellular communications was reached on 1 July 2003. Very few people expected in 1993 that wireless telecommunications would thrive so dramatically. According to UMC forecasts, the company should be providing its services to 1,454,000 subscribers by 2006, but approached the decennial anniversary of the market with 2 million users.

Mobile telecommunications represents one of the largest, fastest-growing and most competitive segments of the Ukrainian telecommunications sector.

Thanks to growing competition, tariffs have fallen drastically over the past few years, making mobile phones affordable to millions of Ukrainians, and the spectrum of services has widened considerably. Robust economic growth that began in Ukraine in 2000 further improved the outlook for the industry, sharply increasing demand for mobile services.

After growing at a rate of about 170 per cent year-on-year both in 2000 and in 2001, the number of mobile phone users in Ukraine was rising less rapidly, but still impressively, in 2002, reaching 3.64 million by the end of the year (up 64 per cent year-on-year). Accordingly, mobile penetration quickly increased to 7.7 per cent as of the end of 2002, as compared with 0.6 per cent at the end of 1999. The current rate is well below that of other Eastern European emerging markets, but is closer to Russia's 12 per cent (at the end of 2002).

Despite Ukraine's relatively low mobile penetration, its mobile market's growth dynamics are much better than in the more saturated markets of its European peers and are expected to remain so in the near term. Provided that economic growth in Ukraine maintains its robust pace, the total number of mobile phone users in the country could top 10 million after 2005, which corresponds to mobile penetration of over 20 per cent (Figure 2.5.2).

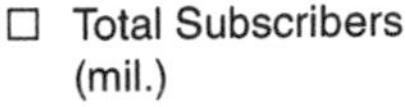

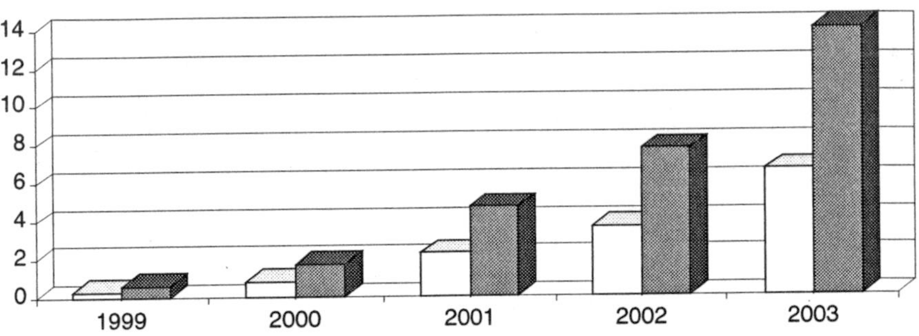

Source: www.mforum.ru

Figure 2.5.2 Mobile operators subscriber numbers and penetration in Ukraine

2.6

IT Sector

Nikolay Royenko, Miratech Software

Overview

The Ukrainian information technology (IT) sector represents a growing and dynamic market. The rate of growth of the IT industry in Ukraine considerably surpasses the world average: in 2000 – 22 per cent, in 2001 – 23 per cent, in 2002 – 25 per cent. Its revenues in 2001 amounted to $2.4 billion: telecommunications – $1.5 billion, technology (computer hardware and software, telecom equipment) – $610 million and media – $300 million. In 2002 the Ukrainian IT sector is expected to reach $2.8 billion: telecommunications –$1.8 billion, technology – $1 billion.

The Internet and data transmission sectors are considered to be the most dynamic according to the growth rates. The number of active Internet users increases by 65 per cent annually in Ukraine. In 1998 there were about 120,000 Internet users, in 2002 there were 900,000. At the end of 2002 the total number of Internet users had increased to 2.5 million. According to expert estimates, the growth rate will stabilize during the next two years and constitute about 40–50 per cent of the population.

The Ukrainian software industry has all the opportunities and capabilities for developing unique products and offering high-quality services that will be competitive in the global market. All these capacities provide Ukraine with ample opportunities for becoming one of the key players in the world's software export market.

At the end of 2002, around 600 companies dealing only with software development, implementation and maintenance had been registered in Ukraine, plus about 800 companies whose main activity is software production.

The past 18 months have been crucial for Ukraine in the area of information policy, taking into account positive enhancements in the formation of the normative-legal field, the development rate of the information and computer technology market, the increase in the quantitative and qualitative figures of Internet use, the initiative of public organizations on both regional and international levels, and the development of the electronic management platform.

The structure of the information technology market has changed. PC production has become a secondary business area because of decreases in PC prices and production profitability. The quantitative growth of PC sales volumes of leading Ukrainian producers is a direct consequence of market redistribution due to small collectors. The market share of network projects has increased considerably. The Ukrainian IT market today is mainly one of complex integration and telecommunications projects.

Legal environment

Statutory legal and statutory technical support of the IT process began after the adoption in 1998 of the Laws of Ukraine 'On the National IT Programme', 'On the Concept of the National IT Programme' and 'On Ratification of Purposes of the National IT Programme for the years 1998–2000'. Moreover, a variety of other standard Acts, issued by the Cabinet of Ministers of Ukraine, and President decrees have been adopted during the years 1997–98 for the solution of IT issues.

The tasks of realization of the state information policy, coordination of the activities of public authorities in the IT area, fulfilment of the functions of the main state customer of the National IT Programme and the organization of international partnerships in the IT area are carried out by the State Committee on Communication and IT.

The current state of the Ukrainian IT area can be characterized by the following results and achievements:

- Public policy in the IT area has been formed and is in the process of implementation.
- Ukrainian laws on the National IT Programme have been adopted.
- Statutory legal and statutory technical bases in the IT area have been created.
- The IT process has stopped being spontaneous and has gained management features.
- The regional IT component is gaining in strength.
- The market for information technologies and services has been created and is gathering force.

- Actions aimed at information protection and information security are being performed in the use of computer technologies.
- International cooperation in the IT field is developing.

At the same time there are some problem areas in the legal environment of the Ukrainian IT sector which are common to the whole international community. These are pirated software and 'grey import' issues. One of directions of state information and telecommunication structure regulation is the struggle with computer and high-tech crimes.

The following bills, providing development of the information branch in Ukraine, have been worked out:

- 'On Electronic Documents and Electronic Document Management';
- 'On Electronic Digital Signature';
- 'On Telecommunications';
- 'On Satellite and Cable Television and Broadcasting';
- 'On National Information Resources';
- 'On Personal Data Protection';
- 'On Control Over Information Security of Data Networks'.

Government sector

The National IT Programme was adopted in 1998. According to this programme, more than 30 information-analytical systems of different levels and about 20 state electronic systems of information resources were to be created and developed during 2000–01.

The aim of the IT policy is to increase the level of information access of every citizen, society as a whole, and public authorities; to use the potential opportunities of IT for comprehensive development of science, culture, art, education, health protection and other areas of public life; to supply the information technology needs of public organizations, subjects of economic activity of any property forms; to realize and to develop basic adjustment, to modernize and to renovate production in a technical way; to develop an information infrastructure; to ensure national security and national sovereignty by means of information technologies.

The main tasks of the state information policy are:

- modernization of the information and telecommunications infrastructure;

- development of information and telecommunication technologies;
- effective formation and use of national information resources and the supply of free access to them;
- preparation of people for life and work in an information society;
- creation of an appropriate information and legal basis for the formation of an information society.

State IT policy anticipates the development of state programmes. The programme of special interest is 'E-Ukraine'. Within this programme, realization of an active dialogue between public agents and the community is anticipated.

The state programme on public school computerization is to be realized by 2004, within which 22,200 Ukrainian schools will obtain around 220,000 computers for educational needs, as well as Internet access.

Financing for projects within the National IT Programme is expected from different funding sources, including international investments and credits. The principal financing of the Programme, according to the Law of Ukraine 'On State Budget of Ukraine for 2001', was aimed at the realization of national projects on IT. Financing of separate projects on IT, including those in the Programme, has been accomplished by branch-wise and local budgets.

Public policy concerning information security is directed at the defence of personal, society and state interests against:

- getting incomplete, tardy and inauthentic information;
- negative information influence;
- negative consequences of the functioning of information technologies;
- unauthorized access and illegal information disclosure.

In terms of the globalization of the use of modern information technologies, the problems of information security will be solved both for each specific project on IT and in the network of the National IT Programme.

The state aims to be at the centre of all actions undertaken in Ukraine with respect to participation in international movements towards harmonization of national legal systems according to the requirements of the digital society. Public organizations in the area of law, professional associations and state profile substructures play the role of performers of accepted programmes and projects both on national and international levels. The same applies to the information transformation of economic relations, education and health systems, the transition of public authorities on all levels to an online regime of interaction with citizens, and other alterations connected with broad IT implementation.

Realization of the state doctrine should be achieved through accomplishment of the following state programmes:

- Internet Development Concept of Ukraine (project);
- Ukrainian White Book of Information;
- Communication Technologies (project);
- programme 'E-Ukraine'.

The developing public initiative includes:

- a forum of public organizations that work in the area of the information society;
- international donor organizations (such as Internews);
- development of a Memorandum and Charter of Information Society;
- the Virtual Party of Ukraine;
- deputy group 'E-Ukraine' in parliament.

Internet

During the past four years the number of Internet users has increased by about 70 per cent annually. (According to different estimates, the growth of the Ukrainian Internet segment amounts to about 40 per cent annually, while the world rate of growth averages approximately 25–30 per cent.)

According to monthly statistics, the number of active Ukrainian Internet users was 1.9 million in August 2001. The number of people using the Internet weekly is 790,000, but only 620,000 users visit Ukrainian Web sites at least once a week and only 130,000 users (6 per cent) use Ukrainian Internet resources every working day.

At the end of 2002 there were about 2.5 million Internet users in Ukraine (5.2 per cent of the population), with about 1.1 million of these visiting the Internet regularly (2.1 per cent of the population). Up to 80 per cent of Internet users are located in the seven largest cities. The majority of Ukrainian Internet users are male (61 per cent). The Internet is regularly used primarily by young people: 43 per cent of users are 25–39 years old, 32 per cent are 18–24, and 25 per cent are over 40 years old.

In terms of education level, people with a university education constitute the majority – 79 per cent of users. The employed constitute 80 per cent of users; most of the remaining 20 per cent are full-time students. Most of the users are white-collar workers, with 55 per cent being specialists of different kinds; 21.5 per cent are managers and 12 per cent are office clerks. Only 6 per cent of users are blue-collar workers.

Up to 20 per cent of Internet users are government employees, 30–40 per cent are corporate customers, 10–18 per cent are medium and small businesses, and 22–30 per cent are miscellaneous customers.

One of the major groups of users of Internet information are pupils and students, namely senior school pupils, students at vocational schools, and students at educational institutions of accreditation levels I–II and III–IV.

There are 23,629 Web servers in Ukraine, and about 380 Internet service providers.

According to different estimates, the capacity of the Ukrainian e-commerce market segment fluctuates from $900,000 to $1.5 million annually.

PC supply and production

The general situation of the world IT industry was characterized by decreased turnover in 2002. The total turnover diminished by 2.3 per cent, to $875 billion. Against this background the computer technologies sector shows good dynamics of growth. The size of Ukraine's market for computer hardware in 2001 was estimated at 450,000 PCs worth $209 million. In 2002 the number of PCs sold was 650,000, worth $400 million. At the end of 2002 the number of PCs had reached 1.2 million (covering 2.3 per cent of the population) in comparison with 980,000 in 2001 (a growth rate of 22 per cent).

During 2002, about 700,000 hard disks were supplied. The leader among suppliers is Samsung with a market share of not less than 40 per cent. The next two suppliers are Seagate (25 per cent) and Maxtor (17 per cent).

Samsung is the leader of the monitor market with a market share of 70–75 per cent. Their main rival is LG (18 per cent). According to their Ukrainian representative, 2002 was an efficient year for this company, with the growth in sales of LG monitors amounting to 145 per cent in comparison with 2001. Third place is occupied by Hansol and Sony (4–5 per cent each).

Production (assembly) for the local PC market continues to grow intensively. The growth rate during 2002 amounted to 35–40 per cent; in 2002 about 620,000 systems of domestic manufacture were sold. The share of foreign PCs in the Ukrainian market did not exceed 3 per cent in 2002.

Characteristic features of the Ukrainian PC market are the following: a low level of brand influence and consumers vulnerable to price. These factors have led to strong price competition and a decrease in producer profitability. In this case, the server and notebook market segments seem to be relatively more attractive. According to the statistics provided by analytical agencies during 2002, the Ukrainian notebook market has increased to 17,000.

In 2002 the corporate segment accounted for about 75 per cent of PCs sold, the remaining 25 per cent being accounted for by the consumer segment. According to forecasts, the share of corporate sales will decrease by 15 per cent by 2006; the share of sales in the private sector will increase by the same amount.

Stable sales growth in the computer market is forecast for the next three years, with a growth rate of 15–25 per cent annually.

Software

Analysts point out that the Ukrainian software market is growing rapidly. The average annual growth rate of Ukrainian software production amounted to 18 per cent during the past two years; income increased to $90 million in 2002 in comparison with 2000 when the profit totalled $65 million. In 2002, the annual growth rate of the Ukrainian software industry was 17 per cent. This exceeded expectations, taking into consideration the deep recession which affected the United States and Western Europe.

The volume of software and related services produced by Ukrainian companies in 2001 was worth around $77 million. The offshore programming segment is a major contributor to the growth of the industry. The volume of licensed software sold in Ukraine by international companies or their distributors is estimated at $13 million, while pirated software sales in 2000 constituted roughly $29 million.

In 2002 the volume of software and related services produced by Ukrainian companies was worth around $90 million. In 2002, the annual growth rate of the whole Ukrainian software market was around 10 per cent. The software development segment was growing very fast – 21 per cent. In 2002, Ukrainian companies working in the software development business area earned $46 million.

The Ukrainian software offshore market increases on average by 15–20 per cent annually. In 2000, the Ukrainian software development sector was worth $32 million; in 2001 it amounted to $39 million. Exports of Ukrainian software were worth $46 million in 2002. The market for licensed software increased by more than 100 per cent in 2002, to $90 million, constituting 10 per cent of total sector turnover.

Microsoft products remained the most used software in Ukraine in 2002. Sales volumes of Microsoft products in financial year 2002 amounted to $22,128 and, in comparison with financial year 2001, increased by 300 per cent.

The popularity of Linux as the platform for corporative systems has increased enormously.

Suppliers drew attention to the growth in sales of electronic switches for protection of the software environment in 2002. Such a tendency can be explained by two reasons: the increase in quantity of Ukrainian developments and copyright protection by their authors.

According to expert forecasts, in the next 1–2 years the growth rate of the Ukrainian software market will not decrease.

IT service demand

Today, the most requested IT services in Ukraine are: system integration, design and construction of computer networks, and the creation of information networks.

In 2001, the IT services market grew by 20–30 per cent and was estimated at $75 million. In 2002, the IT services market grew by 28 per cent and was estimated at $100 million (equipment shipments were not included). This growth primarily took place because of large projects in the bank and public sectors.

The trend of further development of the Ukrainian IT services sector is conditioned on the low-level ratio of profits from IT services and GDP.

The lucrative market has attracted several foreign players – the largest Russian IT services companies have moved to Ukraine.

End users

Information computer technologies are sold mainly in the corporate sector, where demand for such complex products and services as enterprise management systems and large-scale corporate networks is growing extremely fast. The information computer technologies market has new consumers such as renascent industrial giants, entering the market behind public institutions.

The major groups of IT end users are the following:

- government agencies and institutions;
- Ukrainian companies with progressive management, seeking to increase operational monitoring/control efficiency (banking, telecom companies, automobile industry, food processors);
- Ukrainian companies dealing with basic raw materials and commodities;
- educational institutions.

Summary

The Ukrainian software industry has all the capabilities and prerequisites needed to accelerate its growth and start to develop products capable of competing in the world market. Summing up the developments in the Ukrainian IT market described above shows that the main trends are as follows:

- Continued industrial growth spurred IT spending by industrial enterprises.
- State-financed procurement increased considerably.
- Organizational and financial support of the 'E-Ukraine' programme by the Ukrainian government.
- A decline of PC prices resulted in low market growth in dollar terms.
- Laptop and server markets grew faster than the desktop market.
- Distributors are expanding from their traditional markets in centre into Ukraine's regions.
- Demand for enterprise management software increased with local IT companies' expansion deeper into the sector, providing enterprise solutions, not just hardware delivery.
- The emergence and rapid growth of the offshore software development industry.
- The Internet (private and corporate) is booming.
- Significant increase of market share of network projects on the Ukrainian IT market.

Sources: *The High-Tech Navigator Ukraine*, 2002, AVentures; *'E-Ukraine' Country report*; State Committee on Communication and Information of Ukraine, www.stc.gov.ua; Information Society of Ukraine, www.isu.org.ua; *ITC Online* newpaper, http://itc.ua/article.phtml?ID=12214.

2.7

Technology Venture Capital

Serhiy Loboyko, President and CEO, TECHINVEST

Investor interest in the Ukrainian high-tech sector is driven by a large technological and intellectual capital base and impressive technology resources. Some of the most promising segments within the high-tech sector for venture capital include communications, software and IT, and space industry technologies. Of late, an increasing number of emerging and young Ukrainian technology companies have been seeking financing though venture capital transactions.

In Ukraine, the venture capital and private equity industry started to emerge in the middle 1990s, and it is currently at an early stage of its development. The industry is represented mainly by private equity funds with foreign capital. Total capitalization of these funds is estimated at USD800 million. The major portion of this capital has already been invested. The largest venture capital and private equity funds operating in Ukraine are: the Western NIS Enterprise Fund (WNISEF), SigmaBleyzer, Euroventures Ukraine, Commercial Capital and others (see Table 2.7.1).

As can be seen from the table, only a few venture capital and private equity investors, such WNISEF, SigmaBleyzer, Euroventures and AVentures, have made investments in Ukraine's innovative high-tech companies at an early stage of their development. However, in the case of WNISEF, SigmaBleyzer and Euroventures, which are generalist funds, such investments were made during the days of the Internet frenzy during 1999–2001, and eventually they did not live up to the expectations of investors. As a result, the above-mentioned funds have been shying away from investing in technology companies, preferring instead to invest in later-stage venture opportunities in such rapidly developing and less risky industries as food processing, production of building materials, financial services, etc. This has

Table 2.7.1 Major VC and private equity funds investors in Ukraine*

Sl. No.	Company/Fund name and CEO	Contact information	Established	Investment focus	Investee companies
1	AVentures Mr Andriy Kolodyuk	16/15, Vyborzka St., Kyiv, 03056, Ukraine Tel: +38 044 461-8882, Fax: +38 044 461-8883 www.aventures.biz	1994	Telecommunications, hi-tech, media	1994 – 'Unitrade', 1997 – 'MegaCom' 1998 – 'Universal Telecom', 2000 – 'SoftPress' 2002 – US–Ukraine Center for Technology Commercialization, 2003 – Ukrainian Technology Business Incubator; UkrSoft Consortium
2	Baring Vostok Capital Partners Mr Andrey Terekhov	6-A, Bolshaya Zhitomirskaya St., #3, Kyiv, 01025, Ukraine Tel: +38 044 490-5535 Fax: +38 044 490-5512 www.bvcp.ru	1996	Energy, Telecommunications	Zakarpatenergo, Golden Telecom
3	Commercial Capital Group	12/5 Lypska Street Suite 1, Kyiv, 01021, Ukraine Tel: +38 044 490-5667 cce@comcap.kiev.ua	1995	Retail trade, consumer goods, services	Mr. Snack, Ukraine Fund, Euromart
4	Euroventures Ukraine Fund Mr Volodymyr Klymenko	11, Pushkinska St., apt. 4, Kyiv, 01034, Ukraine Tel: +38 044 229-4835 www.evu.kiev.ua	1998	Consumer goods	IDS, Rusnanovsky Meat Factory, P5 Communications
5	SigmaBleyzer Mr Michael Bleyzer	21, Pushkinska St., Kyiv, 01004, Ukraine Tel: +38 044 244-9487 www.sigmableyzer.com	1994	Hi-tech, telecommunications, software, machine building, food processing	Sevastopol Sea Plant, Poltava Confectionary Plant, Kherson Harvester Plant, Kharkiv Machine Building Plant, Softline, Zaprorizhia Meat Factory, Volya Group

6	Ukrainian State Innovation Company Mr Volodymyr Ryzhov	65 B Bogdan Khmelnitsky Str., Kyiv, 01601, Ukraine Tel: +38 044 216-2455 Fax: +38 044 246-8776	2002	Machine building, aviation industry, medicines, energy, food processing	Innovation projects invested: Antonov Aviation Scientific and Technical Complex, Kyiv State Aircraft Factory Aviant, Joint Stock Company Motor Sich, Joint Stock Company Concern Stirol, Joint Stock Company Volynholding (Torchyn Product), Joint-Stock Company Lutsk Foods (Torchyn Product)
7	Western NIS Enterprise Fund Ms Natalie A. Jaresko	4, Muzeyny Provulok, 3rd Floor, Kyiv, 01001, Ukraine Tel: +38 044 490-5580 Fax: +38 044 490-5589 www.wnisef.org	1995	Food processing, production of construction materials, furniture production, hi-tech, financial services	AVK, Ecoprod, Euromart, Microfinance Bank, Ptettl Kable Ukraine, Slobozhanska Budivelna Keramika (SBK), Svitanok, Troyanda

* Data was compiled based on publicly available information.

created a significant early-stage funding gap, as innovative technology companies are finding capital in short supply and established VC and private equity funds are very focused on their current portfolios and late-stage venture opportunities.

This gap in early-stage funding has created a window of opportunity for potentially superior returns that exist for small, technology-focused VC firms and funds that can seek out early-stage ventures. One such VC firm is AVentures, which has been successfully exploiting this window of opportunity, actively pursuing attractive investment projects in Ukraine's high-tech sector. In March 2004, as a result of the re-organization of AVentures and establishment of AVentures Group, AVentures assigned its rights related to the implementation of venture export-oriented high-tech projects initiated in 2002–2003 to the newly established venture capital firm TECHINVEST.

At present, of all the venture capital and private equity investors operating in Ukraine, TECHINVEST is the only one focused on investing in early-stage innovative technology companies within a broad range of high-tech industries.

TECHINVEST's mission is to unlock the true value of the Ukrainian high-tech sector and its huge growth potential to enter global markets by providing smart money for early-stage, technology-focused companies with strong export potential. Leveraging Ukraine's high scientific and industrial potential, as well as its well-educated and technologically qualified talent pool, TECHINVEST promotes and supports Ukraine's transition towards global markets. The company's investment strategy is to take a proactive approach towards its investee companies and make direct contributions to maximize shareholder value via the implementation of managerial and financial value-added measures. TECHINVEST's investment rationale is based on the premise that innovative technologies offer some of the best opportunities for substantial long-term capital gains to those investors who are willing and capable of working closely with investee companies.

Technology venture capital industry perspective

Further development of the technology venture capital industry in Ukraine will depend on such factors as macroeconomic stability, improvement of corporate governance procedures, development of liquid stock markets and long-term capital sources. Such improvements will make investments in Ukrainian companies more attractive to venture capitalists.

Of particular importance is the state policy aimed towards ensuring internal sources of venture capital financing and supporting the development of innovation businesses and the venture capital industry. During the past year, the Ukrainian government took measures to promote venture capital industry and innovations in the country. The Law of Ukraine 'On Joint Investment Institutions', which was adopted in March 2002 and which envisages establishment of resident venture capital funds with a transparent tax structure, as well as Law 'On Non-governmental Pension Funds' which was adopted in July 2003, will create conditions for the development of venture capital in Ukraine and will encourage more local companies to seek venture capital to finance their growth and development. Apart from that, the establishment of the funded pension system in Ukraine will facilitate the development of the domestic venture business, without which economic growth based on innovations cannot be achieved.

The latest package of measures taken by the government, designed to promote enterprise and innovation, will encourage businesses to take advantages of new opportunities in Ukraine's high-tech sector. These measures were embodied in Law of Ukraine 'On Priority Directions of Innovation Activities in Ukraine', adopted in January 2003. This Law envisages substantial tax breaks and other incentives to innovative technology-based companies. As a result, this latest legislation will facilitate the emergence of technology-based startups and their development into profitable innovation businesses, making them attractive targets for venture capitalists.

The experience of leading industrial countries shows that technology innovation cannot go without venture capital. Therefore Ukraine should create a favourable environment for the development of the venture capital industry if she wants to take advantage of new opportunities in the emerging knowledge-based global economy.

2.8

Computer Software and IT Services

Serhiy Loboyko, President and CEO, TECHINVEST

There has been a significant growth in demand for modern information systems and various IT services over the past two years. The corporate and government segment, large industrial enterprises, financial institutions and state agencies have been the major drivers for the growing demand. The Ukrainian corporate sector has entered a new stage of implementation of effective information interchange, data processing and storage after initial computerization.

With a 95 per cent share, foreign software products continue to dominate the corporate market of legal software. Although the share of local products in the corporate segment does not exceed five per cent, it has good growth potential if the economic recovery continues. Microsoft software products are currently the most widely used office software in Ukraine.

Modern technologies of software development in Ukraine allow the production of quality and competitive software products, but significant investments are required for their marketing and promotion on the global market.

The lucrative market attracted several foreign players, with the largest Russian IT services companies expanding their operations into Ukraine.

During September–December 2003, TECHINVEST (which is an assignee of AVentures – www.aventures.biz) jointly with Market Visio (Gartner Group) conducted the first internationally recognized research of the Ukrainian IT export industry (http://research.techinvest.com.ua/eng). Over 60 companies were interviewed during the research. A basic summary of the research is presented below.

The volume of Ukrainian IT services exports in 2003 is estimated to be USD70 million. It has increased by 40 per cent in comparison with 2002.

In spite of the downsizing of the international IT market, 2003 marked a new stage in the development of the Ukrainian IT export industry. The industry recognized its strength and started consolidating and promoting itself internationally. Two business consortia and one network of IT companies have been established. Later they (eSP Consortium and Ukrainian Hi-Tech Initiative) joined forces within the framework of the Ukrainian Software Consortium, which has consolidated the strength of about 25 pre-evaluated companies. Industry leaders, with the support of the Ukrainian Embassy in the USA and the American Chamber of Commerce in Ukraine, cooperated to organize *The US-Ukraine IT Cooperation Forum* on 7 November 2003.

From Market-Visio/Gartner analysts' point of view, Ukrainian exporters of IT services are focused on high-end software engineering due to cumulative intelligent resources, high level of educational systems development and qualification of personnel.

Competition to Ukrainian developers comes from software companies in India, Israel, Russia, Romania, China and Belarus.

According to Gartner analysts' opinion, as an IT services and products exporter Ukraine could be placed in the 'Up and comers' category. Countries in this category have limited offshore IT revenue and they do not yet have sufficient resources and infrastructure to operate at full capacity and sustain good profit margins.

NASSCOM (Indian National Association of Software & Service Companies) see Ukraine between upcoming and potential destinations for offshoring IT services (see NASSCOM: Strategic Review 2004). According to NASSCOM, Ukraine has smart outsourcing ability with main positives in high-quality engineers and low cost.

The market players are quite optimistic about its growth and are forecasting that Ukrainian IT services export revenue will double over the next two years, or 40–50 per cent growth annually. Increased growth rates (even exceeding those stated above) are feasible provided (a) the industry's development is supported by the Ukrainian government and (b) the largest players in the market efficiently consolidate their capacities and efforts for promotion in foreign markets.

Export revenue currently amounts to 50 per cent of the entire market for IT services rendered and will increase to 60 per cent by 2005.

The market is order-oriented, and the 'off-the-shelf' product model constitutes no more than 10 per cent. It is forecasted that its share will grow, and in 2005 will amount to 35 per cent, as products' global competitiveness increases.

There are about 300 companies in Ukraine involved in the IT export business, 30 per cent of them having been established during the past three years. Thirty per cent of Ukrainian IT companies have been

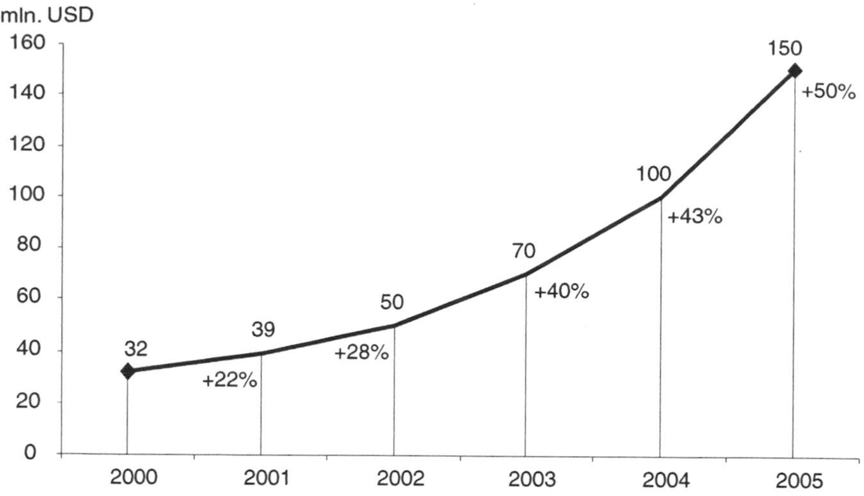

Source: AVentures, Market Visio, 2003

Figure 2.8.1 IT services export revenue

working in the IT export industry for about 10 years. Around 20–25 of Ukrainian companies are 'public' (or known) and are mainly located in Kyiv, L'viv, Kharkiv and Dnipropetrovsk. There are around 200 small companies and independent software developers' groups, whose market share amounts to 50 per cent. In Ukraine there are practically no development centres for large corporations, but there are plenty of development centres for smaller companies, which are often not incorporated as such.

The number of specialists working in the Ukrainian IT services and products export market in 2003 is estimated to range between 8,000 and 10,000 and will grow considerably during 2004–05.

The labour markets annual supply is increasing by 30,000 IT graduates. The previously active immigration of Ukrainian programmers has nearly stopped at present. Some of them are coming back to Ukraine and establishing their own businesses. Since Ukrainian IT companies are working in both low and high levels of the value chain of the IT outsourcing market, other types of specialist (engineers, mathematicians, etc) are to be considered as a potential labour resource, as well.

In Ukraine, the average monthly salary of production personnel involved in software production of IT services and products for export ranges from USD300 to USD1,500, and management salaries range from USD500 to USD$2,500.

Taking into account the growth dynamics of salaries in Russian companies involved in the IT services and products export business, we can say that in Ukraine the average salary in companies engaged in the export business is 30–50 per cent lower than Russian companies.

Also, Ukraine possesses competitive advantage in costs compared with the countries of Central and Eastern Europe, which will be joining the EU in 2004.

The services and products that exporters offer to foreign customers are presented in Figure 2.8.2.

Mostly, the companies oriented towards development of vertical solutions are working in public health and in production industries, as well as for service and commercial businesses (Figure 2.8.3)

Experts note that the market is still developing rapidly, and the market leaders realize the need for consolidation of efforts within Ukraine and cooperation with developers from Russia and Belarus.

The following large companies involved in offshore software development are operating in the Ukrainian market: Miratech, SoftLine, SoftServe and TelesensKSCL.

At the moment the biggest clients of Ukrainian IT companies come from the US. In addition, a significant part of IT services are rendered to the countries of Western Europe and Russia (Figure 2.8.4).

Considering that Ukrainian IT professionals have qualifications similar to Russians, and that their salaries are 30–50 per cent lower, it is not surprising that Russia holds fourth place in the rank of the

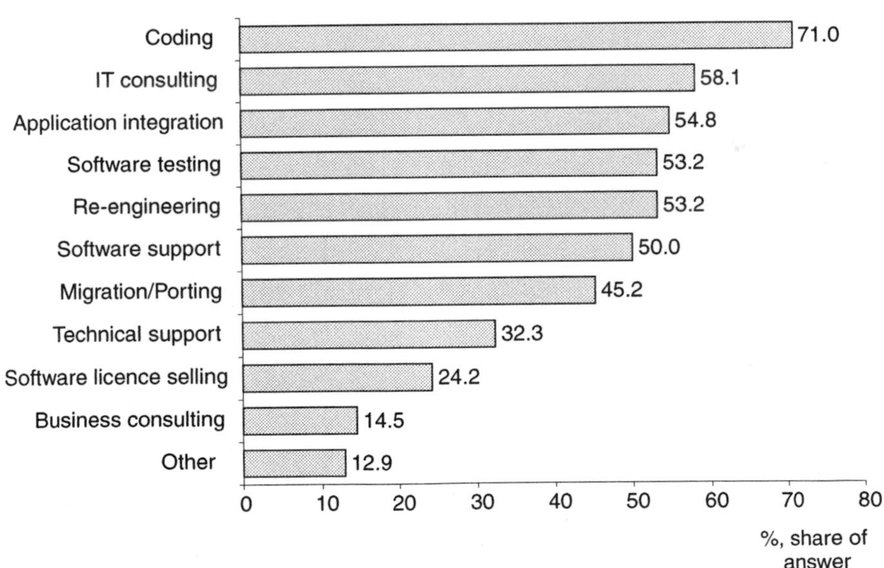

Source: AVentures, Market-Visio, 2003

Figure 2.8.2 Services and products exporters offer to foreign customers

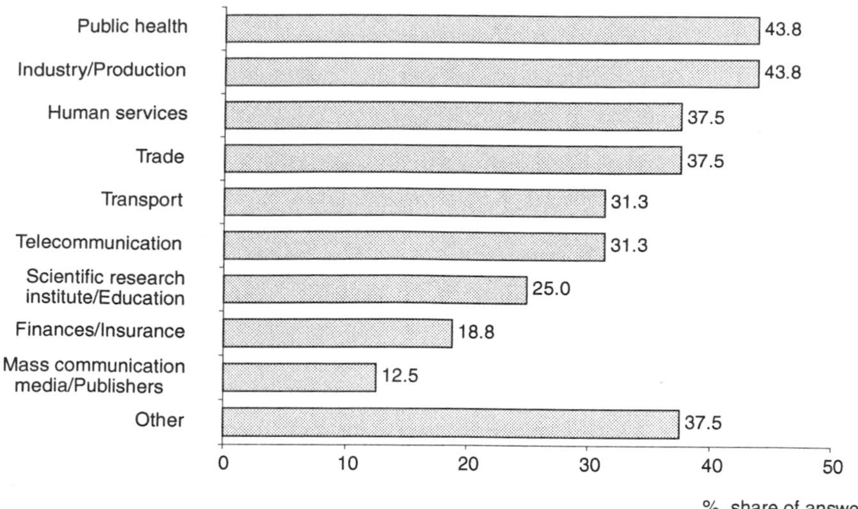

Source: AVentures, Market-Visio 2003

Figure 2.8.3 Sectors in which these companies are based

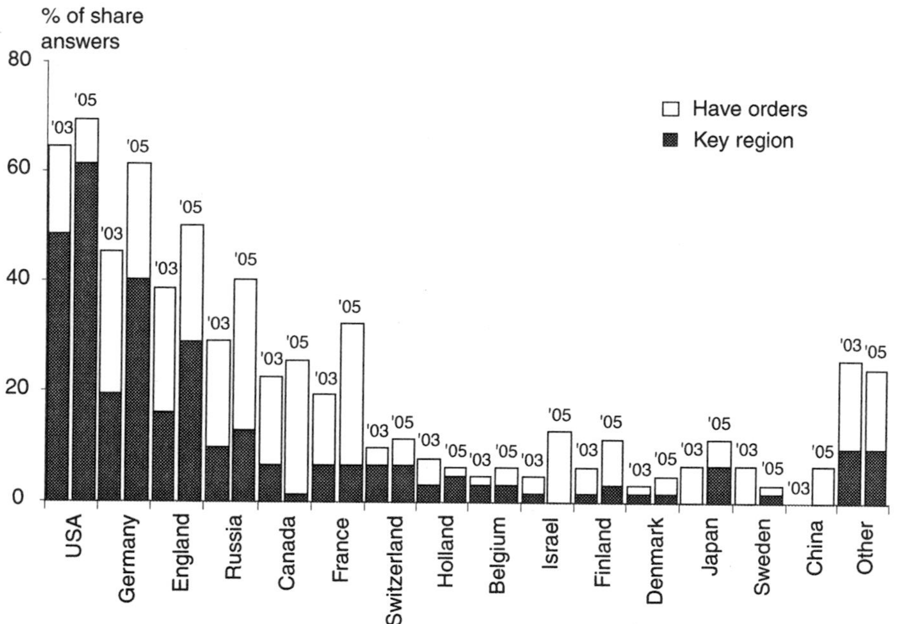

Source: AVentures, Market-Visio, 2003

Figure 2.8.4 Countries to which IT services are rendered

countries where Ukraine's key software development orders are coming from, owing to low international recognition of the Ukrainian IT industry and little on-site presence of software development companies.

Plenty of individual and consolidated activities are expected in this field in the near future. Also, a significant rise of foreign investors' interest in Ukrainian IT companies and the international commercialization of their products is forecast.

The political stability of the state and the dynamic growth of the market are among the positive factors. The telecom sector (dedicated lines, mobile communication) is developing rapidly. The neighbouring EU countries and special cooperation status with the EU are also deemed favourable factors for growth of the Ukrainian IT export industry.

2.9

The Offshore Software Sector in Ukraine – A Special Focus on Western Ukraine

Munk, Andersen & Feilberg

An overview of the software sector

Western European and US software developing companies have, since 1995, faced an increased pressure from the market to reduce their development costs significantly. At the same time, some of these companies are faced with a growing lack of well-qualified programmers and, as a consequence, an upward pressure on salaries. In order to cope with these two problems, software companies have started to outsource tasks to specialists and software companies in Southern Asia and now also Eastern Europe. For some time and perhaps by tradition, India has become the leading country in this field.

Ukraine, together with other former Soviet countries, is usually considered to be an 'up and coming' country, which hasn't gained any big market shares but still has all the potential to do so. Ukraine's big resource pool of qualified IT specialists and the low cost of labour make it a competitive location for offshore programming firms. Along with Russia, it is a country in focus, because it has a large, available and well-qualified human resources pool, willing to work for around 10–20 per cent of the salary level in Western Europe. In this way, low cost and low technology are not necessarily an effect of each other.

Ukraine is slowly emerging as a low-cost site for high quality software development. According to the Ukrainian Association of Software Developers (www.uaswd.org.ua/en), Ukraine's software export market for 2002 constituted $65–70 million, which represents

0.8 per cent of the entire offshore outsourcing market. The domestic software market in Ukraine is estimated at $65 million in 2002.

The Ukrainian software sector is one of the few sectors in the economy that has not experienced a crisis as a consequence of the breakdown of the Soviet Union. Industry insiders believe that this sub-sector of the Ukrainian economy is growing 15–20 per cent annually. Some estimates indicate that this industry employs 10,000–15,000 people, others up to 25,000. This figure might seem low, but taking into consideration that these jobs have been created since 1991 in a recession-like economy, the figure is quite impressive.

Owing to restrictions in society and especially to restrictions in relations with the West, the software sector in Ukraine was under-developed until the late 1980s. At that time, software and computer resources were only used for military or scientific purposes and had very little applicability in everyday life, and were definitely not targeted for commercial use. Gradually, the software sector was redirected to commercial utilization, especially towards customized accounting systems and database development.

Commercialization and application of programming resources was first introduced and developed after 1991. In the early 1990s the sector suffered a backlash in the form of a brain drain. At that time the best-qualified specialists and programmers found jobs abroad or emigrated to the US, Canada or Western Europe.

In Ukraine, the large competence centres for software development are Kyiv, Kharkiv, Donetsk, Odessa and L'viv. Very often programmers are working unofficially in small groups, getting money for work done as private orders, or are registered as private entrepreneurs. Most software companies have experience with subcontracting for European or US companies.

Education and human resources

From a historical perspective, the first computer in the Soviet Union was built in Kyiv. The Soviet Union and Ukraine, as a part of it, managed to organize the educational system on a very high level, enrolling most of the population. Special focus was paid to the exact sciences such as natural science and mathematics. Even though the educational system is now suffering from under-funding, Ukraine continues to possess considerable intellectual potential with its Ukrainian National Academy of Sciences, numerous scientific and technological institutes, universities and R&D companies. Ukrainian scientists have achieved world-class results in such fields as mathematics, physics, computer sciences, biology, electric welding, new materials and space sciences. As an example, it could be mentioned that

Ukraine is the producer of the biggest cargo plane in the world, 'Mriya', and of one of the best brands among space launchers, 'Zenith'.

Ukraine has more students per 10,000 inhabitants than Japan or the UK. Thirty-five per cent choose Information Technology-related disciplines; about 39 educational institutions maintain more than 15 IT-related programmes and produce about 3,000 graduates in IT and related disciplines annually (some sources state 7,000+ of 'software development capable' graduates). Enrolment in IT-related departments is increasing at a rate of 10–15 per cent per year. According to the Ukrainian Association of Software Developers (UASWD), students graduating in IT disciplines will number between 11,000 and 14,000 by 2005.

Competencies

Western specialists active in the sector usually state that the main advantage of Ukrainian programmers is that they are usually not programmers by education. This comes from the essence of Ukrainian education: during their studies, students get quite a wide and strong fundamental education in IT-related fields. Such knowledge enables them easily to master most particular technologies in a very short time. Unlike many Indian programmers, who are often taught some particular technology in short specialized courses, and thus cannot solve problems that arise outside the scope of their knowledge, Ukrainian programmers are usually educated enough to work on non-standard challenges; they are therefore also able to change development platform, technology, etc relatively easy. Technology-wise, virtually all technologies used in the West are also in use in Ukraine.

However, most of the candidates still lack the important skills of project management and an understanding of the need for adaptation to the market. Management and marketing skills are constantly in excess demand in Ukraine. Furthermore, many of the candidates have never worked in actual companies and are therefore not sufficiently aware of the need for documentation of procedures and customization of end products. Therefore, it is highly recommended that the Western company contributes project management and knowledge of how to implement standard operational procedures.

Labour costs and Western involvement

The single most important reason given by companies for entering the Ukrainian software sector is cost savings on development projects, and in this respect Ukraine offers access to vast IT resources at the cost of approximately 10–20 per cent of a US or European IT engineer.

In the 1990s a fairly good salary for a Ukrainian software specialist was around EUR55 a month. Parallel with the positive development in the sector and the rising demand for the best-qualified candidates the standard salary has risen significantly. Table 2.9.1 shows different salary levels in Ukraine. The actual costs as seen from the company will, owing to the taxation structure in Ukraine, be almost twice the amount shown in the table.

The wide spread between minimum and maximum salaries is caused by the differences between rates paid by Ukrainian and Western firms. Wage max. rates stated are for the city of Kyiv – which has the highest salary level – while the lower rates can be expected anywhere outside Kyiv; in western Ukraine in particular salaries will be at the lower end of the scale. The initial net salary for a programmer in L'viv is around EUR100–200 per month, but an experienced specialist will expect to get EUR250–350 per month (or approx. EUR2.2 per hour). The salary level for an experienced local project manager is EUR500–800 per month.

Software development in western Ukraine

In western Ukraine, L'viv is the only, but very interesting, centre for computer technology and software development. This region is especially interesting because it has a large, relatively cheap, and easily accessible human resource potential. L'viv is the economical, cultural and intellectual capital of western Ukraine; it has universities and other educational institutions with specific focus on computer science and software. L'viv has the region's largest and best-consolidated software houses, it has a sufficient and available human resource base

Table 2.9.1 Monthly salary in USD ('in hand', after taxes) for Ukrainian IT specialists

Position	Min.	Average	Max.
IS/IT Manager	500	1,670	4,207
Project Manager	350	1,187	1,927
Systems Analyst	343	654	1,777
Network Administrator	150	631	1,823
Software Development Manager	510	1,071	2,085
Software Administrator	220	429	650
End-User/Customer Support Engineer	252	577	998
IS Service Engineer	448	665	1,010
Software Engineer	120	649	1,275
Programmer Analyst	250	967	1,592

for software development and it has the best communications infrastructure in the region. Furthermore, western Ukraine is known to be culturally more closely related to Western Europe than the eastern part of Ukraine or even Russia, which is likewise very important when managing development projects. Finally, the cultural affinity to Western Europe has proven to be an important factor when achieving efficiency through management. To sum up, L'viv is an interesting target for Western software companies because it still has an unused and available resource of software competencies.

In 2002 some 1,200 companies were registered in Ukraine within software development/programming. The majority of companies have between 20 and 50 employees, with only a few firms having 250 or more. Many of the registered companies employ five programmers or fewer. In L'viv the best-known Ukrainian-owned companies are SoftServe (www.SoftServecom.com) with about 200 programmers, Eleks (www.eleks.biz) employing about 100 developers, and DevCom (www.devcom.com) with about 50 employees. At the moment, software companies employ about 500–600 software specialists in L'viv city. Another 500 people are employed as 'computer specialists' in companies not directly involved in software development, such as insurance companies, banks, energy providers, dispatchers, etc. Furthermore, many specialists are employed to provide customized services in relation to the very popular Russian accounting system '1C:Enterprise'. Altogether, about 2,000–3,000 specialists are working in the software sector in western Ukraine.

DBMS solutions are among the core competencies for both educational institutions and companies in the L'viv area. On the other extreme, there is no institute in L'viv that focuses on such subjects as user interface applicability or design, and these qualifications are therefore scarce.

Intellectual property and copyright protection

Protection of intellectual property in Ukraine is a hot issue not only inside the country, but also outside. Questions about Ukraine's inability to protect intellectual property rights have been brought up very frequently by the US during the past two years. Accusations are primarily related to the production of illegal CDs in Ukrainian factories. Ukraine is number one on the US list of violators, followed by the EU (considered as a single country).

The US has imposed financial sanctions on Ukraine since the beginning of 2002, and changes to the optical media licensing legislation adopted by the Ukrainian parliament have not satisfied the US Trade Representative. The sanctions have thus not been abolished yet.

Currently, the problem lies more in the import of pirate goods into Ukraine, rather than in their production. Microsoft and other software importers report strong sales growth, which is also caused by Ukraine's crackdown on software piracy.

From the perspective of a foreign firm looking into the possibilities in Ukraine there are kinds of copyright infringement that are perhaps more pertinent than unauthorized copying. Here, different kinds of industrial espionage are most on the minds of independent software developers. But such risks are likewise important in any other country, as the end product is costly in development but easy and costless to copy and distribute.

Foreign involvement in the software sector in western Ukraine

Examples of Western companies that have already benefited from the possibilities in this region are American Lohika Systems, Inc (www.lohika.com) and Ulybin (www.ulybin.com). These companies alone are employing about 150 specialists on a full-time basis, plus subcontracting up to 100 specialists on a freelance basis. Not only do these companies develop software offshore, but they are also active on the local market providing services to Ukrainian customers. It is expected that the number of foreign companies in L'viv will rise sharply in the years to come. The other centres for software development – Kyiv, Kharkiv and Donetsk – have already reached a critical mass of software companies, putting an upward pressure on salaries. This situation is still to be seen in western Ukraine.

How to utilize local resources and competencies

Basically, there are two approaches to cost-efficient software development: 1) to outsource processing activities to local companies in low-cost areas; 2) to establish one's own production or development unit in low-cost areas. The approach chosen in the end is often a question of corporate strategy, production volume, market estimates, financial abilities and management skills in the Western company. From a risk point of view the first option puts the business idea at stake whereas the second option is mainly a financial risk.

When only considering the financial aspects of the choice between outsourcing to an external partner and establishing one's own development unit in Ukraine, the decisive factor is the number of programmers to be involved in the project. Based on the market in 2003, the break-even point seems to be around 10 specialists. With fewer than 10 specialists employed full time it will be cheaper to outsource the tasks than to establish one's own development unit. But in the strategic perspective there is more to it than a simple 'visual-cost calculation'.

The market for software in Ukraine

Demand for software in Ukraine remains rather low. The domestic software market in Ukraine is estimated to be around $65 million. This is tightly connected with the local companies' and private consumers' limited purchasing power. But even though the market for software in Ukraine is limited, it is an expanding market.

Among business users there is constant demand for accounting software. The majority of companies use the Russian '1C:Enterprise' system (www.1c.ru). Support for users of '1C', which includes tailoring, implementation and day-to-day maintenance, is also quite a big market in Ukraine. The relatively low cost of Russian software and the inexpensive services of low-paid Ukrainian IT specialists make the cost of owning such financial applications extremely low. This is considered the key to the success and growth of this market segment.

'1C:Enterprise', together with other Russian developments such as 'Parus' and 'Galaktika', has a very strong position on the market for enterprise planning systems. The low cost of local software applications sets a high entry barrier for large enterprise resource planning systems such as SAP R/3 and Oracle Financials. However, there are companies on the Ukrainian market wishing to buy such systems, and implementation and support of ERP solutions is a booming market. The need for similar software – billing systems, merchandising solutions and the like – is realized and growing in Ukraine.

The market for specialized software for public sector organizations such as Ukrainian railways, energy distribution companies etc is growing rapidly, as these are adapting to the competition and expectations in the market.

E-commerce is in its initial stages. The lack of well-proven and secure payment systems in combination with low PC and Internet penetration in Ukraine is the major obstacle. To be sure, the market for software and related services in Ukraine is still very limited. Based on a population comparable to France and a fast-growing market economy, the potential is huge.

2.10

Ukraine's Software Exports

Emmy Gengler, Softjourn Inc

From the latest announcements in IT news, it would seem to be in vogue to announce the opening or expansion of a development centre in India (refer to recent announcements from Oracle, Yahoo, etc), or to announce an increase in a call centre in India (refer to recent announcements by AOL). Owing to the success achieved by India in the software export market, $8 billion for 2002 and an expected $10 billion for 2003 according to Sibabrata Das,[1] many countries are interested in grabbing a piece of the offshore outsourcing pie. Ukraine is no exception. The broader term of software export refers to the export of both services (both IT services and IT enabled[2]) and products. According to the Ukrainian Association of Software Developers (UASWD), Ukraine's offshore software development industry reached $53 million in 2002 and was estimated to be $71 million for 2003. This chapter will focus on the export of services only from Ukraine, and will review the areas that make Ukraine a natural for this type of export.

Detailed criteria to assess a country's potential as a software export location have been developed by analyst firms such as Gartner, and by researchers. To review the natural elements of Ukraine that can make it successful as an offshore software development location, criteria defined by R Heeks and B Nicholson[3] will be used. Instead of concentrating on each of the criteria, this chapter will focus on one of them, domestic input factors, which itself is broken down into several individual components.

---

[1] Software exports to touch $10 billion this fiscal: NASSCOM, ZDNET India. February 11, 2003, found at: http://www.zdnetindia.com/news/national/stories/75907.html.

[2] IT enabled services refers to call centres, data entry services, etc.

[3] Heeks, R and Nicholson, B (2002) *Software Export Success Factors and Strategies in Developing and Transitional Economies*, Institute for Development Policy and Management, University of Manchester.

Domestic input factors

Research and development

Ukraine possesses considerable intellectual potential with its Ukrainian National Academy of Sciences, numerous scientific and technological institutes, universities and R&D companies. It is based on a technical educational structure and research and development structure which have been in place for decades. Ukrainian scientists have achieved world-class results in such fields as mathematics, physics, computer sciences, biology, electric welding, new materials and space sciences. The traditions of the mathematical schools in Ukraine are also very strong. Kyiv had always been the leading centre of computing technologies in the former USSR: the second computer in the world was developed in Kyiv as well as one of the largest schools of cybernetics established – the Glushkov Research Institute. Currently Ukrainian scientists from the company NPO-Yuzhnoye are now working on the Sea Launch project,[4] together with Boeing. Ukrainians are also responsible for putting the largest plane in the world, the Antonov An-225, in the air.

To compare Ukraine on a research and development (R&D) level with other offshore software development locations, Table 2.10.1 has been compiled to show the number engaged in R&D activities by country.

Table 2.10.1 Number engaged in research and development

Country	Number in R&D/mn	Population/mn	Est. total number in R&D
Australia	3,319.8	19.4	64,404
China	459.1	1,271.9	583,802
India	157.9	1,033.4	163,173
Ireland	2,132.2	3.6	8,102
Jamaica	N/A	2.7	N/A
Pakistan	77.7	141.5	10,994
Philippines	156.0	77.0	12,012
Ukraine	2,120.6	49.1	104,121
Vietnam	274.0	79.5	21,783

Source: The World Bank Group, 2002 (www.worldbank.org)

[4] Sea Launch Co, LDC, is a multinational commercial satellite-launching venture formed in 1995 by Boeing Commercial Space Co of the United States with partners Kvaerner AS of Norway, RSC-Energia of Russia and NPO-Yuzhnoye of Ukraine.

Compared to many countries, the number for Ukraine is significant. However, it should be noted that this number has decreased by 1,000 per million since Ukrainian independence was gained at the end of 1991. The decrease is a result of the brain drain that Ukraine has experienced as well as the decrease in government support for many research and development facilities. We can expect the number to go a bit lower in the near term, but hopefully not too significantly.

Human capital

From Ukraine's educational institutes, an estimated 7,000+ students graduate in disciplines that enable them to become software professionals.[5] On average, the number of students entering IT programmes each year is increasing by 10–15 per cent, with many programmes already topped out at the 50 students maximum allowed to enter each year. Many educational institutes are interested in continually improving the education they are able to provide to their students. One way is by establishing relationships with companies. These may be multinationals (MNEs), such as the Kyiv National Technical University (formerly Kyiv Politechnic Institute-KPI) has done with companies such as Motorola, Hewlett-Packard, Dell, Oracle, Microsoft and Cisco, among others. With funding from Motorola, for example, KPI has been able to establish two laboratories where students can practise their skills in digital signal processing. For the universities this is an additional speciality they can offer their students, and for Motorola it means a steady supply of students trained in digital signal processing. KPI, as well as other universities such as the Zaporizhye National Technical University, has also established computer laboratories with the assistance of Samsung.

Continually offering new specialities is another way universities are striving to better prepare their students for the workplace. A speciality in economic-cybernetics is offered now by several universities. The degree programme aims to prepare students for developing applications such as: financial planning systems, market research and market segmentation, production planning, and workflow automation. To improve their course offering and at the same time improve the English language skills of their students, many universities are actively

[5] Given that statistics are hard to come by in Ukraine right now, this is the author's conservative estimate of annual graduates calculated as follows: all educational institutes, all relevant degree programmes, times 25 students per programme. A conservative estimate of 25 per programme was used, even though those university departments interviewed stated that enrollment has been increasing by 10–15 per cent.

pursuing distance education. Many universities now have the bandwidth, equipment and local company support to help make this happen.

Wages

All of the recent articles on the growth of offshore software development point to cost savings as the number one reason to outsource offshore. Therefore a discussion of wage rates is included here. Table 2.10.2 illustrates current labour rates for IT professionals in Ukraine. The wage rates shown are for the city of Kyiv only. Lower rates can be expected anywhere outside Kyiv. For example, in western Ukraine, in the city of Ivano-Frankivsk, rates for a software engineer average $150–200/month. Similar rates can be found in the cities of Zaporizhye in southeastern Ukraine and L'viv in western Ukraine, both cities of approximately 1 million inhabitants. The survey was completed by ANCOR SW Agency, a human resources firm located in Kyiv, in the winter of 2004. Participants in the survey were both Ukrainian and Western firms. Western firms will tend to pay the higher rates and Ukrainian firms tend towards the lower end, which explains the variance between minimum and maximum.

Demand in Kyiv for qualified personnel has driven up wages in the capital, and accordingly higher turnover will be experienced in the capital versus the regions. However, demand for entry-level personnel is not being met at the same rate as it is coming out of school. Demand for those with several years' experience, or with experience in specific technologies, will be tighter.

Table 2.10.2 Salaries for Ukrainian IT professionals

Position	Monthly salary in $ (after taxes)		
	Min.	Average	Max.
IS/IT Manager	346	1,177	4,502
Project Manager	588	964	1,903
Systems Analyst	120	572	1,298
Network Administrator	216	389	748
Software Development Manager	500	1,286	2,273
Software Administrator	350	574	649
End-User/Customer Support Engineer	200	491	935
IS Service Engineer	448	665	1,010
Software Engineer	216	378	606
Programmer Analyst	380	759	991

Source: ANCOR SW Agency (www.ancor-sw.com), winter 2004

Technological infrastructure

There are several types of data connectivity connections now available in Ukraine, such as Digital Subscriber Line (DSL), cable and satellite. Like many offshore software development destinations today, data connectivity is an issue in Ukraine. For comparison purposes, Table 2.10.3 summarizes fees for one type of connection, SDSL (Symmetric Digital Subscriber Line[6]), among various countries. The Ukraine row contains two sets of numbers owing to the common practice of offering limited connections, which involve paying per Mb of usage over a certain limit. As the table shows, the costs for a 1 Mbps connection in Ukraine will be significantly more than a similar connection in the US or the UK.

There are two trends in Ukraine today: improvement of capacity and reduction in fees. Given that the communications industry has received a high level of foreign investment, it can be expected that the communications offerings will continue to increase while the corresponding fees will decrease with competition.

Tips for outsourcing software development to Ukraine

Communications plan

Create a written communications plan, including the means of communication to be used and its priority, and make it accessible to all team members in all locations. The one- to two-hour time difference between Ukraine and Western European countries means a near-shore solution, with most business hours overlapping. However, it may still be necessary to make contact out of hours. Incoming calls on mobile phones are no longer charged, as of September 2003, so they are a great way to get in contact with someone quickly. SMS (Multimedia Messaging Service – MMS) messages can also be used for high-priority messages out of hours in Ukraine, such as: Issue with x project, call me @ +44 555 555 12 34. Or Issue with x project, online chat @ 12:00 (UK time).

---

[6] SDSL: Digital subscriber line: a technology that allows a provider to use the excess bandwidth found in a copper line for the provision of data services. SDSL (symmetric digital subscriber line) is called synchronous because the upstream (customer premise to the network) speed is the same as the downstream (network to the customer premise) speed.

Table 2.10.3 Internet connection cost comparison by country

Country	Business class Digital Subscriber Line (xDSL) in USD[1]							
	Net Install	256/256 Kbps[2]	512/512 Kbps	1/1 Mbps[3]	2/2 Mbps	Router Rental	Traffic cap, GB[4]	Charge per 1 MB after cap
Australia	$501	N/A	$249	$296	$357	N/A	1	$0.12
China	$112	$108	$181	$302	N/A	N/A	Unlimited	N/A
India	$655+	$546	$786	$1,430	N/A	$54	Unlimited	N/A
Pakistan	$2,932+	$1,268	$2,151	$3,425	$5,594	N/A	Unlimited	N/A
Ukraine	N/A	$280	$380	$480	$595	N/A	4–10	$50[5]
United Kingdom	$462	$294	$350	$535	$720	N/A	Unlimited	N/A
USA	$0	$169	$229	$279	$459	$0	Unlimited	N/A

[1] Fees listed in US dollars.

[2] Measure of bandwidth (the amount of data that can flow in a given time) on a data transmission medium: Kbps – Kilobits per second (thousands of bits per second). The number above the line refers to the download speed, the number below the line refers to the upload speed. Thus 256/256 Kbps refers to 256 Kbps upload speed and 256 Kbps download speed.

[3] Mbps – Megabits per second (millions of bits per second).

[4] GB – Gigabyte is a measure of storage capacity. (Roughly a billion bytes).

[5] Pricing for traffic above the cap is based on volume. For example, additional traffic between10–30 GB above the cap costs $50.00/month, for that entire volume.

Sources: Australia: ClariNET, www.clari.net.au accessed July 2004. Pricing for ASDL China: www.shanghaiguide.com. Shanghai Telecom. Pricing for ASDL, accessed July 2004. India: http://www.kelnetonline.net/corp_serv.htm, accessed July 2004. Pakistan: Micronet Broadband Ltd, www.dsl.net.pk. Ukraine: Pricing for ASDL. Global Ukraine: http://www.gu.net, accessed July 2004. United Kingdom: C2 Internet Ltd, www.c2internet.net, accessed July 2004. USA: Transedge, www.transedge.com, accessed July 2004.

Voice connectivity

When working with an offshore location or distributed software development team, telephone conversations are necessary. For voice communications (not Voice Over IP – VOIP), it is possible to pay as little as 18 cents for a call from Ukraine to the US and even less, 13 cents, from the US to Ukraine. It is also now very easy and inexpensive to have several services engaged at one time (for contingency purposes) to ensure constant communications at reasonable cost. Voice Over IP services are also increasingly available; services such as Packet8 (http://www.packet8.net) can reduce the cost of phone calls even further, while enabling your team in Ukraine to be reachable via a US number and to use that US number to make local calls to the US.

Data connectivity

High data connectivity fees require that a tight calculation of capacity needs is made. Work with your Ukrainian vendor and team developer to calculate these needs and plan for usage nearer to actual capacity as opposed to having a lot of unused capacity. Create a contingency plan for how upgrades will be handled quickly as additional capacity is needed. Make sure your vendor has a primary data connectivity provider as well as a backup provider, as well as your company.

Intellectual property

In June of 2004, the Business Software Alliance (BSA), a Washington DC-based group, issued their annual list of the worst intellectual property offenders. China topped the list with 92 per cent of the software sold in China being pirated, Vietnam also had 92 per cent and Ukraine came third with 91 per cent. By definition, piracy refers to the unauthorized copying of software; however, it is most often used in reference to intellectual property. According to the BSA, the rate of piracy is not correlated to the level of industrial espionage in a country. Industrial espionage is more of a concern to companies outsourcing software development than unauthorized copying. Industrial espionage is defined as: employees of a vendor, which was contracted by the client to develop algorithms, moving to the client's competitor and/or the vendor stealing the application code that they wrote and beginning to sell the application in Ukraine or to other countries.

An article in *Computer World Hong Kong* in September 2003 included comments from James Johnson, an analyst at The Standish Group International Inc in Dennis, Massachusetts, about the extent to which industrial espionage is an issue in outsourcing. 'If companies are outsourcing work offshore, there is more risk of an IT worker booby-trapping code or causing some other intentional problem without US laws to protect the client's company', Johnson said.[7] Security risk in outsourcing is not new and certainly risk does not only occur with outsourcing offshore. In December 2002, Roger Duronio, a former UBS PaineWebber, Inc, systems administrator, was charged with planting a logic bomb in the financial services company's network, a perfect example of an internal threat. In another example, Timothy Allen Lloyd, an employee of a high-tech measurement company, Omega Engineering, was sentenced to 41 months in prison for leaving behind malicious programmes that deleted critical data from the servers of his employer.

Incorporating the following steps into the development process can help alleviate issues of industrial espionage:

1. segmenting work so that no one programmer has access to all components of the application;
2. uploading all code, twice a day, to a server that is controlled by the client, with proper measures in place to prevent hacking;
3. conducting periodic code reviews of the code that is uploaded to the server, and peer code reviews during the development cycle (required by CMM level 3 companies, but is also considered a standard software development life cycle process and should be conducted by all companies irregardless of level).

Project management

Project management skills themselves are an area in need of improvement in Ukraine. There is a lack of people who can manage the timeline/budget of a project. While many of the larger vendors will have several experienced project managers, smaller vendors may not, so if you are looking to develop a team with specific technical skills, it may be necessary to build the skills within your team. Having a project led in Ukraine work directly with your project manager will assist in passing on skills to their Ukrainian counterpart.

Hardware

Today, most hardware required can be assembled and purchased in Ukraine. Workstations and servers can be assembled to customer requirements and purchased with service contracts that will guarantee a technician at your office in one hour should there be any problems. While

[7] Weiss, Todd R (2003) IT outsourcing: not just India anymore, *Computer World Hong Kong*, http://www.idg.com.hk/cw/readstory.asp?aid=20030918003.

importing for permanent use within a company is not a problem, unless very specific hardware is needed it is not necessary to import.

Temporary import of hardware

Per the current laws of Ukraine, your outsourcing partner can bring in a piece of hardware, for example a medical device or semiconductor equipment, for use in their office for less than one year, without paying any duties. This may be necessary when specific testing of an application needs to be done. Per the current customs code, there is some leeway given to the customs officer in determining how the equipment will be used and how long the company intends to use it in their office. At times, delays have been known to occur. If you need your partner to import a piece of equipment for testing purposes, for example, allow for adequate time in the schedule in case any delays occur. As Ukraine is pushing towards WTO (World Trade Organization) accession, the customs code is constantly being upgraded. This is one area where improvements can be expected in the very near future.

Language skills

Today English is required from the second grade onwards, which ensures that the next generation of Ukrainians will have the necessary base of English skills. The current generation of IT professionals is not totally lacking in English skills either, specifically in the area of reading comprehension. For years most technical documentation was only available in English. Internet usage continues to ensure that reading comprehension will remain high; it also assists with the practice of English writing skills. Many of the professionals who have graduated in the past few years have completed internships in Europe where English was the common language among their working groups. This enabled them to obtain much-needed practice in speaking and oral comprehension. The technical educational institutes recognize that this is an issue for the global economy and are working on ways to ensure that their students can develop their language skills. Speaking skills are always the hardest to develop though, and this is an issue in Ukraine and one recognized by many companies. To combat this, many companies conduct in-house English language classes.

Travel from Ukraine to your site

Periodically it will be necessary to have your Ukrainian project manager or other team members travel to your location. If you choose a vendor that is a member of the American Chamber of Commerce, then the process to obtain visas to the US and to the United Kingdom, for example, can be expedited. Current agreements with both the American and British Embassies enable member companies to obtain visas for their employees in one day. The British Embassy's Business Express scheme is also offered to members of the European Business Association and the British–Ukrainian Chamber of Commerce. Note: Even though this service is available, do not wait until the last minute. This service is only available one day a week, and if your paperwork is not in order, you will not be able to receive it in one day.

Travel to Ukraine from your site

For team development, transferring the concept of your application, etc, the project manager will want to travel to meet and work with his/her team in Ukraine periodically. For members of the European Union and citizens of the US, invitation letters have not been required for the past three years. Costs of visas have gone down and the length of visas has gone up. Multi-entry visas for up to five years are now available and can be obtained in three to nine days. For example, for $165 a five-year multi-entry visa can be obtained in nine days. Plan ahead, follow up the application procedures and plan for the long term in working with your team in Ukraine.

2.11

Electricity Regulation in Ukraine

Bate C Toms and Tina Radchenko, BC Toms & Co

General regulatory framework

Brief history

Prior to independence, the electricity sector of Ukraine was developed and operated as a part of the united energy system of the USSR. Until the electricity industry was reorganized into its current structure, there were seven regional energy associations. These associations were under the control of the Ministry of Power and Energy of Ukraine. Approximately 65 per cent of all electricity was produced by thermal power stations, 25 per cent by nuclear power stations and 10 per cent by hydropower stations.

During the Soviet period, overall generating capacity of the electricity industry was close to 52,000 mW, with 26,000 mW needed internally. In comparison, the size and number of electricity generating capacities in the UK was similar to this allocation of electricity generation in Ukraine. A World Bank study on how to reorganize the Ukrainian electricity system recommended pooling of generation, citing the practice in the UK and Argentina. During the 1994–1995 period,Ukraine created a new legal framework providing for (1) sales of all electricity to be made to a wholesale electricity market (the 'WEM'), with pooling arrangements to foster competition among electricity generating companies, (2) creation of a state licensing regulatory system, and (3) partial privatization.

Overview of electricity law

The basic legal act establishing the structure for the electricity market in Ukraine is the law 'On Electricity' dated 16 October 1997, No. 575/97 (the 'Electricity Law'). The Electricity Law established the legal basis for the operation of a wholesale electricity market in which, generally, all electricity produced by generating companies is purchased by the market operator and sold to distributors (suppliers).

The Electricity Law regulates the operation of the WEM, state policy and methods of state control over the market, licensing, settlement procedures, pricing on the electricity market, obligations and responsibilities of the market participants, and remedies for violations of the Law.

The Electricity Law confirms the authority of the National Commission for Regulation of the Electricity Industry in Ukraine (the 'NERC') to regulate business activities in the electricity market, including for:

- issuance of licences;
- the regulation of tariffs;
- control over compliance with electricity laws;
- consumer protection.

The Energomarket Members' Agreement

The wholesale electricity market was established under an Agreement between the Members of the Wholesale Electricity Market of 15 November 1996 (the 'Energomarket Members' Agreement' or 'EMA'), which provides for the wholesale purchase and sale of electricity and for electricity system control and high voltage network transmission. The EMA establishes the basis on which each member under the EMA sells output and purchases all the electricity that it requires.

The EMA defines the rights, obligations and responsibilities of the WEM members, the procedure for conducting annual general meetings of market members, and the procedures for electricity market members to join the EMA and terminate their rights and obligations under the EMA.

Structure of the wholesale electricity market

General structure of the wholesale electricity market

The WEM (Wholesale Electricity Market) consists of several groups of market participants. The first group, producers of electricity (generating companies), includes:

- *Thermal power stations (TPS)*. There are four companies possessing and operating 14 power stations with a total capacity of more than 500 mW – Tzentrenergo, Zakhidenergo, Donbasenergo and Dniproenergo.

- *Nuclear power stations (NPS).* Currently, there are five nuclear power stations in Ukraine (Chernobyl, Zaporizhzhya, Rivne, Khmelnytsk and Pivdenno-Ukrainska) operating as one company – the National Energy Generating Enterprise 'Energoatom'.
- *Hydro power stations (HPS).* There are two state companies – Dniprohydroenergo and Dnistrohydroenergo – which hold and operate 11 hydro power stations in Ukraine.
- *Small electricity producers.* These generating companies account for a much smaller share in the production of electricity. They consist of combined heat and power plants (CHPPs), some of which are included in the structure of local electricity distribution companies, and other small power plants.

The second group is suppliers (distributors) of electricity that play the role of intermediaries in the WEM between the generating companies and consumers, and consists of:

- *Wholesale electricity supplier* (this role is currently performed by the SE Energomarket).
- *Local (regional) electricity suppliers (LECs).* LECs purchase electricity on the WEM and resell it at the price (tariff) fixed by NERC and only on the territory specified in their licence. Usually there is one LEC per region (oblast), as well as one LEC in the Crimean Autonomous Republic, one in the City of Kyiv and one in the City of Sevastopol.
- *Independent electricity suppliers.* About 50 licensed independent suppliers purchase electricity on the WEM and re-sell it to consumers at market prices without territorial restrictions.

Consumers form the third group, purchasing electricity from either LECs or independent electricity suppliers.

A separate group of electricity market participants are companies that operate transmission networks. Electricity is transmitted through a high voltage network (220 kW and above) owned and operated by the National Electric Energy Company and then through medium and small voltage networks owned and operated by the LECs. Independent suppliers usually conclude agreements with LECs for the transmission of electricity by the LECs' networks.

NEC 'Ukrenergo' and SE Energomarket

Pursuant to the EMA, sales on the WEM should be conducted through the State Enterprise 'Energorynok' (literally translated as 'energy market', hereinafter 'SE Energomarket'). SE Energomarket was established on the basis of a separate division, named'Energomarket', of the

State Enterprise 'National Energy Company "Ukrenergo"' ('Ukrenergo'), though it received a licence for its wholesale supply of electricity only in 2000. Until SE Energomarket was created, Ukrenergo signed the EMA and undertook the powers of SE Energomarket. Interestingly, the EMA names SE Energomarket as one of its signatories, but in fact it has not been signed by SE Energomarket. This creates an interesting legal issue that might be used to challenge the validity of the EMA, and hopefully will be addressed beforehand by the authorities.

Although the applicable regulations and the EMA entrust SE Energomarket with the task of centralized dispatch management of the united energy system of Ukraine, the Charter of SE Energomarket does not contemplate such a role. Instead, in fact, Ukrenergo continues to perform the role of the National Dispatch Centre servicing the WEM and exercises management of the united energy system.

WEM Board

The WEM is managed by its Board, which serves as the representative of the Energomarket Members in the administration of the EMA.

Under Article 6 of the Energomarket Members Agreement, the Board ('Rada' in Ukrainian) of the WEM is composed of 10 voting directors, of whom 5 are drawn from generators and 5 from suppliers (including independent suppliers) elected annually based on the votes of the companies in each group cast separately as classes using a weighted voting system (in which the votes depend on the volumes of electricity produced or purchased). In addition, the Board includes non-voting directors representing the following entities: SE Energomarket, NERC, a market auditor selected pursuant to the EMA, the Ministry of Fuel and Energy and Energoatom. The Chairman of the Board is selected annually by the voting directors. All matters before the WEM Board are decided by a simple majority.

The quorum required for the meetings of the WEM Board is three directors from the electricity producers and three from the electricity suppliers.

Operation of the wholesale electricity market

General

On the WEM, the generating companies sell their electricity to SE Energomarket which, in turn, sells it to the local (regional) electricity suppliers (LECs) and independent electricity suppliers. At any time, only one supplier may supply electricity to a consumer. Consumers may not purchase electricity from two or more suppliers. Independent suppliers are prohibited from contracting for the supply of electricity with consumers that have any outstanding debts to a LEC; however, LECs cannot refuse to supply electricity to a consumer having outstanding obligations to an independent electricity supplier.

According to the Electricity Law, all electricity produced by power stations must be sold on the WEM, unless the power station has a capacity below 20 mW or has produced less than 100 million kWh in the previous year.

Exception from the WEM for CHPPs

There are two exceptions from the requirement to sell all produced electricity to the WEM, which apply to CHPPs (combined heat and power plants). Any CHPP forming a part of an LEC is permitted by the Electricity Law to supply electricity directly to customers in the territory assigned to the LEC by the terms of its licence. Initially it was understood that the exception applied only to LECs that owned CHPPs. However, NERC broadened this exemption to any CHPP. The NERC Regulation 'On the Sale of Self-Produced Electricity', No. 964, of 23 July 1999 states that CHPPs (either state owned or privately owned) have an option to choose to sell electricity on the WEM or to a supplier or to deliver it directly to customers that are connected to its networks. This, in fact, contradicts the Electricity Law, which provides such options for CHPPs forming a subdivision of a LEC, but not for all CHPPs. Nevertheless, in a letter dated 25 August 1999, NERC stated that its ruling took into account that an essential number of CHPPs were not able to sell electricity at the WEM or to the LECs during previous heating periods, and, therefore the state must consider the peculiarities of the operation of the combined heat and power plants in order not to harm consumers. As a practical matter, the majority of CHPPs obtained a licence to be a 'supplier on a non-regulated tariff basis', which made them independent electricity suppliers.

Pooling/payment arrangements

Generators, that are members of the WEM, price bid each day for hourly generation the next day. These bids are used by the SE Energomarket to set the 'system marginal price' at the price of the most expensive hourly unit. In principle, the bidding process among thermal generators should work so that priority is given to the lowest margin cost generators among thermal producers. In practice, a higher cost block may be dispatched first for practical reasons, such as the availability of fuel for continuous operation, the distance to the consumer and the capacity of the relevant power transmission lines.

The first electricity to be dispatched is that generated under the bilateral agreements. After that, a bidding process is put into place. Generators may also receive a capacity payment irrespective of whether they, in fact, sell electricity.

Power Purchase Agreement

Each LEC must enter into an agreement for the purchase of electricity (a 'Power Purchase Agreement' or 'PPA') with SE Energomarket. The PPA usually reconfirms the parties' obligations under the Energomarket Members' Agreement (EMA) and specifies the procedure for the calculation of the volumes of electricity being purchased under the PPA, payment and exchange of information.

Transaction settlement

Transaction settlement in the wholesale market is carried out in accordance with the Instruction 'On the Procedure for Performing Financial Settlements', which constitutes Annex 3 to the EMA, and the Instruction 'On the Procedure for the Administration of Funds of the Wholesale Market of Electrical Energy in Ukraine', which constitutes Annex 4 to the EMA.

The Energomarket Members' Agreement designates SE Energomarket to be the 'Market Funds Administrator' ('MFA') and the 'Settlement System Administrator' ('SSA') for settlements between the Members. SE Energomarket has performed this function since July 2000, after replacing Ukrenergo. The general duties and responsibilities of the SE Energomarket as MFA are covered in Article 8 of the Energomarket Members' Agreement and Article 4 of the Funds Administration Instruction.

Practical difficulties with settlement and special use accounts

In general, when introduced, the wholesale electricity market system has been only partially effective because of liquidity problems. As a consequence, a number of independent electricity wholesalers entered the market and were purchasing electricity from generators via the wholesale market in return for fuel. In order to facilitate the proper allocation of funds among WEM members, the EMA envisaged creation of so-called 'transit accounts', which were later replaced with 'distribution accounts', currently renamed 'accounts with special use'.

In June 2000, in view of the regular non-payments that plagued the power industry, Parliament introduced Article 15–1 to the Electricity Law to establish a system of distributive accounts for the WEM payments. In accordance with this system, LECs and the wholesale electricity supplier open separate special accounts with an authorized bank. All payments for the electricity purchased on the WEM as well as for consumed electricity must be made to these special accounts. The list of special accounts is approved by the NERC, which is supposed to inform consumers.

Consumers are under an obligation to make all payments for electricity only to the special account of their respective LEC. If this provision is violated, the funds are confiscated and placed in the state budget and are not considered payment for electricity.

All the funds accumulated in the special accounts of LECs are distributed exclusively to:

- the special account of the wholesale electricity supplier;
- a bank account of the company that operates the local power networks;
- a bank account of the LEC.

The algorithm pursuant to which this distribution is carried out is established monthly by NERC.

Several proposals have been made to shift from distributive accounts to regular bank accounts. Currently, in accordance with the NERC Regulation 'On Settlement in Case of the Absence of Debts of an Electricity Supplier under a Regulated Tariff to the Wholesale Electricity Supplier', No. 311, dated 3 April 2001, LECs that pay in full for electricity that they purchase on WEM are allowed to receive all payments for electricity collected from the special accounts into their own bank accounts, and then to pay SE Energomarket and other creditors. However, any modification or elimination of the system of distributive accounts should require amendment of the Electricity Law.

Electricity tariffs

Electricity tariffs for the general population range from 9.6 to 13 kopeks per 1 kWh (not including VAT); however, according to NERC estimates, this tariff reflects about two-thirds of the real value of the electricity supplied to households. This difference in cost is included in the tariffs for purchases on the wholesale market, which consequently increases tariffs for so-called 'non-household' (mainly industrial) consumers. By way of comparison, in developed countries the general public price for electricity is at least twice the price for industrial consumers because much of the electricity is lost in the networks during transmission to households.

The retail price of electricity is established by adding the expenses of each LEC on transmission by local voltage networks and electricity supply services to the wholesale electricity price. Wholesale electricity prices include the cost of electricity generated by producers, expenses on dispatch of electricity (including expenses of Ukrenergo and SE Energomarket) and on transmission by high voltage networks and some additional expenses.

Each LEC has a different retail electricity tariff depending on the length of its voltage networks and the structure of consumption in the region. Therefore, the retail electricity price for non-household consumers is different in each region of Ukraine.

NERC – the primary state regulator

Legal basis for operation

NERC (the National Commission for Regulation of Electricity in Ukraine) represents the executive branch of the Ukrainian government. It was created as an independent state body with special status and is primarily funded by licence fees.

NERC regulates business activities in the electricity market pursuant to the Regulation 'On the National Commission on the Regulation of the Electricity Sector of Ukraine', approved by the Decree of the President of Ukraine 'On Measures to Provide for the Activity of the National Commission on the Issues of Regulation of the Electricity Sector' of 14 March 1995, No. 213/95, and the Decree of the President of Ukraine 'On Issues on the National Commission on Regulation of the Electricity Sector of Ukraine' dated 30 October 2000, No. 1167/2000.

NERC has the following responsibilities:

- issuance of licences for power generation, for the operation of high voltage power lines and low voltage networks and for supplying electricity on either a regulated or non-regulated tariff basis and for wholesale supply;
- regulation of tariffs;
- control over compliance with electricity laws;
- consumer protection.

Authority to regulate tariffs and prices

Under the Electricity Law, NERC is generally responsible for 'insuring implementation of price and tariffs policy in the electricity industry'. The Presidential Decree 'On Issues of the NERC' repeats this provision and further provides that NERC is to 'form within the scope of its authority, the state policy with respect to electricity prices'. One may argue that based on these provisions, NERC may regulate any prices in the electricity industry. However, the Electricity Law only provides for the following specific cases where NERC has such express authority to control prices and tariffs: (a) for the transmission of electricity by local networks (grids), (b) for the supply of electricity by LECs and (c) for the sale of electricity produced by CHPPs owned by LECs to customers within their territorial jurisdiction. According to the Cabinet of Ministers' Resolution 'On Establishing the Authority of the Bodies of Executive Power and the Executive Bodies of City Councils Regarding Regulation of Prices (Tariffs)' of 25 December 1996, No. 1548, NERC also has the authority to 'fix tariffs for electricity supplied to the population for household purposes'.

Other state regulatory involvement

State regulatory involvement in the electricity industry is not limited to NERC. The main function of the Energy Department, a division of the Ministry of Fuel and Energy, is to implement state policy in the electricity sector and to regulate the sector. At the present time, the Ministry of Fuel and Energy also manages the state's shares in the electricity generators and suppliers.

Pursuant to the Electricity Law and the Cabinet of Ministers' Resolution No. 189 dated 15 February 1999, state supervision of the electricity industry is also exercised by the State Inspection on Exploitation of Electric Stations and Networks (Grids) and by the State Inspection on Energy Supervision over the Regimes for Consumption of Electric and Heat Energy. Local authorities also exercise some control. For example, the Electricity Law provides that they participate in the development of the plan for local electricity distribution.

Licensing

General

Under the Electricity Law and the Law of Ukraine 'On the Licensing of Certain Types of Business Activity' dated 1 June 2000, No.1775, business activities in the field of electric energy are licensed in accordance with special laws. The following activities are subject to licensing:

- generation;
- transmission;

- supply on a regulated tariff basis;
- supply on a non-regulated tariff basis;
- wholesale supply.

Under Articles 12 and 13 of the Electricity Law, the state body authorized to license activities is NERC. A separate licence is issued for each type of activity. Production by businesses without a licence is allowed if the installed capacity or the output of electric energy is less than 5 mW (the thresholds set in the licensing terms and conditions for the business activity of electricity production).

A decision on a refusal to issue a licence should be taken within 30 days from the date of receipt of an application and required materials. The period of validity of the licence is determined by NERC; however, it may not be less than three years.

Licensing terms and conditions

Any company interested in working in the Ukrainian energy market should pay special attention to NERC's general licensing terms and conditions, as they contain a number of important restrictions. These restrictions include the following:

- Each LEC and affiliates may only operate within one region (oblast) if the volume of electricity that it supplies exceeds 15 per cent of the total of all electricity supplied in Ukraine.
- Each LEC and affiliates may not own or operate more than 4 per cent of the overall licensed capacity of electricity suppliers in Ukraine without the permission of NERC.
- An LEC may not provide cross-subsidies to affiliates out of profits from licensed activities, and it may not accept any cross-subsidies from its affiliates for its licensed activities.
- Each LEC must guarantee that (1) none of its affiliates is using any information possessed by the LEC in order to gain an unjustified competitive advantage in the market, and (2) such information will not be available to anyone, including any of its affiliates, who may use this information to gain any unjustified competitive advantage.
- In case of the liquidation, certain forms of reorganization or the acquisition or disposal of more than 25 per cent of the shares (or share interest) or assets of a LEC, the LEC must request NERC to confirm that such action is in accordance with the licensing conditions and rules.

Licensing fees

NERC sets monthly fees for all categories of licensees. The fees are calculated based on the expenses that NERC incurres in its activities in a given period of time. This amount is divided in the following proportion between the various groups of the licensees:

- generation of electricity (45 per cent);
- transmission by high voltage networks (5 per cent);
- transmission by low voltage networks (38 per cent);
- wholesale supply of electricity (5 per cent);
- supply on a regulated and a non-regulated tariff basis (7 per cent).

The fee for each licensee within these group varies depending on the capacities and volumes of production or supply of each.

Privatization in the electricity industry

There are now both state-owned and privately owned electricity producers and suppliers. The last major privatization sale in the electricity sector occurred in April 2001, when six LECs were sold at a tender held by the State Property Fund of Ukraine (the 'SPF'). Two of them were purchased by the US multinational AES (AES Washington Holdings BV) and four by the Slovak VSE (Vychodoslovenske Energeticke Zavody). Ukraine received approximately USD160 million from these sales, more than was expected. This privatization was also the first occasion when the SPF involved a sophisticated Western bank, Credit Suisse First Boston ('CSFB'), as its principal adviser. CSFB lobbied effectively for the regulatory framework for the operation of electricity distribution companies to be made acceptable for potential bidders, for example on matters such as the setting of electricity prices.

The major legal problems that investors were facing when participating in the 2001 privatization of six LECs were: (1) uncertainties over the ability to disconnect non-paying customers; (2) lack of clear mechanisms for compensation of the subsidy for electricity purchases by subsidized customers; and (3) uncertainties over tariff formation mechanisms. Due diligence of LECs usually revealed a lack of (or inability to demonstrate, owing to the absence of centralized records) the most important documents, including (1) proof of legal title registration with the Bureau of Technical Inventory ('BTI'), the local body for registering real estate, for most buildings and similar real estate assets listed on their balance sheets; (2) land allocation documents, especially for the smaller land plots used for power lines, etc; (3) project approval documentation required for the operation and the use of facilities (including sub-stations and transformer stations). Hopefully, some of these problems will be resolved for the next 12 state-owned electricity distribution companies, which the SPF intends to sell at a tender in the near future.

Once all the electricity distribution companies have been privatized, it is anticipated that privatization of the state electricity generation companies will follow. In 2001, there were several attempts by powerful Ukrainian corporate groups to take control of these electricity generators by acquiring and enforcing their large debts. This process is commonly known as 'hidden privatization'. Several debts were enforced on this basis and recoveries were made against the assets of these companies, effectively allowing the assets to be acquired to satisfy debts at a small fraction of their true market value. This potentially dangerous trend was halted by the Ukrainian Parliament imposing a temporary moratorium on such recoveries, including through bankruptcy proceedings, against the assets of companies that are 25 per cent or more state owned.

Article 6 of the Electricity Law provides that some power stations are not eligible for privatization. All existing nuclear and hydroelectric enterprises and state companies managing electricity dispatch or operating major electricity transmission networks are not eligible for privatization.

2.12

Ukrainian Law on Oil and Gas Exploration and Production

Bate C Toms and Taras Dumych,
BC Toms & Co

This chapter reviews Ukrainian law on oil and gas exploration and production, considering, in particular, licensing, production sharing, exporting production and the protection of foreign investors.

Ukrainian oil and gas legislation

The principal Ukrainian laws governing oil and gas exploration and production activities are the Subsoil Code adopted on 27 July 1994 ('Code'), the Law on Oil and Gas (12 July 2001) ('Oil and Gas Law'), the Law on Production Sharing Agreements (14 September 1999) ('PSA Law'), the Law on Pipeline Transport (15 May 1996) ('Pipeline Law'), the Law on Licensing of Certain Types of Business Activities (1 June 2000) ('Licensing Law'), and the Law on Rental Payments for Oil, Natural Gas and Gas Condensate (5 February 2004) the entry of which was suspended for the year 2004). Ukraine's corporate, tax, labour safety, environmental, administrative and real property laws also have various provisions that can affect oil and gas activities.

The most important of these laws at present is the Oil and Gas Law, which generally governs the geological study, exploration, development, production, storage, transportation and disposal of oil and natural gas. It establishes the requirements and procedures for oil and gas licensing. The Oil and Gas Law does not apply, however, to activities governed by the PSA Law, discussed below.

Activities by a foreign investor under the Oil and Gas Law, as under previous legislation, typically involve the establishment of a joint venture company by the foreign investor with a local Ukrainian oil and gas enterprise. The joint venture obtains an oil and gas exploration or production licence. Control over the joint venture is exercised on the basis of the corporate rights established by a foundation (joint venture) agreement between the investors and the joint venture company's charter.

The PSA Law, by contrast, creates an alternative legal structure for oil and gas exploration and production based on production sharing agreements ('PSA'). It establishes the basic legal requirements for such agreements as well as a special legal regime concerning, in particular, resource use, taxation and investment protection. However, as of today, the PSA Law has not been generally used in practice, in particular because the tax benefits are not perceived to be sufficiently advantageous.

Oil and gas licensing

Procedure and issuing authority

The legal regime under the Oil and Gas Law is based on licensing. A licence is required for the exploration and production of oil and gas, except where the PSA Law applies. To regulate the issuance of licences, the Cabinet of Ministers adopted Resolution No. 1540 dated 2 October 2003, 'On Approval of the Procedure for the Issuance of Special Permits for the Use of the Subsoil' ('Procedure'). This newly adopted Procedure cancelled the previously applicable 1995 Resolution No. 709 'On the Procedure for the Issuance of Individual Permits (Licences) for the Use of the Subsoil'.

On 10 February 2004, by the Edict of the President of Ukraine, a new State Committee on Natural Resources of Ukraine ('Natural Resources Committee') with authority over natural resources was established. The activities of the Natural Resources Committee extend to geological study (exploration) and the rational use (exploitation) of the subsoil, gathering geological information, and exercising control over how the exploration and exploitation of natural resources is conducted in Ukraine.

The principal role of the Natural Resources Committee is issuance, suspension and termination of licences for the exploration and exploitation of natural resources in Ukraine, including, and in particular, of oil and gas. This role previously was fulfilled by the Ministry of Ecology and Natural Resources Use ('Natural Resources Ministry').

Types and duration of licences

The Oil and Gas Law, in Articles 13 and 17, distinguishes the following four types and duration of licences, depending on the proposed activities of the applicant:

1. the licence for the exploration of oil and gas resources, including to undertake pilot production, for up to five years on land and up to 10 years on the continental shelf;
2. the licence for the exploration of oil and gas, including to undertake pilot production of oil and gas with subsequent extraction (industrial development of the deposits), for up to 20 years on land and up to 30 years on the continental shelf;
3. the licence for the production (extraction) of oil and gas (industrial development of the deposits) for up to 20 years on land and up to 30 years on the continental shelf; and
4. the licence for the construction and use of underground storage facilities not connected with the extraction of natural resources, including for the storage of oil and gas and the wastes from oil and gas exploration and production, for up to 50 years.

The Oil and Gas Law states that these four different types of activities must be separately licensed. This licensing structure is based on past Soviet-era practice when state enterprises operating in the oil and gas sector were divided into either exploration or production enterprises. Following Ukrainian independence in 1991 and the end of the Soviet regime, however, all private and most state entities involved in oil and gas exploration in Ukraine have generally sought to carry out production at the fields that they have undertaken the expense to explore.

The Oil and Gas Law in this respect only provides that the entity that performs the exploration works under the exploration licence has a 'priority right' to receive a production licence. It also provides that, assuming the exploration works were performed at the expense of the licensee, if said licensee wishes to conduct commercial production, a production licence can be issued to it by negotiation without the need for a tender.

As a matter of law, how this priority right is applied in the negotiation of the terms (and state fees) for a production licence leaves great discretion to the government. A company wishing to protect its proposed investment in exploration and ensure that it benefits from this expense by receiving a suitable production licence should therefore, prior to incurring expenses for exploration, negotiate such terms in an Oil and Gas Operations Agreement, as discussed below. Otherwise, a licensee that develops a field under an exploration licence will need to negotiate its production licence after the deposits have been estimated and valued, when the commercial terms for such licence may be quite different. In such circumstances, the government could, in the absence of any prior agreement, effectively force a tender for the production licence, although in the past most private companies have generally been able to move from exploration to production licences.

This licensing issue may now be more serious in view of the amendments to the Oil and Gas Law introduced by the State Budget Law of Ukraine for 2004 (the 'Budget Law'). Based on these amendments, licences may be issued only pursuant to a tender (auction). The procedures for such tenders were established by the Cabinet of Ministers of Ukraine in Resolution No. 694 'On Approval of the Procedure for Conducting Auctions for the Sale of Special Permissions (Licences) for the Use of the Subsoil', adopted on 26 May 2004. Consequently, it became no longer possible under the Oil and Gas Law to issue production licences by negotiation to the holders of exploration licences. However, the Budget Law was amended on 17 June 2004 to permit exceptions to this new tender requirement to be created by 'an executive agency specially authorized by the Cabinet of Ministers', so that it will again be possible for licences to be issued by negotiation rather than tender.

Where an enterprise receives a production licence for a field previously explored at the state's expense, a special tax on exploration works, the so-called 'geological fee' (also referred to below in the section on PSA taxation), is imposed as reimbursement to the state for its prior expense. The timing and amount of this geological fee can vary for a number of reasons, depending in particular on whether the production enterprise also finances further exploration while conducting commercial production under its production licence.

Licence applications

The process of obtaining an exploration or a production licence can be complex. According to the Oil and Gas Law, licences are generally issued on the basis of a tender, participation in which requires the applicant to submit a substantial set of documents (until May 2004, a tender was not necessarily required for issuance of production licences issued based on works conducted under a prior exploration licence). The licence should be issued to the applicant who wins the tender not later than 60 days after the winner is declared. Within this period, all the necessary procedures for the licence issuance stipulated by law must be completed, and an Oil and Gas Operations Agreement (discussed below) must be signed.

To supplement the Oil and Gas Law, the Natural Resources Ministry and the State Committee on Issues of Regulatory Policy and

Entrepreneurship jointly adopted, on 13 February 2001, the Terms for Licensing the Exploration of Natural Resources. According to these licensing terms, an enterprise wishing to conduct exploration or production must meet certain requirements, including having specialists with appropriate geological education and experience and relevant equipment that satisfies Ukrainian technical standards.

Oil and Gas Operations Agreement

As mentioned above, an Agreement on Terms for the Use of Oil and Gas Deposits (an 'Oil and Gas Operations Agreement') must be entered into with the Natural Resources Committee (as successor to the Natural Resources Ministry) as a condition of receiving a licence for exploration or production. The Oil and Gas Operations Agreement is made part of the licence as an exhibit. This Oil and Gas Operations Agreement regulates in detail technical, organizational, financial, economic, employment and ecological aspects of exploration and/or production of oil and gas at the licensed field. (Under prior legislation, such an oil and gas contract was called the 'Licence Agreement', and it was only required where a licence was issued to a joint venture with foreign investment.)

Suspension and termination of licences

The Oil and Gas Law has established a number of circumstances where a licence may be either suspended or permanently terminated by the state and financial sanctions may be imposed. The following circumstances may lead to a licence's suspension:

- violation of the terms of the licence or the Oil and Gas Operations Agreement;
- causing, by the licensed work, a direct threat to the life or health of the licensee's employees or the general population;
- repeated violation of the statutory requirements on environmental protection and inappropriate use of the subsoil;
- performing works not stipulated in the licence, except for exploration of new oil and gas reserves under a production licence within the licensed field.

After a licence has been suspended, the licensee must stop all work. The licence may be reinstated after the licensee has eliminated all of the reasons for its suspension (and paid any fines imposed in connection with the acts that led to the suspension). A licence may be terminated in the following cases:

1. if the licence is suspended and, within the required period, the licensee fails to eliminate the reasons for the suspension;
2. if the licensee does not use the licensed subsoil within 180 days after the licence is granted;
3. if the subsoil is used in a way that contravenes the purpose for which the licence was granted;
4. if the licensed subsoil is withdrawn as permitted by applicable law;
5. if the licence is declared to be void by a court or arbitral tribunal having jurisdiction;
6. if the licensed company is liquidated.

The termination of a licence normally results in automatic termination of the related Oil and Gas Operations Agreement. Any disputes arising out of such termination would be subject to litigation in Ukraine or, if so provided in the Oil and Gas Operations Agreement, to arbitration. Other statutes, like the Code, the Procedure, the Law 'On the Licensing of Certain Types of Business Activities' of 1 June 2000 and certain environmental laws, also provide grounds for a licence to be terminated or suspended, most of which mirror those stipulated in the Oil and Gas Law. In addition to the statutory provisions for the suspension and termination of licences, usually the Oil and Gas Operations Agreement will contain further grounds for the termination of a licence.

Product sharing agreements ('PSAs')

Legal status of PSAs

The PSA Law establishes an alternative legal structure for authorizing exploration and production, but it only applies in specially designated areas, which in principle are those with less appealing prospects. According to the PSA Law, in a production sharing agreement, one party, the state, assigns to another one or more other parties, the investor, the right to carry out the exploration and production of natural resources in one or more designated subsoil areas, together with related works, during a specified period of time. In return, the investor undertakes to carry out such exploration and production and related works at its own cost and risk.

Under a PSA, the investor's expenses may be reimbursed in production ('cost compensation production'). The production ('profit production') remaining after the distribution of this cost compensation production is then shared between the investor and the state. A PSA may include any number of investors, provided that if there is more than one investor, they must bear joint and several liability for their contractual obligations and an operator must be appointed to manage the operations.

The PSA Law requires a PSA to be approved by a special Permanent Interdepartmental Commission (the 'Permanent Commission') consisting of the representatives of the state bodies involved, the local government authorities and some members of Parliament. This Permanent Commission is authorized by the PSA Law and the Resolution of the Cabinet of Ministers 'On the Commission for the Organization of the Execution and Performance of PSAs' of 16 March 2002 to decide all issues concerning the negotiation and performance of a PSA.

A foreign investor (which may be an entity or an individual) wishing to enter into a PSA must prove that it, he or she possesses the required technology, capital and qualifications by presenting appropriate documents issued according to the law of the investor's country.

The terms of a PSA

The PSA Law requires that a PSA expressly contain, among other provisions:

1. a description of the subsoil area (resource deposits) subject to the PSA, and an estimated amount of the natural resources to be produced;
2. the terms for using land for operations, and a plan for restoration of the land after termination of operations;
3. a list of the works to be carried out and the investment and terms for their performance;
4. the rental fees for the use of the subsoil, and the geological fees for the geological exploration works previously completed at the expense of the state;
5. the point for measurement of production ('point of measurement');
6. the method for determining the production that will be used as cost compensation production, and the expenses that can be reimbursed with it;
7. the terms for sharing the remaining profit production between the state and the investor;
8. the rights of the state to supervise the investor's works, and the investor's obligations to report to the Permanent Commission;
9. the terms for any assignment by the investor of its rights and obligations under the PSA;
10. the duration of the PSA.

The PSA Law also requires that the investor, when performing the PSA, should preferentially use Ukrainian products, works and services where they offer equivalent price, quality and compliance with the international standards. Investors are obliged to hire a primarily Ukrainian labour force as well as to provide the necessary training for these workers.

Conclusion of the PSA and the requirements for investors

The right to enter into a PSA is usually awarded on the basis of a tender. The decision of the Cabinet of Ministers to hold a PSA tender should indicate, *inter alia*, the particular subsoil area involved, the terms for the works, the required investment and the tender procedure. The Permanent Commission must approve the tender documentation, and then publish it in official Ukrainian periodicals and the foreign mass media.

The following criteria are, under the PSA Law, intended to be significant in determining the winner of a tender:

1. whether the prospective investor's proposed programme of works ensures the most rational use and protection of natural resources and the environment;
2. whether it uses the most effective technological solutions;
3. whether it proposes the most attractive investment terms;
4. whether the prospective investor has sufficient financial resources and international experience.

The winner of the tender is determined by the Cabinet of Ministers after it takes into consideration the proposals and conclusions of the Permanent Commission.

The PSA Law allows a PSA to be entered into by negotiation, without the need to hold a tender, only in the following circumstances:

1. the prospective investor is the only bidder for a tender, and it fulfils all of the proposed tender conditions;
2. the subsoil area is thought to possess a low level of mineral reserves;
3. the prospective investor already has commercial activities under a licence for the exploration or production of natural resources, in which case the negotiated PSA replaces the licence and related Oil and Gas Operations Agreement;
4. where a tender is held, a PSA should be concluded with the winner of the tender no later than 12 months from the date of official publication of the tender's results. At the investor's request, this time period may be extended for up to a further six months.

Relations between the investor and the state during the performance of a PSA

The distribution of profit production between the investor and the state is carried out in accordance with the PSA and a number of mandatory provisions established in the PSA Law. This distribution must take place at least once every three months, and the quarterly share of the production that is passed to the investor as cost compensation production to reimburse the investor for expenses should not exceed 70 per cent of the total production.

Title to ownership of production (both cost compensation production and profit production) passes to the investor only after the production reaches the point of measurement. After acquiring title to production, the investor is free to choose the manner of its disposition, including by sale or barter in Ukraine or by export.

According to the PSA Law, any such disposal is not subject to export licensing, quota regimes or any other restrictions in Ukraine, unless such limitations have been incorporated in the PSA or were stated as conditions of the tender. However, as discussed below, these export rights for gas are now subject to restrictions pursuant to a Ukrainian treaty with Russia. If the investor is prohibited from exporting by the PSA or the tender terms, then the PSA Law guarantees that the price for domestic sales by the investor shall not be lower than the international market price.

The PSA Law provides that title to the state's share of the profit production is required to be transferred to the state only after the investor has received its cost compensation production. Even after such transfer of title to the state, the investor has a prior right, as necessary, to use this production for the performance of the PSA.

The state is obliged to grant to an investor under a PSA all the approvals, quotas and permissions necessary for its exploration and production activities under the PSA, as well as all site allocation acts and land use documents required for its performance of the PSA. As noted earlier, activities under a PSA are exempt from the need for an exploration or production licence and from regulation under the Oil and Gas Law.

Taxation and foreign exchange regulations

Ukraine's tax laws are generally applicable to companies involved in oil and gas activities. Exceptionally, the PSA Law modifies this tax regime by providing that an investor under a PSA is only obliged to pay the following taxes and fees:

- enterprise profits tax ('Profits Tax');
- value added tax (VAT);

- geological fee in respect of geological exploration works that have been previously performed at the state's expense;
- state, social and pension insurance for the Ukrainian and foreign workers employed in Ukraine;
- a rental fee for the use of the subsoil.

One of the most important tax advantages of a PSA is that it may provide for special depreciation rates, so that highly accelerated depreciation might become possible. The import and export VAT and customs regime under a PSA is very favourable for investors. Neither VAT nor customs and excise duties (except for the customs fee, a minor charge for processing documents) need to be paid when importing into Ukraine goods, works and services for the performance of the PSA. The same duty-free customs regime exists for exports of production under the PSA (subject to treaty restriction on gas exports, discussed below), and VAT on such exports is at a zero rate. However, if production is sold within Ukraine, then VAT must be paid according to the rules generally applicable for domestic sales, although it is possible to substitute production for cash to pay such VAT. These VAT and customs privileges apply as well for an investor's subcontractors.

With regard to Profits Tax (generally assessed on companies at a basic rate of 25 per cent) the PSA Law also permits investors the opportunity to substitute transfers of production for required cash payments, with the possibility that the PSA may define the basis for such transfers. This leaves open the possibility for use of a specially fixed oil and gas price to value such production, so that the amount of production to be used for Profits Tax, as well as VAT, may be more easily budgeted and calculated on a suitable basis. In addition, losses may be carried forward indefinitely.

The amount of the geological fee for geological exploration works previously performed at the state's expense and the rental fee for the use of the subsoil are also to be specified by the parties in the PSA itself, so preferential rates are possible.

Under the PSA law, payments (as well as distributions in kind) abroad to foreign investors are free of withholding tax. Withholding tax is ordinarily applied on payments abroad at a 15 per cent rate, except as may be reduced by applicable tax treaties.

Under the PSA Law, foreign currency may be imported without restriction. The PSA Law also guarantees the right of the investor freely to convert funds received under the PSA into Ukrainian or foreign currency and to transfer such foreign currency earnings abroad according to the PSA. Further, the investor is not subject to the National Bank of Ukraine's mandatory requirements for the compulsory sale of foreign currency receipts in exchange for Ukrainian currency (hryvnia) at the Ukrainian currency markets.

Protection of foreign investment and dispute resolution

A number of special measures aimed at the protection of foreign investors and their investments are provided for in the PSA Law, in particular, and Ukrainian law, in general. One of these measures is Article 27 ('Article 27'), the 'stabilization article', of the PSA Law. Article 27 guarantees that the rights and obligations of the parties established in a PSA shall be governed for the duration of the PSA by the legislation of Ukraine that was effective at the time of the conclusion of the PSA. The only exemptions to this special rule are for changes in law for matters of national defence and security, the maintenance of public order and environmental protection.

Disputes arising out of PSAs, as well as oil and gas licences and Oil and Gas Operations Agreements, may be referred to Ukrainian commercial (state) courts or, if agreed by the parties, to international arbitral institutions or *ad hoc* arbitration. This right to arbitration is supported by Ukraine's being a party to most of the international arbitration conventions, including the New York Convention on the Recognition and Enforcement of Foreign Arbitral Awards and the Washington Convention on the Settlement of Investment Disputes. Ukraine is also a party to a great number of bilateral investment treaties that provide for the arbitration of disputes.

The relative advantages and disadvantages of using a PSA

Using a PSA has a number of advantages, including in particular the following:

1. The duration of the PSA, as determined by the parties, may be up to 50 years from the date of its signing, whereas the maximum duration is 30 years for an oil and gas production licence and 10 years for an exploration licence (although extensions may be possible). The PSA Law also establishes the possibility that the maximum term for a PSA can be extended beyond 50 years if the investor has performed all of its contractual obligations under the PSA and the Cabinet of Ministers consents to the extension. If the PSA is so extended, then the duration of all approvals, quotas, permits, etc, granted in connection with the PSA are also extended.

2. No labour permits are required to employ foreign individuals in Ukraine for works as provided in a PSA.

3. There are tax advantages, as described above, being principally that (a) Profits Tax and domestic VAT can be paid in production in accordance with the PSA, (b) the PSA may provide for special accelerated depreciation rates, (c) there is no import or export VAT and no customs duty (subject to treaty provisions), (d) losses may be carried

forward indefinitely and (e) there is no withholding tax on distributions to an investor abroad.

4. Except for laws concerning environmental protection, security and public order and national defence and for laws arising from new treaties or constitutional amendments, the Ukrainian laws governing the rights and obligations of the investor for the duration of the PSA shall be those in effect when the PSA is signed, including accounting rules on the calculation of expenses. This allows for greater certainty in planning, in particular as it means that no new or higher taxes can apply. However, it also means that an investor may not benefit from improvements in Ukrainian law, at least unless the PSA is amended specially to provide for such benefits. Ideally, a provision in the PSA should be included to allow the investor, as a matter of its contract with the state, to benefit from those subsequent laws that the investor nominates as being beneficial.
5. The PSA Law limits the right of state and local governmental bodies to impose regulations conflicting with the PSA, except where labour safety or environmental protection is concerned.

There are, however, certain disadvantages of operating under a PSA including, in particular, the following:

1. The state acquires title to all equipment and other assets for which the investor's expenses are reimbursed by cost compensation production. Although the investor receives a 'preferential right' thereafter to use such equipment and other assets to perform the PSA, the practical value of this preferential use right, and whether there are limits on it, is not clear.
2. The PSA Law requires that, every five years, the Cabinet of Ministers and the Permanent Commission must carry out an audit of the investor's performance under the PSA and, if 'substantial transgressions' are found to have been committed, then the Cabinet of Ministers is obliged to terminate the PSA. This would appear to pose a great risk.
3. The PSA imposes an express requirement for the investor to compensate fully for all environmental damage caused by its activities, with a binding presumption that the investor is responsible unless it can prove that the damage was caused by natural events or the intentional acts of the victims. Consequently, the investor can apparently be liable for environmental damage resulting from negligent acts by others at its facilities, a form of strict liability.

Limitation on gas exports under the Russian–Ukrainian treaty

Although the Oil and Gas Law, PSA Law and other Ukrainian legislation provide that gas produced in Ukraine may be exported, such exports may be subject to treaty-imposed restrictions. Under Article 9, clause 1, of the Ukrainian Constitution, properly ratified treaties of Ukraine are a part of Ukrainian law. The Law 'On International Treaties' of 22 December 1993 further provides that treaties prevail over statutes and all other legal acts (apart from the Constitution of Ukraine). The PSA Law also expressly provides, in Article 36, that in the event that any provision of a treaty conflicts with the PSA Law, the treaty shall prevail.

Originally, gas export restrictions were imposed in Article 5 ('Article 5') of the Treaty between the Cabinet of Ministers of Ukraine and the Government of the Russian Federation on Guarantees for the Transiting of Russian Natural Gas through the Territory of Ukraine of 22 December 2000 ('Russian–Ukrainian Gas Treaty'). Article 5 established that, in order to prevent the export of natural gas from Ukraine, Ukraine would introduce an export duty on natural gas in the amount of USD140 per 1,000 cubic metres. Such a high export duty effectively prohibited gas exports.

On 4 October 2001, the Cabinet of Ministers of Ukraine and the Government of the Russian Federation signed the Treaty on Additional Measures on Procuring the Transiting of Russian Natural Gas through the Territory of Ukraine, which was ratified on 15 November 2001 ('Treaty on Additional Measures'). This Treaty on Additional Measures generally extends the effectiveness of the prior Russian–Ukrainian Gas Treaty to 2013, but this extension does not apply for certain articles and addenda, including Article 5. Instead, Article 5 of the Treaty on Additional Measures (New Article 5) provides that Ukraine, during the effective term of the Treaty on Additional Measures, will impose an export fee on gas exported from Ukraine.

New Article 5 states that the rate for this new export 'fee', and the amounts of gas to be exempted from the export fee, will be determined by inter-governmental protocols. Currently discussions are taking place between the governments of Ukraine and Russia on the amounts of gas to be exempted from this export fee regime, but no decision has yet been taken on any protocols. While the discussions on the protocols are ongoing, Ukrainian state-owned pipeline companies are, in general, refusing to transport gas exports to the Ukrainian border.

This is an important problem since the domestic Ukrainian gas price is only about half of the price elsewhere in Europe, owing to gas imports into Ukraine from Russia at preferential prices. The restrictions on exports sought by Russia are not necessarily unreasonable; Russia would not want its cheaper gas delivered to Ukrainian state companies to be used by them merely to replace locally produced gas so that the local gas can be exported at higher prices, in competition with other Russian gas exports. Such considerations should not apply, however, to foreign companies that have previously invested in new gas exploration and development in Ukraine in reliance on the provisions in most Ukrainian Oil and Gas Operations Agreements (as well as licence agreements under the prior legislation) and current legislation that their gas production can be freely exported. Hopefully, in recognition of this, the Ukrainian government will obtain exemptions from the new export fee for all foreign-financed gas production.

To encourage foreign investment in gas exploration and production, the PSA Law requires that domestic gas prices paid by the state should be equal to international prices where a PSA itself prohibits exports, but this statutory price protection does not apply where exports are only limited by a treaty. Presumably, in 1999 when the PSA Law was adopted, it was not anticipated that a Ukrainian treaty would override the PSA Law's guarantees on the right to export gas duty-free.

Conclusion

Ukraine possesses considerable potential oil and gas deposits. The government's announced policy will reduce Ukraine's substantial dependence on imported oil and gas by promoting the development of domestic oil and gas. In this context, it is expected that, to encourage major foreign investments, favourable terms may presently be negotiated in Ukrainian Oil and Gas Operations Agreements and PSAs.

Ukraine International Airlines: Twelve Successful Years

History and structure

Ukraine International Airlines (UIA) is Ukraine's leading international airline. It was founded in 1992, a year after Ukraine became an independent state. It was one of the first joint ventures with foreign capital in Ukraine. UIA was the first airline in the CIS to become a full member of the International Air Transport Association (IATA) and the first airline in the former Soviet Union to introduce new Boeing 737 aircraft.

Over the years since its creation, UIA has satisfied all the goals set out in its Foundation documents: creating a high quality, competitive, international Ukrainian airline; expanding and integrating Ukraine's aviation industry worldwide; introducing the best technology and management methods; attracting foreign investment and earning profits.

The founding shareholders of Ukraine International Airlines were the Ukrainian Association of Civil Aviation and Guinness Peat Aviation (GPA), an Irish aircraft leasing company. In 1995, the Ukrainian government's shares in the airline were transferred to the State Property Fund of Ukraine. In 1996, Austrian Airlines and Swissair became shareholders, investing USD9 million in new equity. Then in 2000, the European Bank for Reconstruction and Development (EBRD) invested USD5.4 million and became a shareholder, making UIA the only scheduled airline in the world in which the EBRD owns equity. Ownership of UIA is now as follows: the State Property Fund of Ukraine: 61.6 per cent, Austrian Airlines: 22.5 per cent, debis AirFinance: 6 per cent, EBRD: 9.9 per cent.

Today UIA's fleet consists of seven modern Boeing 737 aircraft. Two more B737–400s will soon be added to these, the first in October 2004, and the second in spring 2005. Although it is 38 per cent foreign-owned, UIA has only five foreign executives, less than one per cent of a total staff of over 800.

Current operations

UIA's headquarters are in Kiev. Its base airport is Kiev-Boryspil International Airport, where it has a joint handling company, 'Interavia'. There are over 40 representative offices in Ukraine and abroad, and tickets for UIA flights are sold in 70 countries worldwide. UIA operates direct flights from Kiev to most major cities in Europe, and has 160 flights per week. Its international destinations include London, Amsterdam, Brussels, Paris, Berlin, Frankfurt, Frankfurt-Simferopol, Vienna, Vienna-Odessa, Vienna-Kharkiv, Vienna-Dnipropetrovsk, Zurich, Rome, Madrid, Barcelona, Lisbon, Helsinki, Copenhagen, and Dubai. This year the airline opened up new markets in the Middle East (Kuwait) and Africa (Tripoli). The airline has also developed a domestic network, which services Ukraine's regions: Lviv, Kharkov, Donetsk, Dnipropetrovsk, Odessa, Ivano-Frankovsk, Zaporyzhya and Simferopol.

In parallel to the expansion of its passenger services, UIA's Cargo Division continues to grow the cargo network. In addition to the capacity of UIA's scheduled network, the airline operates freighter flights to Brussels and Vienna. The direct freighter operations to Vienna were launched in 2003 on An-12 aircraft. The volumes of cargo transportation at UIA increase steadily each year.

Partnerships and standards

UIA works in partnership with Austrian Airlines, with whom it has cooperation agreements on both passenger and freight services from Vienna to Kiev, Odessa, Dnipropetrovsk, Lviv and Kharkov. The airline has similar agreements with Iberia Airlines, KLM Royal Dutch Airlines, SN Brussels Airlines, Swiss International Airlines, TAP Air Portugal, Finnair, Cimber Air and Kuwait Airways. UIA also cooperates with other Ukrainian carriers on a number of domestic routes.

In December 2003, UIA became a full member of the KSAF Insurance Group, the biggest airline alliance for aviation insurance. KSAF stands for the group's key members: KLM, SAS, Austrian Airlines, and Finnair. UIA has worked closely with the group since 1996.

UIA operates to the highest standards: its Technical Division has full JAR-145 certification, which grants the right to carry out full technical maintenance on Western aircraft. UIA supplies technical support to other airlines in the region, for example Belavia (Belarus), Air Zena (Georgia), DniproAvia (Ukraine).

UIA also provides training services to the aviation and travel industries of Ukraine and other CIS countries. The airline works closely with the International Aviation Training Centre in Kiev, where its specialists train pilots and cabin crew for a number of airlines in the region. In addition, UIA sales staff provide IATA training for travel agents. UIA is also a partner of the National Aviation University of Ukraine, which provides training support for technicians and engineers.

UIA has a reputation for reliability: over 88 per cent of all Ukraine International flights depart on time. This is significantly better than the industry average. Technical dispatch reliability for UIA's B737 fleet in 2004 averages 99.67 per cent, which is well ahead of industry norms.

UIA applies best business practice, and actively supports corporate governance in Ukraine. In 2004, UIA co-sponsored a brochure about corporate governance published by the International Finance Corporation. The aim was to educate businessmen in Ukraine about the principles of good corporate governance and business ethics.

Since it began, UIA has competed successfully with some of the best known airlines in the world, including British Airways, Air France, Austrian Airlines, Swissair, Lufthansa, and KLM. UIA has succeeded in the market place: for 10 out of 12 years, the airline has made an operating profit. The airline has grown rapidly in recent years: traffic and revenue grew by approximately 30 per cent in 2003. In 2003, UIA achieved total revenues of over USD100 million and operating profit was USD2.8 million. This growth continues: in the first quarter of 2004, UIA experienced a further 30 per cent growth, in spite of the continuous rise in world fuel prices. In 2004, UIA will carry over 600,000 passengers.

UKRPRODUCT GROUP

Dear Reader,

Hello and thank you for your interest in Ukrproduct Group!

This is one of the hardest tasks I've ever faced: to present Ukrproduct Group to the professional readers of such a well-known business publication as *Doing Business with Ukraine*.

I'll start with the numbers:

- We had over £17 million turnover and £1 million profits in the 2003 financial year.
- We produced and sold 6,500 tons of processed cheese and 5,900 tons of packaged butter in 2003 – more than anyone else in Ukraine.
- We achieved all this within the last three years.
- We ARE publicity-shy – you'll never see us advertise directly.
- We ARE a big company – and growing bigger by the minute.
- We ARE also a brand name company – you'll see our products sold everywhere in Ukraine.

The following pages will provide you with background information about Ukrproduct Group, the company I am proud to serve as Chief Executive Officer. I hope you find this information helpful – I am always ready and willing to deal personally with any questions you may have about us.

May I take this opportunity to wish every success to you personally and to all those who may be interested in learning more about our business.

With best wishes,

Iryna Yevets
CEO

Ukrproduct Group
14th floor, 39-41 Shota Rustaveli, St.
Kiev, 01023, Ukraine
Tel./Fax: +380 44 251 80 14

Ukrproduct Group

The group

Ukrproduct Group is one of Ukraine's youngest, most profitable, and fastest-growing Fast Moving Consumer Goods (FMCG) companies. The group has existed since 2000 and produces milk-based products, such as processed cheese, butter and powdered milk. Its managers say its success is the result of ambition, perseverance and growth: in 2001 they restructured an unprofitable business, the joint stock company, Molochnik, and turned it into what is now a highly successful company. Today it is the group's main production facility.

Sales grew from almost nothing in the year 2000 to over £17 million in 2003. In 2004, the Group aims to double its turnover and is looking at an operating profit of £2.5 million. From zero asset capitalization in 2000, Ukrproduct plans to float on the London Stock Exchange's Alternative Investment Market before the end of this year.

At the moment, the Group is principally involved in the production and supply of brand name milk-based products (packaged butter and processed cheese) to wholesale and retail outlets in Ukraine. The Group's distribution network is the most advanced among food producers in Ukraine and covers the whole country. The second area of business is powdered milk, which the Group produces and exports to Japan, Turkey, Russia and elsewhere. The Group is not involved in retailing.

Brands

Over the years, the Group has built up a range of well-known brand names that are highly regarded in Ukraine:

- **Products associated with tradition**
  This brand category includes processed cheeses marketed under the names 'Nash Molochnik – Druzhba' ('Our Milkman means Friendship'), 'Nash Molochnik Golandsky' ('Our Dutch Milkman'), as well as several varieties of packaged butter, such as 'Nash Molochnik' ('Our Milkman') and 'Vershkova Dolyna' ('Vershkova Valley'). This group of products is mainly geared towards customers in the low- to middle-income brackets.

- **Products for the cost-conscious, quality-oriented customer**
  This brand group includes a wide variety of processed cheeses ('Narodny Product' – 'The People's Product'), as well as individual products aimed at particular consumer groups, eg diet butters with the Frantsuzskoye' ('French') umbrella brand name, directed at the health conscious consumer. This brand group is also primarily designed for middle-income customers.
- **Upmarket products for the discerning customer**
  Products in this brand group include 'Kremlyovskoye' ('Kremlin') butter and a variety of sausage shaped cheeses containing spices and natural condiments. The target audience is the high-income consumer who is looking for a high quality product and for whom the symbol of the Kremlin has appeal.
- **Industrial milk-based products**
  Since January 2003, these products have been promoted under the UKRPRODUCT™ brand name; they are now well known in both European and Southeast Asian markets.

The team

The Group's executive team represents more than 40 years of combined management experience and success in the food industry, both in Ukraine and abroad. It is experienced in every aspect of the business: production, finance, sales & distribution, marketing and human resources. Each individual contributes to the success of the company. Ukrproduct believes it is well positioned to take advantage of continuing economic growth in Ukraine and the recent upsurge of investor interest.

Operating highlights

- two modern manufacturing plants in central and western Ukraine; overall manufacturing capacity: 1400 tons of processed cheese, 1,000 tons of packaged butter and 330 tons of powdered milk a month;
- ISO-certified production and advanced quality control system;
- distribution system with 24/7 delivery capacity across Ukraine;
- full export capability and a range of well-known overseas partners.

The future

Ukrproduct aims first and foremost to enhance shareholder value by delivering what it promises to deliver. Today it is a focused quality foods business, catering for a mass market, and embracing all consumer groups in Ukraine. In addition to expanding its market share in the core sectors, processed cheese and butter, the Group intends to develop new products, such as hard cheese and spreads.

It will not diversify, however. Ukrproduct believes its core strengths are its clear focus, its dedication to excellence, and its meticulous delivery of those simple necessities in life, cheese and butter. Simple necessities they may be, but the Group believes they are more than just commodities: they are brand-name packages full of natural goodness and enjoyment. Ukrproduct produces and delivers these packages. It is a service company and intends to remain one in the future.

How Ukrproduct can help foreign businesses

Ukraine is a promising place to do business. It is politically stable, there is no terrorist threat, and the population's fast-growing affluence means there are many opportunities for new businesses. Ukrproduct has been helping its partners to develop their commercial interests in Ukraine since 2001. The Group has worked with some of the biggest food manufacturers in Germany, France, New Zealand and Russia. It prides itself on relationships built on commercial common sense and mutual respect.

- Ukrproduct encourages **foreign investors** interested in investing in a fast-growing, quality foods company in a stable emerging market to call in and see the Ukrproduct business for themselves. The Group welcomes sensible offers of equity funding to fuel its continuing growth.
- Ukrproduct offers to assist **foreign companies in the FCMG sector that wish to enter Ukraine** by establishing partnerships to support their efforts. Ukrproduct knows the country and its people, runs a highly profitable business, and firmly believes that respectful collaboration is the best way forward for newcomers in Ukraine.
- **Trade partners**: Ukrproduct will consider various forms of Cupertino: alliances, joint ventures, contractual collaboration, and others. It aims to help its partners achieve their goals.
- **Business advice or restructuring**: Ukrproduct offers expertise and organizational know-how in the following areas: FMCG manufacturing, distribution & logistics, branding & differentiation.

Part Three

Getting Established: The Taxation and Legal Environment

3.1

Legal Forms of Doing Business in Ukraine

Bate C Toms and Svitlana Kheda,
BC Toms & Co

Introduction

Since gaining its independence in 1991, Ukraine has been steadily liberalizing its economy and reducing the state's regulation and control. The legal environment for operations in Ukraine by foreign entities has benefited from this general trend.

Presently, foreign persons and entities can conduct business in Ukraine using a variety of different methods. These include operating through a Ukrainian company or a Ukrainian branch or representative office of a foreign company, by engaging in a contractual joint venture with a Ukrainian counterparty, or by having direct business contracts with consumers in Ukraine. The choice of the appropriate method depends on the particular needs and interests of the foreign entity, eg the projected volume of its operations in Ukraine and the extent and type of involvement in the relevant Ukrainian industry. This chapter provides an overview of the relative advantages presented by each of these methods, concentrating primarily on the corporate forms of doing business in Ukraine.

Ukrainian corporate law experienced a revolutionary change when on 1 January 2004 the new Civil Code of Ukraine became effective (replacing the Soviet 1961 Code of the Ukrainian SSR) and the Commercial Code of Ukraine. The results have so far been mixed. The new Civil Code is certainly a significant step forward in regulating all private law matters, generally in a more liberal fashion. It provides detailed regulation on many basic issues of private law and introduces concepts that were not previously covered by the old Civil Code (or even by Ukrainian law in general), like factoring transactions, firm (company) name protection, and non-disclosure of proprietary information (know-how). The Commercial Code to a large extent repeats and generalizes existing legislation, while also introducing a few progressive ideas. However, the drafters of the two codes did not manage to escape a certain overlap, which may result in controversies over the applicability of either of the codes to a particular transaction.

Establishing a company

Presently, the entire registration procedure for a company in Ukraine, including registration with all appropriate local state bodies (eg with the State Statistics Committee, State Tax Inspection, Fund of Social Security in Case of Temporary Disability, Fund of Social Security in Case of Industrial Accidents and Industrial Diseases, State Employment Centre and Pension Fund) in practice takes from two weeks to one month. It usually begins with the collection of the required documents from the foreign founders (ie certificate of incorporation, extract from the trade or court register, etc) and drafting a charter and/or foundation agreement for the Ukrainian company.The charter is, under the new Codei, the only foundation document for most companies, being the main document governing the internal organization and operations of the company. In the past a foundation agreement was also required. The foundation agreement is a type of joint venture agreement that governs the relationship between the founders while the company is being formed. Under the new Codei, it is only required for the relatively rare full liability and mixed liability companies, for which the foundation agreement is the only foundation document.

These documents must be drafted with care, particularly as Ukrainian corporate law now develops so rapidly. For example, traditionally Ukrainian corporate law followed the doctrine of the 'limited legal capacity' of a legal entity, based on which a legal entity only has such rights as are expressly granted by its founders in its charter. Such authorized capacity had to be specifically described. Any contract or other action of a company that exceeded the expressly provided capacity could be declared invalid. The new Civil Code introduces to Ukrainian law the 'general legal capacity' concept under which a company shall be free to engage in any activities (at least, if certain types of activities are not specifically prohibited by the charter). However, activities of the company that do not correspond to the company's 'aims' as stated in its charter, for example, if charitable activity is conducted by a commercial company, should not be carried out on a regular basis, as otherwise there is a risk that a court may terminate the company on the basis that its activities contradict its charter (and/or any foundation agreement). After the state registration is completed, the newly established company may, in principle, engage in any type of business activities, if it is not directly forbidden by Ukrainian law, provided that it obtains where required, all applicable permissions and licences.

On 15 May 2003, the Ukrainian Parliament passed the Law of Ukraine 'On the State Registration of Legal Entities and Individual Entrepreneurs', which came into force on 1 July 2004. This Law establishes a new simplified procedure for the state registration of companies. Although the documents required for state registration remain largely the same, the Law provides for the creation of a new governmental authority, the State Registrar, responsible for the state registration of companies and individual entrepreneurs. The State Registrar database is now on a nationwide basis and is open to the public. At the same time, the Commercial Code envisages a registration procedure almost identical to the existing one, so, it is presently difficult to predict how this conflict will be resolved.

Foreign investment regulation

On 19 March 1996, the Law of Ukraine 'On Regime of Foreign Investment' (the 'Foreign Investment Law') was adopted. The Commercial Code also contains provisions regulating foreign investment. In accordance with the Foreign Investment Law, a company with at least 10 per cent foreign capital in its authorized capital fund is considered to be a foreign investment company. Ukrainian law establishes a national legal regime for investment and any other business activities of foreign investors, subject to any exceptions expressly created by law (including international treaties of Ukraine). The national legal regime gives foreign and national investors equal investment rights and obligations.

Under the Foreign Investment Law, foreign investments can be contributed, without limitation, in the following forms: (1) hard currency; (2) tangible and intangible property and property rights; (3) securities and corporate rights; (4) intellectual property rights; and (5) rights to carry out certain types of business activity (including rights to the use of natural resources, etc).

To help secure its interests in a Ukrainian company, a foreign investor should register its investment with an appropriate state administration. Theoretically, this registration should be completed within three days from the date of filing all the required documents with the registration body. However, the process can take longer, in particular, if the registration body raised any questions.

This state registration gives the foreign investor the right to certain special guarantees and protection mechanisms. These include protection of the foreign investment from nationalization and a guaranteed right of repatriation of the investment and income derived from it, as well as a

10-year moratorium on the effects of any subsequent legislation changing any of these guarantees. A foreign investor also has the legal right to compensation for all losses, including lost profits and moral damages, incurred as a result of an act or omission of any Ukrainian state bodies. As a matter of practice, there are no reported cases where such compensation has been successfully recovered, though as the Ukrainian legal system develops, it should be possible.

Choice of corporate form

The most well-established legal regime for corporate formation is that established under the Law 'On Business Associations' of 19 September 1991, according to which the following types of Ukrainian companies may be founded, including by foreign investors:

- joint stock company (open or closed);
- limited liability company;
- additional liability company;
- full liability company (similar to a general partnership);
- mixed liability company (similar to a limited partnership or *Kommanditgesellschaft* under German law).

Joint stock companies and limited liability companies are the most popular corporate forms among foreign and domestic investors in Ukraine. They both provide for limited liability to share holders or, technically, for limited liability companies, their 'participation' holders, as they do not issue shares, but rather have recorded, participation interests, as explained below (ie the risk is limited to their contributions to the authorized capital of these companies). Additional liability companies are generally regulated in the same way as limited liability companies except that their participants are liable for the company's obligations beyond their contributions to the authorized capital up to a specified amount. Ukrainian general and limited partnerships (unlike the similar legal forms in the 'common law countries') are legal entities under Ukrainian law, and for various reasons, are rarely chosen by foreign investors.

From 1 January 2004, when the new Civil Code came into effect, joint stock companies, limited liability companies and companies with additional liability can exist with only one shareholder. This was previously impossible under the Law 'On Business Associations', which required at least two founders (even if 100 per cent was beneficially owned and controlled by a single corporate group as a 'subsidiary' – as that term is used in the West).

Depending on the legal form of a company, the law requires a minimum amount as paid-up capital. As of 1 September 2004, the required minimum paid-up capital for a joint stock company is 296,250 hryvnias (which is currently equal to approximately USD55,896) and for a limited liability company is 23,700 hryvnias (which is currently equal to approximately USD4,472). The amount of paid-up capital that is required typically increases over time as it depends on the amount of the minimum wage as established from time to time by the Parliament of Ukraine.

A number of other forms of companies that were created in the past on the basis of the Law 'On Enterprises' of 27 March 1991, were abolished by the repeal of this Law by the Commercial Code. The most common of these were the private enterprise founded by one individual and the 'ad hoc' subsidiary enterprise. There were initially merely some ambiguous references in the 1991 Law 'On Business Associations' as the legislative basis for the subsidiary enterprise. Typically, such a subsidiary enterprise was founded by one legal entity. The Commercial Code introduces detailed classifications for enterprises, but it is not yet clear whether these enterprises will exist as separate forms or whether they must now use one of the forms for a business association, which is the most likely outcome.

Selected forms of Ukrainian companies

Joint stock company

The legal form and functioning of a Ukrainian joint stock company is similar to the joint stock company of the continental legal system. This corporate form has the following characteristics:

- the authorized capital fund is divided into a certain number of shares (as determined in the charter), each having equal nominal value;
- the company's liability is limited to its assets;
- the risk of the shareholders is limited to their shares in the company.

Under the Law 'On Business Associations', there are two types of joint stock companies: open and closed. The Commercial Code also provides for open and closed joint stock companies (the new Civil Code does not distinguish between these two types).

A Ukrainian open joint stock company is a public issuer of shares, which implies that the company has a right to distribute its shares among an unlimited number of persons. It can issue registered or bearer shares.

The legal status of a closed joint stock company is not clearly defined by Ukrainian law. In a closed joint stock company only registered shares may be issued, which can be distributed only among the founders and cannot be freely distributed, including on a stock exchange. During the past two years, there has been a lot of controversy and litigation over whether the foundation documents of such a company may impose certain limitations on the shareholders rights to dispose of shares (pre-emption rights, etc). The Commercial Code, effective from 1 January 2004 adopted the position that the shareholders of a closed joint stock company have a pre-emption right to purchase shares from the other shareholders before they can sell to third parties. A similar provision is also included in the draft Law 'On Joint Stock Companies'. Nevertheless, it is still ambiguous whether such a pre-emption right applies if a shareholder wishes to dispose of his, her or its shares other than by sale, for example by gift. There is also no legal procedure on how to execute such a pre-emption right and there is still an issue as to what sanctions apply for violations of the pre-emption right, issues that presumably can be addressed by a company's charter.

For joint stock, liability and additional liability companies, Ukrainian law provides for two foundation documents, a foundation agreement and charter. From a legal standpoint, the foundation agreement is a joint venture agreement, and under the new Civil and Commercial Codes it is optional, as it is no longer required to found these companies. For full liability and mixed liability companies, which do not have a charter, the foundation agreement is their only foundation document.

One of the important issues related to the operation of joint stock companies is corporate governance. A joint stock company has a multilevel management structure. The highest managing body is the general meeting of shareholders that must be convened at least once a year to decide the main issues for the company's activities. At a general meeting of shareholders, most decisions must be adopted by a so-called 'simple majority vote' (ie 50 per cent plus one vote) of the shareholders present. However, decisions on amending the charter and to decide on the company's liquidation must be adopted by a 3/4-majority vote of the shareholders present. For a meeting to be validly held, there must be a quorum of shareholders attending who represent 60 per cent of the outstanding shares.

Ukrainian law also provides for the possibility to create a supervisory council, and for joint stock companies having more than 50 shareholders, the creation of this body is obligatory. The supervisory council is supposed to permit the shareholders to exercise more control over the company's management. The executive body of a joint stock company that manages its day-to-day activity is usually its board of directors, although under the new Civil Code, it can be any other collective body or even a single director, as determined by the charter.

Under the Law 'On Business Association', a company's activities are reviewed by the audit commission, which must consist of at least two members. The new Civil Code does not establish a requirement for any such special auditing controlling body, but instead only requires an obligatory annual independent audit inspection for those open joint stock companies that are public issuers of shares. As the Law 'On Business Associations' continues in effect, presumably audit commissions continue to be required, even for open joint stock companies.

By law, there is a list of issues that are referred to the competence of a general meeting of shareholders, some of which may be delegated to the supervisory council or the board of directors by the shareholders.

On 11 December 2003, the State Commission of Ukraine on Securities and the Stock Exchange adopted the 'Principles of Corporate Governance', which were developed to reflect generally accepted international standards of corporate governance. This should be viewed as a guidebook intended to recommend practices. In practice, minority shareholder rights are generally poorly protected in Ukraine in the absence of special charter provisions and other protections.

Limited liability company

A Ukrainian limited liability company is similar to a Ukrainian joint stock company in that its shareholders benefit from limited liability; however, it does not issue shares (stock). Instead, it has an authorized capital divided into a certain number of participation shares, the value of which is determined by the charter together with the foundation agreement, if one is used.

The profits of a limited liability company may be distributed in dividends pro rata to each participant's contributions to the company's authorized capital. In case a participant of a limited liability company withdraws its participation, then the participant's contribution must be returned in the form specified in the charter (and foundation agreement if any).

A limited liability company also has a simplified management structure. The highest body of the company is the general meeting of participants, which should be convened at least twice a year unless otherwise provided in the company's charter. The day-to-day management is handled by a collective executive body, or by a sole director, as the participants may decide. Under the Law 'On Business Association', a limited liability company's activities are reviewed by an audit commission, which must consist of at least three members; however, the new Civil Code does not require the creation of any such audit bodies.

Most decisions of the general meeting of participants must be adopted by a simple majority vote of the participants present at a meeting. However, decisions to determine the main types of the company's activity, to approve its plans and accounts, to amend the charter and remove a participant from the company (permitted in certain circumstances) must be adopted by participants holding more than 50 per cent of all of the votes of participants. The limited liability company is the most common form of doing business in Ukraine and is typically used for creation of a Ukrainian subsidiary by foreign multinationals.

Nevertheless, this form also has certain disadvantages, which for some investors may be crucial. One of the major drawbacks in using the limited liability company structure for some investors is the pre-emptive right of participants to purchase the participation share of the other participants that want to sell. Any participant has the right to withdraw from a limited liability company, resulting in cancellation of the participation share and a corresponding reduction of the authorized capital, so that the participant becomes entitled to compensation in respect of its participation share. As a practical matter, unless the charter and foundation agreement (if any) have been drafted specifically to anticipate such a situation, disputes often arise with respect to the methods of valuation of the withdrawing participant's share.

Another problem for any minority investor in a limited liability company is the provision of the 'Law on Business Association' allowing exclusion of a participant who 'systematically fails to comply with his, her or its obligations or prevents the company from reaching its goals'. A vote in favour of exclusion by participants holding a total of more than 50 per cent of all of the votes of participants is sufficient to exclude a participant.

Private enterprise

Private enterprises were previously formed on the basis of the Law 'On Enterprises' and based on ownership by one individual. Under the Commercial Code, a private enterprise can now be founded by one or several individuals or by one legal entity. As a separate legal entity, a private enterprise should give its owner/shareholder the full benefits of a limited investment risk, provided that its charter is drafted appropriately. One of the benefits of the private enterprise form is that the law does not require that any authorized capital be formed, so there is no minimum capital funding requirement, and in addition there are virtually no corporate formalities that must be complied with. The private enterprise is simply governed as provided by its charter.

Subsidiary enterprise

A subsidiary enterprise, also sometimes translated as a 'subsidiary company', is another unusual corporate form, which was created in the early 1990s and continued until adoption of the new Civil and Commercial Codes. A subsidiary enterprise is wholly owned by one founder, and should not be confused with the general Western term 'subsidiary' as applied to a company owned by a parent company. There was no detailed legislation or regulations defining how such enterprises must be organized or run. For example, there were no legislative provisions on the minimum amount of the charter fund for such entities or on what are their governing bodies. There have been a number of cases where issues on these matters have caused difficulties and misunderstandings between the founders of a subsidiary company and the state authorities. The operations of a subsidiary enterprise were therefore based largely on what the charter provided. Major multinationals and other large investors usually preferred to avoid this corporate form because of the lack of predictability in interpretations from the state authorities as to how it should be legally regulated. In this respect, the subsidiary enterprise was similar to the private enterprise described above.

The new Civil and Commercial Codes do not provide for any such 'subsidiary enterprise (company)' as a separate legal form. In defining a subsidiary company, the Commercial Code focuses on the economic and/or organizational dependence of a subsidiary enterprise to a controlling (holding) company. Therefore, the authors of the Commercial Code have finally reflected the Western concept of the term 'subsidiary company'. Under the Commercial Code, the company created in any legal form established by law is now considered a subsidiary company if the other (holding) company owns a controlling block of shares in such subsidiary company. Presumably, companies currently registered in the form of a 'subsidiary enterprise' will have to be re-registered into one of the existing corporate forms.

Other forms of doing business in Ukraine

Representative offices

A foreign legal entity may also operate in Ukraine through a representative office. This form of business activity is arguably the best option to have a minimal presence in the country. In Ukraine, a representative office of a foreign company does not, for most purposes, have the status of a separate Ukrainian legal entity and, therefore, is treated similarly to a branch of a resident Ukrainian company. The head of a representative office acts on the basis of a power of attorney issued by the mother foreign legal entity, and all contracts are concluded on behalf of the mother company. Unlike a resident Ukrainian legal entity, registration of a representative office is required with the Ministry of Economy of Ukraine.

Certain activities of representative offices of foreign companies may be exempt from income taxation in Ukraine, depending on the relevant tax treaty. Most tax treaties with Ukraine provide for tax exempt status for a number of representative office functions, such as market research, storage of certain goods, marketing and other ancillary activities. Often foreign companies trading in Ukraine from abroad by contract establish local representative offices to assist with the proper performance of their contracts. If, however, instead of merely providing tax exempt ancillary assistance for its foreign mother company, the representative office itself trades, for example generally buying and selling goods commercially, then it will be subject to corporate income tax on its Ukrainian source income like any Ukrainian company.

When compared with merely concluding business contracts without any Ukrainian presence, operation through a representative office provides a foreign legal entity with a number of rights and obligations. By way of illustration, a foreign legal entity may purchase and re-sell goods within Ukraine only if it has a duly registered Ukrainian representative office. A foreign company may purchase land in Ukraine from the state only if it has a Ukrainian representative office. A representative office has the obligation to withhold all taxes payable in Ukraine from the proceeds of transactions that it conducts that are payable to its head office.

Contractual joint venture

Another alternative for a foreign legal entity to conduct business in Ukraine is the contractual joint venture – known in Ukraine as a 'joint venture without the establishment of a legal entity'. Such a contractual joint venture must be created on the basis of a joint investment activity agreement between qualified subjects of business activity, such as legal entities and individuals specially registered as entrepreneurs.

Often foreign legal entities use joint investment activity agreements as a first step in a business relationship with a resident company or where it is difficult for them to obtain a necessary licence. For example, in the sphere of oil and gas exploration and production and for a certain construction activity, a foreign company may be unable as a practical matter to obtain a licence, but the foreign company could effectively use a local company's licence through a contractual joint venture. Since such a joint activity agreement may be drafted so as to be relatively easily suspended or terminated, such joint investment activity is often particularly suitable for the initial stages of a business project for a party that is uncertain that it will want to fully proceed with the other party.

Such joint investment activity is treated for Ukrainian tax and many other purposes separately from the general activities of the various parties to it. Both the property contributed to the joint investment activity and the proceeds arising from it must be accounted for on a separate balance sheet, and special bank accounts must be opened for the transactions of the joint investment activity. It is advisable to determine in the joint investment activity agreement who will be responsible for keeping the records, representing the interests of the joint investment activity and filing special reports on the joint investment activity to the relevant state bodies. Otherwise, it will be considered that all parties are jointly responsible for operating the joint investment activity, resulting in every transaction having to be approved by all of the parties of the joint investment activity. The parties to a joint investment activity agreement share profits as agreed among themselves or, if not so agreed, based on the relative value of their contractually specified contributions to their joint venture.

Direct contracting

A foreign legal entity may also conduct business in Ukraine by concluding direct business contracts with Ukrainian legal entities or individuals, whether or not it has any local presence. Most such business contracts fall within the legal criteria for special treatment under Ukrainian law as being 'foreign economic contracts'. In comparison to domestic business contracts, such foreign economic contracts may be governed by any law, Ukrainian or foreign, as chosen by the parties. There are relatively strict requirements as to the form for foreign economic contracts. A failure to satisfy form requirements may, as a matter of Ukrainian law, render such foreign economic contracts invalid, even if such matters of form are irrelevant under the foreign law stated to govern the contract. Numerous foreign investments have been cancelled on this basis, with the foreign party losing the benefits of its investments and sometimes the investment itself.

Conclusion

Although the increasingly liberal legal regime in Ukraine facilitates foreign investment, Ukraine has become a legalistic society and close attention must be paid to legal details when structuring and documenting any investment. The importance of full due diligence, including on compliance with corporate organization and other formalities, cannot be underestimated. Provided that the legal aspects are properly handled, a foreign company should be able to use any of the various legal forms for doing business to take advantage of investment opportunities arising as Ukraine's economy develops into a full, Western-style market economy.

3.2

Corporate Income Tax

KPMG

Corporate residence

Ukrainian corporate income tax law distinguishes between domestic companies and foreign companies based on their place of incorporation. Domestic companies (those incorporated in Ukraine) are taxed on their worldwide income whilst foreign companies are subject to corporate income tax on profits from business activities performed via a permanent establishment in Ukraine.

Permanent establishment of foreign legal entities

Non-residents engaging in business activities via a permanent establishment (PE) in Ukraine are subject to Ukrainian corporate profits tax. However, there are several methods for determining tax liability of a PE, including the direct method, split balance method and gross income method. According to the direct method, taxable profit is determined as gross taxable income (ie income of the permanent establishment received offshore or onshore) less allowable expenses incurred by the permanent establishment (ie expenses incurred offshore) and depreciation charges. Such taxable profits are subject to the applicable corporate profit tax. According to the split balance method, a non-resident should provide the tax authorities with financial and other data on the company's activities worldwide and particularly in Ukraine (eg number of staff in all countries where the company operates). On the basis of these data the local tax office apportions some part of the net overall profit to the Ukrainian operations. Such deemed profit will be subject to the applicable corporate profit tax liability. According to the gross income method, taxable profits are considered as the difference between gross income and deemed gross expenses. Gross expenses are calculated as gross income multiplied by 0.7. Accordingly, the formula for the taxable profits calculation is $TP = GI - 0.7 \times GI$. Given this, profit calculated using this method is subject to tax at the (current) rate of 30 per cent, and the effective taxation is 9 per cent of the gross income.

Taxable base

Taxable profit is determined based on adjusted gross income reduced by deductible costs and tax depreciation. For corporate income tax purposes, adjusted gross income means gross income (ie a company's worldwide income) received (accrued) during the reporting period either in cash, in kind or in intangible form. Gross income includes total income from the sale of goods (work, services), fixed assets and receipt of gratuitous transfers.

Ukraine uses an accrual and cash method to record expenses, although there are some anomalies that should be looked at closely. Revenues are recognized at the earlier of goods or services being provided or cash being received (eg if there is a prepayment).

Deductions

The existing law generally allows reasonable business expenses as tax deductible, with the exception of expenses explicitly disallowed or restricted by the law in a detailed list.

The disallowed or restricted expenses include the following:

- 50 per cent fuel for cars and car rental costs (except where the company's business is transportation, then such expenses are fully deductible);
- contractual penalties;
- expenses associated with warranty repairs (deductibility is restricted to 10 per cent of the total price of such goods sold and still under warranty);
- expenses incurred in connection with receptions, celebrations and similar events held for advertising purposes and connected with business activity (deductibility is limited to 2 per cent of the taxpayer's taxable profit for the respective period);
- other expenses not connected with business activity.

Tax rates and payment dates

The basic corporate income tax rate is currently 30 per cent, but will be reduced to 25 per cent from 1 January 2004. Special tax rates apply to certain types of income (eg income earned from Ukrainian sources by non-residents not engaged in business activities in Ukraine through a permanent establishment).

Corporate tax liabilities are self-assessed by taxpayers. Tax is payable on a quarterly basis.

Quarterly tax returns are due within 40 days from the end of the reporting quarter.

For corporate income tax purposes the tax year is the calendar year.

Payments to related parties

Transactions between related parties should be executed on the basis of 'fair market' prices, which generally would be paid under similar conditions to third (non-related) parties.

In order to be deductible, expenses should be supported by documentary evidence. In respect of payments to individuals or entities related to the taxpayer, the law explicitly states that the absence of documentary evidence concerning payments for services rendered can lead to disallowance. In practice this requirement becomes particularly important in respect of management fees, payments under secondment contracts and other inter-group cost (re) allocations.

Payments to non-residents in deemed tax havens

A restriction applies to the deductibility of payments made to non-residents in deemed tax haven locations. Such payments, provided that they are allowable deductions, can only be deducted at 85 per cent of their total amount. Tax haven locations are referred to as those which are listed in the relevant resolution of the Cabinet of Ministers of Ukraine.

Interest

Interest payments on loans required for the taxpayer's business are deductible. The Corporate Profit Tax Law of Ukraine restricts the tax deduction available for interest paid by Ukrainian resident companies where 50 per cent or more of their charter fund is owned or managed (directly or indirectly) by non-residents or those entities which use other than basic tax rate. This restriction applies provided that the interest is paid to non-resident entities or resident entities that meet similar foreign ownership tests (ie 50 per cent or more of the charter fund of residents is owned or managed directly or indirectly by non-residents) or taxpayers that are exempted from profits tax and entities which use other than the basic tax rate. In general terms, this restriction is set at 50 per cent of the available taxable profits of the taxpayer, adjusted for any interest received, interest paid and tax depreciation charges. Interest expenses thus disallowed can be carried forward to subsequent periods indefinitely. Some double taxation treaties may override this domestic provision, but each case should be examined separately.

Exemptions

The following are not included in taxable profit:

- capital contributions in return for an equity interest (ie in return for corporate rights);
- contributions in cash or in kind under joint activity agreements in Ukraine without creation of a legal entity;
- share premium received by a share issuer (the difference between the price of a share and its nominal value);
- dividends received (except for the dividends received from non-residents).

Foreign tax credit

A tax credit system is effective to avoid double taxation of income derived from abroad. A credit is allowed for foreign taxes paid up to the amount of Ukrainian tax due on such income, provided there is a tax treaty with the state in which the tax was paid (and proof of taxes paid can be obtained).

Ukrainian repatriation tax

Under current Ukrainian tax legislation Ukrainian source income, such as dividends, interest or royalties payable to non-Ukrainian residents, is subject to 15 per cent withholding tax upon repatriation. However, the rate of 15 per cent can be reduced based on the provisions of a relevant double tax treaty.

It should also be noted that certain cross-border payments and transactions are subject to National Bank of Ukraine approval.

Group/consolidated tax returns and loss relief

Group/consolidated tax returns are allowed for resident taxpayers and their branches or other units without legal entity status. There is no group relief for losses and profits of separate Ukrainian legal entities. An application to switch to payment of tax on a consolidated basis should be filed before the new reporting year. The detailed procedures for paying consolidated tax are established by the State Tax Administration of Ukraine.

Resident taxpayers are allowed to carry losses forward without any time limitations (previously there was a time limit of five years). The carry-forward can be started subsequent to the year in which such losses occur. Different tax treatment is provided in respect of losses accumulated as at 31 December 2002; the carry-forward of such losses is subject to a three-year limitation. If the three-year period expired by 31 December 2002, the available losses (which are not more than five years old) can be carried forward only to the first quarter of 2003.

Dividends

Dividends distributed to Ukrainian legal entities or individuals are taxed in the form of advance payments of profits tax. An advance payment is made by a taxpayer who distributes dividends (ie currently a 30 per cent tax applies for the full amount of dividends declared for distribution, which means that the tax is not withheld at source). This tax is paid prior to or at the moment of distribution of dividends and can be set off against the taxpayer's liability arising in the reporting period in which the tax is paid. A recipient of dividends is generally free from tax obligations on the received dividends.

Value added tax

The VAT law provides for the uniform treatment of both production and merchandising entities: under the VAT law VAT due to the state is assessed as the difference between VAT collected from customers and VAT paid to suppliers.

All turnover from the sale of goods and services in Ukraine is within the scope of the tax (but subject to specific exemptions or exclusions as noted below), as are imports of goods and services.

VAT rates

The law distinguishes between the following major types of transactions which are:

- Subject to VAT and are taxed at the standard rate of 20 per cent (but there is a draft law which proposes to reduce this rate to 17 per cent). This applies to all goods and services apart from the exceptions set out below.
- Subject to zero-rate VAT. The list of transactions primarily includes: sales of goods outside Ukraine (export of goods); sales of services which are intended to be used or consumed outside Ukraine etc.
- Non-VATable transactions, such as: fixed assets contributed in exchange for a share in the equity of enterprises with foreign investment; transfer of property for leasing from a Ukrainian lessor to a lessee and its return to the lessor on the termination of the lease; rent payments under financial leases; insurance and reinsurance transactions, social and pension insurance; most banking services, etc.
- VAT-exempt transactions: education services; artistic and cultural services; healthcare services; certain mass media services; privatization services, etc.

In general, VAT is payable by: an entity with a volume of VATable transactions in excess of UAH61,200 (currently approximately USD11,550) for any preceding 12 months of operation; an importer of goods, services or works; or an entity that is engaged in trade for cash regardless of the volume of sales.

VAT registration is compulsory for all Ukrainian limited companies that qualify as VAT payers. A voluntary registration as a VAT payer is also possible under the current legislation. Foreign legal entities engaged in production or other commercial activity on the territory of Ukraine are considered to be VAT payers and are required to register for VAT purposes. Foreign legal entities registered as VAT payers are required to collect and remit VAT in the same manner as Ukrainian entities.

Under Ukrainian law, VAT is recoverable provided that the goods (works, services) are deductible for corporate profits tax purposes or, in the case of fixed assets, are subject to depreciation. VAT incurred on business expenses may normally be recovered as a credit against output VAT or as a refund, with the following exceptions: VAT on inputs corresponding to exempt supplies; VAT on certain expenses, which by virtue of the corporate tax legislation are not deductible for corporate profits tax purposes.

There is no clear or effective mechanism for VAT refund by foreign entities that are not registered as VAT payers in Ukraine. Also, currently it is a significant issue that the government rarely provides cash refunds of VAT credits.

Usually the reporting period for VAT is monthly. If VATable transactions do not exceed approximately UAH122,400 (currently approximately USD23,100) for the preceding year, a taxpayer can at its discretion use either monthly or quarterly reporting periods for the future calendar year. If the taxpayer chooses a quarterly reporting period, it is obliged to inform the tax authority one month before the new calendar year.

For VAT payers whose reporting period is one month, VAT returns are required to be filed no later than the 20th day of that month. For those VAT payers whose reporting period is quarterly, VAT returns are required to be filed within 40 days of the end of that quarter.

Under VAT legislation, all VAT-liable transactions must be properly documented with tax invoices. The VAT law provides for an explicit list of items to be included in a tax invoice, primarily including the selling price, VAT amount, registration number of the tax payer, etc.

To be treated as a tax credit (ie deductible from VAT), VAT paid to suppliers should be properly supported with tax invoices. Tax invoices can only be issued by entities (individuals) registered as tax payers for VAT purposes.

Taxation of individuals

Personal income tax

Individuals are subject to personal income tax in Ukraine. Currently, income tax rates range from nil to 40 per cent. Non-residents are subject to a fixed withholding tax of 20 per cent on their incomes from Ukraine unless another rate is mentioned in the relevant double tax treaty. From 1 January 2004 a new personal income tax will come into force, and a 13 per cent flat tax rate will apply to income received by taxpayers (this rate is scheduled to increase to 15 per cent from 1 January 2007).

While many aspects of the new personal income tax law still need to be clarified, the new law clearly suggests good news with respect to lower tax rates and additional tax deductions. However, the new law also presents important new considerations for individuals who receive interest and/or dividend income; or who work as private entrepreneurs; or foreign individuals who spend less than 183 days in Ukraine.

Payroll contributions

The employer, whether a Ukrainian business entity or a permanent establishment of a foreign entity, is generally required to make monthly contributions to the State Pension Fund, Employment Fund, Disease Security Fund and Accident Insurance Fund.

The taxable base for the employer's and employee's contributions to social funds is currently capped at UAH2,660 (approximately USD502) per employee per month. In other words, salary amounts exceeding UAH2,660 are not subject to these contributions.

The statutory payments are made in one lump sum for all employees and are calculated as a percentage of the employee's gross monthly salary. Total employer's contributions to the social funds are equal to approximately 37.67 per cent[1] of gross payroll. Additionally, the employer is obliged to make withholdings from the employee's salaries to the above funds. The withholding rates are from 2 per cent to 3 per cent[2].

An employer must make the above payments directly to the tax authorities at the same time or before payment of salary.

Excise duty

Excise duty is an indirect tax on profitable and monopolized goods (products), which is included in the price of these goods (products). All business entities producing or importing excisable goods (products) are the payers of excise duty.

The list of excisable goods currently includes the following items: alcoholic beverages, tobacco and tobacco products, imported cars, tyres, fuel and jewellery.

Rates of excise duty are uniform for the whole territory of Ukraine. For example, the excise duty on alcoholic drinks currently ranges from UAH0.25 to UAH16 (approximately from USD0.05 to USD3) for 1 litre.

The amounts of excise duty levied on transport vehicles depend on their engine capacity.

Excise duties are not levied when excisable goods are exported for foreign currency.

---

[1] The tax rates for contributions to the Accident Insurance Fund are based on the type of activity in which an entity is engaged (the rates are from 0.86 per cent to 13.8 per cent). Normally, this rate is 0.87 per cent.

[2] Tax withholdings include contributions to the Pension Fund of Ukraine, in respect of which a 1 per cent tax applies to salaries not exceeding UAH150 and a 2 per cent tax applies to salaries exceeding this threshold.

Other major taxes and charges

Customs duties

In addition to excise tax (if applicable), the following customs duties are payable by an importer on importation of goods into Ukraine:

- customs fees at the rate of 2 per cent of the customs value of the good but not more than USD1,000 (for goods whose customs value exceeds USD1,000);
- customs duty in accordance with the Unified Customs Tariff;
- under Ukrainian law, there are relieved and full rates of customs duties applied depending on the country of manufacture or origin;
- the relieved duty rates apply to goods manufactured in countries that have signed trade agreements with Ukraine for most-favoured-nation status.

Tax on owners of motor vehicles

Legal entities and individuals who own motor vehicles registered in Ukraine pay this tax. The tax rate depends on the power output of the vehicle's engine and currently varies from UAH0.5 to UAH30 per 100 cc of engine displacement.

State duty

State duty is levied on legal entities as well as on individuals for the issue of certain documents by specified authorities (ie notaries, state authorities). The rate of duty varies depending on the deed executed.

Hop- and vine-growing tax

The payers of this tax are legal entities that are wholesalers and retailers of alcoholic beverages and beer. The amount of the tax is 1 per cent of the revenues from the sale of such products.

Geological tax

Payers of this tax are all subsoil users, which extract minerals on the territory of Ukraine. The rate of this tax depends on the kind of minerals extracted. For example, for gold ore the tax rate is currently UAH3 (approximately USD0.6) per ton of extracted gold ore.

Payment for the use of natural resources

There are some payments for the use of natural resources (eg water use, forest use, wild animal use etc). Payers of such payments are entities that use these natural resources. Payments for the use of natural resources are generally immaterial.

Rent payments

Entities that conduct business activity connected with gas and oil extraction on the territory of Ukraine are payers of rent payments. Currently, the rate for rent payment is UAH28.9 (approximately USD5.5) per 1,000 cubic metres of gas extraction and UAH52.02 (approximately USD10) per ton for oil extraction.

Entities that transport either oil or gas by pipeline on the territory of Ukraine should also pay rent payments specified in the current legislation.

Land tax

Land tax is paid by owners or users of land. The rate depends on the nature and location of the land and is paid monthly.

Local taxes and duties

There are some immaterial local taxes and duties in Ukraine, the important ones being advertising tax and municipal tax. Advertising tax is levied at a rate from 0.1 to 0.5 per cent based on the value of advertising installation and placement services. Municipal tax is currently paid monthly at the rate of UAH1.70 (approximately USD0.3) per each employee.

3.3

Ukrainian Tax Law

Bate C Toms, Zoya Mylovanova and Igor Posypayko, BC Toms & Co

Introduction

Ukraine has a relatively complex system of taxation. The general principles of Ukrainian tax law are established by the Law 'On the System of Taxation' No. 77/97 dated 18 February 1997 (the 'Tax System Law').

Under the Tax System Law, Ukraine imposes state and local taxes. In addition, numerous fees are provided for, such as payments to social security funds, fees for the exploration and production of natural resources, stamp duty on notarial acts, and import and export duties. Even though they are not called taxes, such payments are mandatory and apply in the same way as taxes. Under the Tax System Law, when provisions of a double tax treaty or other international treaty of Ukraine contain tax rules different from those created by domestic legislation, the provisions of the treaty prevail.

The state taxes, fees and duties established pursuant to the Tax System Law presently include 24 national and 14 local taxes and other charges. At the national level, the principal taxes are the corporate profits tax, personal income tax, value-added tax (VAT), excise tax, import and export duties, stamp duty (fees for notarial services, court proceedings, marriage, divorce, etc), various social security withholdings and land tax.

Local taxes and duties are of lesser importance. Their rates and payment procedure are established by local governments within the limits provided in the Decree 'On Local Taxes and Duties' of 20 May 1993 (the 'Local Tax Decree'). The Local Tax Decree specifies the persons and entities subject to local taxes, as well as the maximum rates and the procedure for tax payments. Under the Tax System Law and the Local Tax Decree, local taxes and duties include such diverse levies as those on advertising, retail trading, tourism and dog ownership.

In addition, several state bodies, mainly the State Tax Administration and the State Customs Service, regularly issue regulations, instructions and interpretations to fill in the gaps in the tax legislation. Application of these supplemental acts is often complicated because of inconsistencies with the statutes that they are intended to implement as well as with older regulations and other administrative acts. Often new regulations may appear to replace previously adopted rules, but if the prior rules are not expressly withdrawn, ambiguities may arise as to their continuing legal effect. Moreover, regulations often go much further than the underlying statutes and establish additional burdensome requirements for taxpayers, some of which may be of questionable validity.

In general, Ukrainian tax law is becoming more sophisticated and the regulations more complicated as the law evolves, largely to mirror Western practice. A turning point in Ukrainian tax policy took place on 1 January 2004, when several new tax laws (unofficially referred to as the 'Small Tax Code') came into force. Even though an attempt to adopt a comprehensive tax code failed the year before, through this Small Tax Code Parliament implemented a number of significant changes affecting the following major aspects of taxation. To begin with, the amendments reduced the corporate tax rate from 30 per cent to 25 per cent, and considerably revised the taxation of dividends, interest-free loans, bad debts, income from leasing, and insurance. The transfer pricing rules and rules on depreciation charges, deductions and filing and payment procedures were also significantly modified. Second, a new personal income tax law was adopted that fundamentally changed the taxation of natural persons. The previous scheme of progressive tax rates (from 10 to 40 per cent) was replaced with a flat rate 13 per cent tax with a greatly extended tax base. In addition, significant amendments to the existing VAT law are being currently considered by the Ukrainian Parliament which, if adopted (as is expected), will result in reduction of the VAT rate and will considerably change the Ukrainian VAT regime.

An interesting tax-related development over recent years has been the introduction of about 20 free economic zones (the exact number depends upon whether related zones in particular areas are counted separately). The zones vary in size and available benefits, but all are characterized by some sort of privileged taxation regime. The special tax benefits usually include a package of temporary exemptions, for qualifying investment projects, from business profits tax, VAT and import duties. To qualify, the investment project must meet a number of requirements, such as minimum investment criteria, and be in the areas of business activity covered by the particular privileged taxation regime. Ordinarily, both foreign and domestic investments can benefit from these privileges.

The principal taxes in Ukraine that affect companies and individuals are described below.

Corporate profits tax

Taxpayers and tax rates

Ukrainian companies are taxed on their worldwide profits. Beginning from 1 January 2004, the basic profits tax rate is 25 per cent (reduced from 30 per cent). Special rates apply to certain types of income, for example, insurance income. Non-resident companies are taxed only on their Ukrainian source income, unless they have a permanent establishment in Ukraine, in which case their Ukrainian branch will be taxable as a Ukrainian resident. The general withholding tax applicable to Ukrainian source income is 15 per cent, with special rates existing for freight, certain insurance, and advertising income as well as interest or discount income received from certain state securities. Withholding tax rates are generally significantly reduced by tax treaties where applicable.

Calculation

The tax base for the calculation of profits tax is determined as the difference between gross income (the total income from all revenue sources, whether in cash or in kind) and allowable gross expenses and deductions for depreciation related to the taxpayer's production and other business activities incurred during the reporting period.

The Law 'On Taxation of Profits of Enterprises' of 28 December 1994 (the 'Profits Tax Law') broadly lists the types of expenses that are non-deductible or partially deductible. These include contractual penalties, expenses in connection with warranty repairs (deductible up to 10 per cent of the total sales price of such goods when originally sold), representation expenses in connection with holding receptions and celebrations, etc, travel expenses exceeding the relatively low limits provided for business trips within Ukraine and abroad, and many other expenses that are normally fully deductible in the West. Additional limitations exist in certain cases for the deductibility of interest expenses paid to non-residents or persons taxable at a reduced tax rate.

The Profits Tax Law also limits deductions for expenses on transactions with companies in 'offshore' jurisdictions. Any company incorporated or resident in a country officially listed as being an 'offshore' jurisdiction is presumed to have an offshore status. Unless this presumption is refuted, a Ukrainian taxpayer making payments to a company with such offshore status, through the company or through its banking account, is entitled to deduct only 85 per cent of the expenses thereby paid. The list of jurisdictions considered by Ukraine to be 'offshore' is published annually by the Cabinet of Ministers of Ukraine and generally includes countries often referred to in the West as 'tax havens'. The current list of such offshore states is shown in Table 3.3.1.

Special provisions also exist for the calculation and taxation of income from specific transactions, such as insurance income, foreign exchange gains (losses), gains from operations with securities and other corporate rights, and income from leasing transactions.

If deductible expenses for a current tax accounting period exceed the gross income of the taxpayer, the recognized loss can be carried forward indefinitely. Losses cannot, however, be carried back.

Transfer pricing rules

At the end of 2002, and then in the middle of 2004, the Profits Tax Law was amended to include more detailed rules regulating the determination of the so-called 'usual prices'. These rules apply to provide for the VAT and profits tax consequences for a number of transactions. Their main purpose, however, as in most Western jurisdictions, is in

Table 3.3.1 The 2003 Cabinet of Ministers' list of offshore jurisdictions

British Islands	Caribbean	Africa
Alderney	Anguilla	Liberia
Guernsey	Antigua and Barbuda	Seychelles
Jersey	Aruba	Pacific
Isle of Man	Bahamas	Vanuatu
Middle East	Barbados	Samoa
Bahrain	Bermuda	Marshall Islands
Central America	British Virgin Islands	Nauru
Belize	Virgin Islands (USA)	Niue
Panama	Cayman Islands	Cook Islands
Europe	Granada	Southern Asia
Andorra	Montserrat	Republic of Maldives
Gibraltar	Netherlands Antilles	
Monaco	Puerto Rico	
	St Kitts and Nevis	
	St Lucia	
	St Vincent and Grenadines	
	Commonwealth of Dominica	
	Turks and Caicos	

transactions between related parties to avoid overstated expenses or understated income resulting in a reduction of the income taxable in Ukraine.

Under the new rules, a rebuttable presumption exists that the contractual price set by the parties is the usual price and corresponds to a fair market price. The burden of proof is on the tax authorities to show that the contract price is not a fair market price. A taxpayer can be requested to substantiate the level of the prices it pays.

The usual price for a transaction is ascertained utilizing the comparable uncontrolled price (CUP) method, with certain exceptions. Under the CUP method, the normal price is established based on the prices that would be payable for the same or similar goods in comparable uncontrolled transactions (ie transactions between unrelated persons). For natural monopolists, the usual price can be established by the resale price method or, in certain cases, by the cost plus method, regulations for which are to be promulgated by the Cabinet of Ministers of Ukraine.

Dividend taxation

Recent amendments to the Corporate Profits Tax Law introduced a classical system of corporate taxation. Under this system, the profits of a company are subject to double taxation, as they are taxed first at the corporate level and then, upon distribution of dividends, at the level of the shareholders. To avoid taxing the same income more than twice, corporate shareholders are entitled to exclude Ukrainian source dividends from their gross income.

When a company distributes dividends, it pays an advance tax of 25 per cent from its own income without reducing the amount of the dividends due to its shareholders. The company is entitled to a tax credit for the amount of the advance tax paid against its corporate tax liabilities. If the advance tax paid exceeds the current tax liabilities of the company, the excess may be carried forward indefinitely.

In addition, the company must withhold a 15 per cent tax on the dividends it pays to non-resident companies and a 13 per cent tax (15 per cent tax starting 1 January 2007) on the dividends it pays to a non-resident individual. Relevant tax treaties can significantly reduce the withholding tax rate applicable to dividends paid to non-residents.

Leasing of real estate

According to the recent Law of Ukraine 'On the Income Tax of Natural Persons', No. 889-IV, adopted on 22 May 2003 and which took effect on 1 January 2004, the leasing of real property belonging to a non-resident legal entity or individual may be conducted in Ukraine exclusively through either its permanent establishment, if one exists, or a legal entity resident in Ukraine which, based on a written agreement, performs representation functions on behalf of such non-residents.

Tax periods

Taxpayers are obliged to file quarterly tax returns and to remit the amount of tax due by the 50th day following the end of the relevant accounting quarter.

Taxation of representative offices

Traditionally, 'representative offices', those set up as non-trading branch offices, carried on their activities in Ukraine without paying tax. Representative offices involved in trading, and therefore receiving income from their activities, are taxed at the standard corporate tax rate and required to register as taxable permanent establishments.

Thus, where some of the profits of a non-resident may be attributed to the activities of its supposedly non-taxable representative office, tax liabilities may arise on the basis of its representative office's trading activity. For example, where a non-resident sells equipment to a Ukrainian purchaser and employees of the non-resident's representative office handle the installation, the representative office would be liable to pay tax on the installation work, unless an applicable tax treaty exempts these activities from taxation.

For most representative offices in Ukraine, there should be little risk of taxation, owing to provisions of applicable tax treaties. Most tax treaties follow the Organization for Economic Cooperation and Development (OECD) model tax treaty in allowing a representative office to perform auxiliary functions such as marketing, storage, information support, etc, without subjecting the income from such commercial activities to taxation. Nevertheless, problems can arise. For example, where marketing is in fact one of major activities of a non-resident and not an ancillary function, its representative office in Ukraine will not, for its marketing activities, ordinarily be able to take advantage of the above exemption for auxiliary activities.

It is also important for companies from tax treaty countries to limit the power of attorney they grant to the local management of their representative offices as well as the office's internal regulations to exempt activities. This is usually achieved by excluding all trading and limiting the office's activities to those listed in a relevant tax treaty as not creating a taxable permanent establishment.

Taxation of non-residents: withholding tax

Certain Ukrainian source income of non-resident legal entities is subject to withholding (repatriation) tax. Ukrainian source income includes the following items: dividends, interest, royalties, rents, lottery winnings (except from the state lottery), real estate sales proceeds, remuneration for certain cultural, entertainment and sports activities, charitable donations, freight payments, proceeds from sales of securities and other corporate rights, brokerage fees, commission and agency fees and certain other income of non-residents. The income received as consideration for goods and services provided to a resident is excluded from the definition of Ukrainian source income.

A general 15 per cent withholding tax rate applies to the majority of Ukrainian source income, with the exception of (i) freight income, which is taxed at 6 per cent, (ii) certain insurance-related income, which is taxed either at a 0 per cent or 15 per cent rate depending on the financial stability of the insurer, (iii) income from advertising services provided in Ukraine, which is taxed at 20 per cent and (iv) interest or discount income received from certain securities issued by the state, which is exempt from taxation.

The tax is levied on the so-called repatriation of income (hence, it is often referred to as the 'repatriation tax'). The resident Ukrainian payer of such income is required to withhold and remit to the state the amount of the tax before the actual payment to the non-resident is made. The applicable withholding rate for dividend, interest and royalties and sometimes certain other payments is usually reduced by the double tax treaties entered into by Ukraine or, in some cases where a new Ukrainian treaty has not been concluded, by those USSR tax treaties that Ukraine still applies as a successor of the USSR (see Table 3.3.2).

The procedure for the application of a tax treaty exemption or rate reduction has been recently modified, to facilitate an outright elimination or reduction, as may be applicable, of the tax obligation. In order to benefit from a double tax treaty, a Ukrainian company paying a dividend, interest or a royalty merely needs to show a certificate from the tax authorities of the country where the recipient is located confirming that the recipient is a resident of that country that has a double tax treaty with Ukraine.

Personal income tax

General

The recent Law of Ukraine 'On the Income Tax of Natural Persons', No. 889-IV, adopted on 22 May 2003 (the 'Personal Income Tax Law'),

Table 3.3.2 Withholding tax rates for treaty countries on income paid from Ukraine

Country	Dividends(%)	Interest (%)	Royalties (%)
1 Armenia	5/15	0/10	0
2 Austria	5/10	0/2/5	0/5
3 Azerbaijan	10	0/10	10
4 Belarus	15	10	15
5 Belgium	5/15	0/2/5	0/5
6 Bulgaria	5/15	0/10	10
7 Canada	5/15	0/10	0/10
8 China	5/10	0/10	10
9 Croatia	5/10	0/10	10
10 Cyprus*	0	0	0
11 Czech Republic	5/15	0/5	10
12 Denmark	5/15	0/10	0/10
13 Egypt	12	0/12	12
14 Estonia	5/15	0/10	0/10
15 Finland	0/5/15	0/5/10	0/5/10
16 France	0/5/15	0/2/10	0/10
17 Georgia	5/10	0/10	10
18 Germany	5/10	0/2/5	0/5
19 Hungary	5/15	0/10	5
20 India	10/15	0/10	10
21 Indonesia	10/15	0/10	10
22 Iran	10	0/10	10
23 Italy	15	0	0
24 Japan*	15	0/10	0/10
25 Kazakhstan	5/15	0/10	10
26 Korea	5/15	0/5	5
27 Kyrgyzstan	5/15	0/10	10
28 Latvia	5/15	0/10	10
29 Lithuania	5/15	0/10	10
30 Macedonia	5/15	0/10	10
31 Malaysia*	15	0/15	10/15
32 Moldova	5/15	0/10	10
33 Mongolia*	0	0	0
34 Netherlands	0/5/15	0/2/10	0/10
35 Norway	5/15	0/10	5/10
36 Poland	5/25	0/10	10
37 Romania	10/15	0/10	10/15
38 Russian Federation	5/15	0/10	10
39 Slovakia	10	10	10
40 Spain*	18	0	0/5
41 Sweden	0/5/10	0/10	0/10
42 Switzerland	5/15	0/10	0/10
43 Turkey	10/15	0/10	10
44 Turkmenistan	10	0/10	10
45 UK	5/10	0	0
46 USA	5/15	0	10
47 Uzbekistan	10	0/10	10
48 Vietnam	10	0/10	10
49 Yugoslavia	5/10	0/10	10

* Based on Ukrainian application of a USSR double tax treaty.

In addition, Ukraine has concluded double tax treaties that have not yet been ratified (treaties with Luxemburg, Slovenia, Syria and the Republic of South Africa) or are not yet in force (treaties with Brazil, Cuba, Portugal, Lebanon, Algeria, Kuwait, United Arab Emirates and Mongolia).

fundamentally reformed the system of personal income taxation. This new legislation replaced a former progressive tax rate scale (from10 to 40 per cent) with a flat tax rate of 13 per cent (starting in 2007, this flat rate will rise to 15 per cent). The legislation also launched a wholly new system of deductions; substituted the non-taxable minimum income amount with a social tax allowance; substantially altered the taxation of dividends, deposit interest, winnings, inheritances, operations with real estate, and sale of movables; greatly expanded the tax base; modified exemptions and revised the tax administration procedures.

Taxpayers

The Personal Income Tax Law is applicable to residents of Ukraine as well as non-residents receiving income from sources in Ukraine. Residents are defined as individuals who have their place of abode in Ukraine and are further categorized as follows:

- where an individual has a place of abode in another country as well, he or she is considered to be a resident of Ukraine if he or she has a domicile (a permanent place of living) in Ukraine;
- where an individual has a domicile in another country as well, he or she is considered to be resident of Ukraine if his or her centre of vital interests (such as the place of abode of his or her family members) in Ukraine;
- where an individual's centre of vital interests cannot be determined or the individual has no domicile in any country, he or she is considered to be a resident of Ukraine if he or she stays in Ukraine for at least 183 days during the tax year;
- where residency status cannot be determined based on the above rules, an individual is considered to be a resident of Ukraine if he or she is a citizen of Ukraine.

Non-residents are defined as individuals who do not qualify as residents of Ukraine.

Taxable income

The Personal Income Tax Law defines the taxable income of a resident taxpayer as gross worldwide income *either accrued or received* by the taxpayer during the reporting year, less applicable exemptions and deductions. A non-resident's income is subject to Ukrainian personal income tax only to the extent it originates from sources in Ukraine.

The new law specifically includes in the gross income of an individual the following items:

- salary accrued or paid to a taxpayer by an employer;
- interest and dividend income, investment income, and royalties;
- insurance payments and premiums;
- income from the renting or disposal of movable and immovable property;
- fringe benefits (including the value of received rent, property, food, domestic assistance, expense reimbursements, amounts of financial aid);
- amounts of punitive damages received (not including compensation for actual damages);
- forgiven debts and obligations;
- gifts, winnings and inheritance.

Income is taxable irrespective of whether it is received in cash or in kind. For benefits received in kind, the tax base is computed at the usual (market) price of the benefits, increased for VAT and excise tax where applicable, and grossed up to give the *pre-tax* value.

Any amount of taxable income received by a resident from foreign sources should be specified in the taxpayer's annual tax return and taxable in Ukraine. Where Ukraine has a double tax treaty with the country that is the source of the income, the taxes paid outside Ukraine may be offset as a credit against Ukrainian taxes due if the taxpayer provides written proof from the foreign tax authorities that such foreign taxes have been paid. The total foreign tax credits may not exceed the amount of the Ukrainian personal income tax due for the reporting period.

A tax credit is not available for any capital tax, property tax, postal tax, sales and other indirect taxes.

Exemptions

The Personal Income Tax Law exempts the following key types of income from taxation:

- investment income on securities issued by the Ministry of Finance;
- winnings from state lotteries;
- obligatory insurance payments by state social funds;
- alimony payments;
- most income received as inheritance from immediate family;
- state compensation for nationalized property;

- shares received from the capitalization of undistributed profits, provided the allocation of shares between the shareholders remains unchanged;
- income from the sale of a car, motorbike, yacht or engine-driven boat, though stamp duty must be paid upon sale;
- income from certain operations with property and investment assets;
- cost of employee training paid by an employer within the limit of 1.4 times the subsistence minimum (at present UAH510) per month; and
- certain insurance payments.

Deductions

The Personal Income Tax Law also created a new right for taxpayers to claim certain deductions from their annual taxable income for certain documented expenses incurred in the reporting year. It specifically allows the following deductible expenses:

- a certain portion of mortgage interest payments (available from 2005);
- educational expenses for the taxpayer and his or her immediate family (up to 1.4 times the subsistence minimum income per month, currently UAH510);
- certain medical expenses not covered by insurance for the taxpayer and his or her immediate family (subject to adoption of the Obligatory Medical Insurance Law);
- charitable contributions in an amount of 2 to 5 per cent of the individual's taxable income;
- non-state pension insurance premiums (available from 2005) as well as life insurance premiums (up to 1.4 times the subsistence minimum income per month); and
- adoption and artificial insemination expenses.

The new law also allows low-income individuals (those having a salary below 1.4 times the subsistence minimum income per month) to reduce their monthly taxable income by an amount known as the 'Social Tax Concession' (this equals one minimum income). The Concession was introduced starting from 2004 at 30 per cent, rising in 2005 to 50 per cent, in 2006 to 80 per cent, and in 2007 to 100 per cent. Some privileged categories of taxpayers (for example, disabled persons, Second

World War veterans, and single mothers) nevertheless retain the amount of UAH17 for the application of other laws that refer to the Non-Taxable Minimum Income. The Social Tax Concession replaces the Non-Taxable Minimum Income for qualification purposes for administrative misdemeanours and criminal offences. Consequently, the threshold for an amount evaded to qualify as felony tax evasion rose from the previous UAH17,000 to UAH61,500 as of 2004. This will be increased further in subsequent years.

Tax rates

The new Personal Income Tax Law 2003 eliminated the progressive scale of personal income tax established by the 1993 Decree 'On the Individual Income Tax' (the 'Decree on Individual Income Tax') and introduced a flat tax rate as of 1 January 2004. During the period from 1 January 2004 to 31 December 2006, this flat personal income tax rate is fixed at 13 per cent. The rate will increase to 15 per cent as of 1 January 2007. This standard flat rate is applicable to nearly all types of income, including salaries, investment income, dividends, royalties, fringe benefits, and most gifts. A double tax rate (26 per cent until 31 December 2006, then rising to 30 per cent) applies to gifts from abroad, winnings and prizes (except for cash prizes in the state lottery) to Ukrainian residents as well as to most Ukrainian source income received by non-residents (exceptions generally include dividend, interest and royalty income).

Taxation of income from the sale of real estate

Under the Personal Income Tax Law, any income from the disposal of living quarters acquired before 1 January 2004 is subject to income tax at a 1 per cent rate (and 5 per cent for the portion of the income from the disposal of living quarters attributable to floor space exceeding $100m^2$). If more than one similar immovable property is sold during a reporting year, and for all real estate other than living quarters, the rate of applicable income tax is 5 per cent.

Income from disposal of real estate acquired after 1 January 2004 is subject to income tax at a standard rate of 13 per cent, based on the gain realized from the sale. This taxable gain can be reduced by 10 per cent for each calendar year of possession if the individual sells no more than one living quarter in a taxable year.

Taxation of real estate rental income

A lessee that is a legal entity is required to withhold income tax from rent payments to a lessor who is an individual at the standard rate of

13 per cent (15 per cent starting 2007). Where the lessee is an individual, it is the lessor's duty to pay the applicable tax on a quarterly basis. The taxable income from a rental agreement is based on the rental contract, but shall not be lower than the minimum rental approved by the local government. Such an agreement must be notarized, with notaries reporting the agreement to the tax authorities.

Taxation of insurance income

Where an employer contributes an amount for voluntary insurance in favour of employees, such amount is included in the employees' taxable income. However, premiums under long-term life insurance or non-state pension insurance are exempt up to 15 per cent of an employee's monthly salary, but no more than 1.4 times the subsistence minimum income per month.

The tax rate for insurance payments is the standard 13 per cent (15 per cent starting 2007), with the tax levied on 60 per cent of the amount received by the individual under a non-state pension scheme or long-term life insurance. The standard income tax rate also applies to the amount of redemption in case of earlier termination by the individual of a pension insurance or long-term life insurance agreement. Insurance payments to individuals over 70, or upon an insurance event that resulted in a first-category disablement of the insured individual are exempt from tax.

Payments under other life/health/property insurance policies, with minor reservations, are generally exempt from personal income tax.

Taxation of inheritance and gifts

As a general rule, inheritance and gifts are subject to income tax at the standard 13 per cent rate (15 per cent starting 1 January 2007). The rate of applicable tax is substantially reduced for such transactions between immediate members of a family. Any property inherited or received as a gift from a spouse is subject to a zero-rated tax (except for securities, corporate rights and intellectual property). The value of real estate, movables and insurance payments as well as a limited amount of cash and deposits is taxed at a 5 per cent rate when inherited or presented as a gift from an immediate member of family other than a spouse (ie parents, parents-in-law and children).

Any property inherited or received as a gift from non-residents is subject to double the standard rate of personal income tax (26 per cent rising to 30 per cent in 2007).

Taxation of non-residents

Income of non-residents received from any activity in Ukraine is subject to Ukrainian personal income tax.

If such income is paid to a non-resident from sources in Ukraine by another non-resident, it must be credited to an account with a resident bank, which will act as a tax agent on behalf of the non-resident. Where income is paid in cash or in kind, it is the non-resident's duty to pay the applicable amount of tax to the state within the next 20 days, but before he or she leaves the country.

As a general rule, income accrued to non-residents is taxed at double the standard rate (26 per cent until 31 December 2006, and 30 per cent thereafter). This includes salary, investment income, rental income, insurance payments, income from disposal of real estate, etc. The only exceptions are dividends and royalties, which are taxed at the standard 13 per cent rate (15 per cent starting 2007), as well as interest from bank deposits and deposit certificates, which are taxed at a 5 per cent rate starting 1 January 2005. These tax rates may be reduced under provisions of applicable tax treaties.

Tax administration

Any business entity (defined by the new law as a 'tax agent') that accrues salary or certain other types of income to an individual is responsible for withholding the amount of tax due and remitting it to the state. Payments of income and of applicable tax should be made simultaneously. When income is accrued in cash or in kind, the tax should be paid the following banking day. Thus, such business entities alone are required to settle individual tax liabilities and file monthly reports on income paid to individuals and the amount of tax remitted to the state. Consequently, individuals only receiving their annual income from such business entities acting as tax agents are not obliged to file a tax return. They may, however, wish to do so in order to claim tax deductions.

Ukrainian residents, as well as non-residents, receiving income from persons other than such business entities acting as tax agents (ie in principle, from non-resident entities and individuals and resident individuals not registered as entrepreneurs) are required to file a tax return by 1 April of the year following the reporting one. The Law 'On Settlement of Tax Liabilities', No. 2181-III, adopted on 21 December 2000, requires the tax to be paid within 10 days after the last day for filing the tax return.

Where an individual engages in entrepreneurial activity, he or she must register to be specially taxed as an entrepreneur and file an initial tax return based on an estimated annual income. The entrepreneur must then, on a quarterly basis, file tax returns and make tax payments, which are reconciled in an end-of-year tax filing and reconciliation payment. Such registered entrepreneurs are taxed as individuals except that, as noted earlier, their business expenses may, in general, be deducted on the same basis as is permitted for legal entities.

Value added tax

Background

Value added tax, or VAT, is an indirect tax currently levied at a rate of 20 per cent on most business transactions, domestic retail sales and imports. The Law 'On Value Added Tax' (the 'VAT Law'), adopted on 3 April 1997, which presently governs VAT, represents an attempt by Ukraine to move closer to European VAT norms. Significant amendments to the VAT Law are now being considered. The amendments considered include, *inter alia*, the reduction of the VAT rate, elimination of certain exemptions, changes to the VAT export refund mechanism, and increasing the threshold for registration as a VAT-taxable person.

Taxable persons

VAT-taxable persons generally include:

1. any legal entity or registered individual entrepreneur if the total amount of the person's taxable transactions exceeds 3,600 minimum non-taxable income units (about USD11,000) over the most recent 12-month period;
2. any entity or registered individual entrepreneur importing goods into Ukraine or receiving services (including all 'works', to use Ukrainian terminology) from non-residents for usage or consumption in Ukraine;
3. any entity or registered individual entrepreneur trading in Ukraine for cash, irrespective of the amount of its taxable transactions.

As a practical matter, a non-resident cannot be registered as a VAT-taxable person unless he, she or it has a permanent establishment in Ukraine, even if the criteria mentioned above are otherwise met.

Furthermore, a person may be exempt from any obligation to register as a VAT-taxable person, and to collect and remit VAT if he, she or it is subject to the alternative 10 per cent small business single tax.

Taxable transactions

Most business transactions involving the supply of goods or services are taxable transactions for VAT purposes, including:

1. the sale of goods and the provision of services carried out in Ukraine;
2. the import of goods into Ukraine, and the receipt of services intended for use or consumption in Ukraine;
3. the export of goods and provision of services for consumption outside of Ukraine (although, as described below, presently a 'zero' VAT tax rate generally applies to such transactions).

A number of transactions are specifically excluded from VAT, including:

1. the issuance, placement and sale of securities as well as derivatives issued by legal entities and the government of Ukraine;
2. rental payments under finance leasing, transfers of property pursuant to operating lease and pledge agreements, and repayment of principal and interest payments under mortgage loan agreements;
3. the provision of insurance and reinsurance services;
4. the transfers of fixed assets as a contribution to the authorized statutory fund of a legal entity in exchange for corporate rights in the entity (including the import of such assets into Ukraine, unless such import is subject to the excise tax), provided that the assets are necessary for the business of the entity;
5. the sale of the aggregate gross assets of an enterprise, which is defined as the sale of an enterprise as a separate business or the inclusion of the enterprise's assets into the assets of another enterprise, provided that the seller's rights and liabilities are transferred to the buyer;
6. the sale of goods and provision of services designated for the needs of diplomatic and consular representations of foreign countries and representations of international organizations in Ukraine, as well as for their diplomatic personnel and family members in residence.

Rates

The two VAT rates currently existing in Ukraine are 20 and 0 per cent. The 20 per cent rate is the standard VAT rate applying to all VAT-taxable transactions other than transactions taxable at the zero tax rate. As indicated above, it is possible that the 20 per cent VAT rate will be reduced by new legislation in the near future. The zero tax rate applies to most exports of goods and sale of services intended for use or consumption outside of Ukraine.

Deciding when the zero tax rate should apply to the provision of services can be complicated as the law does not contain specific criteria to determine when services are to be considered intended for use and consumption outside of Ukraine. Administrative practice is also somewhat ambiguous on this point. As a result, the state tax authorities often insist on application of the 20 per cent tax rate to the sale of services provided by Ukrainian residents to non-residents even though the report or other service is sent abroad to the non-resident.

Calculation

General sales transactions

The VAT liability for a sales transaction generally arises at the earliest occurrence of either (a) the transfer of the goods or the performance of the services (as evidenced by a document, usually an 'act of transfer-acceptance', confirming completion of the services); or (b) the receipt of actual payment.

As there is no legally mandated period within which the act of transfer-acceptance or other document confirming the completion of services should be executed, it is, as a practical matter, often possible to postpone the date on which the VAT tax liabilities arise until payment is made for the services. Special rules for the calculation of VAT apply to finance leasing, long-term contracts and certain other transactions.

Import of goods and services

For goods imported into Ukraine, the VAT tax liability arises when an import customs declaration is completed by the taxable person. Ordinarily, the VAT must be paid along with import duties and any excise tax when the goods cross the Ukrainian customs border. Instead of paying VAT at the border, however, the VAT-taxable person can issue a promissory note to be redeemed at the end of the VAT tax accounting period.

This right to pay using promissory notes is, however, severely restricted at the present time. Promissory notes cannot be issued by companies with foreign investment (a discrimination that should be ended with time), nor for the importation of goods subject to excise tax and many other products. In addition, a person can issue a promissory note only if, at the time of importation, the taxable person is entitled to a VAT refund for input VAT paid and only as long as the goods are imported on the basis of direct contracts for the actual industrial needs of the VAT taxpayer. Thus, in general, resale of the imported goods would preclude the use of such VAT promissory notes. Even though questions exist as to the legality of such restrictions and several possibilities appear to be available to overcome them, the use of VAT promissory notes remains limited in practice.

When services are imported, the VAT liability arises on the first occurrence of either (a) payment for the services or (b) execution of a document confirming the performance of the services. The Ukrainian purchaser importing the services is responsible for reporting and withholding the VAT that is payable.

Calculation of VAT liabilities

The amount of VAT to be paid at the end of each tax accounting period is determined as the general amount of such VAT liabilities, less the VAT tax credits that arise over the period. A VAT credit for a tax accounting period generally arises for the total amount of input VAT paid or accrued (whichever occurs first) by the taxable person during the period for the purchase of goods or services, provided their costs are either deductible or depreciable.

Neither is a VAT taxpayer entitled to a tax credit for input VAT paid, if the goods or services purchased are used further in any VAT-exempt transactions. Instead of being credited, the amount of such input VAT is deducted.

If the amount of VAT credit exceeds the amount of VAT liability for the relevant period, the excess VAT credit (referred to as 'Excess VAT') is supposed to be either (a) refunded to the VAT taxpayer by the state after a three-month period from the date of filing of the VAT tax declaration in respect of the Excess VAT or, (2) at the request of the taxpayer, used to decrease future VAT or, in limited cases, other tax liabilities. A special procedure (and limitations) exists for the refund of input VAT paid to purchase goods used for re-export.

As a practical matter, at present, it usually proves extremely difficult to obtain a cash refund of the Excess VAT. The state tax authorities are reluctant to grant such refunds and the existing procedures invariably take a long time to complete and, even then, legal action may be necessary to compel compliance. Certain amendments to the VAT Law are currently being considered by Parliament that are intended to simplify the procedure for obtaining an Excess VAT refund and to preclude abuse of the Excess VAT refund system. Meanwhile, however, VAT taxpayers in Ukraine need to be careful with their VAT planning to avoid, where possible, accumulating Excess VAT and, should Excess VAT accrue, to offset it against their future VAT and other tax liabilities as much as possible.

Tax periods

Under the VAT Law, VAT returns must be filed on a monthly basis, unless the taxpayer's annual taxable turnover is below 7,200 minimum non-taxable incomes (currently approximately USD22,000), in which case the taxpayer may choose to file returns quarterly. The tax should be paid no later than on the 20th day following the relevant reporting period.

This deadline for payment of VAT should have changed, based on the generally applicable provisions of the Law 'On the Procedure for Settlement of Liabilities of Taxpayers before Budgets and State Special Purpose Funds' of 21 December 2000 (the 'Tax Settlement Law'). Pursuant to the Tax Settlement Law, if the tax is paid monthly, the tax return should be filed within 20 days following the end of the reporting period, and if the tax is paid quarterly, the tax return should be filed within 40 days following the end of the reporting period. The tax should then be paid within 10 days after the expiration of the term for filing the tax return.

The conflict between the VAT Law and the Tax Settlement Law initially resulted in a great number of controversies, with many tax authorities insisting on the application of the shorter 20-day period for filing and paying VAT even on a quarterly basis. This position has since been generally abandoned, but until the VAT Law is amended, the issue may still be disputed by the tax authorities.

Excise tax

Background

The excise tax was imposed by the Decree of the Cabinet of Ministers 'On Excise Duty' in 1992. The tax rates as well as the categories of goods subject to excise are regularly updated by Parliament. Currently, the list primarily includes alcohol and tobacco products, gasoline and certain other fuels, vehicles and jewellery. The rates are calculated either as a percentage of the sale price or as a fixed amount in euros, based on the type, quantity, and volume or weight of the goods.

Taxable transactions

Excise taxable transactions include the sale or other transfer of ownership of any goods subject to excise tax ('excise goods'), whether imported or produced in Ukraine. Both resident and non-resident legal entities and individuals that produce or import excise goods are subject to excise tax.

Exemptions

Excise tax is not levied on the export of goods for foreign currency, or on the import or purchase of excise goods for the production of other goods that will be subject to excise tax. Nor does it apply to the sale or other disposal of certain specially designed vehicles (eg for handicapped people, ambulances and police cars). Other exemptions exist for goods in transit, temporarily imported goods subject to an obligation for their re-export, humanitarian aid and certain other goods. If any of the exempt goods are later sold or otherwise disposed of within Ukraine, then the excise tax must be paid.

Accounting procedure

Excise tax calculations must be filed on a monthly basis, and the excise duty must be paid monthly, although certain special procedures exist for payment by the producers of alcohol and tobacco products.

Other taxes

Customs duties on imports and exports

Goods imported into Ukraine are subject to customs import duties in accordance with the Law of Ukraine 'On the General Customs Tariff of Ukraine' of 5 February 1992, with the actual rates being presently fixed in the Law 'On the Customs Tariff of Ukraine' of 5 April 2001. The rates of custom duties are set either as a percentage of the customs value of the goods or as fixed amounts in euros, or as a combination of these two methods of calculation. There are three types of customs duty rates imposed under the tariff: preferential, privileged and full, depending on the country of origin of the goods. Goods from most countries are subject to privileged rates ranging generally from 5 per cent to 10 per cent, provided that the ultimate origin of the goods is proven.

Ukraine still retains customs export duties aimed at restricting the export of several types of goods, including oilseeds (mainly sunflower seeds), livestock (eg cattle and sheep) and animal hides. Although this issue attracts great attention from both Ukrainian exporting companies and a number of international organizations, it has so far proved politically impossible to abolish these export duties.

Social security payments

Social security payments are generally borne both by an employer (paid on the overall amount of its salaries and other remuneration disbursed to its employees (the 'salaries')) and by its employees (withheld by the employer from the salary of each employee). These payments are made to four separate state funds, at rates (as a percentage of the salaries) as described in Table 3.3.3.

Table 3.3.3 Social security payment rates

	Paid by the employer	Paid by the
employee	(% of all salaries)*	(% of gross salary to be deducted)*
Pension Fund of Ukraine**	32	1 to 2
Social Security Fund for Unemployment***	1.9	0.5
Social Security Fund for Occupational Accidents and Professional Diseases***	0.84 to 13.8****	–
Social Security Fund for the Temporarily Disabled***	2.9	0.25 to 0.5

* Only generally applicable rates are shown; the rates that apply for a particular category of employer or employee may, in certain cases, be different.

** The rates are subject to annual revision by the Ukrainian Parliament (as part of the annual budget). Until the law on annual budget sets the new rates, the currently existing rates should apply.

*** Rates are subject to periodical revision by the Ukrainian Parliament.

**** The rate depends on the type of business. Sample rates: finance, credit and insurance businesses – 0.84; trade and public catering – 1.02; and production of construction materials and

Table 3.3.3 shows that the most important payments are those made to the Pension Fund of Ukraine. Currently, the payments to the Fund for the employer amount to 32 per cent of the salaries and for an employee (1 to 2 per cent of the salary, with the actual rate depending on the taxable amount of the income of the individual).

Under the newly adopted Law 'On Mandatory State Pension Insurance' of 9 July 2003, No. 1058-IV, which became effective on 1 January 2004, the tax rates for payments to the Pension Fund are to be established each year in the annual budget of Ukraine, and thus may differ from the current rates. Until the new rates are adopted, the current rates of 32 for the employer and 1 to 2 per cent for the employee continue to apply.

All of these social security payments should be made prior to the payment of salaries. The payments borne by the employer are included in the gross expenses of the employer and thus are deductible from its taxable income when determining its business profits tax. From 1 January 2004, the monthly taxable income of an employee likewise is reduced by the mandatory payments to the social security funds borne by the employee, including pension payments.

In addition to the Pension Fund payments cited above and collected as a percentage of salaries, a number of specific transactions are also currently subject to a Pension Fund payment, with the applicable rate of such contributions based on a percentage of their value. These transactions, with the applicable rate, are as follows: (1) transactions covering the non-cash purchase of hard currency – 1.5 per cent, (2) the sale of jewellery – 5 per cent; (3) the sale of cars – 3 per cent; (4) the sale of immovable property – 1 per cent; and (5) the sale of mobile telecommunication services – 6 per cent. These special payments were originally introduced in 1998 as a temporary measure to cover the Pension Fund's debts for the payment of state pensions. It is expected that these payments will be abolished in the future as the Ukrainian economy develops and the ordinary withholdings from salaries become sufficient.

Land tax

The land tax is levied under the Law of Ukraine 'On Payment for Land' of 3 July 1992, as amended on 22 March 2001. The tax is paid by both owners and users of land. The land tax payable is based on a percentage of the monetary value of the land and is determined according to government-established formula. The land valuation varies depending on the purpose of the land use, ie whether it is for agricultural, urban or recreational use. The amount of any profit earned from commercial activity involving land has no bearing on the amount of the tax.

Other miscellaneous taxes

The taxes described above are generally those of most interest to foreign entities and individuals investing, doing business or residing in Ukraine. There are, however, numerous other payments and fees of which one should be aware.

These include the state duties, duties on certain security and commodity transactions and fees to permit certain types of trading activities. An example of a state duty is the fee payable on the commencement of legal proceedings in commercial courts (equal to 1 per cent of the amount at issue, but no more than 100 non-taxable minimum income units, presently equal to approximately USD300). Notaries also charge duties for conducting many transactions. There are also special taxes on certain assets, such as the automobile tax, as well as taxes on certain types of activities, for example the rental and geological fees for oil and gas production activities and the fee for the use of natural resources.

The single tax option for small businesses

The Presidential Decree of 3 July 1998 introduced an option for small businesses to pay a single tax instead of most of the generally applicable taxes, including:

- business profits tax;
- individual income tax;
- VAT, except if the 6 per cent tax rate applies (see below);
- land tax;
- payments to certain social security funds; and
- certain other obligatory payments specified by legislation.

This option is available to any legal entity engaged in business activity or any form of organization and ownership that employs no more than 50 persons per year and whose annual earnings from the sale of goods and services do not exceed UAH1 million (approximately USD182,000). Further, to qualify for this single tax, no more than 25 per cent of the taxpayer's charter fund (authorized capital) may be held by (1) entities that do not also qualify as small businesses; and (2) an individual registered as an entrepreneur who employs no more than 10 persons per year and whose annual earnings from the sale of goods and services do not exceed UAH500,000 (approximately USD91,000).

A qualifying legal entity also has the choice of two rates of single tax: (1) 6 per cent of the amount of the earnings from the sale of goods and services, plus excise tax and VAT; or (2) 10 per cent of the amount of earnings from the sale of goods and services, plus excise tax.

The single tax rate for registered individual entrepreneurs is specified by the relevant local authorities as a fixed amount of between UAH20 and UAH200 (approximately USD3.8 and USD38), plus half of that amount for each employed person, irrespective of the individual's actual earnings.

A new social security payment was introduced in 2001 to the Social Security Fund for Occupational Accidents and Professional Diseases, which must also be paid in addition to the single tax, although this is contrary to the announced purpose of the single tax. A similar problem exists in respect to the Pension Fund payments because of the new Law 'On the Mandatory State Pension Insurance' of 9 July 2003. However, for the time being there is no general requirement to make payments to the Pension Fund payment in addition to a single tax. Instead, the payments due to the Pension Fund are being offset against certain portions of single tax payments made by the taxpayer, which go to the Pension Fund.

The single tax was intended to enable small businesses to pay a single amount and operate legally, instead of hiding income to avoid an excessive tax and accounting burden. While this new approach to taxation has largely proved to be successful, the future of the single tax remains unclear, as it allows small businesses, and especially individual entrepreneurs, to minimize their tax obligations significantly compared with the tax rates generally applicable to all other business entities in Ukraine. It has been criticized because it is allegedly being used by larger businesses to escape much tax by artificially operating as collections of small businesses.

Currently, the Parliament is considering a draft of a new law intended to regulate the application of the single tax instead of a President Edict. Its introduction is likely to change the existing single tax system and regulate the issues remaining unsettled under the President Edict.

Tax enforcement and penalties for tax violations

Compared to Western standards, Ukraine has very high penalties for even inadvertent tax violations. As an example, errors in calculating tax liabilities, if revealed during inspections by the tax authorities, may result in the fine of as much as 50 per cent of the amount of the tax underpaid or of tax underestimated. The fine is payable even when the violations did not result in the taxpayer actually paying less tax to the budget. In addition to the fines, the taxpayer is under an obligation to pay an interest on the amount of tax due if the payment is delayed. As a matter of practice, Ukrainian tax authorities are rigorous in enforcing compliance with the tax law and payment of various fines and penalties due. Taking into account this, as well as inconsistencies in Ukrainian tax laws and their vague working, even minor non-compliance may lead to extremely severe consequences for a taxpayer. Thus, professional tax advice should always be sought for planning specific transactions.

Conclusion

Despite the difficulties of its transition to a market economy, Ukraine has now developed a generally profits-based tax system founded on international tax and accounting principles that resembles those found in developed countries. This represents a great step away from the Soviet-style gross revenue, production-based taxation methods where the level of profit was irrelevant.

Much still remains to be done, especially to develop detailed regulations to address the many ambiguities in the legislation. Many commentators believe that tax rates need to be further lowered in order to encourage compliance by large and medium-sized businesses, rather than push them towards tax evasion. In the future, the Ukrainian system of taxation will likely follow Western trends, in particular by increasing indirect taxation and social security withholdings and by developing and enforcing further anti-avoidance measures.

This review of Ukrainian tax law should be read for general guidance only, as many special rules and exceptions apply and the actual application of tax laws is subject to special practices and is being continuously revised. Tax enforcement in Ukraine can be especially draconian, with very high penalties for even inadvertent violations. Professional tax advice should always be sought for planning specific transactions.

3.4

Banking and Exchange Control Regulation

Bate C Toms and Zoya Mylovanova,
BC Toms & Co

Banks in Ukraine

The banking system of Ukraine consists of the National Bank of Ukraine (the 'NBU'), banks that can function as universal banks and specialized banks such as saving, investment, mortgage and clearing banks.

A bank is regarded as specialized if more than 50 per cent of its assets are of one type. Currently, there are no specialized banks except for Oschadnyi bank, the state savings bank, where more than 50 per cent of deposits are from individuals. A bank is considered to be a state bank only if 100 per cent of its authorized capital is held by the state.

As of 1 September 2004, there were 183 registered banks in Ukraine, of which 159 are banks that are actually functioning in the market and have an NBU licence to conduct banking activities. Among these 159 banks, 19 have foreign capital, including the following six banks with 100 per cent foreign capital: Citibank Ukraine (USA), Raiffeisenbank Ukraine (Austria), Calyon Bank Ukraine (France), Bank Pekao (Ukraine) Ltd (Poland), ING Bank Ukraine (Holland) and HVB Bank Ukraine (Germany).

The NBU is the central bank of Ukraine, with an authorized capital of 10 million Ukrainian hryvnyas[1] ('UAH'). It is 100 per cent state

---

[1] Hryvnya is the national currency of Ukraine and is the only legal tender for cash payments in Ukraine. One Hryvnya consists of 100 kopecks. The currency exchange rate of the UAH to the US dollar has generally remained stable since the introduction of the UAH in 1996. Currently 1 US dollar roughly equals UAH5.3.

owned and has the exclusive right to issue cash in UAH. The primary function of the NBU is to ensure the stability of the national currency.

Among other roles stipulated in the Law of Ukraine 'On the National Bank of Ukraine' dated 20 May 1999, the NBU is responsible for general banking regulation and supervision, including regulating currency and exercising currency control over banks. It establishes rules for the conduct of banking operations, including the systems, procedures and forms of payment. Additionally, the NBU controls the state registration of banks and the licensing of banking activities, as well as having authority for approval over the selection of the head of the board of directors and the chief accountant of commercial banks. Finally, the NBU acts as a lender of last resort to banks, and organizes the system of bank refinancing.

The NBU establishes the rules, standards and forms of settlements for banks as well as for other legal entities and individuals, and coordinates the organization of settlement procedures. It grants approvals for the performance of clearing operations and settlements. The NBU also provides for the performance of interbank settlements through its institutions, and grants approvals for interbank settlements through direct correspondent relationships between banks and through their own settlement systems.

The banking system of Ukraine has employed international accounting standards since January 1998. Ukrainian banks are required to submit to the NBU annual financial reports, which must be audited by an authorized independent auditor holding a special certificate issued by the NBU.

Establishment of a bank in Ukraine

The establishment of a bank in Ukraine is governed by the Law of Ukraine 'On Banks and Banking Activity' of 7 December 2000 (the 'Law on Banks and Banking Activity'), pursuant to which a bank can be established by resident and non-resident individuals and legal entities, as well as by the state acting through the Cabinet of Ministers of Ukraine or other state bodies authorized by the Cabinet of Ministers for this purpose.

A bank can be created as (1) a joint stock company, (2) a limited liability company or (3) a cooperative bank. As of 1 September 2004, 131 banks had been formed as joint stock companies, of which 107 were constituted as open joint stock companies (including two state-owned open joint stock companies) and 28 had been formed as limited liability companies.

Presently, at the time of its registration, a bank that conducts activities in only one oblast (region) must have a minimum authorized capital of 3,000,000 euros, while banks that conduct activities throughout Ukraine must have at least 5,000,000 euros. In order to establish or increase a bank's authorized capital, the shareholders that are residents of Ukraine must deposit the necessary funds in UAH, whereas non-residents may make such deposits either in convertible foreign currency or in UAH.

In order to register a bank (other than a state-owned bank), the founders must submit the following documents to the NBU:

1. the application for bank registration;
2. a foundation agreement;
3. the bank's charter;
4. a decision on establishment of the bank (usually the minutes of the founder's meeting);
5. a business plan, prepared in accordance with NBU criteria, defining the types of activities that the bank plans to conduct during the coming year and the strategy for the bank's activity for the next three years;
6. information on the financial standing of each founder having a significant participation in the bank. If a founder is a legal entity, information is also required on the members of the Board and on all persons having a significant participation in such legal entity;
7. accounting and financial reports for the last four reporting periods for the founding legal entities that would have a significant participation in the bank, and a State Tax Administration certificate on income for the last reporting period for individuals who would have a significant participation in the bank;
8. information on the proposed members of the Supervisory Board, the Board of Directors and the Audit Commission;
9. a copy of the receipt for payment of the registration fee (currently about UAH5,100 or approximately USD953);
10. copies of the foundation documents of participants that are legal entities having a significant participation in the bank, certified by a notary;
11. a copy of the report on any initial public offering for the bank (being in the form of an open joint stock company);
12. information on the professional adequacy and business reputation of the chair and the other members of the board and the chief accountant of the bank.

The Law on Banks and Banking Activity requires that registration of a bank should be completed within three months from the date of submission of the full package of the required documents to the NBU, although this is not often achieved. A bank becomes a legal entity once its registration is recorded in the State Register of Banks.

Following the state registration of the bank, it must obtain a banking licence. This licence gives the bank a right (1) to attract deposits and other funds subject to return, (2) to provide loans, and (3) to maintain settlement accounts for clients. Only banks have the right to conduct all three activities at the same time, this being the key feature distinguishing banks from other financial institutions.

In addition to the three major activities mentioned above, a bank having a banking licence may also provide certain other services without obtaining any further permits from the NBU, including providing guarantees and leasing services and issuing credit cards. A bank also requires a special permit from the NBU in order to conduct certain other banking operations, such as certain transactions with currency valuables, trading in securities on the instructions of clients or on its own behalf, underwriting, and trust management of the funds and securities of its clients.

There are strict requirements that a bank must meet in order to obtain a banking licence and NBU permits, including, but not limited to, obligations to have a fully paid-in capital of a specified amount, to be equipped with the necessary banking equipment, computer systems and software, and communication facilities, and to have proper premises and employees with relevant knowledge and expertise. The specific requirements depend on the type of NBU permit sought.

Special rules for establishing a foreign-owned bank in Ukraine

Currently, foreign banks can operate in Ukraine only through their representative offices or through ownership of a Ukrainian bank. The representative offices of a foreign bank cannot conduct any banking operations, whereas a foreign-owned Ukrainian bank can act like any other Ukrainian bank providing full banking services.

In order to establish a bank with 100 per cent or partial foreign capital, the founders of such a bank must obtain the prior permission of the NBU. No such requirement applies for establishing a representative office of a foreign bank. For the registration of a foreign-owned bank, in addition to the documents normally provided for establishing a bank in Ukraine, each corporate foreign investor acquiring a significant participation share in the bank must submit certain documents confirming its status and financial standing, and each individual investor must submit a consent of the appropriate controlling body of the investor's country of residence for making the investment (if required) and documents confirming the absence of criminal convictions.

If the NBU refuses to register a bank with significant foreign participation, based on documents required by the law being missing or not being properly drafted, such a refusal must be in writing and indicate the grounds for the refusal.

Relatively recently a draft law was proposed to Parliament aimed at making the Ukrainian banking market more open to foreign capital by allowing foreign banks to operate in Ukraine through a Ukrainian branch instead of having to incorporate a subsidiary bank in Ukraine. This initiative, however, has encountered serious resistance from certain banking circles, and thus the prospects for its adoption remain unclear.

The banking payment system

The Ukrainian banking mechanism for settlements is relatively efficient. The function of the main clearing bank is performed by the NBU, which holds correspondent accounts of all banks established in Ukraine. All transactions in Ukraine must be conducted between banks within three operational days. As a matter of practice, however, money transferred from one bank to another in Ukraine does not remain in the NBU for more than 20 minutes. Transactions are completed, as a rule, within one hour. A Ukrainian bank, as a correspondent of the NBU, can select the manner of settlement as well as the means of transfer of payment documents and notifications from among those means for settlement and communication provided for in the agreement establishing the correspondent relationship concluded between the bank and the NBU.

Many Ukrainian commercial banks have also joined the international Society for Worldwide Interbank Financial Telecommunications (SWIFT) for their international transfers.

Regulation of cash payments

In order to discourage the use of cash in commercial transactions, the NBU has set limits on the amount of cash payments that may be made between (a) legal entities other than banks and/or (b) individuals trading as entrepreneurs. Currently, cash settlements between one entity (or an individual trading as an entrepreneur) with another entity (or an entrepreneur) may not exceed UAH10,000 per day. Payments exceeding this limit must be conducted by bank (wire) transfer. However, this rule does not apply to (1) settlements by legal entities with individuals (other than entrepreneurs), state budgets and state special funds, (2) small and middle-sized enterprises using cash obtained under certain credit lines with the European Bank of Reconstruction and Development, (3) voluntary donations and charitable contributions received by state tax bodies, (4) settlements for consumed electricity, (5) cash provided for business trips, and (6) settlements of legal entities (including individual entrepreneurs) among themselves for certain agricultural products, as provided by law.

Certain limitations applicable to cashless transfers abroad

In order to control foreign currency outflows and prevent tax avoidance and money laundering, the NBU has introduced limits on certain payments abroad, including interest payments and payments under contracts for services rendered or intellectual property rights provided by non-residents.

It has been a general requirement for a number of years that prior to receiving a loan from a non-resident, a resident company or individual was under an obligation to register a loan agreement with the NBU. Such agreement could be registered only if the interest charged under such contact did not exceed the weighted average interest charged by Ukrainian banks, as published by the NBU from time to time. Recently this system has been amended. As before, loan agreements with non-residents must be registered with the NBU, and the loans may be received only by bank transfer. The limitation of the maximum interest that may be charged by a non-resident, however, now appears to extend not only to loans but also to certain other forms of indebtedness.

This interest limitation, rather than being a statistical figure, is now set by the NBU and generally reflects conditions existing in the world financial markets. It varies depending on the term of the credit extended to a resident as well as on the type of currency used. Currently, the limitations on fixed annual interest on indebtedness in currency such as US dollars or euros are set at 9.8 per cent if the credit is extended for less than a year, at 10 per cent if the loan term is more than a year but less than three years, and at 11 per cent if the credit is extended for a longer period. The loan registration requirement does not generally apply to banks that are permitted to conduct foreign currency operations in the international market.

In addition, relatively recently the NBU introduced regulations intended to limit such traditional methods of capital repatriation and tax optimization as the use of payments to non-residents for services and various intellectual property rights. First, under the new rules banks and non-bank financial institutions are allowed to transfer funds to non-residents for services or intellectual property rights provided to non-residents only on the basis of (1) an agreement or any other document that under Ukrainian law is treated as a contract, and (2) documents that confirm that the services were rendered or that the work was performed, or the intellectual property rights were provided. Such documents should be made available either at the time of the fund transfer or, if the services are provided under a deferral of payment scheme, within a 90-day period after the fund transfer.

Second, if the amount of transfers to a non-resident under the same contact exceeds 50,000 euros or the equivalent of this sum, such amount may be transferred only if the transferor receives an act of price examination issued by the State Information-Analytical Centre for Monitoring the External Goods Markets confirming that the contract price corresponds to the market situation. For purposes of calculating whether the above-mentioned threshold is met, the contract prices of all contracts entered between the same parties for the provision of the services and intellectual property rights of the same class, as defined by law, are aggregated. This limit does not apply to transactions that require an individual NBU licence, to certain operations of residents under intergovernmental agreements, to payments for financial, tourist, transport and communication services where the residents hold a licence for conducting commercial activity in these fields, and to certain other payments.

Exchange control regulations

Ukraine has an elaborate system of exchange control regulations, which contains more limitations than what is typical in the West. The Decree of the Cabinet of Ministers of Ukraine 'On the System of Currency Regulation and Currency Control' (the 'Decree'), which establishes the groundwork of the Ukrainian exchange control regulations, was introduced in 1993, and many of its provisions now appear to be somewhat outdated. Even though drafts of a law intended to replace this Decree have been under consideration by the Ukrainian Parliament for a number of years, it is not clear what form such a law would take, if adopted, and when, or if, it might take place.

Under the Decree, all payments for transactions conducted in Ukraine must be made in UAH. Settlements between residents and non-residents for trade transactions must be made in foreign currency through authorized banks. Under the mandatory sale requirement currently in force, 50 per cent of all foreign currency revenues from export operations must be sold by the resident in exchange for UAH, with some minor exceptions.

For currency control purposes, a licensing requirement exists for certain operations with currency valuables, which are defined to include Ukrainian and foreign currency, payment documents and other securities denominated in Ukrainian or foreign currencies and banking metals. Specifically, a licence is required for the following operations, conducted on a one-time basis:

- the export or transfer outside of Ukraine of any currency valuables, with certain exceptions;
- the transfer into Ukraine of Ukrainian currency, except if such currency was previously legally taken outside of Ukraine;
- any use of foreign currency in Ukraine as a means of payment or for a mortgage;
- the allocation of currency valuables to accounts and the making of deposits outside of Ukraine, except if held by Ukrainians residing abroad and for certain correspondent accounts;
- investing abroad, including the purchase of securities, except for securities or other corporate rights inherited by individuals or received as a gift.

The Decree also provides for certain exceptions. Other than the general exception from the licensing requirement for currency transactions entered into between Ukrainian residents where only Ukrainian currency is involved, the following operations do not require an NBU licence:

- The taking or transfer abroad from Ukraine of foreign currency by an individual resident in Ukraine in an amount stipulated by the NBU. Currently, this sum for individuals, both residents and non-residents, travelling abroad from Ukraine for tourism or private matters is USD6,000 or its equivalent in another foreign currency. However, the law requires that (1) non-residents declare all amounts taken abroad exceeding USD1,000 in a custom declaration, and (2) residents declare amounts taken abroad exceeding USD3,000.
- The taking outside of Ukraine of amounts up to USD10,000 by residents and non-residents going abroad for business reasons, provided such amount is declared in a custom declaration.
- The transfer or sending abroad of foreign currency that was legally brought into Ukraine earlier, as evidenced by an import custom declaration.
- Payments in a foreign currency made by a resident outside Ukraine to satisfy liabilities in that currency to a non-resident for services, goods, works involving intellectual property rights and other property rights, except for payment for currency valuables and payments under life insurance agreements. As mentioned above,

however, special limits were imposed on payments for services provided by a non-resident.

- Payments of interest in foreign currency on loans made into Ukraine as well as the repatriation of profits earned on a foreign investment in Ukraine.
- Repatriation of the amount of a foreign investment made in Ukraine upon termination of the investment activity.

Banks and certain other financial institutions are not required to obtain separate licences to conduct each of the operations mentioned above, as long as they, as financial institutions, have general licences and permits for conducting currency operations.

As mentioned above, Ukrainian legislation in the area of the exchange control regulations is not flawless. Specifically, there are a number of requirements in the Decree that, in principle as a matter of law should be enforced in Ukraine, but in reality cannot be complied with by individuals and companies as there are no procedures for doing so. They are therefore not enforced.

An example is the requirement to obtain a licence for making deposits or allocations of 'currency valuables' into accounts outside of Ukraine. Since the term 'currency valuables' is defined to include securities, the above-mentioned requirement also applies to the opening of accounts in securities abroad. Unfortunately, at present the NBU has not made public any procedure for obtaining such licence for the opening of a securities account abroad. This, causes difficulties where, for example, Ukrainian employees working for a multinational corporation in Ukraine are to be allocated shares of the parent companies incorporated abroad under an employee incentive plan. Another example is the broad requirement for Ukrainian residents to declare currency valuables held abroad. Under the existing system, the procedure established by the NBU applies only for legal entities and individuals trading as entrepreneurs, so that individuals other than registered entrepreneurs are not able to comply with the declaration requirement since there are no such procedures applicable to them.

Money laundering

A new system of financial monitoring, identification of persons conducting financial operations and reporting requirements for financial operations was introduced by the Law 'On Preventing and Countering the Legalization (Laundering) of Criminal Proceeds' of 28 November 2002 (the 'Anti-Money Laundering Law'). This Law creates a two-tier system of financial monitoring that consists of so-called initial financial monitoring and state monitoring.

The responsibility for initial monitoring has been imposed on banks, insurance companies and other financial institutions as well as other organizations, including exchange markets, professional securities dealers, investment funds and those financial organizations that conduct financial transactions. State monitoring is conducted by the Financial Monitoring Department of the Ministry of Finance of Ukraine, central bodies of government and the NBU. Significant penalties are stipulated for the violation of the anti-money laundering provisions.

3.5

Ukrainian Securities Laws

Bate C Toms, BC Toms & Co

The past several years have witnessed the development of a Ukrainian securities market and, in response, more effective regulation. Yet, the capitalization of the Ukrainian securities market does not exceed 2 to 3 per cent of its annual GDP, and the volume of securities trading remains insignificant. While stock exchanges and over-the-counter trading systems have been in existence for almost a decade, most transactions are still carried out directly between companies, and the liquidity of Ukrainian securities is mostly a theoretical issue, subject to few exceptions. Thus, it would be inappropriate to compare the Ukrainian securities market to any of those existing in the West. Despite privatization, a steadily growing economy and the existing basic legal framework, both the securities market and its regulation are still at an early stage of development.

Legal framework

The basic legal framework for the issuance and circulation of securities in Ukraine is created by the Law of Ukraine 'On Securities and the Stock Exchange' of 18 June 1991 (the 'Securities Law'), and the newly adopted 'Civil Code' of Ukraine of 16 January 2003 (the Civil Code), which became effective on 1 January 2004. The Law of Ukraine 'On the State Regulation of the Securities Market in Ukraine' of 30 October 1996 (the 'Securities Market Regulation Law') specifies types of professional activities on the securities market and establishes a rule that such professional activities can only be performed under a specific licence. The Law of Ukraine 'On the National Depositary System and Peculiarities of the Electronic Circulation of Securities in Ukraine' of 10 December 1997 (the 'Depositary System Law') defines the depositary system and its participants, and the procedure for the issuance and circulation of securities.

A number of other legislative acts exist, which govern certain types of securities or particular issues on their circulation. These include the Law of Ukraine 'On the Institutes of Joint Investment (Shared and Corporate Investment Funds)' of 15 March 2001, the Decree of the Cabinet of Ministers of Ukraine 'On Trust Companies' of 17 March 1993, and the Law of Ukraine 'On the Circulations of Bills of Exchange' of 5 April 2001.

The general procedure for the establishment of different types of companies, including joint stock companies, and their operation by shareholders and management, including the issuance of shares, is determined by the Law of Ukraine 'On Business Associations' of 19 September 1991, the Civil Code and the Commercial Code of Ukraine of 16 January 2003.

There are also numerous regulations adopted by various state bodies that implement general legislation in the securities area. Most such regulations came from the State Commission of Ukraine on Securities and Stock Market (the Securities Commission). However, in certain cases, regulations of the State Property Fund of Ukraine, the National Bank of Ukraine and the Antimonopoly Committee of Ukraine among other state bodies may be relevant to securities transactions.

In addition to domestic law, international treaties ratified by Ukraine may be applicable. These include the 1930 Geneva Convention providing a Uniform Law for Bills of Exchange and Promissory Notes, the 1930 Convention for the Settlement of Certain Conflicts of Laws in connection with Bills of Exchange and Promissory Notes and the 1930 Geneva Convention on the Stamp Laws in connection with Bills of Exchange and Promissory Notes.

Securities Commission

The Securities Commission was established in 1995 as the primary state regulator of the securities market. Its authority was substantially broadened after the adoption of the Securities Market Regulation Law in 1996. The Securities Commission is composed of a Chairman and six members appointed by the President of Ukraine subject to approval by the Parliament and serve for a term of seven years. In addition to its national office in Kyiv, the Securities Commission has 27 regional departments.

The powers of the Securities Commission are enumerated in the Regulation 'On the State Commission on Securities and the Stock Market' approved by the Presidential Decree of 14 February 1997, No. 142/97, and other legal acts, including the following:

- establishing the requirements for the issuance and circulation of securities, including for registration of such issuances and prospectuses;
- granting permissions to Ukrainian issuers for circulation of their securities abroad;
- establishing the requirements for the admission of securities of foreign issuers for circulation in Ukraine;
- establishing the requirements for licences for professional activities in the securities market, including licences for depositaries, custodians, registrars, brokers and dealers;
- establishing the procedure for and conducting the registration of stock exchanges and over-the-counter trading systems, as well as professional self-regulatory organizations of the participants of the securities market;
- establishing the requirements and standards for the disclosure of information by issuers and by professional securities market participants.

Definition and types of securities

Definition of securities

Securities are defined in the Securities Law as 'monetary documents that certify relationships between the issuer and their owner and envisage, as a rule, income repayment in the form of dividends or interest and also the possibility to transfer the monetary and other rights that stem from these documents to other persons'. It is obvious that this definition is far from perfect and a better definition is now available in the Civil Code, which provides that: 'A security is a document in the established form with appropriate details, which certifies a monetary or other property right, determines the relationship between the person that issued it and the owner, and provides for the performance of obligations in accordance with the conditions of the issuance as well as for the possibility to transfer the rights arising out of this document to other persons.'

Classification of securities

The Civil Code classifies securities by dividing them into groups and types. According to Article 195 of the Civil Code, the following groups of securities exist in Ukraine:

1. Participation securities (ie equity securities), which confirm participation in the authorized capital and entitle the owner to take part in the management of the issuer and to receive profit distributions (including dividends) and a share of the issuer's assets in case of liquidation. This type of security currently mainly covers shares (stock), but also includes investment certificates.
2. Debt securities, which confirm lending relationships and envisage an obligation of the issuer to pay the funds back within a defined period of time. The typical securities that fit this description are corporate bonds, treasury bonds and certificates of deposit (as well as, arguably, promissory notes, bills of exchange and cheques, although as a matter of legal theory, they are usually put into the separate category of 'payment securities').
3. Derivative securities, the mechanism for the issuance of which is related to the right to buy or sell securities and other financial or commodity resources during a contractually agreed term. This should cover all the various forms of derivatives, the most common of which are options, futures, forwards contracts and warrants.
4. Securities of title, which give their holder the right to dispose of the property indicated in these securities. Examples of this type of security are bills of lading, warehouse receipts and mortgage notes (bonds).

This list of groups of securities is not exclusive. The Civil Code does not list any particular types of securities and rather provides that the types of securities should be established by legislative acts.

The Securities Law lists the following types of securities:

- shares (stock);
- state and municipal bonds;
- corporate bonds;
- treasury obligations;
- savings certificates;
- bills of exchange and promissory notes;
- privatization certificates; and
- investment certificates.

Although the Securities Law was an important and progressive legal act when it was adopted in 1991, it no longer reflects the economic realities, and its limited list of securities is a good illustration of this problem. Derivatives are not mentioned in this list, although the State

Regulation Law contains a definition of derivative securities. Among the other types of securities that are not identified in the Law on Securities are bills of lading, cheques, mortgage notes and warehouse receipts.

Mortgage notes, a relatively new security for the Ukrainian legal system, were introduced by the Law of Ukraine 'On Mortgage' of 5 June 2003, No. 898. They allow mortgages to be freely transferable, for example by sale or pledge to third parties. This should create an opportunity for big mortgagors, such as banks or construction companies, to enter the Ukrainian securities market with new instruments, such as mortgage bonds in which the mortgage is represented by a number of mortgage notes that can separately be sold to different investors.

Among the various types of securities, the most commonly used in Ukraine are shares, bonds, promissory notes and bills of exchange.

Issuance and characteristics of the most common securities

Shares

Shares can be issued by joint stock companies ('JSCs'), but not by limited liability or any other type of companies existing in Ukraine. Two types of JSC exist in Ukraine: closed and open. Shares of an open JSC can be publicly traded. Shares of a closed JSC cannot be publicly traded and are initially distributed among the founders, who may subsequently sell them in private transactions. Open JSCs can issue both registered and bearer shares, while closed JSCs can issue only registered shares.

Shares can be issued either in certificated form (called 'documentary' under Ukrainian law), where physical certificates are distributed among the shareholders, or in non-certificated (electronic) form (called 'non-documentary' under Ukrainian laws), where only electronic entries are maintained to certify ownership of shares. Title to securities issued in non-documentary form is confirmed by an extract from the 'securities account' issued by a custodian, which extract is itself not a security and cannot be traded.

The issuance of shares must be registered with the Securities Commission before the circulation of shares can begin.

In 2002–03, there was much litigation over whether charters of closed joint stock companies may impose limitations on the rights of shareholders to dispose of shares (ie, to create pre-emption rights, etc). The prevailing view appeared to be that such restrictions could not be imposed by the charter of a company. The Commercial Code has partially resolved this controversy. Part 3 of Article 81 of the

Commercial Code states that 'shareholders of a closed joint stock company have a pre-emptive right to acquire shares, which are being sold by the other shareholders of the company'. To be effective this provision requires that detailed implementation rules be established in the charter of a company. Furthermore, the cited provision leaves numerous loopholes, for example, because the pre-emptive rights apply only to sales of shares, and not to transfers by gift or inheritance (or possibly not even to barter transactions). These deficiencies would be corrected if the Law 'On Joint Stock Companies' is adopted in its current draft by Parliament.

Bonds

During the past three years, the corporate bond market has made a giant leap, as Ukrainian companies have tried to make up for the lack of equity funding by issuing corporate bonds. To respond to this market trend, the Securities Commission adopted its Regulation 'On the Issuance of Bonds by Enterprises' of 17 July 2003 (the 'Bond Regulation'), which is intended to balance the need to protect investors by requiring wider disclosure of information on the issuer with the need to simplify the procedure for the non-public issuance of bonds, though some important issues have not been addressed.

Until recently, one of the most frequently cited impediments to the development of the corporate bond market was the limitation on the value of their issuance set forth in Article 11 of the Securities Law, which provides that the value of bonds issued by a joint stock company may not exceed 25 per cent of its authorized capital. Article 158 of the Civil Code has increased this limitation to permit bonds up to 100 per cent of the authorized capital of the issuer or the value of security granted to the issuer for this purpose by third persons, whichever is greater. This limitation can, however, easily be overcome by having a joint stock company establish a special purpose vehicle in any form other than a joint stock company so that this vehicle may issue bonds without regard to the amount of its, or its parent's, authorized capital.

Promissory notes and bills of exchange

Promissory notes and bills of exchange are commonly used in Ukraine for settlements in commercial transactions. The Law of Ukraine 'On the Circulations of Bills of Exchange' of 5 April 2001, which implements the 1930 Geneva Convention providing for a Uniform Law for Bills of Exchange and Promissory Notes, to which Ukraine is a party, establishes a general legal framework that is not much different from what one would find in other countries following the 1930 Geneva Convention. One of the important peculiarities is that promissory notes and bills of exchange in Ukraine can be issued only in evidence of debt for goods that were actually delivered or services rendered. Thus, for example, promissory notes cannot be used to provide evidence of debt under loan agreements. Payment under promissory notes and bills of exchange must be made by wire transfer. Promissory notes and bills of exchange cannot be used for investment (contribution) in the authorized capital of Ukrainian companies.

The national depositary system

Depositary activities and the depositary system

Depositary activity is defined as the provision of services related to keeping custody over securities in any form, to operating and maintaining accounts in securities, to conducting operations with such accounts (including clearing and settlements under agreements) and to servicing the issuer's operations in respect of issued securities. Clearing means the receipt, verification and updating of information, and the preparation of the accounting documents necessary both for transactions with securities and for making payments.

The depositary system consists of custodians that maintain accounts of securities, and registrars that maintain registers of shareholders. This creates a dual system of registration, depending on whether securities exist in certificated or non-certificated form. Custodians keep only those securities that exist in a non-certificated (electronic) form. These shares could either be issued in a non-certificated form or, if originally issued in a certificated form, they could be transferred into a non-certificated form by a process known as 'dematerialization'. Registrars keep registers of shareholders if shares are issued in certificated form. However, if such shares are later dematerialized, then the custodian keeping the shareholder's shares would be listed in the register as the nominal shareholder.

On top of the custodians and registrars, there is a national depositary that maintains accounts in securities for custodians and performs clearing and settlements in security transactions.

Depositaries

A depositary is a legal entity in the form of an open joint stock company created by at least 10 custodians, provided that one custodian cannot hold more than 25 per cent of the depositary's authorized capital fund, the paid-in amount of which must be not less than the equivalent of 400,000 euros. The depositary can only provide depositary activities.

In addition to the requirements on the legal form of the depositary and the minimum amount of its authorized capital fund, other Ukrainian rules are aimed at protecting the rights of holders of securities. For example, a depositary is formally prohibited from treating securities that belong to its client as being its own assets and cannot use them for its own interests or the interests of third parties (eg by pledging such securities). In addition, a depositary cannot hold securities in trust or, without the special permission of its client, transfer them in trust or for the management of third parties. Prior to the adoption of the Depositary System Law, a depositary could also clear securities and make cash settlements. Now, financial settlements can only be provided by depositaries using the services of a settlement bank (a bank that has an agreement with the depositary for providing such settlement service). This separation of clearing and financial settlement is another attempt to provide more protection to securities holders.

All information regarding securities must be kept by the depositary both in electronic form and on hard copies. The Securities Commission has established a rule that a depositary must preserve its archives, including electronic data and the hard copies, for five years.

As a practical matter, creation of a national depositary in Ukraine proved to be a difficult and controversial task. The first national depositary was created in 1996 by a number of banks and other securities market players under the name of the Open Joint Stock Company 'Interregional Stock Union' (for further details, please see http://www.mfs.kiev.ua).

After the adoption of the Depositary System Law in 1998, the state initiated the creation of a national depositary in which the Securities Commission and the National Bank of Ukraine would hold a shareholding of up to 25 per cent. This national depositary was created under the name of the Open Joint Stock Company 'The National Depositary of Ukraine' (for further details, please see http://www.ndu.gov.ua). However, as it was deemed inappropriate for this company to compete with the Interregional Stock Union, the functions of this National Depositary of Ukraine are currently limited to the codification of securities (in order to ensure compliance with international standards) and the standardization of the documentation used in securities transactions. Depositary functions with respect to state securities are performed by the National Bank of Ukraine.

Custodians

Custodians maintain accounts in securities for investors. Commercial banks and securities traders can be custodians and provide custodial services for securities and perform registration of title to securities, provided that they have received an appropriate licence. The

Depositary System Law prohibits custodians from performing clearing and the registration of securities that are in the custody of the custodian. If a custodian receives a licence to perform registrar activities, then it must cease performing custodial services in respect of the securities for which it serves as a registrar. Clearing of securities, as mentioned above, can only be performed by depositaries.

Registration and registrars

Registration plays an important role in the circulation process for securities in certificate form because the rights of new owners of registered securities can only be exercised after the appropriate changes are made to the register to reflect the change of title.

Under the Depositary System Law, every legal entity issuing shares in certificate form must either maintain its own share registry or have its share registry kept by an independent registrar licensed to carry out such activity. If the number of shareholders exceeds a threshold amount determined by the Securities Commission (currently 500 shareholders), then the issuer must have its share registry kept by an independent registrar pursuant to a written agreement.

According to Ukrainian law, registration consists of the maintenance of a register system that contains: (1) the register of registered securities owners; (2) individual accounts of the issuer and the registered persons (owners and nominal holders); (3) books that reflect records made in the register; and (4) documents that are the basis for the register's records (title documents, etc). Such a system is required by law and is supposed to make it possible to retrieve lost information regarding registered persons and their securities because information lost from one part of the system can be renewed based on information from another part.

Registration can be performed by registrars – legal entities that have a licence issued by the Securities Commission to maintain a register of the owners of registered securities. If the issuer of securities held by a register is also a founder of the registrar, then such issuer cannot own more than 10 per cent of the authorized capital of the registrar. Ukrainian law also has a number of requirements regarding the maintenance of technical equipment and keeping confidential information in respect of the registrar's activities.

Circulation of securities

Transactions in securities

Securities transactions can be concluded on an organized market (the stock exchanges or trading systems) or on a non-organized market (ie directly between parties). The depositary system allows professional market participants and their clients to trade much like in the West, with 'payment against delivery' and other effective protections for purchasers.

Almost 90 per cent of all securities transactions on the organized market in Ukraine are conducted through the First Securities Trading System, better known under its Ukrainian abbreviation of PFTS. PFTS is the oldest and the largest self-regulated organization in the Ukrainian securities market that performs the functions of an over-the-counter trading system, similar to NASDAQ in the United States (for further details, please see http://www.pfts.com).

Even for direct transactions between two parties, it is usually recommended to engage a securities broker as an intermediary. Article 4 of the Law of Ukraine 'On the State Regulation of the Securities Market in Ukraine' of 30 October 1996 states that a licence is required for 'trading in securities', which is defined as being '... the purchase of securities on one's own behalf and at one's own expense with an aim of future resale of such securities (dealer activity)'. While a single transaction in securities should not raise issues regarding the need for a professional dealer license for activity in the securities market, assuming an intention to resell the securities cannot be demonstrated, the transaction has a potential risk of challenge based on interpretations by the Securities Commission. This risk can be avoided by using a professional intermediary.

Transfer of ownership

One of the essential issues for a purchaser of shares is to determine at what moment title to the shares is actually transferred. The Depositary System Law introduced a clear rule that title to securities in non-certificate form (including immobilized securities) passes to the buyer at the moment when they are credited to the buyer's securities account with its custodian (ie when the custodian of the buyer makes an appropriate entry in the registration records of the buyer). The title in this case is evidenced by the extract from the securities account issued by the custodian, which, however, is not a security itself and cannot be traded.

With respect to certificated securities, the Depositary System Law merely states that they are transferred by way of endorsement, without specifically saying that title passes upon such endorsement. This should allow the parties contractually to establish the moment when title passes to the buyer. Such a flexible approach may, however, also create a potential legal risk that title may be secretly passed to another buyer, unknown to the purchaser receiving an endorsed security, which could result in litigation between two bona fide purchasers.

As a practical matter, no actual endorsement is made on share certificates. Instead, as mandated by the Securities Commission, by signing a transfer order that is given to the registrar, the seller fulfils the requirement for endorsement of a registered security.

Although legally the title to certificated registered securities may pass upon endorsement or at some other moment, the rights to participate in general meetings, to receive dividends, etc, which arise out of ownership of these securities, can be exercised only when the appropriate entry is made to the register of the owners of the registered securities.

Circulation of foreign securities in Ukraine

Special rules apply for the circulation of shares and bonds of foreign companies in Ukraine. Such securities must be registered with the Securities Commission in accordance with the procedure specified in the Securities Commission Regulation 'On the Procedure of Registration of Shares and Bonds of Foreign Issuers in Ukraine' of 20 November 1997 (the 'Foreign Securities Registration Procedure'). (This must be done in addition to any registrations and other actions made to comply with requirements for the issuance of securities in the foreign issuer's home jurisdiction.) Presently, only securities issued in non-certificate form and listed on at least one of the following stock exchanges – New York, Tokyo, Toronto, Hong-Kong, Frankfurt or London – will be permitted to circulate in Ukraine.

The application to the Securities Commission must include a prospectus containing a detailed description of the issuer and the securities intended for circulation in Ukraine, as specified in the Foreign Securities Registration Procedure. After Ukrainian registration of the securities' issuance (which should usually be completed within 60 days of submitting all required documents), this prospectus must be published in the specified official Ukrainian periodicals.

The foreign issuer whose securities circulate in Ukraine will also have a number of continuing obligations, similar to those of domestic issuers, including making regular disclosures to the Securities Commission and in the qualifying publications.

All transactions with securities of foreign issuer must be conducted within the national depositary system, through stock exchanges or through trade-information systems, such as PFTS.

A Ukrainian company or an individual may also purchase securities issued abroad directly, even if they are not specially registered for circulation in Ukraine, subject to compliance with Ukrainian exchange control rules (in particular, subject to the receipt of a licence from the National Bank of Ukraine, which is usually difficult to obtain). Such a transaction would usually be outside of the reach of Ukrainian securities laws, subject to certain controversial issues if such security is resold by one Ukrainian resident to another Ukrainian resident.

Exchange control considerations

Ukraine continues to maintain a restrictive system of currency rules and exchange control requirements that impede transactions with securities. The Decree of the Cabinet of Ministers 'On the System of Currency Regulation and Control' of 19 February 1993 treats securities as 'currency valuables' and requires that a National Bank of Ukraine (the 'NBU') licence be obtained, in particular, for:

- any investments abroad, including the purchase of securities of a foreign issuer (excluding securities acquired as a result of inheritance or gift);
- any purchases of securities of Ukrainian issuers by residents from non-residents (before 2003, all such transactions were done without a licence, relying on the exemption for the return of investments, but on 29 January 2003, the NBU adopted the procedure for the issuance of licences for such purchases);
- any physical movement of share certificates and other certificated securities out of Ukraine.

In theory, the opening of any securities accounts abroad should also require a separate licence from the NBU, but no licensing procedure has been established for this purpose. This, together with the unreasonably burdensome procedure for the receipt of licences for the purchase of securities of foreign issuers, is one of the reasons why the usually exceptionally generous employee share plans used by many Western multinational companies across the world cannot be implemented in Ukraine for the benefit of Ukrainian employees without creating a risk that these plans will be challenged.

Competition law considerations

Acquisitions of shares in excess of 25 per cent or 50 per cent of the authorized capital of the issuer and certain other transactions with securities may require the approval of the Ukrainian Antimonopoly Committee, provided that established jurisdictional thresholds are met.

Disclosure of information

One of the main directions in which the Securities Commission is currently moving is to promote full disclosure of information by the issuers of securities. Currently, the issuers of securities are required to disclose the so-called 'regular information' on an annual basis, including the results of business activities for the previous year and balance sheet. Issuers must also, within two days of an event, disclose any 'special information', defined as any change in the business activity that influences the value of the securities or the income derived from them, including:

- any changes in the rights of the shareholders;
- any changes in the managing or controlling bodies of the issuer;
- any arrests of the issuer's bank accounts;
- any decisions on the reorganization or liquidation of the issuer;
- any destruction of more than 10 per cent of the issuer's assets;
- any lawsuits the value of which exceeds 10 per cent of the issuer's authorized capital or fixed and current assets;
- any receipt of a loan or the issuance of securities for an amount exceeding 50 per cent of the issuer's authorized capital or fixed and current assets.

The failure of the issuer to disclose relevant information promptly may allow an investor to rescind a transaction in securities. Pursuant to Article 37 of the Securities Law, an investor who subscribed for securities or purchased them before information affecting the value of securities or the income derived from them is published may unilaterally terminate the agreement for the purchase of such securities 15 days after such information is published.

Insider trading

Ukraine has virtually no insider trading laws and transactions based on inside information are the prevailing practice, not the exception. The need to regulate insider trading was raised in Ukraine during the second half of the 1990s, but with little success. Relevant provisions on this were added to the draft of the new Securities Law, but this has not yet been adopted.

Currently, only employees of direct participants in the depositary system and certain state officials supervising the depositary system are prohibited by Article 18 of the Depositary System Law from purchasing and selling securities based on inside information.

Prospective developments

Significant further development of the Ukrainian securities law is expected over the next several years. In 2000 and 2001, a draft of a proposed comprehensive Securities Law was presented to Parliament, but failed to receive the necessary votes. This draft was prepared with the participation of domestic and foreign experts from various branches of government and the private sector. It would cover in greater detail the functions of the various market participants, the procedure for the issuance and the registration of securities, the disclosure of information and the prohibition of insider trading. It is expected that this draft law will be modified and resubmitted to Parliament.

The Securities Commission can also be expected to improve its regulations. It is often stated that investors are not protected by the current licensing standards for professional securities market intermediaries because they fail to ensure that only well-capitalized, qualified market intermediaries receive a licence. These requirements are likely to change in the near future, which should result in licences being withdrawn from those who are not able to meet the higher standards.

Another current trend is to decrease the regulatory burden for small companies, which are clearly over-regulated by current law and by the Securities Commission's activities and rules. The focus of both law and regulation is likely to be on the market for the securities of large, actively traded companies. Small private businesses with only a handful of shareholders will probably be forced to change their corporate form to become a limited liability company or some other business form, and the Securities Commission will probably concentrate their investor protection activities on those large joint stock companies with diversified shareholdings.

Part Four

Business Development: Operating an Enterprise

4.1

Ukrainian Real Estate Law

Bate C Toms, Taras Dumych and Svitlana Kheda, BC Toms & Co

This chapter examines the principal features and problems of Ukrainian real estate law (other than Land Law, which is covered in the next chapter), focusing on recent legislative developments. At the outset, it should be noted that Ukrainian law is still in the process of development, particularly as to acquiring and leasing residential and office space in urban areas. Despite improvements, there remain several significant, but little-noticed problems, discussed below. These problems make confirmation of title to premises difficult, if not impossible, and have resulted in losses to unsuspecting purchasers.

Most significantly, some title transfers and mortgages may not be reflected in the public registries. It is expected that these problems will be resolved in the near future, but for now, they present legal as well as practical problems for many transactions.

The most important legislative developments of 2003 include adoption of the Civil Code ('New Civil Code') and the Law 'On Mortgages' (both of which came into force on 1 January 2004). Amendments have also been enacted to the Law 'On Leasing of Land' and to the Land Code, which were intended to solve various issues such as the right of companies with foreign investment to purchase land plots in Ukraine, but which still leave unresolved issues. The newly adopted Law 'On Individual Income Tax', which came into effect on 1 January 2004, may also affect the rights of foreign companies and individuals to lease real property in Ukraine.

The New Civil Code establishes for the first time a legal definition of real estate (real property): land plots and constructions located on land plots, relocation of which is impossible without reducing the value and changing the purpose of the use of such constructions. This regime of real property is also extended by the law to aircraft, vessels and space objects. The Code establishes that the integral property complex of an enterprise is real property and may be subject to sale, purchase, pledge, lease and other transactions.

Privatization of residential apartments by Ukrainians

During the past 13 years, most residential apartments in the cities of Ukraine have been privatized by individuals. The right of Ukrainian urban residents to privatize the apartments they rent from the state arose from the Law 'On Privatization of the State Dwelling Fund' (19 June 1992). This Law allows such privatization by purchase of the lessee's apartment for a state-appraised value, and then effectively crediting each Ukrainian individual with certain assets, so that whether any payment above the value of these assets is due from the occupier depends on a valuation based on the location, type, condition and size of the premises and on the number of family members or other occupiers involved.

For example, in Kyiv, a family of three may ordinarily privatize an apartment of $73m^2$ or less for free. For a larger apartment, an additional payment would usually be required for the extra space. The additional payment is based on a formula. Such an owner might therefore choose to continue to rent the premises rather than pay for privatization. Once privatized, the owner may deal with the premises as he or she wishes, including selling, leasing, mortgaging or otherwise disposing of them.

This legislation allows buildings, and the apartments and offices in them, to be owned privately by both Ukrainians and foreigners. An active real estate market has resulted.

Purchases and leasing of premises by foreigners – specially required permissions

Under Soviet law, until 1991, foreigners were prohibited from purchasing any real estate interests in Ukraine. This changed with the adoption in 1991 of the Law 'On Property', which permitted foreigners to purchase buildings, as well as offices and residential premises. However, since June 1997, in order to be valid, certain purchases of such real estate by foreign companies and other foreign legal entities must be authorized by a permit, as required by the Regulation of the Cabinet of Ministers of Ukraine 'On Changes and Amendments to the Resolution on the Procedure for Locating Diplomatic Representations,

Consulate Offices of Foreign Countries and Representations of International and Foreign Organizations', No. 670, of 28 June 1997 (the 'Regulation').

The Regulation is, in practice, being used to prohibit any purchase or leasing of apartments, offices or other real estate by foreign companies, except with the permission of a designated governmental body. The Ministry of Justice has expressed its opinion to notaries that the Regulation applies to all foreign legal entities (notaries in Ukraine, as under most other European civil law systems, are a type of lawyer with special statutory qualifications and powers to handle certain types of transactions, including, in particular, those involving the sale or mortgaging of real estate).

In addition, the General Direction for Services to Representative Offices (known by its Ukrainian abbreviation as 'GDIP'), which issues such permissions in Kyiv (elsewhere in Ukraine, the appropriate oblast administrations and the city administration of Sevastopol grant such permissions), has implemented the Regulation, on the instructions of the Ministry of Justice, to require GDIP's approval for all purchases or leases of premises by foreign companies in Kyiv. In principle, this should apply equally to require GDIP approval for leases of property. On this basis, GDIP has refused to permit numerous proposed purchases by Western companies. GDIP's position that any purchase or lease by a foreign entity without its permission is void and subject to legal challenge is, however, questionable since the Regulation only obliquely refers to 'foreign firms, etc' in its definition of what constitutes a 'representation of a foreign organization' that is reached by its requirements. (The Regulation otherwise generally focuses on the diplomatic representations of countries and international organizations.) Furthermore, the literal wording of the Regulation requires GDIP approval *only* if the premises are being purchased 'to locate a representation of a foreign organization', which should exclude the need for approval of purchases of premises for other purposes, such as for further development with a view to sale or lease.

The requirement for receipt of such GDIP permission used to be also provided for in the Instruction of the State Construction Committee of 9 June 1998 'On the Procedure for the Registration of Title of Legal Entities and Individuals to Immovable Property' (which ceased to be effective as of 15 February 2002). It stated that the Bureau of Technical Inventory ('BTI', the agency for registration of title to real estate other than land) will register agreements for the purchase of real estate by foreign organizations only if the relevant permissions have been obtained. (This had caused a problem for one Embassy in Ukraine, which was subsequently obliged to give up premises because of the lack of the GDIP's permission.) Under the currently effective Order of the Ministry of Justice of Ukraine of 7 February 2002 'On the Approval of the Temporary Regulation of the Procedure for Registration of Title to Real Estate', the registration of real estate premises sale-purchase contracts for the location in such real estate premises of embassies may be carried out only upon the receipt of the Note of the Ministry of Foreign Affairs of Ukraine; as to the foreign and international non-governmental organizations, the GDIP approval letter is required.

Procedure to purchase offices and apartments

Documents required of the seller

The title documents that should initially be presented by the seller for the buyer's review ordinarily include: (1) a certificate of privatization, a purchase contract (which will usually be notarized showing the number and bearing the seal of the notary before whom it was executed), or evidence of inheritance or gift; (2) a certificate from the appropriate BTI office stating that the seller is the owner and citing the BTI registration number; and (3) a certificate from the Unified Register of Prohibitions on Disposal of Immovable Property verifying the absence of mortgages, arrest or other encumbrances (however, for the reasons discussed below, such a document will not necessarily provide conclusive proof that the property is, in fact, owned free of adverse claims). Individuals should also provide a passport and tax identification number.

In addition, an investigation should be conducted regarding any residency registrations (formerly known as *propyskas)*. They are residency permits for individuals stating in which locality and where they live. In particular, a buyer should confirm that all individuals who could have residential rights to the premises (including children through their representatives) have relinquished their rights. Therefore, a certificate from the local state dwelling management enterprise (known as ZHEK, discussed below) should also be obtained to confirm who is listed as residing at the premises, and the status of utility payments.

A corporate seller will need to prove that it is a validly existing and registered entity and that its representatives are properly authorized to enter into the sale transaction. The foregoing is usually accomplished for a foreign company by providing a fully notarized and legalized set of the following documents, with certified translations into Ukrainian: (1) resolutions on the appointment of the company's officials who have signatory authority or other documents that confirm the authority of the company's representatives; (2) a copy of the certificate of incorporation of the company; (3) a copy of the foundation documents (charter, memorandum and articles of association or similar document) or extracts thereof confirming the authority of the company to sell real property; and (4) a power of attorney from the company's officials authorizing any individual representing it to sign on its behalf, if applicable.

Documents required of the buyer

An individual buyer must provide a passport. A corporate buyer will need to prove that its representatives are authorized to enter into the purchase transaction, which is usually accomplished with documents paralleling those indicated above for a corporate seller. In addition, a foreign company should hold the permission from GDIP (discussed above) for a purchase in Kyiv, or of the relevant oblast or Sevastopol City administration, as applicable. The notary should also require submission of receipts confirming that the state duty and pension fee (each constituting 1 per cent of the amount of the transaction) have been paid.

BTI documents and purchase contracts

Review of BTI documents and purchase contracts

The buyer should, to begin with, verify the seller's title by reviewing the BTI and other title documents and checking these with the notary or exchange (auction) house (if one was used) responsible for the conveyance. The purchase contract that is registered with the BTI must contain a Ukrainian version, but it may be made in two or more languages.

Traditionally, state notaries and the BTI would ordinarily only register a transfer of title based on a short-form type of contract generally used in Ukraine. This short-form contract consisted of one or two pages (with annexes) and documented only the bare conveyance of title, with no guarantees or other protections and often leaving critical ambiguities. Typically, such agreements merely state the names of the parties, the address of the premises with a brief description of the floor plan, the price and the current registration number for the premises allocated by the BTI. The agreement will also contain the signature of the parties, and the signature, seal and number of the notary. The authorities in the past have usually resisted the typical Western-style, longer, detailed contract as being unusual and unnecessary.

Full contract protections should be sought

However, the laws on misrepresentation and fraud are not well developed in Ukraine, and there is only very limited recourse against sellers under the typical short-form contract. For protection under

Ukrainian law, it is advisable to have all agreements, guarantees and indemnities as fully documented as possible in the purchase agreement. Fortunately, attitudes are changing, and a number of state and private notaries and other state officials now accept contracts that contain covenants similar to those one would expect in the West. Increasingly, more elaborate agreements, like those common in the West, are being used for substantial transactions, especially where foreign buyers and their lawyers are involved and the Ukrainian seller has substantial assets and can be held accountable. Agreements guaranteeing, for example, absolute and unconditional title, the good physical condition of the premises, and the absence of any knowledge of adverse claims and defects may often be obtained by negotiation.

Due diligence for purchases

Review of the BTI certificate and other documentation cited above is all that is usually done in Ukraine as a matter of practice, but it is often not sufficient. Before a purchaser completes any acquisition of a substantial real property in Ukraine, a complete due diligence of the state of title (including a mortgage verification) should be conducted, starting with the original transfer from state ownership (if applicable). If a building or other structure was built by the owner, the necessary construction documentation, including, but not limited to, the permission for construction and project approval documentation, and the Governmental Act (discussed below), should also be verified, since the absence of any of the required documents may subsequently lead to a prohibition of any use of a structure that was improperly constructed.

The importance of exhaustive due diligence for title transfers for substantial transactions in Ukraine cannot be over-emphasized. The seller should not merely rely on the BTI and notarial documents of the seller, although typically Ukrainian sellers will not initially volunteer more than these. In addition to verifying the title legally, certain practical verifications should be made as to the complete chain of title.

These practical verifications should include a physical site inspection and enquiries into past residents. For example, if a building was initially built, or was entirely rebuilt, without a right of land use first being obtained from the local council, the purported owner would have illegally constructed premises on the state's land. The state could require that the premises be moved or destroyed, or possibly confiscated. Likewise, approvals must be granted for most modifications to premises, for example to subdivide a room or remove a dividing wall. A sale of premises with unapproved modifications may be subject to fines, and this could even be a basis for voiding the prior sale. As a practical matter, such problems can normally be cured if effectively handled with the relevant authorities in a timely manner.

The technical description of the property to be purchased should correspond exactly to all official records, including the BTI certificate. In addition, the purchaser should inspect the technical passport for the property, which is a description of the property with drawings prepared by the BTI for each property. For a corporate party to a sale, it is also important to verify that the company's actions were properly authorized. In connection with this, its charter and foundation agreement (or equivalent documents), and documents on appointment of the person signing for such party, should be reviewed. In Ukraine, however, the charter and foundation agreements are not available for public inspection and verification.

Lease-purchase option agreement to protect the purchaser pending completion

In the meantime, while the process of due diligence proceeds, in order to protect the purchaser's right to acquire the property on the agreed terms, a long-term lease with a purchase option might be signed. Such a lease-purchase option document could give the purchaser the right to hold in escrow the prior purchase contract or other evidence of title, which makes a transfer to others more difficult if, for example, a third party offers the seller a higher price before completion. While not required, it would be preferable to have this lease-purchase option document executed before the notary (if one was used) who was responsible for the previous sale of the property, and who holds one of the original copies of the prior purchase contract.

A seller will often require a down-payment before parting with its original copy of the prior purchase contract, usually in the amount of 1 to 5 per cent of the purchase price. Ordinarily, such contracts provide that if the seller sells to a third party in violation of the down-payment terms, then the seller suffers a penalty, such as being obliged to pay to the purchaser double the amount of the down-payment under the purchase option.

Completion of the purchase

Once good title has been verified as far as possible through the due diligence process, and the price and other sale terms agreed, the purchase contract (usually called in Ukraine a 'purchase-sale agreement') must be executed before a notary, and the transaction listed in the notary's register of notarial acts. Usually two original copies of the purchase contract are prepared, with one copy for the buyer and one for the notarial records, and a notarized copy is provided to the seller.

The buyer should then apply for the transfer of the property to be registered at the appropriate BTI office and obtain a registration number and an appropriate certificate or stamp on the purchase contract. Once a BTI certificate and registration number exist, the documentation formalities are completed, although under current law the moment when title actually passes is established solely by the contract of purchase.

Notarization and state registration of real property purchase contracts

It should be emphasized that, according to Article 657 of the New Civil Code, a contract for the sale and purchase of real property, including a land plot, an integral property complex, or a residential house or apartment must be executed in writing, certified by a notary and registered at a state registry. Unlike the Civil Code of 1963, the New Civil Code does not establish any exceptions allowing legal entities to validly execute real estate purchase contracts between themselves without notarization.

According to the recently adopted Resolution of the Cabinet of Ministers of Ukraine of 26 May 2004 'On Approval of the Temporary Procedure for State Registration of Agreements' ('Temporary Procedure'), registration of contracts for the purchase and sale of real estate must be performed by the notary who notarized the contract, by submitting the necessary information concerning the contract to the State Registry of Agreements simultaneously with the contract's notarization, assuming that the notary is a registrar and, for this purpose, is connected to the state registry computer system. If the notary does not have access to the State Registry of Agreements computer system, he or she should send one copy of the agreement to the State Registry on the same day that the agreement is notarized.

Further changes to the current title registration procedure have been introduced by the Law of Ukraine 'On State Registration of Proprietary Rights to Real Estate and their Limitation' ('Registration Law'), which was passed by the Ukrainian Parliament on 1 July 2004. Pursuant to the Registration Law, registration of title to all real estate will be carried out by a new State Registry of Rights to Real Estate and their Limitation ('State Registry of Rights'), which is to be created within the State Committee of Ukraine on Land Resources. Unfortunately, the Registration Law left some unresolved issues and doubts concerning the registration of title to real estate, in particular, as to the timing of registration and how the State Registry of Agreements, the State Registry of Rights and other state registries related to real estate and property rights will be integrated. It also appears that the New Civil Code does not solve the old title registration problems completely. Although a purchase agreement must be notarized and submitted by the notary for registration, delays in the actual registration can occur, especially where a notary is not integrated into the State Registry of Agreements computer system; so it may still be possible in the time required to register such a contract and the transfer of title under it, for an unscrupulous seller, using duplicate title documents, to sell the same real estate to other buyers before the first sale appears publicly in the Registry. It is also unclear what protection or remedy a purchaser has if the notary fails to comply with the legal requirement that the notary carry out such registration or if the Registry makes a mistake. In both cases, the risk still exists because Ukrainian law does not provide that by registration, title can be valid as against unregistered title claims. Hopefully, this weakness in the title legislation will be remedied in the near future. Presently, in order to minimize these risks the purchaser should apply to the Registry for registration of the purchase contract immediately after execution of the purchase contract and verify that such registration has been made before payment is unconditionally made.

Mortgages

Under the mortgage regulations provided by Chapter 3 of the Law 'On Pledge', which ceased to be effective as of 1 January 2004, a mortgage was understood as being a type of pledge that covers real property. During the duration of a mortgage, such property remained in the possession of the mortgagor or a third party. Now, the Law 'On Mortgages' dated 5 June 2003 (the 'Mortgage Law'), which currently governs mortgages, defines a mortgage as a kind of performance security for an obligation, whereby (1) real property that remains in the possession and use of the mortgagor is used as security, and (2) in the case of non-performance of the obligation secured by the mortgage, the mortgagee has a priority right to satisfy its claim from the mortgaged property.

Under the Mortgage Law, a mortgage agreement must be in writing, certified by a notary and registered. Mortgagees should be aware that, although the mortgagee's rights under a mortgage agreement take effect from the moment of its notarization, the priority right of the mortgagee over other possible claims to the mortgaged property, including other mortgages, only takes effect from the moment of state registration of the mortgage agreement as against subsequently registered claims. A mortgage may be created in a separate mortgage agreement, or it may be created by being included in a contract establishing a principal obligation, for example a loan agreement.

The Mortgage Law lists the following four material provisions for an agreement to create a mortgage, in the absence of which the parties will be deemed to have failed to reach such an agreement: (1) the details of the parties (as required by the Mortgage Law) – their names, addresses, the Unified State Register code for a Ukrainian legal entity, for a Ukrainian citizen an individual taxpayer number, and for a non-resident entity the country registration details; (2) a description and the amount of the principal obligation; (3) a description of the mortgaged property that allows identification of such property; and (4) a reference concerning the issuance of a mortgage note or its absence.

In order for the new mortgage regime to be implemented, a number of additional laws and regulations should be adopted, including, in particular, regulations governing the mortgage registration procedure. Currently, the registration of mortgages is governed by the Resolution of the Cabinet of Ministers of Ukraine of 31 March 2004 'On the Temporary Procedure for the State Registration of Mortgages' ('Mortgage Registration Procedure'). Under the Mortgage Registration Procedure, the State Registry of Mortgages, to be created under the Ministry of Justice, will be the public record of mortgages.

Special considerations for the acquisition of buildings – ZHEK and project approvals

To acquire a building, either by outright purchase or by purchasing all of the apartments, special considerations apply. For formerly state-owned buildings, the state typically retains ownership of the non-privatized apartments and the common parts. The state's title is usually held by the Executive Committee of the appropriate local council, which in turn delegates management to the appropriate local state dwelling management enterprise (known by its Ukrainian abbreviation as ZHEK). The owners of all the apartments of a building are required to enter into maintenance agreements with the ZHEK. Each apartment owner under such agreement is obliged to pay ZHEK for its maintenance role, regardless of whether any services are actually provided, at rates that vary depending on the size of the apartment, the number of occupants and whether the apartment is for business or residential use.

It is, however, possible for the private owners of all of the apartments and other premises in a building, following their complete acquisition by privatization, to form an association of owners (a condominium) to take over ownership and responsibility for maintenance of the common parts. The condominium can either retain ZHEK or independently contract for building maintenance.

If the entire building is acquired through the condominium process, or is otherwise acquired or owned outright (including by 'greenfield' new construction), then the new owners will be required either to purchase the land or to obtain a right of use of land by entering into a lease for temporary use, and pay rent. In either case, they would then have to pay the land tax in respect of the land. Where the common areas of an apartment building remain in state ownership, there is no charge under current law to any private owners of the apartments in the building for the land use for the building.

To document the rights to the land under the building (or the construction site), for foreign purchasers, in the past meant that the rights to the use of the land by temporary use allocation, or lease, or permanent use allocation had to be confirmed or established. Based on the new Land Code, a foreign purchaser should be able to obtain ownership rights to the land, either by purchasing land from the seller of the building, or if the seller only has land use rights, by having these rights relinquished and then purchasing the land from the state.

Another important consideration for purchasing a building, especially one used commercially, is to verify that the approval process for its construction was properly followed. As part of the project approval process for most new construction, a Government Act on acceptance of the building into operation must be executed by the appropriate governmental commission to permit the use (especially if the premises were formerly part of an industrial enterprise or complex). The governmental commissions that provide such Governmental Acts are normally made up of specialists and governmental officials competent in a number of fields relevant to the proposed activities at the new structure, as well as in other areas that may be potentially affected by its contemplated use, such as the authorities responsible for health and safety, fire and labour protection.

One of the principal legal acts of such governmental commissions is the Instruction 'On the Acceptance into Operation of the Completed Objects of Construction', adopted by the Cabinet of Ministers of the USSR on 23 January 1983 ('Instruction'), which remains in force (Soviet laws continue in effect in Ukraine to the extent that they are not inconsistent with or replaced by Ukrainian law). The Instruction creates a general procedure for the establishment of such commissions as well as the project approval process that must be followed for a commission to authorize the entry into operation of facilities or other constructions.

The Instruction prohibits start-up of operations of any facility or construction without the execution of the Governmental Act by each of the representatives of the 'state supervision authorities' (clause 8, paragraph 3). This is interpreted as referring to the state health and safety, fire, labour protection and all other authorities or commission. Most of the sanctions that may be imposed by these governmental authorities for non-compliance mirror each other. Thus, if health and safety, fire or labour protection authority approval is lacking, the owner of the building or other facility in question may be liable for penalties, or the authority may close down the building or facility, either temporarily until compliance with the order of the authority, or indefinitely.

Surprisingly, a significant number of buildings and facilities in Ukraine, including those of some major Ukrainian enterprises, have been found to lack the appropriate Governmental Act, especially those buildings that were built or renovated in the aftermath of the Second World War. Usually, these sorts of problems can be readily corrected, especially if they arise while the building or facility is still owned by a state enterprise. However, difficulties can arise, particularly if such issues are not appropriately handled before completion of a transaction. Requirements like these underline the need for thorough due diligence before a purchase is made.

Leasing of premises

Leases of offices, residential dwellings and buildings may be validly granted, including to foreigners, as noted above. Unlike land leases, no restrictions currently exist to limit the duration of such leases. However, permission from the appropriate state agency, in Kyiv from GDIP, is apparently required, as discussed above.

Typically, a lease should define the rent, the term, and the extent and type of permitted refurbishments. It may also provide for first refusal rights should the premises be offered to a third-party purchaser. In general, the lease provisions can cover whatever else the landlord and tenant agree. Leases must be in writing in the Ukrainian language (but may also be in one or more other languages). According to Article 793, paragraph 2, of the New Civil Code, a lease agreement for a term of more than one year must also be notarized. Furthermore, Article 794 of the New Civil Code establishes a requirement for state registration of lease agreements executed for a term of one year or longer. Currently registration of such lease agreements is governed by the above-mentioned Temporary Procedure and should be registered at the State Registry of Agreements.

According to Article 770 of the New Civil Code, if the lessor conveys title to the leased premises to a person other than the lessee, then unless the lease provides otherwise, the transfer is subject to the lessee's continuing rights to the leased premises under the existing lease.

It should be noted that according to Article 9.1.3 of the recently adopted Individual Income Tax Law, the leasing of Ukrainian real property by a non-resident to another non-resident legal entity or individual should be exclusively conducted by the non-resident lessor through either (1) a permanent representative office in Ukraine of such non-resident or (2) a legal entity resident in Ukraine that, based on a written agreement, performs representation functions on behalf of such non-resident. In the case of a non-resident individual, his or her representative in Ukraine also acts as a tax agent to withhold tax from lease payments. Note that a non-resident that violates the forgoing requirement will be considered as committing tax evasion. However, the law does not specify whether property 'belonging' to a non-resident applies not just to real property owned by the non-resident, but also to property held under use rights.

Zoning

All Ukrainian real property, including premises and undeveloped land, is ordinarily subject to use zoning. Most urban offices and apartments in urban buildings will be zoned for either residential or non-residential use. Changes in zoning can be difficult to obtain, and therefore the zoning status should always be confirmed prior to any acquisition or renovation.

According to Article 6 of the Housing Code of Ukraine of 30 June 1983 (the '1983 Housing Code'), residential premises may only be used for the accommodation of individuals. Therefore, if residential premises have been purchased and their status has not been changed to non-residential, their use for offices or other non-residential uses will violate the 1983 Housing Code and make the parties to the lease subject to substantial penalties as well as court orders prohibiting further non-residential use. According to Article 8 of the 1983 Housing Code, a change of use from residential to non-residential is prohibited save for exceptional cases. Therefore, where a non-permitted use is anticipated, the necessary change in zoning should always be carried out before the property acquisition is completed and payment is made.

4.2

Ukrainian Land Law

Bate C Toms and Taras Dumych,
BC Toms & Co

The Land Code

The principal Ukrainian legal act governing the status of and transactions in land is the new Land Code of Ukraine, which came into effect on 1 January 2002 (the 'Land Code'). It should be emphasized that the new Land Code represented a fundamental change to Ukrainian real estate law. It introduced new rights to private land ownership and land use, as well as the principle that land can be freely bought and sold. Although private land ownership is permitted under the Ukrainian Constitution of 1996, this was made subject to further implementation '*as may be provided by law*', and previous statutes on ownership were very restrictive. Under the Land Code of 1992 (the '1992 Land Code'), only Ukrainian individuals were entitled to their own land, and only in very limited circumstances, such as for rural homes, garages, farms and gardens.

Ownership of land

The Land Code greatly expands the list of permitted land purchases. It allows land intended for non-agricultural use to be purchased by Ukrainian and, in certain cases, foreign individuals and legal entities. However, for these fundamental changes to be implemented and applied in practice, a number of supplemental legal acts should be adopted on issues such as land valuation and the creation of the proposed Register of Land Plots and land surveys. Such supplemental legislation is presently under discussion.

The Land Code establishes transitional periods (moratoria) before certain land transactions can take effect. Until 1 January 2005, land plots that are owned by legal entities for agricultural purposes or by individuals cannot be sold or otherwise transferred except by exchange or inheritance. The reference to the 'exchange' of land plots is ambiguous. The Land Code fails to define 'exchange', presumably the provision refers to an exchange for other land plots. This might provide a way around the moratorium for many transfers depending upon the details of the anticipated implementing legislation.

Beginning 1 January 2005, land may be used as a contribution to the charter fund (authorized capital) of a company. Until 1 January 2010, acquisitions of land for agricultural use are limited to 100 hectares per owner. However, even upon completion of these transitional periods, the rights of land owners may still be limited. For example, land may only be mortgaged to secure bank loans, and land plots may only be contributed to the charter funds of those companies that are exclusively founded by Ukrainian individuals or entities (although, apparently, these Ukrainian entities can be owned by foreigners). In addition, the Land Code expressly states that further limitations of land ownership rights may be imposed by subsequent legislation.

Owners of land

The new Land Code provides that the following persons may be owners of land in Ukraine: (1) the state (which exercises this right through the Cabinet of Ministers of Ukraine, the Cabinet of Ministers of the Republic of Crimea, and the relevant oblast as well as the Kyiv and Sevastopol city state administrations), (2) municipalities (which exercise this right through local councils, which are local self-governing bodies) with respect to most land in cities and villages and (3) individuals and legal entities, with respect to land in private ownership.

The Land Code provides that municipal land may be allocated to a private person on the basis of an appropriate decision of a local council. In Kyiv, such authority was granted to the Kyiv City Council. State land owned by the state directly (rather than by municipalities) may be allocated on the basis of a decision of the local state administration where the land plot is located.

Prior Presidential Decrees

Prior to the adoption of the Land Code, with a view to encouraging entrepreneurship, a number of Decrees were issued by the President of Ukraine to allow privatization of land by individuals and legal entities. One of these decrees, the Decree of the President, No. 608/95, 'On the Privatization and Leasing of Non-Agricultural Land Plots for the Purpose of Entrepreneurial Activity' dated 12 July 1995 (the '1995 Decree') is particularly important. These Decrees remain effective to the extent that they are not contradicted by the Land Code or other subsequent legislation.

The 1995 Decree provided for the privatization of land by sale to Ukrainian individuals and legal entities for the purpose of carrying out entrepreneurial activity. However, the validity of the 1995 Decree has been questioned by numerous commentators because it contradicted the then applicable 1992 Land Code, which should have prevailed.

Nonetheless, in the past a number of land sales were conducted on the basis of the 1995 Decree and were later registered. It is likely that these transfers are invalid and cannot be the basis for genuine ownership or for any further transfer of good title. Apparently in recognition of this issue, the 1995 Decree was never implemented as would have been expected.

The Decree of the President, No. 32/99, 'On the Sale of Land Plots of Non-Agricultural Designation' dated 19 January 1999 (the '1999 Decree') also provided for the sale of land owned by state and municipal authorities to Ukrainian individuals (including, in particular, those registered as entrepreneurs) and legal entities. This right to purchase land only applies under the 1999 Decree for land plots underlying buildings, constructions or unfinished constructions. It did not permit undeveloped 'greenfield' sites to be sold or otherwise privatized.

The 1999 Decree created a right for a privately-owned Ukrainian legal entity to purchase the land underneath an unfinished construction only if the unfinished construction was (1) on a non-agricultural site, and (2) such unfinished construction had been previously privatized or purchased by the legal entity. The 1999 Decree should have applied to Ukrainian entities that were, in whole or in part, foreign owned, as no distinction was made in the 1999 Decree between Ukrainian companies that are Ukrainian, rather than foreign owned.

Initially, as was the case for the 1995 Decree, the 1999 Decree was not fully implemented in practice. Possibly this reflected some early doubts expressed as to its constitutionality. However, now most commentators accept that it was validly adopted (an issue that turns on whether the 1999 Decree lawfully filled in 'gaps' in legislation, or instead improperly addressed matters governed by the 1992 Land Code). As a consequence, a number of acts and resolutions of local councils have recently been adopted to clarify the procedures for the sale of land pursuant to the 1999 Decree. For example, the Kyiv City Council has confirmed that land plots and unfinished construction sites may be sold to 'appropriate' real property owners, including those Ukrainian entities that own the structure above a land plot or site.

The procedure for purchases under the new Land Code

Under the new Land Code, most of the land within residential city areas and land intended for industrial use can be sold, except for land for streets, parks, beaches (some of which may be leased), cemeteries, other city areas that are in public use, railways, highways, pipelines and the radiation-affected Chernobyl zone.

In cases where the land underneath a building was previously allocated for temporary or permanent use to a Ukrainian entity (including if foreign owned or controlled), the procedure for the entity to obtain ownership over such land plots is quite simple. To obtain such land ownership an application must be submitted to a local council or local state administration, as appropriate, together with a current state act for permanent use of the land plot or a land lease agreement (confirming a temporary right of use) with the local council or state administration, as appropriate, a plan of the land plot, an expert valuation of the land plot and a copy of the certificate of state registration of the applicant.

The local council is supposed to review the application within a one-month period. As expressly provided in the Land Code, the only permitted reasons for refusal of such an application for a land allocation are: (1) the absence of any documents required for the allocation of the land plot; (2) the discovery of false information in the submitted documents; and (3) the initiation of bankruptcy or liquidation proceedings against the applicant. This should leave no discretion for a council to refuse to give its approval.

If a company wishes to purchase a land plot that was not previously allocated for its permanent or temporary use, it must submit additional documents that constitute a 'project for land allocation'. In this case, the process of land allocation by the local council may take a longer time because several state agencies are involved in drafting and providing the consent to the purchase. For example, the local Department on Land Resources, the State Agency on Architecture, the local Sanitation-Epidemic Station, the State Department of Environmental Safety, and the Department on the Protection of Historical Heritage must all issue required permissions for such consent. Several land-surveying agencies must also prepare project estimates and define the borders of the land plot. Each of these agencies is allotted between 20 and 30 calendar days to consider the application and accompanying documents. The whole process can take up to four months by statute. Each state inspection body named above requires the payment of fees for the issuance of the necessary documents.

A notarized agreement on a purchase of a land plot must also be concluded between the purchaser and the local council or state administration, as appropriate, and registered with the State Registry of Agreements. Pursuant to the agreement, the land purchaser must pay for the land, unless the purchaser is a Ukrainian individual who qualifies for a so-called 'unpaid privatization'. Payment to the local council for a land plot may be made in instalments. Following execution of the land purchase agreement and payment of the purchase price, the land purchaser receives a state ownership act to confirm ownership of the purchased land plot.

The land underneath a building (including under any adjoining structures and territory forming an integral part of it) will initially be allocated to the organization that administers the building (commonly referred to by the Ukrainian abbreviation 'ZHEK'). However, if the building's ownership is privatized by a condominium, an association composed of all of the building's apartment owners, the condominium can also privatize or obtain use rights over the land plot underneath at no cost.

As discussed above, until procedures for implementation of the new Land Code are established, presumably the existing procedures for the sale of land that were established by the Cabinet of Ministers Resolution No. 440, of 24 March 1999, pursuant to the 1999 Decree (described above), will continue to apply.

Purchases by non-residents

The new Land Code also allows foreign individuals and companies to purchase land plots underneath buildings and other constructions that they own, whether located in city areas or outside of a city. They can also purchase land plots for construction within city areas. The basis for obtaining ownership rights to such a land plot is: (1) a notarized private land purchase agreement (or certain other types of agreements) that has been registered with the local council, which must include such clauses on the land plot size, the amount of the payment, the purpose of the use of the land plot, etc; (2) inheritance; or (3) purchase of the land plot from a local council or local state administration.

Foreigners still cannot own land intended for agricultural use. However, the Land Code simplifies the procedure for changing the specified intended use of land. Local councils and state administrations now have the authority to determine what the intended use of a particular plot of land is. This authority previously rested with the Parliament. It is therefore the local councils and state administrations who decide on any change of the specified intended use of land, when deciding on the allocation of land to a foreign person. The new Land Code provides that a procedure for making such a change of use will be established by the Cabinet of Ministers.

However, in order to purchase land underneath real property, a non-resident will need to register a branch office in Ukraine that will carry out business activity (a taxable 'permanent establishment'). A foreign person or entity that wishes to purchase a land plot that has been previously leased to it will need to submit an application to the relevant state administration or council, as the case may be, with copies of the land lease agreement and, if applicable, the certificate of state registration of the branch office, and a confirmation that such office is 'operational' (the Land Code fails to identify the documents that should confirm this). In addition, the local council or state administration may only consider such an application with the approval of the Cabinet of Ministers, which must be given separately for each transaction (as required by Article 129, Sections 2, 5 and 6 of the Land Code). This will greatly increase the time required for non-residents to purchase state-owned land (and probably will effectively prevent many transactions).

Recent amendments to the Land Code

On 10 July 2003, the Ukrainian Parliament passed an amendment to Article 82 of the Land Code, then one of the Land Code's most controversial articles. Prior to this amendment, Article 82 defined Ukrainian legal entities as being those established by Ukrainian citizens and Ukrainian legal entities, thus apparently excluding Ukrainian companies founded with foreign investment from buying land plots.

The amended Article 82 provides that joint ventures established with the participation of foreign legal entities and individuals may also acquire ownership rights to non-agricultural land by using the same procedure used for purchases by foreign persons and entities as described above. By adopting this amendment, Parliament has, however, created a new controversy, since on a literal reading it still appears that 100 per cent foreign-owned Ukrainian companies may not acquire ownership rights to land plots from local councils or state administrations. For a foreign-owned Ukrainian company to avoid the current restriction, a minority share should be owned by a Ukrainian company or individual when the company is founded and, although not actually required, preferably also when the purchase is made. Article 129 of the Land Code, which establishes the procedure for foreign legal entities to purchase non-agricultural land plots, applies only in those instances where state or communal non-agricultural land is the object of the transaction. It appears that if the land plot is not state or communal property, then no additional approval for the foreign legal entities or joint ventures with foreign participation is required. Therefore, in order to avoid this, when a wholly foreign owned Ukrainian company wishes to buy land from a local council or state administration, then an intermediary company created in whole or in part by Ukrainian nationals should be used to buy the land and subsequently resell it to the wholly foreign-owned Ukrainian company.

Land auctions

Amongst its new tools for allocation, the new Land Code has introduced public land auctions. Land plots not already privatized or sold in accordance with the procedures discussed above may be sold through public land auctions. These auctions are largely expected to facilitate new construction.

To take part in such a land auction, potential purchasers must pay a registration fee and guarantee payment of certain minimum amounts based on criteria that will be established in the future. A land auction can be initiated by a local council, or state administration, or by the State Enforcement Service to implement a court order. If the land for sale belongs to the state or a municipality, the local state or municipal authorities must prepare all the required documentation for the land allocation by auction, in particular to define the borders of the land plot and prepare its so-called 'technical passport'.

Information on a land auction with a detailed description of the land plot that is to be sold must be published in a local newspaper no later than 30 days prior to such auction, and a billboard with this information must be placed on the land plot. The land auction will only be valid if there is more than one potential purchaser and the proposed bids exceed the initially stated minimum bidding price.

Leasing of land

In addition to land ownership, the Land Code provides for land leasing as another basis for use of a land plot. The Land Code also continues to permit permanent land use rights for state lands to be granted to state or municipal entities by local councils and local state administrations for any purposes (the old Code also permitted temporary use rights, but these have been abolished). In addition to the Land Code, land leasing is regulated by the Law of Ukraine 'On Land Leasing' dated 6 October 1998, No. 161-XIV (the 'Lease Law'), as amended on 2 October 2003.

Under the Land Code, land can be leased from private, state or municipal owners. According to the Lease Law, individuals and legal entities that own land may be lessors. Foreign individuals and legal entities may lease land on the same basis as Ukrainians. The three-year limitation on leases to individuals under the 1992 Land Code was eliminated in the new Land Code.

There are now short-term and long-term leases. A short-term lease may run for up to five years. A long-term lease may run up to 50 years less one day, and arguably may be prolonged (including by agreement at the outset). The Law provides that an existing lessee has a priority right to extend a land lease, but only if it matches all terms proposed by others, such as the offered rent.

To be valid, a land lease must contain a number of provisions, including on matters such as (1) the location and borders of the land plot, (2) the duration of the lease, (3) the lease rent (amount, inflation indexation and payment procedure), (4) the purpose and conditions for the use of the land plot, and maintenance of the quality of the land, (5) the conditions for returning the land plot to the lessor, (6) possible limitations and burdens on the use of the land and (7) the liabilities of the parties under the lease.

It should be noted that according to the wording of the Lease Law prior to its amendment in 2003, the lease contract had to be executed before a public notary in the jurisdiction where the land plot was located. However, under the 2003 amendments, this notarization requirement was abolished, so lease contracts are now notarized only where the parties want to.

Thus, if a Ukrainian or foreign entity would like to execute a lease agreement for the use of land under a building (or other construction) that it owns, the following steps, based on the example of an application to lease municipal land in the city of Kyiv, must be taken in order properly to document such lease: (1) submission of a letter to the head of the Kyiv City Council requesting conclusion of a lease agreement for the land underneath the building for any period up to 50 years less one day; (2) obtaining a resolution from the Kyiv City Council confirming its agreement to allocate the land plot for such lease, which resolution should order the applicant to make a further application to the local Department on Land Resources of the Kyiv City State Administration within one month; (3) filing the application to the Department on Land Resources, with the following documents: (a) a notarized copy of the purchase agreement as proof of title to the building, (b) copies of the building's registration with the Kyiv Bureau of Technical Inventory ('BTI') and the Kyiv City State Administration (if applicable) and (c) any other required technical information; and, (4) upon receipt of a favourable response from the Department on Land Resources, entering into a lease agreement with the Council for the requested period, being up to 50 years less one day.

The applicant may, if needed for reconstruction of the acquired property, request that an adjacent land plot be temporarily granted to it for such construction (for example, to site a crane or other equipment, for storage, etc). Such leases of adjacent land can only be granted on a short-term basis of up to five years.

If the land is leased from a local council, then the lease would likely be based on the standard form of land lease agreement that was adopted by the Resolution of the Cabinet of Ministers on 17 March 1993, No. 197. Generally, local authorities are reluctant to include any additional clauses into or otherwise modify this form of lease agreement, but modifications are sometimes possible.

After the lease agreement is executed, it must be registered with the relevant Department on Land Resources of the state administration. In Kyiv, such registration is carried out by the Department on Land Resources of the Kyiv City State Administration in accordance with the Regulation of the Cabinet of Ministers of Ukraine of 25 December 1998, No. 2073. The following documents, *inter alia*, must be submitted for such state registration:

- an application for registration;
- the lease agreement (the failure of the lease agreement to cover any required matters, as described above, may constitute a basis for the state authorities to refuse registration);
- a plan of the land plot; and
- a decision of the local council or state administration, as appropriate, confirming its agreement to lease the land plot if the said local council or state administration is the lessor, or a copy of the state act or results of a land auction confirming the land ownership rights of the lessor, if it is a private entity or an individual.

Under the Land Code, leased land can be sub-leased; however, the Lease Law makes sub-leasing conditional on the written consent of the lessor. Arguably such consent can be given in the original lease agreement. Such sub-lease agreements also must be registered with the relevant Department on Land Resources. There is no requirement for a sub-lease agreement to be notarized, but the parties may do so if they wish.

If the land plot beneath a building is leased from the state or municipal authorities by the owner of the building and the building is subsequently sold to a third party, the land use rights should, in principle, be given up by the former building owner so that they can be granted to such new third party purchaser of the building, subject to the terms of a new land lease contract. It is recommended, however, that purchasers of buildings cover this point in express clauses in their purchase agreements so that the prior building owner does not try to retain any land use rights after the building is sold. Usually, sellers are anxious to give up land use rights in order to avoid applicable land taxes. Finally, it should be noted that the Lease Law does not permit sub-leasing of land plots under an integral property complex of a state-owned or communal enterprise or organization.

4.3

Dispute Resolution: Arbitration in Ukraine

Bate C Toms and Dmytro Korbut,
BC Toms & Co

Arbitral tribunals

The parties to any civil or commercial dispute may agree to submit to the jurisdiction of an arbitral tribunal. In Ukraine, an arbitral tribunal (called a '*treteyskiy*', literally meaning a 'third-party tribunal') may be an institutional arbitral tribunal created to handle some or all types of commercial disputes or an ad hoc tribunal specifically created by the parties to resolve a particular dispute. These tribunals may be located in Ukraine or abroad, and the location affects how the arbitral award will be enforced in Ukraine.

The parties to an ad hoc arbitration can establish their own tribunal and rules. Resolution of a dispute by ad hoc arbitration (either for international or purely domestic disputes) is carried out based on principles and rules chosen by the parties in their discretion. Such ad hoc rules can provide for the nomination of any arbitrator, whether a Ukrainian or foreign resident, whom the parties desire to decide a particular dispute. The parties can also determine the location of the tribunal and subject the arbitral proceedings to any rules, including those based on any internationally accepted arbitration rules. As a practical matter, ad hoc arbitration is not widely used in Ukraine, in particular owing to frequent problems with enforcement of such arbitral awards.

If a foreign investment dispute arises between a foreign investor and the State of Ukraine, then the foreign investor may choose to submit the dispute for resolution to a commercial court in Ukraine according to Ukrainian laws if international treaties of Ukraine do not provide otherwise. As a rule, the bilateral treaties on mutual protection of investments provide for the opportunity for a foreign investor to submit any dispute that arises in relation to an investment in Ukraine to the jurisdiction of an international arbitration tribunal, whether institutional or ad hoc, and Ukraine submits to the jurisdiction of this court waiving its state immunity. Enforcement of decisions of foreign arbitral tribunals in investment disputes are ensured through procedures set forth in the New York Convention on Recognition and Enforcement of Foreign Arbitral Awards of 1958, to which Ukraine is a party.

Ukraine is also a party to the Washington Convention on the Settlement of Investment Disputes between States and Citizens of Other States of 1965, ratified by the Ukrainian Parliament in March 2000. Therefore, any legal dispute arising directly from an investment between Ukraine (or any constituent agency of Ukraine) and a national of another contracting state may be submitted to the International Center for Settlement of Investment Disputes established by this Convention, if the parties to the dispute so agree in writing at any time. When the parties have given their consent, no party may unilaterally withdraw its consent.

The activity of tribunals established in Ukraine that resolve disputes involving foreign parties or Ukrainian companies with foreign investment is, as a matter of Ukrainian law, governed by the Law 'On International Commercial Arbitration' of 24 February 1994 (the 'International Arbitration Law'). The International Arbitration Law lays down general rules on the jurisdiction of an arbitral tribunal, appointment of arbitrators, procedural rules, choice of language and place of arbitration, and how an award is rendered and enforced. The International Arbitration Law is based to a large extent on the UNCITRAL (United Nations Commission on International Trade Law) model law. It generally provides for the principles that govern commercial arbitration in Ukraine. Many of the International Arbitration Law's rules apply only to the extent that the parties to such an international arbitration do not decide on such issues themselves.

Arbitral tribunals that resolve domestic disputes where both parties are Ukrainian entities that have no foreign investment are governed by the Law 'On Treteyskiy Tribunals', adopted by the Ukrainian Parliament on 5 May 2004. This Law governs issues on establishing domestic arbitral tribunals in Ukraine and resolving disputes submitted by parties to their jurisdiction.

Jurisdiction of arbitral tribunals

The jurisdiction of an international arbitral tribunal is primarily based on the parties' arbitration agreement, subject to certain mandatory legal rules. The form for an arbitration agreement in an international contract is governed by Article 7 of the International Arbitration Law. The importance of drafting a clear and precise arbitration agreement cannot be underestimated. Article 7 provides that 'an arbitration agreement', which can validly replace the state court jurisdiction that would otherwise apply, is 'an agreement of the parties on submitting to an arbitral tribunal all or certain disputes that have arisen or may arise between them in connection with any definite legal relations, whether or not contractual in nature'. This is ordinarily interpreted to mean that there must be a written agreement to submit specified disputes to arbitration and not a mere agreement on arbitration as one of several non-exclusive dispute resolution procedures.

Furthermore, the submission must be to a specific arbitral tribunal, and not simply reflect an agreement to resolve disputes by 'arbitration'. Failure to follow this rule may render the arbitration agreement void. Arguably, this problem can be cured by the Geneva European Convention on International Commercial Arbitration of 1961 (the 'Geneva Convention'), which was ratified by Ukraine. The Geneva Convention provides a mechanism whereby, if the parties to a contract have merely agreed to arbitration without specifying a tribunal, the claimant shall be entitled, at his option, to apply to the president of the competent Chamber of Commerce of the country of the respondent's habitual place of residence or seat for the necessary action to create an arbitration tribunal.

On this basis, in theory, the failure to specify a tribunal in an arbitration clause in a contract governed by Ukrainian law might not render it void, since there is a mechanism for selection of a specific tribunal. However, it is not clear whether the president of the Ukrainian Chamber of Commerce will in fact agree to be under any obligation to appoint such an arbitration tribunal. For example, even if the president of the Ukrainian Chamber of Commerce appoints the International Commercial Arbitration Court under the Ukrainian Chamber of Commerce, it is not clear whether the chairman of this tribunal (who has the ultimate authority to decide on the jurisdiction of the tribunal under its Rules) will accept the appointment under an arbitration clause that is otherwise defective in absence of any provision in the clause expressly selecting the Rules for the tribunal. Thus, in the absence of a clear mechanism and any established history of implementation of the Geneva Convention, it may provide a good theoretical argument but cannot yet be relied upon by practitioners. It is therefore highly recommended for parties to use the arbitration clause recommended by a particular tribunal as it may be carefully modified in accordance with any special wishes of the parties to avoid any challenges to its validity.

Where a contract properly refers disputes to arbitration, Article 80(5) of the Code of Commercial Procedure requires the state commercial courts to close any proceedings covering the same dispute at the request of any of the parties, provided such request is made in a timely manner by a party that has not already acquiesced to the state court's jurisdiction. Therefore, great care must be taken, where a party prefers and has an agreement for arbitration, not to appear or submit any motions on the merits of a case in any state court proceedings for any purpose other than to request that such proceedings be terminated.

An agreement to submit a claim to arbitration may be made in an arbitration clause in a contract on a commercial or other matter or in a separate agreement specifically entered into to provide for arbitration of some or all disputes between the parties. In either case, the agreement on arbitration must be in writing and can take the form of a single document signed by the parties or an exchange of letters, faxes or other means of communication that provide for the unambiguous choice of arbitration. An arbitration clause that forms a part of a contract between the parties is, under Ukrainian law, considered an independent agreement and will not necessarily be declared invalid if the contract in which it is contained is invalid.

Even if an arbitration clause is defective, for example by being too ambiguous on important points, a party may still try to enforce it. The party could, for example, file a statement of claim to the selected arbitral tribunal and send a copy of the claim to the other party. If the other party responds to the merits of the claim without raising the issue of the jurisdiction of the arbitration tribunal, this should create a sufficient basis under Ukrainian law for the tribunal to accept the case and for its decision to be binding on the parties.

In the case of ad hoc arbitration, it is advisable to indicate in the arbitration agreement the number of arbitrators, the procedure for appointing the arbitrators, the language and place of the arbitration, and the procedure for sharing the expenses between the parties. The parties should also provide for rules to govern the arbitration, which preferably should be based on a developed system such as those of the International Chamber of Commerce or UNCITRAL.

The leading arbitral tribunals used in Ukraine

The principal international arbitral tribunals cited for large transactions involving a Ukrainian counterparty are the International Chamber of Commerce (ICC) and the Arbitration Institute of the Stockholm Chamber of Commerce (usually applying UNCITRAL rules). The local International Commercial Arbitration Court under the Ukrainian Chamber of Commerce is also becoming increasingly popular. In addition, Ukrainian cases are heard by the International Commercial Arbitration Court of the Russian Chamber of Commerce, the London Court of International Arbitration, the International Arbitral Centre of the Austrian Federal Economic Chamber in Vienna, the American Arbitration Association and the International Centre for Settlement of Investment Disputes. More detailed information on certain selected tribunals is provided below.

ICC

The ICC, with its head office in Paris, is recommended for major disputes. It has national committees in approximately 60 different countries, including Ukraine. Each national committee keeps a list of arbitrators with appropriate qualifications who may be chosen for a particular dispute. Unlike some institutions, the ICC does not require that arbitrators be selected from their established list. In order to ensure that the arbitrators properly act within their powers, the ICC's headquarters in Paris supervises all arbitral proceedings from commencement to the rendering and enforcement of a final award. This level of attention comes at a price, however, so the ICC tends to be used more for important matters.

An ICC arbitral tribunal may be composed of one or more arbitrators, depending on what the parties decide. If the parties do not decide on the number of arbitrators, the ICC Rules provide that the ICC may appoint a sole arbitrator 'save where it appears to the Court that the dispute is such as to warrant the appointment of three arbitrators' (article 8). If the tribunal is to be composed of three arbitrators, then each party (assuming there are only two) nominates an arbitrator and the ICC nominates the third arbitrator who serves as the chairman of the arbitral tribunal (unless parties agree otherwise).

In order to initiate an arbitration with the ICC, a party must file a Request for Arbitration and pay USD2,500 to cover the initial administration expenses. As soon as the arbitral tribunal is formed, the ICC Secretariat transfers the files to it. At the initial stage of the arbitration process, the arbitral tribunal composes its 'Terms of Reference' – a document that contains an overview of the facts and arguments as they are then perceived by the arbitrators. Sometimes disputes can be amicably settled on the basis of such Terms of Reference. The plaintiff may be asked to make an advance payment for the arbitrators' time to prepare these Terms of Reference, and periodic advances may be required from the parties thereafter. After studying the parties' written submissions, the tribunal may ask the parties and their experts and other witnesses to appear.

In addition to arbitration, the ICC provides other dispute resolution options for the parties to a dispute. For example, the ICC has established a procedure by which the parties can appoint a pre-arbitral referee, who can evaluate a dispute and grant preliminary measures before the convocation of an arbitral tribunal. It is also possible for parties that have decided to resolve their disputes by ad hoc arbitration to use the ICC as their 'appointing authority' to appoint qualified arbitrators.

The Arbitration Institute of the Stockholm Chamber of Commerce

The Arbitration Institute of the Stockholm Chamber of Commerce (the 'SCC Institute') is also one of the well-known and established international arbitral institutions frequently used in Ukraine. The SCC Institute is an independent entity within the Stockholm Chamber of Commerce and is located in Stockholm, Sweden. The SCC Institute principally conducts arbitrations on the basis of its own rules ('the SCC Rules') and those of UNCITRAL, depending on the choice of the parties. For Ukrainian contracts, UNCITRAL rules appear to be the most common choice, following the practice adopted during the Soviet era.

To initiate an arbitration before the SCC Institute, a Request for Arbitration must be submitted to its Secretariat, which will then decide whether the SCC Institute is competent to hear the dispute. A €1,000 Registration Fee must be paid at the outset by the plaintiff. From time to time during the proceedings, the SCC Institute may request the parties to pay advances on costs to cover the fees of the one or more arbitrators and the other arbitration expenses, which are split equally among the parties.

If the parties decide that the arbitral tribunal will be limited to a sole arbitrator, the SCC Institute will appoint the arbitrator unless the parties mutually decide to appoint this arbitrator themselves. If the tribunal is composed of three arbitrators, each party (if there are only two) nominates one arbitrator and the third arbitrator, who chairs the tribunal, is appointed by SCC Institute, unless the parties agree otherwise. The SCC Institute does not require parties to limit their choice of arbitrators to those on its recommended list; the only requirement is that the arbitrators chosen be unbiased and independent of the parties.

As a rule, in addition to exchanges of written statements, an SCC Institute arbitral tribunal will hold hearings. The tribunal's decision must be made not later than one year following appointment of the arbitrators, though this time period may be extended.

Recently the SCC Institute adopted rules for expedited arbitration, which is recommended for disputes involving relatively small amounts. Expedited arbitration should be faster and less expensive since (1) only one arbitrator hears the case, (2) oral hearings are only held if the arbitrator so decides and (3) the parties are allowed to submit only one written explanation in addition to the plaintiff's statement of claim.

ICAC

The International Commercial Arbitration Court at the Chamber of Industry and Commerce of Ukraine ('ICAC') is the leading Ukrainian-based arbitration institution. The ICAC acts according to its procedural Rules that are based on the UNCITRAL Model Law. The number of Ukrainian disputes that are heard by the ICAC exceeds that of any other arbitration tribunal and is growing steadily. The ICAC has already rendered more than 4,000 awards during the more than 11 years of its existence, including more than 3,500 awards in the past 6 years.

ICAC may settle a business dispute arising between parties, provided that either the principal place of business of at least one of the parties is either located abroad or is a Ukrainian company with foreign investment. If the jurisdiction of ICAC in a particular case is disputed, then the chairman of the ICAC decides whether it can accept or must reject the case.

Traditionally, the ICAC has only accepted proceedings under arbitration clauses that directly specified it as the sole arbitration tribunal. However, recently a tendency has developed for the ICAC to permit arbitration even where the arbitration agreement is somewhat vague, unless the respondent immediately objects. The ICAC has a 'recommended' list of arbitrators, which in theory does not appear to limit the choice of arbitrators under its Rules. However, as a practical matter, the ICAC insists on using its recommended arbitrators. The list of arbitrators consists of over 50 individuals from 17 countries, some of whom also act as arbitrators for a leading international tribunal.

Under ICAC's Rules, the parties are authorized to specify the number of arbitrators, including a sole arbitrator. If parties do not specify a particular number of arbitrators and fail to provide a procedure for their appointment, then under the ICAC's Rules, each party (assuming there are only two) nominates one arbitrator, and these two arbitrators appoint the third arbitrator, who is the chairman of the arbitral tribunal. If within the required periods any of the parties fails to nominate its arbitrator or the two nominated arbitrators fail to agree on the third arbitrator, then the president of the Ukrainian Chamber of Commerce appoints such arbitrator. Similarly, the president of the Ukrainian Chamber of Commerce appoints a sole arbitrator where a contract provides for the parties to select a single arbitrator but they fail to agree on a selection.

Arbitration under the ICAC Rules is initiated when one party to a dispute files a formal statement of claim. Upon receipt of such statement of claim, the ICAC notifies the claimant of the amount of fees due for handling the arbitration. The approximate amounts of fees are listed in the Schedule of Arbitration Fees and Costs (with payment details) posted on ICAC's website (http://www.ucci.org.ua/arb). These fees tend to be substantially lower than those charged by the leading international arbitration tribunals. An ICAC arbitration is normally conducted in either Ukrainian or Russian, but the parties may also agree to hold the proceedings in English or any other language.

Maritime Arbitration Commission

The Maritime Arbitration Commission at the Chamber of Industry and Commerce of Ukraine (the 'Maritime Commission') is the other leading arbitration institution based in Ukraine that handles disputes where at least one party is either foreign or a Ukrainian company with foreign investment. It operates on the basis of rules and regulations similar to those applied by the ICAC, is headed by the same chairman, and consists largely of the same arbitrators as the ICAC. The Maritime Arbitration Commission has a limited role however, as in principle it only handles disputes under contracts concerning maritime transactions.

4.4

Dispute Resolution: Enforcement of Court Judgments and Arbitral Awards

Bate C Toms and Dmytro Korbut,
BC Toms & Co

Enforcement of decisions of the commercial courts

A commercial court decision is subject to mandatory enforcement within Ukraine. Enforcement of a commercial court decision is carried out pursuant to the court's order, which is an enforcement document that supplements the actual decision of the court. The court is supposed to deliver this order to the plaintiff either personally or by mail when the decision comes into force. When a commercial court decision comes into effect, after all appeals, and an enforcement order has been delivered to the successful plaintiff, the plaintiff can require performance by the debtor during the three-month period following the rendering of the court decision or from when any suspension of enforcement has expired if later. This limitation period for submission of the order for enforcement is suspended by delivery of the enforcement document to the State Enforcement Service, a state agency acting under the Ukrainian Ministry of Justice, or by partial performance of the decision by the defendant. The limitation period for submission may be prolonged if the plaintiff can persuade the commercial court that it has good reason for missing the three-month deadline, such as the absence of the defendant and its assets in the jurisdiction. If the decision is not performed voluntarily within the period as stipulated, then the plaintiff (or any other interested party) may apply (during the three-year period following the court decision) for enforcement by the State Enforcement Service.

The State Enforcement Service enforces court judgments following procedures primarily established by the Law of Ukraine 'On Enforcement Proceedings' of 21 April 1999 and the Code of Commercial Procedure. Enforcement of a decision by any means other than a sale of the defendant's property should be implemented by the enforcement officer within six months from the date when the order commencing enforcement proceedings was issued, and in other matters not related to monetary claims, within two months.

In order to enforce a judgment, the State Enforcement Service may, among other measures, seize the defendant's property, including any funds in bank accounts and any salary or other income of the defendant. It may also take from the defendant any items stipulated in the court's decision. When enforcing a monetary claim against a legal entity, the State Enforcement Service normally should begin by collecting any cash in the defendant's possession and in its bank accounts, as well as any other valuables deposited in banks. If such funds and valuables are not sufficient, then enforcement can be made against other property of the defendant, although the defendant has the right to determine which such property items are to be subject to seizure in the first instance. There is a list of property against which a court decision cannot be enforced, adopted by the Law 'On Enforcement Proceedings'. For individuals, enforcement against real estate, such as an apartment, house or land plot, is only allowed if the defendant does not have sufficient movable property to satisfy the claim.

Property of a legal entity can be recovered in the following order of priority: (1) property that is not engaged in actual production processes (eg securities, money in bank accounts, foreign currency, cars and office furniture, and final products – such as produced goods); (2) other valuables that are not engaged in actual production processes; and (3) real estate, production equipment and other fixed assets and raw materials. Recovery against property in pledge or mortgage is allowed only at the request of the holder of the pledge or mortgage. Otherwise enforcement can only be levied against such property if it was pledged or mortgaged after the court decision had been rendered, or if its value exceeds the pledge or mortgage debt (in this case, a levy can be made against money received from property sold after the proceeds are first used for payment of the secured debt). Following appraisal of the defendant's property by the enforcement officer (or, if the value of the property is more then UAH1,700 (approximately USD320), by an appraiser), the subject property may be sold by specialized companies at special auctions.

In connection with such enforcement, the defendant will be charged an enforcement fee of 10 per cent of the actual amount recovered, which represents the collection expense. Out of this amount, the enforcement officer who successfully enforces the court judgment on a timely basis may receive up to 2 per cent of the collected amounts personally, but not more than UAH 510 (approximately USD100). As a practical matter and as is expressly permitted by law, the plaintiff may need to advance some funds to the State Enforcement Service to cover its collection expenses, which advances should in principle be reimbursed after the enforcement is completed.

It should be noted that there are many procedural faults in the Ukrainian enforcement process that help a defendant to try to avoid debt payments. For example, it is always very difficult for an enforcement officer, whose jurisdiction is limited by the relevant district that he is responsible for, to arrest the bank account of a debtor in other districts or to monitor any activity of a debtor, such as opening new accounts in other banks and transferring money or the proceeds from sales of property that has not yet been seized. Practical problems can occur if, for example, enforcement is attempted against an apartment or other premises of the debtor and the property owner or building security does not allow the enforcement officer to enter the relevant building. Parliament tried to address these problems by adopting the amendments to the Law 'On Enforcement Proceedings' in July 2003, permitting an enforcement officer to monitor compliance with a court decision by a debtor and to enter unimpeded the premises of a debtor or another person possessing the debtor's property and securing enforcement, where the amount of debt exceeds UAH10 million, by transferring the assets to the jurisdiction of the central department of the State Enforcement Service.

Enforcement of foreign court judgments

According to the Law of Ukraine 'On Recognition and Enforcement in Ukraine of Foreign Court Judgments' of 2001, a foreign court judgment may only be enforced in Ukraine pursuant to a written application to a competent court, and only if there is a bilateral or multilateral agreement to which Ukraine is a party providing for recognition and enforcement of such decision, or if there is an ad hoc agreement on reciprocity with the foreign country on this matter. Ukraine is not a party to the Lugano Convention on Jurisdiction and the Enforcement of Judgments in Civil and Commercial Matters of 16 September 1988 or the multinational treaty on reciprocal enforcement. Consequently, only court judgments from a very limited number of countries can be enforced in Ukraine based on bilateral treaties, including those with the CIS countries (Russia, Azerbaijan, Armenia, Georgia, Kazakhstan, Kyrgyz Republic, Moldova, Turkmen Republic and Uzbekistan), as well as Albania, Algeria, Bulgaria, China, Cuba, Cyprus, Czech Republic, Estonia, Finland, Greece, Hungary, Iraq, Italy, Korean NDR, Latvia, Lithuania, Macedonia, Mongolia, Poland, Romania, Serbia and Montenegro, Tunisia, Turkey, Vietnam and Yemen.

The procedure for enforcement of foreign court judgments is determined by the applicable international treaty, as well as by the Law 'On Recognition and Enforcement in Ukraine of Foreign Court Judgments' and the Law 'On Enforcement Proceedings'. According to the Law 'On Recognition and Enforcement in Ukraine of Foreign Court Judgments', a foreign court judgment may be enforced within three years from the date it came into force, or within the entire period that may have been established by a court judgment for periodic payments if longer than three years, but only in relation to debt covering the last three years. Foreign court judgments must be enforced through the Ukrainian appellate common courts having jurisdiction where the defendant (regardless of whether it is an individual or a legal entity) is permanently or temporary located, or where the defendant's property is located if the defendant has no permanent or temporary location in Ukraine, or such location is not known to the court.

Application for enforcement of foreign court judgments may be filed in the relevant court by the plaintiff or through the appropriate governmental institution if the applicable international treaty so provides. A list of documents that must be attached to the application as well as grounds for refusal of enforcement of a foreign court judgment is determined by reference to the applicable international treaty. If an applicable international treaty makes no reference to such a list, the following documents must be attached to the application: a legalized copy of the foreign court judgment; an official document confirming that the foreign court judgment is currently in force; documentation confirming that the defendant against which the foreign court judgment was made was properly informed about the time and place of the court hearings; a document determining within what time the foreign court judgment must be enforced; a power of attorney if the application is filed by a representative; and a legalized translation of all of the documents listed. If grounds for refusal are not set forth by the applicable international treaty, then recognition and enforcement of the foreign court judgment may be refused if:

- the defendant was denied a fair hearing; or
- a Ukrainian court has exclusive jurisdiction over the issue in question; or
- there is a Ukrainian court decision in force on the same issue between the same parties, or court proceedings on the same dispute

between the same parties had been commenced in a Ukrainian court earlier than in the relevant foreign court; or

- the limitation period for enforcement of the foreign court judgment has expired; or
- the issue in question cannot be litigated according to Ukrainian legislation; or
- enforcement of the foreign court judgment would threaten the interests of Ukraine; or
- any other grounds as may be envisaged by Ukrainian legislation.

Enforcement of arbitral awards

According to the International Arbitration Law, an award of the ICAC, the Maritime Commission or any other international commercial arbitration tribunal properly convened either in Ukraine or abroad shall be recognized as binding and, upon application in writing to the competent court, shall be enforced. The party relying on an award or applying for its enforcement shall submit to the court a duly authenticated original of the award or a duly certified copy thereof, with the original arbitration agreement or a duly certified copy thereof. If the award or agreement is made in a foreign language, the party must submit a duly certified translation thereof into the Ukrainian or Russian language.

The International Arbitration Law provides that recognition or enforcement of an arbitral award, irrespective of the country in which it was made, may be refused only for a limited number of grounds as follows, with the burden of proof resting on the party who wishes to rely upon the exception: incapacity of the party or invalidity of the arbitration agreement; denial of a fair hearing; excess of authority or lack of jurisdiction by the arbitral tribunal; or procedural irregularities. There are two other circumstances in which an award may be deemed invalid and which can be considered unofficially by the judicial authority requesting recognition or enforcement of the decision: if the subject matter that formed the basis of the arbitration was not capable of settlement by arbitration according to the law of the country where the arbitration took place; or recognition and enforcement of the award would be contrary to the public policy of Ukraine. In principle, no review of the merits of an award is allowed.

Thus, the International Arbitration Law in this respect follows the provisions of the Convention on the Recognition and Execution of Foreign Arbitral Awards signed in New York on 10 June 1958 (the 'New York Convention'), which has been in force in Ukraine since January

1961. Under the New York Convention, arbitral awards obtained in Ukraine can be enforced in any of the countries that are signatories to this Convention, and similarly, arbitral awards rendered in any of these foreign countries are enforceable in Ukraine. This Convention also applies to arbitration agreements and establishes the general principle that an arbitration agreement must be in writing, and that a tribunal in a contracting state must refer the parties to arbitration if their dispute is subject to an arbitration agreement.

According to Article V of the New York Convention, recognition and enforcement of an award may be declined at the request of the party against whom it is invoked only if that party furnishes to the competent authority, where the recognition and enforcement is sought, proof of any of the following:

- the parties to the arbitration agreement were, under the law applicable to them, under some incapacity, or the said agreement is invalid under the law that the parties agreed shall govern the agreement or, failing any agreement of the parties on the governing law, under the law of the country where the award was made; or
- the party against whom the award is invoked was not given proper notice of the appointment of the arbitrator or of the arbitration proceedings or was otherwise unable to present its case; or
- the award deals with a dispute not contemplated by, or not falling within the terms of, the requirements for submission to arbitration, or it contains decisions on matters beyond the scope of the submission to arbitration, provided that, if the decisions on matters submitted to arbitration can be separated from those not so properly submitted, that part of the award which contains decisions on matters properly submitted to arbitration may be recognized and enforced; or
- the composition of the arbitral authority or the arbitral procedure was not in accordance with the agreement of the parties or, failing such agreement, was not in accordance with the law of the country where the arbitration took place; or
- the award has not yet become binding on the parties, or has been set aside or suspended by a competent authority of the country in which, or under the laws of which, that award was made.

Recognition and enforcement of an arbitral award may also be refused if a competent authority in the country where recognition and enforcement is sought (ie a Ukrainian court for enforcement in Ukraine) finds that:

- the subject matter of the dispute is not capable of settlement by arbitration under the law of that country; or

- the recognition or enforcement of the award would be contrary to the public policy of that country.

However, one should also note that Ukraine inserted a reciprocity reservation when it ratified the Convention, declaring that it shall apply only to the other contracting states. This creates a contradiction, as described below, between the International Arbitration Law of Ukraine adopted in 1994, and the reservations to the Convention made by the former Ukrainian Soviet Socialist Republic in 1961, to which Ukraine is the legal successor.

According to the Law of Ukraine 'On the Recognition and Enforcement in Ukraine of Foreign Court Judgments', an arbitral award of a foreign arbitration tribunal may only be enforced in Ukraine if there is a bilateral or multilateral agreement to which Ukraine is a party providing for recognition and enforcement of such decision, or if there is an ad hoc agreement on reciprocity with a foreign country on this matter. Based on Ukraine's reciprocity reservations to the New York Convention, an arbitral award made in a state which is not a party to this Convention, or to a bilateral treaty on mutual assistance with Ukraine, should not be recognized and enforced in Ukraine. Such an approach conflicts with provisions of the Law on International Commercial Arbitration providing for the recognition and enforcement of every arbitral award, irrespective of where it was rendered.

The Resolution of the Plenum of the Supreme Court of Ukraine of 24 December 1999 resolves many of the ambiguities that previously existed concerning enforcement of arbitral awards. This Resolution summarizes the law in this area based on the Civil Procedure Code of Ukraine and the other laws, rules and regulations and international treaties ratified by Ukraine on this subject, including, in particular, the New York Convention, the European Convention on International Commercial Arbitration, the Law of Ukraine 'On Enforcement Proceedings', and the International Arbitration Law among other treaties. The Resolution explains that the International Arbitration Law applies to the recognition and enforcement of arbitration awards rendered by a commercial arbitration or a third-party tribunal established according to an arbitration agreement between parties. Nevertheless, Ukrainian judges appear to believe that the restrictive reciprocal approach of the Law of Ukraine 'On the Recognition and Enforcement in Ukraine of Foreign Court Judgments' prevails anyway. Thus, it is highly unlikely that recognition and enforcement of an arbitration award made in a state that is not a party to the New York Convention, or any bilateral treaty on mutual assistance where Ukraine is a party, may be granted by a Ukrainian court.

Providing that the conditions of the Law 'On the Recognition and Enforcement in Ukraine of Foreign Court Judgments' are met, an award by a foreign arbitral tribunal may be enforced with the same procedure as described above for a foreign court judgment. Such procedure should take place through the Ukrainian appellate common court having jurisdiction where the defendant is permanently or temporary located, regardless of whether the defendant is an individual or a legal entity, or where the defendant's property is located, if the defendant has no permanent or temporary location in Ukraine or if such location is not known to the court.

In contrast to the procedure established in Ukraine for foreign arbitral awards, the Law 'On Enforcement Proceedings' provides that decisions of a 'third-party tribunal' established according to the laws of Ukraine (which include both international arbitration tribunals in Ukraine and the 'Treteyskiy' tribunals established to hear cases where both parties are Ukrainian residents or companies) shall be directly enforceable by the State Enforcement Service (which, as observed earlier, is responsible for enforcing state court judgments) without the need to make any additional application to a state court for enforcement. Although theoretically this should mean that the awards of all international arbitration tribunals established in Ukraine should be directly enforceable, as a matter of practice, only decisions of ICAC and the Maritime Commission can be so enforced at present. Because foreign arbitral awards are not so directly enforceable, it has been argued that this creates an unfair preferential treatment for the ICAC and Maritime Commission arbitral awards.

According to the International Arbitration Law, enforcement of a Ukrainian domestic arbitral award (such as a decision by ICAC) may be appealed to the state common courts (those that primarily hear cases involving individuals, as discussed above) on grounds similar to those that would apply to prevent a request for enforcement of a foreign arbitral award. The important difference is that where such direct enforcement is available to the plaintiff through the State Enforcement Service for a domestic award, the burden is shifted to the defendant who must initiate state court proceedings if it wishes to prevent or halt such enforcement.

4.5

Dispute Resolution: Litigation in Ukrainian Courts

Bate C Toms and Dmytro Korbut,
BC Toms & Co

Overview of the judicial system in Ukraine

Disputes in Ukraine, including those that involve a foreign party, can be resolved either in state courts or by arbitral tribunals. Within the state court system, if one party to a dispute is an individual, then ordinarily the state common courts ('common courts') have jurisdiction. Disputes among legal entities and those individuals registered as entrepreneurs (sole traders) fall within the jurisdiction of specialized state commercial courts ('commercial courts').

Marking the end of a five-year transition period under the Constitution of Ukraine, the court system was substantially modified by the so-called 'small' judicial reform in 2001. During the course of this reform over a dozen laws governing the court system, civil and criminal procedure were amended to adapt Ukrainian legislation to more universally recognized principles as developed in Western civil law countries. As a result, the revised Law 'On the Judicial System of Ukraine' of 7 February 2002 provides that the judicial system is composed of (1) courts of general jurisdiction and (2) the Constitutional Court of Ukraine, which is the sole institution having constitutional jurisdiction.

In turn, the separate commercial court system (misleadingly referred to earlier as 'state arbitration courts') was integrated into the system of courts of general jurisdiction as specialized commercial courts, which is reflected in the revised Ukrainian Code of Commercial Procedure of 4 June 1991 (the 'Code') and the amended Law of Ukraine 'On Commercial Courts' of 4 June 1991. Finally, the other specialized court system to be established pursuant to the Law 'On Judicial System of Ukraine' is for the administrative courts to deal with challenges to administrative actions and administrative violations (misdemeanours).

Therefore, the system of courts of general jurisdiction in Ukraine shall consist of the following levels:

- local courts, including common, commercial and administrative courts;
- appellate courts, including appellate common, commercial and administrative courts, and the Court of Appeals of Ukraine;
- Higher Specialized Courts of Ukraine, which are higher bodies in the system of specialized courts, namely, the Higher Commercial Court of Ukraine and the Higher Administrative Court of Ukraine;
- the Supreme Court of Ukraine, the highest judicial organ in the system of courts of general jurisdiction.

The Court of Appeals of Ukraine and the Higher Administrative Court of Ukraine are not as yet operational, although the Decree of the President of Ukraine on their establishment was issued in October 2002. In addition, as a transitional measure, pending the organization of the proposed administrative courts, the common courts are handling most cases concerning challenges to administrative action and administrative violations. The Law 'On the Judicial System of Ukraine' also provides for the creation of a Court of Cassation of Ukraine, but this will not happen under current law because the Ukrainian Constitutional Court recently decided that these provisions contradict the Constitution of Ukraine.

Presently, there are many conflicting views and opinions of leading lawyers, judges and government officials regarding future reform of the judicial system in Ukraine. This is reflected in numerous debates taking place in the press and in Parliament. Many of these controversies should be resolved when the new 'Large' Judicial Code is eventually adopted by parliament.

As observed, provided that at least one of the parties to a dispute is an individual, cases that deal with civil, commercial, family, administrative and labour law are heard in the common courts in accordance with the Code of Civil Procedure of Ukraine. Criminal proceedings in these courts are governed by the Code of Criminal Procedure of Ukraine. In Kyiv and other major cities, local common courts are located in every administrative district. There is also, for each administrative region ('*oblast*') and the cities of Kyiv and Sevastopol, an appellate common court, to which decisions of the local common courts can be appealed. In a few relatively rare instances, these second-level courts can also act as courts of first instance.

The third level of the common courts system according to the Law 'On the Judicial System of Ukraine' was intended to be the Court of Cassation of Ukraine. However, taking into account that the recent decision of the Ukrainian Constitutional Court that these provisions contradict the Constitution of Ukraine, until satisfactory legislation is adopted to provide for this, if ever, appeals from the appellate common courts will continue to be heard by the Supreme Court of Ukraine. In certain instances the Supreme Court of Ukraine may directly hear appeals against decisions of a common court of first instance. Finally, the relevant Chamber of the Supreme Court of Ukraine may also review decisions of the common courts on the grounds of exceptional circumstances revealed even after a cassation appeal is denied, such as:

- the ambiguous application by the common courts of the same provision of law; or
- the application of any law contrary to the Ukrainian Constitution; or
- a ruling of an accepted international tribunal finding that the decision contradicts an international obligation of Ukraine.

Disputes where all parties are legal entities or individuals registered as entrepreneurs (sole traders) fall within the jurisdiction of the commercial courts. The commercial court system consists of three levels, beginning with the local commercial courts. Each oblast of Ukraine and the cities of Kyiv and Sevastopol (separately from their respective oblasts) have one local commercial court. The second level consists of the appellate commercial courts, each having jurisdiction over the territory of several oblasts or the cities of either Kyiv or Sevastopol and an oblast. The appellate commercial courts largely hear appeals from decisions of the local commercial courts. Currently, there are eleven appellate commercial courts in Ukraine following the establishment of two new appellate commercial courts in the Luganska and Kyivska oblasts in June 2003. The jurisdiction of the Kyiv Appellate Commercial Court consequently covers just the territory of Chernihiv oblast and the city of Kyiv.

At the top of the commercial court hierarchy is the High Commercial Court. It serves as a secondary level of appellate jurisdiction, referred to as 'cassation'. In principle, as discussed below, the High Commercial Court, in considering cassation appeals, may review only issues on the application of law by lower courts and may not review findings of fact or accept new evidence. In a limited number of cases, as discussed below, the decisions of the High Commercial Court may be appealed to the Supreme Court of Ukraine, which is the highest court of general jurisdiction.

It was anticipated in legislation that the foregoing system would be replaced with a three tier system of local courts, Courts of Appeal and the Supreme Court in which the lower courts and Courts of Appeal would be divided into civil, commercial, criminal, and administrative chambers. However, no implementing legislation for these further reforms has been pursued.

Statutory jurisdiction of the commercial courts

The jurisdiction of commercial courts is governed by the Code. Their authority is limited to disputes among legal entities and independent entrepreneurs registered as such, as well as certain disputes between them and state bodies. In rare cases, the Code permits individuals to participate in a commercial court trial, such as in bankruptcy cases.

Through the end of 1993, only the High Commercial Court (at that time called the 'High Arbitration Court') heard cases involving foreign entities. Until 1997, it also initially heard cases where the amounts in dispute exceeded certain sums (from UAH150,000 to 1,500,000, or approximately USD75,000 to 750,000 in 1997) depending on the subject matter of the dispute, except if all the parties to the dispute were situated in the same oblast or within the cities of Kyiv or Sevastopol. This is no longer the case. All parties, including foreign entities, must now go through the full procedure (irrespective of the amounts involved), beginning with the local commercial courts.

Beginning on 1 January 2004, the jurisdiction of Ukrainian courts was significantly expanded to cover any lawsuits brought against non-residents. Previously, Ukrainian courts had jurisdiction over non-residents only in limited cases, for example where a non-resident had a branch or a representative office in Ukraine, or where the dispute concerned immovable property located in Ukraine. The Law of Ukraine 'On Securing Claims of Creditors and the Registration of Encumbrances' of 18 November 2003 amended Article 16 of the Code to provide for the jurisdiction of Ukrainian courts at the plaintiff's location if the respondent was a non-resident. Although decisions of Ukrainian commercial courts against non-residents having no property in Ukraine could not usually be enforced in any other country in the absence of a relevant bilateral treaty on mutual recognition of court decisions, such judgments could often have the effect of creating many other problems for the non-resident defendant and often provided the basis for a settlement. While this Ukrainian legislation oddly limited the choice of forum for Ukrainian residents exclusively to Ukrainian courts, nevertheless, this choice of forum limitation could not be given effect in most foreign jurisdictions, which would treat jurisdiction as a procedural matter not affected by Ukrainian law.

Astonishingly, in June 2004 the Code and the Law of Ukraine 'On Securing Claims of Creditors and the Registration of Encumbrances' were amended by the Ukrainian Parliament so that the jurisdiction of the Ukrainian commercial courts was limited again only to cases against non-residents that have a branch or a representative office in Ukraine or immovable property located in Ukraine. Consequently, Ukrainian companies, for which bringing litigation abroad may be prohibitively expensive, will now not be able to take any action if their rights are abused by foreigners having no representative or branch office or real property in Ukraine.

Parties may also contractually provide for arbitration by a specified tribunal as the exclusive forum for the resolution of their disputes, thereby avoiding the jurisdiction of Ukrainian commercial courts that would otherwise exist. The parties may even agree on arbitration after a conflict arises. In addition, a bilateral or multilateral international treaty on legal assistance to which Ukraine is a party, can establish that a Ukrainian court shall have jurisdiction even if the Code provides otherwise, and can also provide for enforcement of Ukrainian decisions. Ukraine presently has signed bilateral treaties with the CIS countries (Russia, Azerbaijan, Armenia, Georgia, Kazakhstan, Kyrgyz Republic, Moldova, Turkmen Republic and Uzbekistan), as well as with Albania, Algeria, Bulgaria, China, Cuba, Cyprus, Czech Republic, Estonia, Finland, Greece, Hungary, Iraq, Italy, North Korea, Latvia, Lithuania, Macedonia, Mongolia, Poland, Romania, Serbia and Montenegro, Tunisia, Turkey, Vietnam and Yemen.

Commencing litigation in the state commercial courts

Commercial court proceedings are initiated by the plaintiff filing a formal written statement of claim (the 'statement of claim') stating the facts of the dispute and the plaintiff's allegations. The statement of claim must be filed within the limitation period prescribed by applicable law. The Civil Code of 1961, applicable until 1 January 2004, provided for a limitation period of three years after the discovery by a party that its rights had been violated. This limitation could not be modified by contract and was applied by state courts as well as arbitral tribunals, irrespective of any agreement by the parties to the contrary. For certain types of cases, there was a shorter limitation period, such as for the discovery of product defects following a sale or quality claims, claims for visible defects in services, claims for the payment of penalties and fines and claims regarding the carriage of goods and passengers. The limitation period could be extended by the courts in exceptional circumstances, for example owing to circumstances beyond the plaintiff's reasonable control that prevented the filing of a claim, such as where a sole entrepreneur was unconscious and therefore unable to act in time.

The new Civil Code of Ukraine, which entered into force on 1 January 2004, establishes new rules on limitation periods. These new rules are applicable to any claim arising after January 2004, if the limitation period previously established for this claim has not then expired. Thus, there remains a general three-year limitation that cannot be reduced by parties; however, the period can be extended if parties so agree. If a claim refers to the quality of work performed by a contractor under a construction agreement, the limitation period is one, two, three, 10 or 30 years depending on which type of construction performed is the subject matter of the claim. A five-year limitation period will apply to claims for transactions performed under coercion or to fraud to declare an agreement null and void, and a ten-year limitation for claims affecting the consequences of a null and void transaction. The limitation period for claims concerning international carriage of goods must be established according to international treaties in force for Ukraine, transport codes and statutes. There is also a one-year limitation period for claims concerning payments of penalties and fines; defamation in the mass media; violation of the right of first refusal in respect to joint ownership; an after-sale product defect; cancellation of a donation; the postal services or the carriage of goods; acts by an executor of a will; damage to leased property; the quality of the work performed by a contractor; and demands to pay under a cheque.

In any contractual dispute with a foreign element, Ukrainian courts should apply the limitation period based on the law governing the contract. An ambiguity arises if applicable foreign law considers the statute of limitations to be a matter of procedure, thus making it impossible for Ukrainian courts to apply foreign rules of procedure. Ukraine is also a party to the Convention on the Limitation Period in the International Sale of Goods, which has been in force since April 1994 and provides for a four-year limitation period for claims arising from international contracts of sales of goods. This Convention applies, subject to its other provisions if, at the time of the conclusion of contract of international sale of goods, the places of business of all of the parties to the contract are in contracting states, or if under the rules of private international law, the law of a contracting state is applicable to the contract. This Convention does not apply when the parties have expressly excluded its application.

Prior to the June 2001 judicial reform, a mandatory pre-trial dispute settlement procedure was applied to most types of cases, requiring the plaintiff to send its claim to the defendant at least one month before court proceedings could be initiated. The defendant was required to provide a response within this one-month period. Currently this pre-trial dispute settlement procedure is required only for relatively few types of cases, including those in matters relating to transport services (carriage of goods, postal services and transportation of passengers), communication services and state procurement, or where the contract at issue so provides. Even in these cases, the mandatory nature of this procedure is questionable based on the position taken by the Constitutional Court of Ukraine in the case on the Campus Cotton Club.

To initiate proceedings, copy of the statement of claim with copies of all relevant documents supporting the claim must be sent to the defendant. The following documents must be attached to the statement of claim filed with the court:

- confirmation of the transmittal of a copy of the statement of claim to the defendant;
- confirmation that mandatory pre-trial dispute settlement procedures, if applicable, have been complied with;
- confirmation of the payment of the statutory filing fee and the fee for informational and technical support for the court hearings;
- information about application of preventative measures, if any;
- power of attorney or other document confirming the authority of the signatory, if the statement of claim is signed by a representative.

The filing fee (state duty) is 1 per cent of the value of the claim, subject to the requirement that it may not be less than UAH51 (approximately USD10) or exceed UAH1,700 (approximately USD330). If the value of the claim cannot be determined (such as a claim to declare a decision of a state organ null and void), then the filing fee is only UAH85 (approximately USD16). The claimant *must* also pay in advance for the information services of the court in the amount of UAH118. Upon acceptance of the case, the court must send an official notice to the parties.

A commercial court, according to the Code, is supposed to resolve a case within two months of the filing of the statement of claim. As a practical matter, Ukrainian courts are overloaded and are often unable to meet such deadlines. Within this two-month period, a court may also, at the request of one party, postpone the deadline for completion of the judicial proceedings by one month based on a demonstrated inability of the party to be able to adequately prepare its case and represent its interests. Prolongation is also possible if mutually approved by both parties to a lawsuit.

Usually, a local commercial court case is heard by one judge. However, any case, depending on its category and complexity, may be heard by a three-judge panel led by one judge acting as the chairman, if the court so decides at the request of a party or on its own motion.

Appellate and cassation proceedings

A decision of a local commercial court takes effect on the tenth day following its announcement in full, or if a decision is not announced in full (Ukrainian law allows a court initially to announce the conclusion for a decision only, with the full decision provided in writing later on), then on the tenth day after it is formed and signed by the judge (Article 85 of the Code). If a party believes that the local commercial court's decision is wrong, it then has 10 days to lodge an appeal by filing a written statement of appeal (the 'statement of appeal') with this local commercial court. The local commercial court must then forward the statement of appeal to the appellate commercial court responsible for its jurisdiction within five days.

In practice, it may take the judge or judges more than 10 days to document a decision, after it is announced in the courtroom at the last hearing. If the full decision is dated as of the date of the last hearing, as opposed to when the decision is actually issued and registered by the court's administrative office for delivery to the parties, then assuming the parties wait to receive a copy of the written decision to evaluate the bases for an appeal, the 10-day period for appeal may be missed. This is a frequent problem as a practical matter.

In this situation (or if, for any other reason, the appeals deadline is missed), the party wishing to appeal the lower commercial court decision must file an extension petition setting forth the reasons for missing the 10-day period. The appeals period may, at the court's discretion, be extended for up to three months after the decision was rendered. In practice, where the 10-day appeals period is missed because the local commercial court failed to issue its decision in time, an extension to the appeals period is ordinarily granted, and if not, the decision to deny the extension can usually be successfully appealed.

The rules for the appellate commercial court provide that on appeal it may re-examine the circumstances of a case and verify the legal grounds for the decision taken by the local commercial court. In practice, this amounts to a new trial, although in theory the appellate commercial court is supposed to accept additional evidence for consideration if the party introducing it can prove that it was unable to present such new evidence to the court of first instance for reasons outside of that party's control.

As a result of the appellate review, the appellate commercial court may:

- let the decision of the local commercial court stand;
- partially or fully reverse the decision and make a new decision;
- partially or fully reverse the decision and close the proceedings;
- amend the decision.

The Code lists the following four grounds for reversing or amending the decision of a local commercial court:

- incomplete analysis of circumstances that were material to the case;
- lack of proof of circumstances accepted by the local commercial court that were material to the case;
- the conclusions reached did not correspond to the circumstances of the case;
- violations or improper use of substantive or procedural laws that led to an incorrect decision.

A decision of the appellate commercial court may be appealed to the High Commercial Court for supervision ('cassation'). In certain situations, the losing party in a local commercial court may appeal directly to the High Commercial Court, bypassing the appellate commercial court, provided that it does not need to submit any additional evidence.

Such supervisory review by the High Commercial Court is supposed to be limited to issues on the correct application of substantive law by lower courts to the proven circumstances of the case, or the observance of the rules of procedure and the general analysis of the case by the lower courts. In principle, the High Commercial Court should accept the lower court's factual decisions and should not review the established evidence or accept new evidence. The High Commercial Court has the authority to:

- deny an appeal;
- leave the decisions of either the court of first instance or the appellate court intact;
- partially or fully reverse the decision and render a new decision, return the case for a new hearing to the court of first instance or close the proceedings;
- amend the lower court's decision.

The 2001 amendments to the Code also created an additional limited appeal option for the parties to a commercial dispute. A decision of the High Commercial Court may now be further appealed to the Supreme Court of Ukraine, the highest court of the courts of general jurisdiction. Such an appeal to the Supreme Court may only be lodged based on any of the following grounds:

- the High Commercial Court applied legislation or secondary law contrary to the Ukrainian Constitution;
- the decision of the High Commercial Court is contrary to a prior decision of the Supreme Court or of another specialized court of the same level;

- the decision is inconsistent with the application of the same provision of the law or other legal act by the High Commercial Court in other similar cases;
- the decision of the High Commercial Court is contrary to an international treaty of Ukraine that is in force and agreed to be binding by the Parliament of Ukraine;
- there is a ruling of an accepted international tribunal finding that the decision contradicts an international obligation of Ukraine.

In such proceedings, the Supreme Court of Ukraine has the authority to:

- deny the appeal and leave the court decision intact;
- reverse the decision and return the case for a new hearing to the court of first instance or the High Commercial Court;
- reverse the decision and close the proceedings.

These multiple levels of judicial review are aimed at increasing the predictability of the judicial system, making it more reliable and less vulnerable to mistakes and corruption. In addition to this appellate review, the parties are afforded the opportunity to request review of their case based on any new material circumstances of which the party could not have been aware. Within two months after such new circumstances have become known, a petition for review may be filed with the commercial court of first instance that rendered the decision or the appellate commercial court that sustained, amended or reversed the previous decision.

Preventive measures

In June 2003, the Commercial Litigation Procedure was amended to introduce a new procedural instrument for securing claims. One must take into account that this procedure is new to the Ukrainian judicial system and has so far been applied on a very limited basis. However, it may become an important vehicle for the protection of the rights and interests of an applicant in court. Thus, even before commercial court proceedings are initiated, a party, having both a reason for concern that required evidence would be impossible to obtain afterwards and a reason to believe that there is an infringement or a serious danger of infringement of his, her or its rights, can submit an application for 'preventive measures' to the commercial court. Such preventive measures may include summoning evidence; examining the premises where actions in connection with an infringement of rights have or are taking place; and seizing property belonging to a person subject to preventive measures even if such property is in another person's possession.

The application must include the reasons why such measures are required, and all the documents and evidence supporting the application, as well as a confirmation of the payment of the statutory filing fee. The local commercial court having jurisdiction over the territory where the preventive measures will be applied should consider such application not later than two days after its submission. The local commercial court then should inform all interested parties prior to its consideration of the application except if the applicant has serious grounds to request that the court not inform the party that will be subject to preventive measures. The commercial court may also request a relevant deposit from the applicant to prevent abuse of this form of application.

If the commercial court decides to initiate preventive measures without informing the person subject to those measures, the latter may apply to the same commercial court for cancellation of preventive measures, which then should consider such application and may cancel the preventive measures, change them or leave them intact. A commercial court's decision to apply or deny preventive measures, as well as to change or annul a decision to apply preventive measures, may later be appealed to a higher court. Filing of an appeal to a decision cancelling or changing preventive measures should result in a suspension of such preventive measures until a decision is taken in the appeal.

Not later than 10 days following the issuance of a court decision commencing preventive measures, a statement of claim must be filed by the plaintiff to the commercial court, whereupon the preventive measures become measures to secure the claim. The application of preventive measures should be cancelled if: a statement of claim is not filed in due time, the commercial court rejects the claim on grounds provided by the Code, or the commercial court annuls the decision commencing the preventive measures. If the application of preventive measures is cancelled or a plaintiff withdraws the claim, the person subject to preventive measures has the right to compensation for damages resulting from such measures, and the deposit paid by the applicant can be taken for this purpose.

Securing claims during trial and suspending enforcement pending appeals

Ukrainian law provides for several measures to secure a claim pending the resolution of a case (hereinafter referred to as 'interim relief'). According to the Code, a commercial court at any level has the right to take measures to secure a claim, if so requested by one of the parties or at its own discretion, but it is not obliged to do so. A commercial court may secure a claim at any stage of the proceedings 'if failure to do so may make the enforcement of a court judgment in the case difficult or impossible' (Article 66 of the Code). The Code provides that a claim can be secured by:

- arrest (freezing) of property or funds of the defendant;
- forbidding the defendant to take certain actions;
- forbidding other persons to take actions with regard to the subject matter of the litigation;
- suspension of the collection of debts by a party to the proceedings (including by a state body, such as the State Tax Administration).

A court has full discretion to determine whether interim measures are necessary to secure a claim. To justify requiring security for a claim, reasonable grounds should be proven by the plaintiff, to show that the defendant's property or funds existing at the time that the proceedings are commenced would cease to exist or would materially diminish in value or in quality before enforcement may be made of any decision. The standard of proof of such a request is ordinarily relatively high. In a case involving a claim for damages, a court is likely to agree to arrest some or all of the funds in a defendant's bank account only to the extent that this appears necessary to ensure satisfaction of the claim.

After a decision is made, pending appeal by one of the parties or at the court's own discretion, enforcement of the verdict may be suspended by the appellate commercial court or the High Commercial Court, whichever is hearing the case. The High Commercial Court or appellate commercial court may order the parties to return any property previously received as a result of any enforcement process or interim relief.

Hearing cases in common courts

As has already been mentioned above, disputes involving at least one individual as a party, including foreign individuals, must be settled by the state common courts. Basically, court proceedings in the common courts are similar to those in the commercial courts, with a few distinctions. For example, the rules for the territorial jurisdiction of the local courts, including both the local common courts and the local commercial courts, provide that disputes shall be heard by the local court at the place where the defendant is located. However, in addition, the Code of Civil Procedure provides that, for most civil law and certain other cases before the common courts, jurisdiction may also be (1) at the location of the plaintiff or where the contract was performed, where the damage occurred or where property involved in the case or owned by the defendant is located, at the option of the plaintiff, or (2) at any location in Ukraine as the parties may agree. These criteria may sometimes also vary depending upon the subject matter of the case, so that, for example, labour law cases may only be tried at the location of the plaintiff or the defendant.

4.6

Intellectual Property Protection in Ukraine

Bate C Toms and Olga Prokopovych, BC Toms & Co – Kyiv and London

Introduction to the system of intellectual property protection in Ukraine

The system of intellectual property protection in Ukraine has developed significantly since independence. The system is primarily based on the principles and general rules established by the major international treaties on intellectual property to which Ukraine is a party. To the extent that these duly ratified international treaties conflict with Ukrainian legislation, the provisions of the treaties prevail.

The international treaties to which Ukraine is a party and that form the basis for the international system of intellectual property protection include the following: the Paris Convention for the Protection of Industrial Property of 1883 (the 'Paris Convention'); the Berne Convention for the Protection of Literary and Artistic Works of 1886 (the 'Berne Convention'); the Madrid Agreement on International Registration of Marks of 1891; the Universal Copyright Convention of 1952; the Nice Agreement on Classification of Goods and Services for the Purposes of the Registration of Marks of 1957 as amended in 1979; International Convention for the Protection of Performers, Producers of Phonograms and Broadcasting Organizations (the 'Rome Convention') of 1961; the Convention Establishing the World Intellectual Property Organization (WIPO) of 1967; the Patent Cooperation Treaty of 1970; the Geneva Convention for the Protection of Producers of Phonograms Against Unauthorized Duplication of Their Phonograms of 1971; Nairobi Treaty on the Protection of the Olympic Symbol of 1981; the Protocol Relating to the Madrid Agreement on International Registration of Marks of 1989; the Geneva

Patent Law Treaty of 1990; the Geneva Trademark Law Treaty of 1994; the WIPO Copyright Treaty and the WIPO Performances and Phonograms Treaty of 1996; and the Budapest Treaty on the International Recognition of the Deposit of Micro-organisms for the Purposes of Patent Procedure as well as other agreements and global treaties.

National legislation on intellectual property protection is comprised of laws and numerous governmental regulations. The major laws include: the Law of Ukraine 'On the Protection of Rights to Inventions and Utility Models' of 15 December 1993 (the 'Inventions Law'); the Law of Ukraine 'On the Protection of Rights to Marks for Goods and Services' of 15 December 1993 (the 'Trademarks Law'); the Law of Ukraine 'On the Protection of Rights to Industrial Designs' of 15 December 1993 (the 'Industrial Designs Law'); the Law of Ukraine 'On Copyright and Neighbouring Rights' of 11 July 2001 (the 'Copyright Law'); the Law of Ukraine 'On the Protection of Plant Varieties' of 21 April 1993 (the 'Plant Law'); the Law of Ukraine 'On the Protection of Rights in Layouts of Integrated Circuits' of 5 November 1997 (the 'Integrated Circuits Law'); the Law of Ukraine 'On the Protection of Rights to Appellations of Origin' (the 'Appellation of Origin Law'), and other laws. Certain laws whose direct subject is not intellectual property issues *per se* may also contain relevant provisions on the protection of intellectual property rights. For example, the Criminal Code of Ukraine, the Ukrainian Code on Administrative Offences, and the Law of Ukraine 'On the Protection Against Unfair Competition' of 7 June 1996 (the 'Unfair Competition Law') all impact on intellectual property rights.

Recent changes in the Ukrainian legislation upon the protection of intellectual property rights

Ukraine has taken several important steps aimed at strengthening its intellectual property rights protection system, harmonizing it with the EU and WTO intellectual property protection standards and avoiding accusations by various intellectual property organizations and governments that its policies to combat intellectual property piracy, especially in the area of compact disc production and distribution, are ineffective.

The Ukrainian Parliament adopted the Law 'On the Peculiarities of the State Regulation of Activity in the Field of the Production, Export and Import of Discs for Laser Systems for Sensing Information' on 17 January 2002. This Law provides for licensing the production, export and import of laser compact discs. It also establishes a number of additional requirements to further protect copyright and neighbouring rights to works on compact discs. For example, requirements will be imposed that a special identification code be added to each disc and that discs be manufactured only in licensed premises, which are subject to periodic checks by the licensing bodies. These steps are intended to indicate that Ukraine treats its international reputation in the area of intellectual property protection seriously and is eager to combat effectively any illegal production and distribution of audio and video products.

The latest changes in the Ukrainian system of intellectual property rights protection include the Law 'On Amendments to Several Legislative Acts of Ukraine Concerning the Legal Protection of Intellectual Property' dated 22 May 2003. This Law is another step in the process of harmonization of Ukrainian intellectual property protection rules with international protection standards and the multilateral Agreement on the Trade-Related Aspects of Intellectual Property (TRIPS). It is especially important in light of Ukraine's intention to enter the WTO in the very near future. Among other novelties, this latest Law introduced the mechanism of the so-called 'preventive measures' (TRIPS referred to them as 'provisional measures') into Ukrainian civil and commercial procedures aimed at preventing intellectual property infringements and securing evidence against actual or potential infringers of intellectual property rights. Upon a motion to the court by an individual who believes that his or her rights have been or are in threat of being infringed, the court may grant preventive measures prior to the actual filing of a lawsuit. The motion may be filed either on notice to the alleged infringer or *ex parte* (TRIPS uses the term *inaudita altera parte*, ie without giving notice to the other party). These newly introduced preventive measures include: (1) a court order to produce evidence; (2) an inspection of the premises where alleged actions related to infringement took or are taking place; and (3) the seizure of the assets of the person subject to such a preventive measure. Although this Law ensures additional intellectual property protection, it contains some provisions that may bar its effective application by the Ukrainian judiciary.

Among several important amendments, the Law added a separate article on the protection of well-known trademarks to the Trademarks Law. Previously, the protection of such trademarks was based on Article 6-bis of the Paris Convention and could be granted only against similar goods or services. The amended Trademarks Law has taken the important step of broadening this protection to all goods and services.

Finally, one of the most important legislative events for the Ukrainian system of protection of intellectual property rights in 2003 was the adoption of the New Civil Code of Ukraine (the 'New Civil Code') that became effective on 1 January 2004. The New Civil Code contains a separate Book IV titled 'Intellectual Property Rights' outlining the legal framework for the protection of intellectual property rights and establishing general principles and rules for such protection. Generally, the New Civil Code retains the approaches envisaged in prior legislation and Ukraine's international treaties. However, it also introduces certain improvements and innovations that strengthen and broaden the protection of intellectual property rights.

For example, the New Civil Code explicitly regulates the legal protection of a 'commercial name' (presently called a 'firm name' and protected by the old Soviet statute of 1927). The New Civil Code introduces new general rules on the protection of a scientific discovery and envisages the adoption of a new law that will regulate the protection of a scientific discovery in detail. The New Civil Code also expressly lists commercial secrets as objects of intellectual property rights, provides a definition of a commercial secret and sets out the legal conditions for its protection. It should be noted that adoption of the New Civil Code will not result in the termination of previous intellectual property protection laws. These will remain in force to the extent that they do not contradict the provision of the New Civil Code.

The Commercial Code of Ukraine (the 'Commercial Code'), adopted in 2003 and effective beginning 1 January 2004, also touches upon intellectual property issues. However, it cites the New Civil Code as being a higher primary source for rules on the protection of intellectual property rights.

In general, all intellectual property rights can be classified into certain categories based upon the objects (intellectual products) in which they subsist. Some of these types of intellectual property rights are discussed below.

Copyright and neighbouring rights

The Ukrainian Copyright Law sets down a non-exclusive list of works by authors to which copyright protection is extended. For example, verbal and written literary works, dramatic works, musical works, architectural, audiovisual and photographic works, computer programmes and databases as well as other literary, artistic and scientific works are protected under the Copyright Law.

Copyright protection is generally provided to: (1) nationals of Ukraine, individuals who are not Ukrainian nationals but are permanently resident in Ukraine and legal entities having a place of business in Ukraine irrespective of the country where the work was first made public or the country where the work is in fact located; (2) individuals and legal entities irrespective of their nationality, permanent residency or place of business provided that the work is first made public in Ukraine or, if not made public, is in fact located in Ukraine; (3) individuals and legal entities irrespective of their nationality, permanent residency or place of business whose work is first made public outside of Ukraine but then within 30 days is made public in Ukraine; and (4) individuals and legal entities irrespective of their nationality, residence or place of business whose works are protected in accordance with the international treaties to which Ukraine is a party.

According to the Copyright Law, copyright subsists in an authorial work as a result of the creation of such work. Under Ukrainian law, a work must exist in a certain objective form of expression (verbal or written) to be given protection for ideas, theories, principles etc, which are not themselves protected under the Copyright Law even if they are contained in such a work. There are no formalities (registration, notification etc) required for a copyright to subsist or for its exercise by the author or another copyright owner (heir or a person to whom the copyright was transferred by the author or his or her heirs).

However, the author or another copyright owner may register its copyright with the Ukrainian Agency of Copyright and Neighbouring Rights within the time period provided by law in order to certify and secure evidence of its copyright. The time period for the protection of copyright is longer than the term established by the Bern Convention. Generally, a copyright owner enjoys protection from the moment of the work's creation throughout the life of the author and for 70 years after the author's death, beginning from 1 January of the year following the author's death. In the case of joint authorship, the death of the last surviving author is taken as the starting point for calculating the 70-year period. Although not requested, to put the public on notice of his or her copyright, the copyright owner can use a copyright notice that consists of the symbol © followed by the name of the copyright owner and the date of the first publication of the work. The copyright notice can be placed on the original as well as copies of the protected work.

Ukrainian Copyright Law recognizes two types of rights inherent in copyright: moral rights and economic rights. The moral rights that belong to an author include: (1) the right to demand recognition of his or her authorship; (2) to prohibit revealing the author's name during public performances of the work if he or she wishes to remain anonymous; (3) to use a pseudonym instead of the author's real name; and (4) to demand respect for the integrity of the work and to prevent any deformation, distortion, alteration or other derogation of the work that may threaten the author's reputation and dignity. Moral rights belong to the author independently of the economic rights to the work and they may not be transferred to others or inherited by the author's heirs and are permanently protected. The author's heirs are, however, entitled to protect the author's right to authorship and the author's work against any reputation-damaging derogation for an unlimited period of time. The expiration of a copyright term means that the work enters into the public domain.

Works that have never been protected in Ukraine are deemed to have passed into the public domain and may be freely used in Ukraine by any person or entity without payment of remuneration. However, the author's moral rights, such as the right to be recognized as an author, and the right to protect an author's reputation, must still be respected.

Contrary to moral rights, economic rights provide: (1) an exclusive right to use a work and (2) an exclusive right to allow or to forbid the usage of the work by other persons. Economic rights may be transferred or licensed by the copyright owner to another individual or entity. Upon any such transfer, a transferee becomes the owner of the copyright or neighbouring rights, and upon any licensing, the licensee obtains such rights of use as are provided in the license agreement, which may be exclusive or non-exclusive.

Under the Copyright Law, if a person creates a work during an employment agreement, he or she is considered to be the author of the work and shall have the moral rights to such work. However, the exclusive economic rights to the work created by an employee belong to the employer, unless otherwise provided in an employment agreement. The employee shall nevertheless be entitled to remuneration for the creation and use of the work, the amount of which should be established in the employment agreement. These rules have been attended to by the New Civil Code, which provides that the economic rights to a work created by an employee in the course of employment belong jointly to the employee and employer, unless established otherwise by an employment agreement.

As pointed out above, computer programmes are specifically included in the list of copyright protected objects under the Copyright Law. The Copyright Law also states that computer software programmes are protected as literary works. Such protection applies to computer programmes, whatever may be the mode or form of their expression. However, the protection of computer programmes solely under copyright is not considered sufficient. Many Western countries now use the system method of computer programme protection. This means that, in general, computer programmes are protected under copyright and, in addition, patents are obtained for the inventions reflected in the computer programmes. Under the Ukrainian Inventions Law, however, there is no express patent protection for computer programmes.

Similar to copyright, neighbouring rights do not need any formal procedures to be recognized and protected. Producers of phonograms and videograms, broadcast organizations and performers may use the symbol of protection of neighbouring rights, (®), together with the name of the owner of the neighbouring rights and the year of first performance, publication or broadcast of the work, to inform the public about their rights.

Trademark protection

Under the Trademarks Law, legal protection is granted to any mark for goods or services that does not contravene the public interest or principles of humanity and morality and does not fall within the list of marks that cannot be registered as a trademark set out in the Trademarks Law (ie because they are identical or similar to previously registered trademarks for the same or similar goods and services or well-known trademarks for any goods and services, generic marks etc). To be protected in Ukraine, or to be protected under international treaties duly ratified by Ukraine (trademarks registered under the Madrid System for the International Registration of Marks or trademarks recognized as being well known), a mark must not only meet the Trademarks Law's requirements but also must be properly registered with the State Department of Intellectual Property (the 'SDIP') in accordance with legally established procedures. According to the Trademarks Law, the rights of a trademark owner, as confirmed by a certificate, constitute an exclusive right to use such a trademark, and are valid from the application date as determined by SDIP upon the filing by an applicant of the documents required by the Trademarks Law. After completion of the registration process, an applicant is granted a certificate that acts as a title document confirming the applicant's ownership to the trademark. However, there is some uncertainty as to the moment when an applicant may actually seek protection of its exclusive rights to use a trademark and to forbid its exploitation by others. According to a recent interpretation by the Ukrainian judiciary, such exclusive rights arise and may be protected only after an applicant is granted a trademark registration certificate. A fee must be paid for the submission of the registration application as well as a state duty for the issuance of the registration certificate for a trademark.

In the event that several persons or entities have the right to obtain a certificate, they are collectively granted a single certificate, and their mutual rights to its use must be determined thereafter by an agreement amongst themselves. In the absence of such an agreement, each of the joint owners has the right to use the trademark at his, her or its own discretion. However, none of them has the right to license the use of the trademark or transfer ownership (except of a joint owner's share by inheritance) without the consent of all other joint trademark owners under the certificate.

The trademark certificate is issued for a period of 10 years and may be renewed upon application of the owner to SDIP for a successive additional 10-year period, provided that all fees and duties for such renewal are paid.

Protection for the name of a company or commercial name

The right of a legal entity to the exclusive use of the name of its company is, in particular, protected by the Paris Convention, Commercial Code of Ukraine and Civil Code of Ukraine, as well as other documents, including the Joint Resolution of the Central Executive Committee of the USSR and the Council of the People's Commissaries of the USSR 'On the Name of Firms' dated 22 June 1927 (the 'Firm Name Resolution').

According to the Paris Convention, Ukraine must guarantee protection to the company name of a legal entity, irrespective of whether any special registration has been made of such company name and regardless of whether the company name constitutes an integral part of its registered trademark. Furthermore, the legislation of Ukraine provides that the state registration of a legal entity having a company name identical to a company name of another legal entity registered earlier in an appropriate register is forbidden. Registration of a legal entity with an identical name in violation of this requirement may result in the judicial cancellation of the state registration of such legal entity.

According to the Firm Name Resolution, a legal entity has an exclusive right to use its firm name for transactions, advertisements, goods, etc, from the date when the legal entity first actually starts to 'use' its firm name. The intellectual property right to the firm name usually referred to under Ukrainian law as a 'commercial name' becomes protected from the moment of first use of this name and does not require any application to state bodies for its protection or registration, and does not depend on whether this firm name is a part of the firm's mark for goods and services. The exclusive right to a firm name also includes the power to permit or forbid the use of the firm name by other persons. Priority in the use of a commercial name should belong to the company that first commenced using the name. It might be argued that the date of such first use is the date of the official registration of the company with this name, but there is no recognized rule on this.

Under Ukrainian legislation, the usage by one legal entity of a firm name identical or similar to the firm name of another legal entity having a prior right to such firm name based on prior use constitutes an infringement of the exclusive right to the firm name. Such infringement may be remedied by the termination of the infringing use as well as by compensation for any damages suffered. It is also possible to prosecute an infringer under the Criminal Code of Ukraine.

Legal protection is granted to a commercial firm name to enable a company to distinguish itself from other legal entities, provided that it does not mislead consumers as to the real activities of this company. The New Civil Code provides that identical names may, however, be used by different companies, provided that, 'it does not mislead consumers as to the goods produced and services rendered by these companies'.

Patent protection of industrial property

Invention and utility models are protected in Ukraine according to the Inventions Law and international conventions ratified by Ukraine.

According to the Inventions Law, to be protected, an invention (product or process) must meet the requirements of patentability set forth in the Inventions Law, namely to possess: (1) novelty (the invention is not part of the body of existing global technical knowledge); (2) an inventive step (the invention is not obvious to a person with average knowledge in an applicable technical field); and (3) industrial utility (the invention is of practical use in the relevant industry or another field of activity). For a utility model to be patentable, it is enough to possess novelty and industrial utility.

The right to ownership of an invention or a utility model is certified by a patent. There are two types of patent established by the Ukrainian Inventions Law: (1) a patent – granted after a qualification examination (a substantive examination of patentability) establishes that the invention meets the conditions of patentability; and (2) a declaratory patent – granted after a formal examination of the invention and an examination that confirms the local (for Ukraine only) novelty of the proposed invention.

The formal examination is a simplified procedure to establish whether the subject proposed for a patent registration may be recognized as an invention or a utility model and whether the patent application satisfies all of the formal filing requirements, including the requirement to pay the application fee. The declaratory patent for an invention can be converted into a regular patent after the successful completion of a qualification examination at the request of the initial applicant or any other person. Such request must be made within three years after the initial application date. The declaratory patent is the only kind of patent granted for utility models in Ukraine.

The duration of a patent for an invention is 20 years from the application date, defined according to the provisions of the Inventions Law.

For a declaratory patent, the duration is six years; a declaratory patent for a utility model lasts for 10 years. The validity of these periods is subject to payment of an annual fee. Failure to pay the fee on time results in the termination of the patent.

Rights of foreigners

Under Ukrainian law, foreign legal and private persons (including stateless individuals) generally enjoy the same rights to protection of intellectual property rights as Ukrainian nationals under the applicable intellectual property laws and international treaties ratified by Ukraine. However, foreign persons who reside or have a permanent place of business outside of Ukraine must deal with the Ukrainian SDIP through registered Ukrainian-based patent attorneys, called 'representatives in intellectual property matters' ('IP representatives').

Under Ukrainian intellectual property laws, foreign nationals, as well as Ukrainians, have the right to register objects of intellectual property, to be a transferor and a transferee of intellectual property rights, to grant and to be granted licences, to enjoy legal protection of their intellectual property rights and to enforce their rights against any infringement.

Types of ownership-confirming documents and terms for validity

The ownership and legal protection of certain intellectual property rights in Ukraine is confirmed by a patent or a certificate. Summary information on the types of ownership- confirming documents and the terms of validity for different intellectual property rights is provided in Table 4.6.1 categorized by the SDIP's subdivisions responsible for issuing such documents.

Obtaining a patent or a certificate

A person wishing to obtain a patent or a certificate confirming his or her intellectual property rights must file an application with the appropriate subdivision of SDIP in accordance with the applicable procedures. The requirements for preparing the application documents and the application procedure itself are relatively complex; therefore, it is advisable to use a patent agent for the filing. The general scheme of governmental agencies and others involved in the process of obtaining an ownership-confirming document is provided in Figure 4.6.1.

Table 4.6.1 Summary information on the types of ownership-confirming documents and their terms of validity

Object of intellectual property	Type of ownership (years) confirming document	Term of protection (years)
Ukrainian Institute of Industrial Property (UkrPatent)		
Inventions	Patent	6 for declaratory patent; 20 for regular patent
Utility model	Patent	10
Industrial design	Patent	10 + 5
Layout of integrated circuits	Certificate	10
Trademarks; Geographical indications of the origin of goods	Certificate	10 +
Ukrainian Agency on Copyright and Neighbouring Rights		
Works of art, literature and science; computer programmes; databases.	Certificate *(registration is optional)*	During the life of the author and 70 years starting from his or her death
Ukrainian Institute of Plant Variety Expertise		
Varieties of plants	Patent	Protection of rights during 30 or 35 years

Dealings in intellectual property rights

The owner of a patent may transfer the right of ownership to an invention or a utility model to any person or entity on the basis of an agreement. The transferee under such an agreement becomes the successor in title to the patented invention. The owner may also grant exclusive or non-exclusive licences to use the invention or utility model to any person or entity in accordance with the conditions established by a licence agreement. The Inventions Law also provides for the possibility of mandatory licensing by court order if the patented invention or utility model is not used or is insufficiently used in Ukraine for a period of three years.

A trademark owner may transfer its certificate-confirmed ownership rights to a trademark to any person or entity on the basis of an agreement. However, such transfer of ownership is not permitted if the transfer may mislead consumers as to goods or services, or as to the entity that produces goods or renders services connected with the trademark.

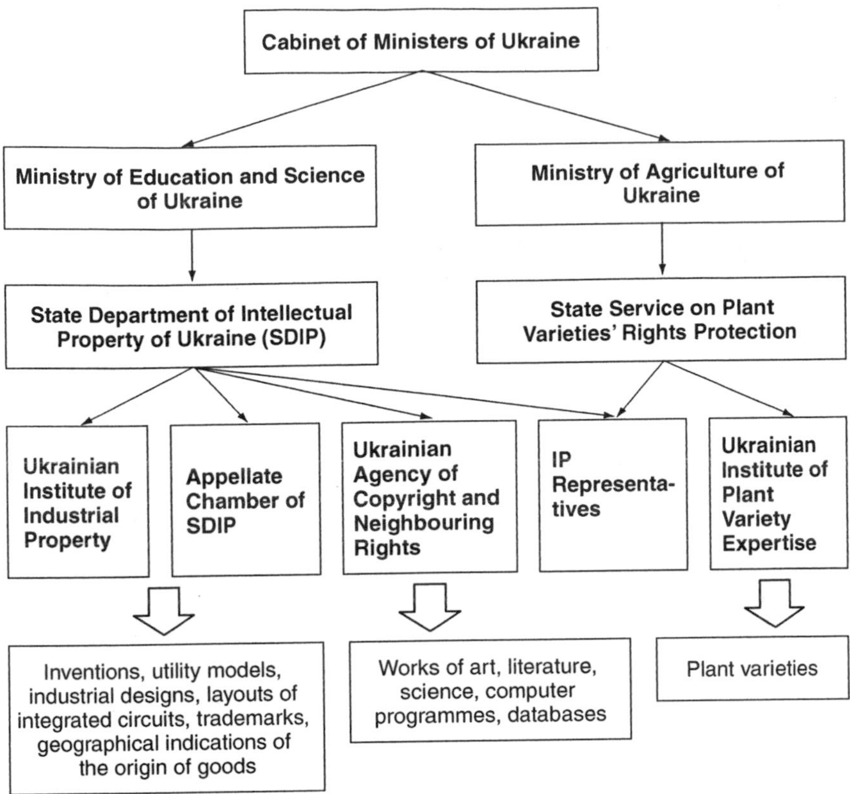

Figure 4.6.1 Agencies and actors involved in the process of obtaining an ownership-confirming document

The certificate owner may also give any person or entity the right to use a trademark by granting a licence under a licence agreement. Such a licence agreement must include a special condition that the quality of goods produced or services rendered under the licence agreement shall not be worse than the quality of goods produced or services rendered by the certificate owner and that the certificate owner will exercise control over compliance with this requirement.

A certificate owner that conducts intermediary activity, for example wholesale distribution and reselling of goods and services, may use its trademark together with, or instead of, the trademark of the manufacturer of goods or the provider of services that it distributes only on the basis of an agreement between them.

A copyright owner may assign its economic rights to a work or may grant a licence to use such work to any person or entity. The assignment of a copyright or the grant of a licence is accomplished through a so-called 'author agreement'. Economic neighbouring rights may also be transferred to other persons and entities pursuant to an agreement. To be valid, an agreement providing for the transfer of rights of use must be in writing, except that an agreement on the use (including publishing) of a work in periodicals may be either oral or in writing. The agreement must provide for a term, the mode of use of the work, the amount of the author's remuneration and other essential provisions as prescribed by the Copyright Law. The extent of the author's remuneration should be fixed by the parties, but may not be less than the minimum rates established by the Cabinet of Ministers of Ukraine (for example, the author of a film screenplay must receive at least two per cent from the total amount collected for showing the film).

Remedies for infringements of intellectual property rights

Pursuant to the Inventions Law, a patent infringement means any action violating the rights of a patent owner or licensee, such as the use of the invention without the owner's or licensee's permission. Thus, the manufacturing, exploitation, offering for sale, sale, importation or storage of a patented product without the permission of the patent owner or a licensee is considered an infringement. Ukrainian patent protection legislation provides for various remedies to a patent owner or licensee.

The patent owner or licensee may request a court to order an infringement to be terminated and to hold the culpable party civilly liable for the damages caused by such illegal use, including lost profits and moral damages. Any licensee has the right to demand restoration of the violated rights on behalf of the patent owner unless otherwise stipulated by the licence agreement. Ukrainian legislation also provides for criminal liability for unlawful use of another person's invention or utility model if such use results in 'substantial' damages (currently this threshold is satisfied by damages equal to at least at 200 individual non-taxable 'minimum' incomes, the equivalent of approximately USD640).

According to the Trademarks Law, any actions violating the exclusive rights of a certificate owner constitute an infringement. At the certificate owner's request, such infringement must be stopped and the infringing party will be obliged to remedy any damages caused, including through moral damages. In addition, the owner may request the deletion from any goods and packages of any trademark that is used unlawfully, or of any other mark that is so similar to the registered trademark that it may cause confusion. A licensee may request protection of any infringed rights on behalf of the trademark's owner if the latter agrees. The unlawful use of a trademark is also criminally punishable, provided that the unlawful use results in 'substantial' damages as defined above.

In the case of infringement of a copyright or neighbouring rights, the Copyright Law provides that the owner is entitled to file a claim for copyright protection and is entitled to various remedies, (including an award of damages, moral damages, termination of the infringement, possible criminal prosecution etc).

The Copyright Law also provides that a copyright or neighbouring rights owner has the right to request, in civil proceedings, one of the following remedies: (1) reimbursement of damages caused to the owner as a result of the infringement of the copyright or neighbouring rights, including lost profits; (2) transfer of all profits gained by the infringer as a result of the infringement of the copyright or neighbouring rights (this remedy is similar to an equitable accounting of profits in common law legal systems); or (3) payment of compensation in an amount determined by the court (such amount may range from 10 to 50,000 minimum monthly salaries, currently equal to about USD450 to USD2,240,075). In addition to reimbursement of damages, transfer of profits or award of compensation, the court may impose a fine for copyright or neighbouring rights violation in an amount equal to 10 per cent of the total awarded by the court to the plaintiff. The person owning the copyright or neighbouring rights may, in addition, claim the award of moral damages.

A Ukrainian court also has the power to respond to infringements of copyright by issuing an injunction against the infringer: (1) prohibiting the release of a work, the staging of a performance, the playback of a sound recording or any transmission on air or by cable; (2) stopping distribution of the work, and ordering (a) the confiscation of all copies of the work, including sound recordings, as well as of all equipment and materials used for their improper production and reproduction; and (b) that a public announcement of the offence be published.

If an infringement of an intellectual property right constitutes unfair competitive action, the Unfair Competition Law provides that the person whose rights have been infringed may apply to the Ukrainian Antimonopoly Committee (the 'AMC') for protection of the constitutionally guaranteed competitive environment in the field of commerce. This right is in addition to the remedies available through issuing civil proceedings. Among other remedies, the AMC may be requested to seek termination of such infringements and impose penalties on the infringer through separate legal proceedings brought by the AMC.

Conclusion

Legal protection for intellectual property rights order in Ukrainian legislation, for the most part, meets the international intellectual property protection standards established by treaties to which Ukraine is a party. In some aspects, Ukrainian law provides for even better statutory protection. However, the use of Ukrainian intellectual property protection laws by a foreign investor can sometimes be quite difficult as a practical matter. Therefore, an experienced Ukrainian lawyer should usually be retained to ensure the protection of an investor's intellectual property rights in Ukraine.

4.7

Import and Export Procedures in Ukraine

Munk, Andersen & Feilberg

Introduction

Eastern Europe has been renowned for its complicated import and export procedures, functioning as a non-tariff barrier to trans-regional trade. At first sight, the procedures in Ukraine also seem to be complicated, but the system has proven to be effective and trouble-free if all the regulations are followed carefully.

The general and simple recommendation is to study carefully all customs procedures, regimes, payments, taxes, and other obligations related to the export–import procedures of Ukraine. It pays to do it right the first time in Ukraine, as it does everywhere else.

Import–export operations involve several authorities – not only the customs service (www.customs.gov.ua) but also a number of different state and public organizations such as the tax administration (www.sta.gov.ua), the sanitary and epidemiological service, and the Chamber of Commerce and Industry (www.ucci.org.ua), depending on what kind of external economic activity is undertaken.

In Ukraine all state bodies work according to the principle of 'zero tolerance'. This means that during import–export operations, any incorrectness in documentation such as the contract, packing list or Load Customs Declaration (LCD), the absence of an original stamp or absence of some periphery documents can result in days-long customs clearance or even confiscation of goods, since they are considered as contraband. As a rule, the more mistakes made in documents and procedures, the more costly and time consuming it becomes for all parties.

Referring to the experience of foreign manufacturers who have worked in Ukraine for the past 10 years, the import–export procedures have definitely become less complicated over the years. Today, it is possible to provide customs clearance in a couple of hours, even during the evening and at weekends – there is always a chance to get consent from customs.

Fulfilling conditions for joining the World Trade Organization (WTO), Ukraine introduced a new Customs Code from 1 January 2004, one that will comply with the main requirements of the WTO. The information below describes import–export procedures according to the new Customs Code of Ukraine, effective from 2004.

General principles of export and import procedures

All Ukrainian companies, including legal entities with foreign investments, have a right to import and export goods and services. In order to undertake import–export operations several conditions must be considered:

- Practising of import–export operations has to be stipulated in the company's charter.
- The enterprise that is planning to import or export products has to be registered at the customs office.
- The import–export contract according to which the products are imported (exported) has to be in written form and meet certain well-defined requirements.
- Payment for goods exported from Ukraine must be made within 90 days from the day of submitting the export customs declaration.
- Such legislative limitations as quoting and licensing have to be taken into account when defining the subject of an import–export contract.

In order to avoid problems with customs clearance of products it is necessary to define the main provisions and terms of the contract very clearly, and to take into account all requirements of the legislation regarding certain types of activity.

Even though such contracts are often considered by the partners to be merely a formal document, the Ukrainian customs officer will likely study it carefully, down to the last bullet point.

Customs regimes

Depending on the purpose of use, the goods may be imported (exported) according to different customs regimes. Each regime has its peculiarities in customs clearance procedures, taxation, tariff rates and non-tariff measures applied. The most important regimes are described below.

Import

Import of goods for free circulation in Ukraine provides a company with the opportunity to deal with imported products in the country without any limitations.

The company must submit the following to the customs service: a Loading Customs Declaration (LCD); contract; invoice; certificate of origin; Ukrainian certificate of correspondence; CMR; TIR-carnet; and a document confirming payment of import taxes.

To import goods into Ukraine the company has to pay customs duty, fees, VAT and excise duty (if goods are subject to excise duty).

Re-import

This regime applies to goods previously exported out of Ukraine and imported for free circulation into Ukraine if such goods:

- originate from Ukraine;
- are imported into Ukraine within one year of export;
- have not been used for obtaining profits outside Ukraine;
- have not been changed outside Ukraine except for normal wear;
- can be identified as those that were exported from Ukraine.

The company may be reimbursed the amount of duty paid upon export of re-imported goods.

The company is exempted from paying customs duty upon import of the goods but it must pay VAT and excise tax (if applicable) for these goods.

Export

Export of goods for free circulation enables a company to deal with exported products beyond the territory of Ukraine without any limitations or obligation to bring it back.

The company must submit to the customs service the same documents as for import except for the certificate of correspondence.

To export goods it is necessary to pay only customs fees. Certain types of raw materials such as sunflower seeds, leather, and metal scrap attract a special export duty. VAT is imposed at a zero rate.

Re-export

Goods which have previously been imported into Ukraine may be exported outside Ukraine if:

- there is a permit for re-export issued by competent authorities;
- the goods are of foreign origin;
- they are exported outside Ukraine within one year of import;
- they have not been used for obtaining profits in Ukraine;
- they have not been changed in Ukraine except for normal wear.

The re-exported goods are free of licensing and quoting.

Like other imports, re-exported goods attract all the usual duties and taxes upon import. Export of such goods attracts only customs fees.

Temporary import–export of goods

Temporary import–export of goods is very similar to re-import and re-export – the goods may be imported/exported into (out of) Ukraine for a definite period of time (up to one year, with the possibility of prolongation) with a commitment to send them back.

The goods that may be admitted for temporary import–export are as follows:

- goods intended for demonstration or use at exhibitions, seminars, conferences, etc;
- professional equipment needed for those coming (leaving) Ukraine to make films, media programmes, etc;
- containers, pallets etc used for transportation of wares;
- samples of goods and items on condition that they remain in the ownership of a person situated outside Ukraine, and are not used for commercial transactions;
- goods imported for educational, scientific or cultural purposes;
- personal items belonging to passengers and goods imported for sporting purposes;
- materials for tourism and advertising;
- transportation vehicles used for the conveyance of passengers and goods across the Ukrainian border.

The customs office may prohibit temporary import–export if the goods cannot be identified or their return is not guaranteed.

Goods imported for temporary use are exempted from customs duty, VAT and excise duty.

Processing in the customs territory of Ukraine

According to this regime, raw materials originating and imported from abroad may be processed in the territory of Ukraine and the finished goods exported within 90 days.

This regime may be applied only after obtaining a permit from the customs service and includes the following operations:

- processing of goods;
- installation, assembling, mounting, setting up, which results in getting other goods;
- repair of goods, including renovation and adjustment;
- use of other goods, which are not products of processing but fully consumed during processing.

The company that is going to import goods for processing under this regime has to develop and submit the following documents, in addition to usual package of import documents:

- economic calculation of finished goods output, approved by the local Chamber of Commerce;
- sanitary service conclusion on raw materials;
- tax bill of exchange.

If the company exports all finished goods it is exempted from paying customs duty and VAT for imported raw materials. Otherwise, the company must pay duty and VAT for that ratio of raw materials which corresponds to the ratio of finished products sold in Ukraine. Finished products are not subject to licensing and quoting.

This regime is very popular within the textile sector, which imports all materials to Ukraine for processing, processes and packs the products and sends them back within 90 days from the date of import. This enables the companies to take full advantage of the low salary levels in the country, without paying customs duty and VAT when passing the borders.

Import of equipment as contribution to share capital

Foreign companies with a subsidiary company in Ukraine may import equipment (fixed assets) as a contribution to the share capital of the Ukrainian subsidiary company. Though it is not considered as a separate customs regime in the new Customs Code, this has more favourable tax and customs regulation than ordinary import.

Fixed assets imported into Ukraine as a contribution to share capital are exempted from customs duty and VAT. Where excisable goods (eg car or bus) are contributed, the goods will be exempted from customs duty but VAT and excise duty will be levied.

Unlike ordinary imports, the foreign company must not present Ukrainian certificates on correspondence for the goods contributed to share capital.

It is necessary to mention that in the case of alienation of the fixed goods within three years from the date of contribution, the subsidiary company will have to pay full customs duty.

Customs clearance

Goods being transferred across the border of Ukraine have to undergo customs clearance. Regardless of the type of customs regime chosen, the customs clearance procedure is uniform and includes the following stages.

Preliminary note and declaration

Goods cross the Ukrainian border at customs entry points. In order to accelerate this procedure, the Ukrainian company that receives or sends the goods should inform a customs office at a certain entry point about upcoming import–export by submitting a preliminary note. If the transported goods are subject to excise tax, the company has to submit a preliminary declaration, which is more informative.

On the border, the customs officer checks the goods against the preliminary note (declaration) and stamps the container in order to prevent the use of the goods until they are cleared.

Load customs declaration

Customs clearance is done by the customs office located in the same district as the company. It includes the following steps:

- presentation of the goods to the customs officer;
- submission of the documents necessary for customs clearance (load customs declaration, transport way bill, copy of the contract, certificates of origin, etc);
- payment of the customs duty, customs fees and other taxes if import–export of these goods is a subject to those payments.

The declaring procedure is done by the authorized officials of the company or customs broker who acts according to a power of attorney.

The company has the right to declare the goods used only for its own production or commercial purposes.

Load customs declaration (LCD) is a document that contains information about the goods, their value, quantity, the purpose of import–export, temporarily or permanently, and the customs regime of those goods.

The LCD is filled for the whole batch of goods. Should the consignment have goods with different codes or different identities (country of origin, evaluation currency) this information has to be reflected on additional pages of the LCD.

Filling out the LCD requires an appropriate level of knowledge from the declarer. Therefore, if a company brings goods in and out of the country regularly, it is necessary to have one or two customs clearance specialists at the company. Companies that transfer goods across the border less often usually choose to use a customs broker service instead of employing another administrative official. The average price for filling out one page of the LCD by a customs broker is €35 for the first page and €11 for each subsequent page.

Taxes and payments levied upon import–export

When importing goods into the territory of Ukraine, the owner (recipient) of goods (resident or non-resident) has to pay customs duty, customs fees, VAT, and excise tax if the goods attract excise duty. When exporting goods, as a rule, only customs fees must be paid.

Customs duty

According to the general rules, goods that are imported into the territory of Ukraine attract customs duty according to the rates fixed by the Consolidated Customs Tariff. There are two types of rates – privileged and full. Privileged rates of import duty apply to the goods originating from countries that have signed treaties with Ukraine on provision of most favourable status (EU, US, all East European countries, China, etc). Goods from other countries are taxed at the full rate, which usually is twice the privileged rate.

All CIS countries have signed the Treaty on Free Trade, therefore goods from CIS countries are exempted from customs duty when imported into Ukraine and Ukrainian goods do not attract import duty in CIS countries.

Export duty is not applied in Ukraine. Only for certain types of goods such as sunflower seeds, leather, and metal scrap is a temporary export duty applied. This is done to protect Ukrainian producers from the lack of raw materials.

Customs fees

Customs fees are paid for the clearance of goods that cross the border of Ukraine. For customs clearance of goods imported for permanent use the customs fees amount to 0.2 per cent of the customs value of goods, but should not exceed USD1,000.

In the case of customs clearance of temporarily imported property, with a given obligation to re-export it later, the company should pay: for each LCD – USD30; for each additional page of the LCD – USD15.

Value added tax and excise tax

VAT and excise tax are paid when importing goods into the territory of Ukraine. The rate of VAT is 20 per cent of the customs value of goods; the rate of excise depends on the type of goods being imported.

Licensing and quoting

The Ukrainian government determines a list of goods and services that are subject to licensing and quoting upon export and import. In order to export–import certain goods it is necessary to receive a licence and/or quota beforehand.

A licence is written permission to import or export certain goods. A quota is a document stating the quantity of licensed goods that may be imported (exported). Duty is not imposed upon goods that are exported within received quotas.

For 2003, the Ukrainian government determined licensing procedures for the following types of export products to EU countries: flat and sorted rolled products from ferrous metal (with determined quotas); textile goods (shirts, suits, dresses, sweaters, etc). There are no quotas on wood and wood processed products.

Distribution of quotas and licences is done by the Ministry of Economy of Ukraine. To receive a licence it is necessary to submit the following documents to the Ministry:

- application letter;
- petition letter, concerning issuing the licence, which includes an obligation to pay state duty;
- copy of the contract;
- document on quota receiving;
- certificate of origin, issued by the Chamber of Commerce and Industry of Ukraine;
- copy of a state registration certificate.

4.8

Ukrainian Labour Law

Bate C Toms and Svitlana Kheda,
BC Toms & Co

Introduction

Ukrainian labour law evolved during the Soviet era from civil law as a result of shifting views on the role of labour in society. Although after Ukraine's independence, it underwent numerous changes to make it more market economy oriented and less complex, it remains highly biased in favour of employees and is frequently rigidly enforced against employers by Ukrainian authorities. However, the complexity and bias of Ukrainian labour law can be managed through a thorough knowledge of its provisions and the pitfalls it holds for unwary employers, combined with careful compliance with its requirements.

An individual can be engaged to work for a company, institution or organization in Ukraine based either on (1) an employment agreement governed by Ukrainian labour law provisions or (2) a civil law agreement governed primarily by the Civil Code of Ukraine. It is important to differentiate between these two types of agreements because they create relations that are very different in nature.

An employment agreement subjects both the employer and the employee to the strict rules of labour law that are generally very protective of employees. To the contrary, a civil law agreement is an independent services agreement that does not result in any employment relations. A civil law agreement is entered into for the performance of a certain defined task or the rendering of a defined scope of services at the entrepreneur's own risk.

The majority of labour law provisions apply equally to Ukrainian and foreign employees in Ukraine. However, there are special procedures for hiring a foreign national that must be followed to avoid administrative liability or even deportation of the foreign national. These procedures are outlined below.

Labour law relations and employment agreements

Labour relations and agreements are subject to regulation by the Labour Code of Ukraine of 10 December 1971 (the 'Labour Code'), as amended since its adoption, and a large number of related statutes and regulations. They are also governed by the internal regulations of the employer and may be subject to the provisions of a collective bargaining agreement concluded by an employer with a labour union or other elected representatives of the employees.

Employment agreement

An employment agreement is an agreement between an employee and an employer establishing terms of employment. Employment agreements are ordinarily concluded in a written form, though they may also be entered into verbally. There are a number of special cases where the agreement must be concluded in written form, including, among others, (1) to enter into an 'employment contract', a special type of employment agreement; (2) if the employee so desires; or (3) if the employee is under 18 years of age.

The duration of an employment agreement can be for the following terms: (1) indefinite; (2) fixed (the use of which is relatively restricted under Ukrainian labour law); and (3) for a period which continues until the completion of agreed-upon works (for example, when the specific character of a company's business activity makes it impossible to determine in advance the time necessary to complete agreed-upon works).

Under the Labour Code, employment agreements may only be entered into for a fixed term when the employment relationship cannot be established for an indefinite term because: of the nature of the work or conditions of its performance (for example, when the company charter sets a one-year term of service for an elected director) or the fixed term is in the employee's interest, or the fixed term may be used in those other cases specifically set forth by Ukrainian legislation.

Employment contract

Ukrainian labour law provides for a special form of an employment agreement, called an 'employment contract', that may be concluded either for a fixed term (including until the completion of certain works) or for an indefinite period of time. The employment contract, unlike an ordinary employment agreement, (1) allows the employer to establish employment relations for a fixed period of time even where the nature and conditions of employment would not ordinarily warrant the conclusion of an employment agreement for a fixed term, and (2) may contain additional grounds for an employee's dismissal in addition to the list of grounds set out in the Labour Code. An employer and employee may also agree on additional rights, obligations and liabilities, as well as conditions for financial remuneration apart from those set out in Ukrainian labour law. However, the employer's ability to add additional terms is limited by Article 9 of the Labour Code, which states that such additional agreed upon terms shall not diminish the rights of an employee as guaranteed by Ukrainian labour law.

It is also worth noting that an employment contract can be used only in cases specifically provided for by *Parliamentary statutes* of Ukraine, as opposed to secondary legislation and regulations. Before the amendments to the Labour Code adopted on 24 December 1999 entered into force, employment contracts could be regulated by any Ukrainian *legislation,* so that state bodies like the Ministry of Labour and Social Policy could define the scope of use of employment contracts. This is no longer the case. Currently, an employment contract is used to govern labour relations in certain branches of the economy, for certain types of companies or for certain positions, for example, for company directors, directors of public educational establishments, teachers and scientific research employees, etc.

Distinguishing employment agreements from civil law agreements

Employment agreements should be distinguished from civil law agreements with independent contractors, which are independent services agreements and do not create an employment relationship.

Unlike an employment agreement that is aimed at regulating the process of work in general, the subject matter of a civil law agreement is a specific product to result from the work or other services to be performed. Therefore, it is necessary to state in a civil law agreement the specific works and services agreed upon by the parties and the results that must be achieved to comply with the civil law requirements. It is also necessary for the parties to agree on the value of the work to be done and the price to be paid to the contractor upon completion of the work. Unlike an employee, a person engaged to work on the basis of a civil law agreement does not have to follow the internal rules regulating labour procedures of a company to which he or she provides services and only needs to respect the terms of the civil law agreement concluded with him or her.

During the past several years, there has been a tendency for employers to replace their employment agreements with civil law agreements. This was done primarily to take advantage of the favourable tax treatment that applied until recently for small individual entrepreneurs.

However, there is a high risk that Ukrainian courts, the Ministry of Labour and Social Policy and the tax authorities will treat any such civil law agreement as being in fact an employment agreement if, under the civil law agreement, the contractor is in fact treated like an employee rather than an independent contractor. (For example, if the contractor has to work at a company's office on a regular 9am to 6pm schedule under the company's close control, has to comply with the internal regulations of the company, and uses exclusively the company's facilities and resources for completing contractual tasks, the relationship may be viewed as resulting from an employment agreement.

Until recently, there were no legally established objective criteria for distinguishing an employment agreement from a civil law contract. These criteria were usually taken from legal theory and applied by courts using their wide discretion. However, on 26 December 2003, the Ministry of Labour and Social Policy of Ukraine issued its Letter 'On the Use of Employment Agreements and Contractor Agreements', which stated criteria developed in legal theory for distinguishing between employment agreements and civil law agreements.

The use of civil law agreements was substantially affected by the Law of Ukraine 'On the Taxation of Incomes of Individuals' (the 'Income Tax Law') of 22 May 2003, which came into force on 1 January 2004. According to the Income Tax Law, an individual registered as a private entrepreneur who performs work (renders services) on the basis of a civil law agreement is taxed as an employee rather than an independent contractor if, according to such civil law agreement: (1) services are provided on a constant and regular basis for a period exceeding a monthly tax period and/or (2) all benefits and remunerations are received (except for a salary and connected payments) and all risks related to provision of such services are borne by the client of the independent contractor under the civil law agreement. As interpreted by the State Tax Administration of Ukraine, however, this provision does not apply to individuals registered as entrepreneurs provided that they perform works (render services) in their capacity as entrepreneurs and pay a single tax. On the other hand, neither the Income Tax Law itself nor any interpretations of this law by the tax authorities provide criteria to be used in the determination of whether an individual performs works (provides services) as an entrepreneur rather than an individual. Therefore, in order to minimize the risk of an individual being taxed as an employee rather than an independent contactor, the civil law agreement for the performance of works needs to be carefully drafted.

Collective bargaining agreements

Under Ukrainian labour law, all employer companies must enter into a collective bargaining agreement with the company's trade union or other elected representatives of the employees of the company. However, the need for a collective bargaining agreement can be avoided. To accomplish this, a director of the employer company initiates, in writing, a proposal for the collective bargaining agreement and, if the company's trade union (or other elected representatives of the company's employees) refuses to enter into or negotiate it, stating that the employees prefer for employment relationships to be regulated only by labour legislation. This refusal should be documented by minutes signed by the company's director and the head of the trade union (employees' representative). This will ensure that the company's director will not be held liable for not entering into a collective bargaining agreement.

Hiring procedure and general employment conditions

Hiring procedure

Under Ukrainian law, the conclusion of an employment agreement is documented by an internal hiring order stating the employee's position and salary (which customarily is a statement that an employee will have a salary in accordance with the company's manning table) issued by the director of the employer company, on the basis of the written application of an employee stating the position that he or she wants to be hired for. However, an employment contract is deemed to have been reached even if a hiring order is not issued, but the employee was *de facto* admitted to work.

Labour books

Another important document formalizing employment relations and the employment record of an employee is a labour book. Under Ukrainian law, the labour book is the primary document regarding the activities of an employee. The labour book must be filled out and maintained by an employer for each employee who works for the employer for more than five days. For those who are entering into employment for the first time and do not have a labour book, the employer must set one up within seven days after issuing an internal hiring order regarding an employee. Ukrainian labour law requires all labour books to be registered in a special internal register of the company. The procedure for setting up and maintaining labour books is established by the Resolution of the Cabinet of Ministers of Ukraine 'On Labour Books of Employees' and joint Labour Ministry, Ministry of Justice and Ministry of Social Protection of Population of Ukraine Instruction

'On the Procedure for Maintaining the Labour Books of Employees' (the 'Instruction') specifying the provisions of the Regulation.

Violation of the rules for setting up and maintaining labour books can result in disciplinary as well as administrative sanctions against the director of a company or the person designated by him or her as being responsible for setting up and maintaining the labour books (these functions are ordinarily performed by the head of the company's personnel department). According to the Ukrainian Administrative Code, the sanction can be a fine of 15 to 50 non-taxable minimum incomes (currently, 255 to 850 hryvnias, which equals to approximately USD48 to 160).

A special procedure for the maintenance of labour books applies to Ukrainians employed by foreign representative offices, foreign correspondents, international organizations and other similar employers. In Kyiv, these labour books are kept and maintained by the General Directorate for Servicing Foreign Representative Offices (customarily referred to as 'GDIP'). All such foreign representative offices must enter into an agreement with GDIP and compensate GDIP for these services. A similar problem exists in cities outside of Kyiv, where local authorities are granted the same powers held by GDIP in Kyiv.

However, it is not clear, based on the wording of the Instruction, whether GDIP indeed has such powers regarding the representative offices of foreign companies operating in Kyiv. Arguably the wording of the Instruction warrants the conclusion that only diplomatic, consular and other representations of foreign states and international organizations should have to conclude such agreements on keeping the labour books of their Ukrainian employees with GDIP, so that representative offices of foreign companies should not be legally required to do so. The interpretation of this Instruction is presently unsettled.

General employee protection

In accordance with Ukrainian labour law, after entering into an employment relationship, the employee is protected by the legal provisions regulating the conditions of employment. This means that the agreed-upon conditions cannot be worse than those guaranteed by law. For example, pursuant to Ukrainian law:

- The working week generally shall not exceed 40 hours.
- The employee's salary shall be not less than the minimal monthly salary guaranteed by law (237 hryvnias as of 1 September 2004, which currently equals approximately USD45) and must be paid twice a month.

- An employer can establish an initial probation period for an employee that cannot exceed one month for workers, and three months for most other employees as a general rule (in certain circumstances, it can be six months).
- An employee is entitled to annual paid holiday, generally of 24 calendar days. Special types of holiday allowance of longer duration are also possible under the Labour Code and the Law of Ukraine 'On Vacations'.
- An employee is entitled to paid maternity and sick leave.
- An employer cannot demand an employee to perform work not covered by employment agreement.
- The transfer of an employee to other work, another enterprise or another locality with the same enterprise is generally not permitted without the employee's consent.

Maternity leave

Article 179 of the Labour Code provides that women are entitled to take paid maternity leave for a period of 70 calendar days before delivery and 70 calendar days after delivery (56 in the case of an abnormal delivery or giving birth to two or more children) This is irrespective of the number of days actually necessary for delivery. In addition, at a woman's request, she is entitled to partially paid leave in order to take care of a child until the child is three years old, together with an entitlement to social security payments.

If the baby needs additional home care, a woman is also entitled to the unpaid leave for a period that is defined according to her doctor's medical opinion, but which should not last longer than the child's sixth birthday. Article 179 also provides that companies, at their own expense, may give partially paid leave or unpaid leave to women employees in order for them to take care of their children for a longer period of time, if this is deemed necessary. (In general, an employer is always free to increase, but not decrease, benefits provided by statute.)

During maternity leave, if a woman wishes (or if one of the relatives who will take care of the child so wishes), she or he may work part-time or from home. Article 180 of the Labour Code provides that the regular holiday allowance to which a woman is entitled should be added to the maternity leave at a woman's request, irrespective of how long the woman has worked at the company.

Work permits for foreign nationals

Legal requirements and the responsible agency

According to the Resolution of the Cabinet of Ministers of Ukraine 'On the Enactment of the Regulation on Work Permits for Foreigners and Stateless Persons in Ukraine' of 1 November 1999 (the 'Resolution'), foreign nationals, including foreign directors, intending to work in Ukraine for Ukrainian or foreign companies, as well as foreign nationals sent to perform specific work in Ukraine on the basis of civil law agreements entered into by a foreign company with a Ukrainian counterpart, must obtain work permits. Foreign nationals permanently residing in Ukraine and foreign nationals hired by an investor under a production-sharing agreement do not require work permits. A work permit is also not required if there is a provision to this effect in an international treaty entered into by Ukraine with a foreign nation. However, currently, according to the information obtained from Ukrainian labour authorities, there are no such provisions.

The Resolution identifies the Employment Centre of the Ministry of Labour and Social Policy (the 'Employment Centre') as the state agency responsible for granting work permits to foreign nationals. The Resolution also contains the list of documents required to be submitted by the inviting company to the Employment Centre. These include an application letter, substantiation of the necessity to use the work of the foreign national, notarized copies of the inviting company's charter and certificate of state registration, documents evidencing the foreign national's education and qualifications, copy of a draft employment agreement. The decision to issue or reject a work permit must be made within 30 days from the date the application package is submitted.

In practice, the Employment Centre holds a special meeting at the end of each month to consider applications for which all required documents have been submitted at least one week before the meeting. The Employment Centre will then notify the employer in writing of its decision.

Procedural issues and practical problems

A work permit may be issued for a term of up to one year with the possibility of extension. To obtain an extension, the employer must apply to the Employment Centre not later than one month before the expiration of the work permit. Prior to adoption of the Resolution of the Cabinet of Ministers of Ukraine of 17 May 2002, No. 649 ('Resolution No. 649'), a foreign national could only remain on the basis of a work permit for up to four consecutive years. Following this four-year period, he or she had to cease to work or to leave the country for at least six months before applying for a new work permit. Resolution 649 eliminated this provision, and now there is no maximum time constraint on employment of a foreign national. It should be noted, however, that the termination of an employment contract between an employer and its foreign national employee results in the termination of the work permit. Therefore, each time a foreign national changes employer, his or her new employer must obtain a new work permit for the employee. The work permit will also be terminated if the foreign employee is declared *persona non grata* by the Ukrainian government.

As a practical matter, subsidiaries of foreign companies usually obtain work permits for foreign nationals for the first year when they apply. However, during the second and the third year, the number of refusals increases, as the Employment Centre begins to scrutinize the uniqueness of the foreign employee's qualifications, the correlation between the number of foreign and the number of local employees, etc. The Employment Centre holds substantial discretion in deciding whether to issue a work permit, and can be influenced by local factors. Thus, Ukrainian investors in a number of shareholder conflicts have removed previously elected top managers representing foreign shareholders based on their inability to obtain work permit renewals. Very often this sort of issue needs to be resolved by litigation, but where timing is crucial, careful negotiation with the authorities may provide the more viable solution.

Violation of work permit regulations can subject a company and its management to administrative liability, and its foreign nationals can be subject to deportation.

Termination of employment

General legal basis

According to Article 36 of the Labour Code, employment relations can be terminated in a number of ways. Termination at the employee's initiative is relatively easy. Termination at the employer's initiative is often more problematic for an employer and deserves special attention.

The employer's right to terminate an employee hired on a limited or unlimited terms is generally restricted by Ukrainian law, which requires an employer to provide a specific, legally justifiable ground for termination of the employment agreement, whether it was written or arose by law. Article 40 of the Labour Code provides for an extensive list of grounds based on which an employment agreement can be terminated at the employer's initiative. These Article 40 cases are as follows:

- if required by changes in the activities of the company, including its liquidation or reorganization, changes in its profile, or necessary reduction in the company's staff;

- non-compliance of the employee with his or her position or improper performance of his or her duties as a result of inadequate qualifications or a state of health that interferes with the continuation of his or her performance;
- systematic failure by the employee to fulfil his or her duties or to comply with the internal rules of the company without good reason if the employee has been previously reprimanded;
- failure to appear at work for more than three consecutive hours in one working day without a good reason for such absence (eg sick leave, etc);
- failure to appear at work for more than four months in a row due to a temporary incapacity for work, excluding time for maternity leave, unless permitted for that special type of disease. If, however, the employee has lost his or her capacity for work as a result of a work-related illness or severe injury received while performing his or her employment duties, the position must be maintained for this person until he or she is capable of working again or until a disability status is obtained and the person becomes entitled to state benefits;
- if the employee was appointed temporarily to replace the person who used to perform this work, and this person is being reinstated to his or her old position;
- appearance at the workplace drunk or in a narcotic or toxic state;
- theft of the property of the employer that is confirmed by a court decision or by a resolution of a competent administrative body.

Article 41 of the Labour Code provides for the following additional grounds for dismissal of an employee at the employer's initiative:

- a single gross violation of employment duties by an employee holding a managing position (eg chairman of the board, director, deputy director, chief accountant, etc). It should be borne in mind, though, that there is no legal definition of what constitutes a 'gross violation of employment obligations', which leaves it to the appropriate court in each case to decide on whether the violation was 'gross'.
- the guilty actions of the company's directors resulted in late salary payment or the payment of salaries in amounts lower than the minimum wage established by law;
- the guilty actions of the employee who operates the company's funds or handles its commodities if such actions resulted in the lost of trust in such employee;

- the immoral misconduct of an employee performing pedagogical functions that prevents the employee from further holding the position.

It should be noted that in accordance with Article 235 of the Labour Code, if an employee is fired without a legitimate reason (ie one of the reasons specified in the Labour Code), the appropriate court will require an employer to re-employ them and to pay damages in the amount of his or her average wage for the period of the employee's so-called forced absence from work (such period, however, generally should not exceed more than one year). The company's directors must therefore ensure that each dismissal is legally justified and properly documented in accordance with the applicable labour law regulations governing a particular dismissal (or, if a director is being dismissed, the highest governing body of a company (eg a general meeting of shareholders, etc) that elected and hired this director should justify the employment termination based on the grounds for dismissal provided for in the Labour Code and then properly document such dismissal.

Limitations on the dismissal of employees

Under the Labour Code, it is not possible to fire an employee during his or her temporary incapacity for work, except pursuant to Article 40, Section 5 of the Labour Code (failure to appear at work for more than four months in a row due to a temporary incapacity for work), or while the employee is on holiday. This rule does not apply in the case of a complete liquidation of a company or if the employee files an application requesting earlier termination of the employment relationship.

Under Article 184, Section 3 of the Labour Code, it is prohibited to dismiss pregnant women, women who have children under three years of age (or under six years of age for special categories of employees), or single mothers having at least one child younger than 14 years of age or a disabled child, except in the case of (1) the full liquidation of the enterprise, or (2) the expiration of a fixed-term employment agreement for the relevant employee. In these cases, such dismissal is permitted subject to an obligation to find the employee a job elsewhere. It should be remembered that until a new job for such employees is found, the employer is subject to payment of the employee's average salary, except that for expired fixed-term employment agreements, this obligation is limited to only three months of payments. Ukrainian law also prohibits dismissing an employee on the basis of his or her reaching pensionable age.

The Labour Code sets forth certain statutory procedures that may be applicable to any termination for any of the foregoing reasons. For example, an employee must, at the time of dismissal, be subject to a disciplinary penalty (imposed by the company) or a public reprimand (for example, as might be declared by the workers collective of an enterprise) in order for a dismissal to be made under Article 40, Section 3 of the Labour Code. Under some of the above reasons, the dismissal of an employee may also require the preliminary consent of a trade union functioning at the company. The termination of employment relations under any of the above-mentioned grounds and the procedures used must also be properly documented in strict compliance with the labour law rules. Legal advice should normally be sought if there is any doubt over whether grounds exist for a valid termination and what procedures should be followed. Quite frequently, in such cases, a voluntary, negotiated termination at an employee's initiative may be the best course of action.

Legally required steps in a redundancy procedure

Ukrainian labour law is extremely formalistic, and Ukrainian courts in most cases favour employees and care more about the observation of the required termination procedures than the substance of the employer–employee relationship. Therefore, it is necessary to be extremely careful when firing employees, especially when reducing a company's staff.

Under applicable law, in order to reduce the company's staff, the following steps must be performed:

1. Preparation of the list of potential candidates for dismissal. The Labour Code provides priorities for the retention of certain categories of employees by a company when dismissals are carried out because of a reduction of staff or other changes in the organization of the work of the company. Employees with higher levels of production or qualifications are given priority to stay. It should be kept in mind that the employer must have sufficient proof of an employee's high qualification in order to avoid any problems that may arise if any of the dismissed employees go to the court claiming his or her wrongful dismissal.

   Between employees with equal qualifications and production output, priority is given based on various criteria, including a preference for an employee who is the only working person in a family, who is married and has two or more dependants, who has long-term working experience at the company, who is working while studying in secondary or higher schools (including 'evening students'), who participated in a war or is a war-disabled veteran, who is an inventor of new inventions, utility models, industrial designs and efficiency proposals, or who was made disabled while working at the company or who has developed a work-related disease due to his or her employment.

2. Preparation by the company's director of the order on the redundancy, which should include an economic justification of the potential redundancy (eg changes in the production technology, unprofitable activities, etc).

3. Informing the company's trade union on the potential redundancy. Staff redundancy can be carried out only with the prior consent of the company's trade union (if the company has one, and only if any of the employees subject to dismissal are its members). If an employer does not meet this requirement, the court, in case of any claims by employees on their unlawful dismissal, is supposed to suspend the consideration of the case and request the trade union's opinion, and only after receiving its response may the court continue considering the case.

   A trade union must, within 15 days, consider an employer's written petition on a proposed staff redundancy. The employer's petition must be considered in the presence of each employee to be dismissed. This requirement can only be disregarded at an employee's written request. The trade union must notify the employer in writing of the adopted decision within three days. If the trade union fails to meet this deadline, it is deemed to have agreed in full with the proposed dismissal of employees.

4. Proposing employees subject to dismissal to be employed in other positions, if available, or explaining in writing why it is not possible to appoint them to other positions.

5. Providing the district State Employment Centre with a notice on the reduction of the company's staff, stating the grounds for the pending dismissal of the company's employees, as well as the positions, qualifications and amount of salary of each employee. This notice must be submitted at least two months prior to the proposed dismissal of the company's employees.

6. Personally informing each employee of his or her dismissal at least two months prior to such dismissal. It is possible to reduce this two-month term at the employee's written request. Even though, under Ukrainian law, the employer is prohibited from worsening the employee's conditions in comparison with applicable law, the employee's written request can serve as a waiver of the employee's rights.

7. Providing each employee on the day of actual dismissal with his or her labour book where the reason for termination is properly documented, and paying each employee all amounts due (as discussed below) as of the day of his or her dismissal.

8. Providing the district State Employment Centre with a list of employees that have been dismissed within 10 days after their actual dismissal.

Exit (dismissal) compensation

Whether unlawfully or lawfully terminated, the former employee has the right to obtain from his or her employer compensation consisting of an exit grant and compensation for unused holiday.

An employee is usually entitled to a so-called 'exit grant' if he or she was dismissed for certain reasons (excluding dismissal for causes such as drunkenness and other serious misbehaviour), and in particular where he or she was dismissed as a result of a serious illness preventing the employee from performing responsibilities in the future, upon liquidation or reduction of the enterprise's staff, or where the employment agreement is terminated by the employee because of violation of labour protection rules by the employer. The amount of the exit grant ranges from one to three times the average monthly salary of the employee, depending on the circumstances.

All sums due to the employee must be paid on the day of dismissal as specified by the internal dismissal order. In the event that an employee does not work on the dismissal day, then the sums due shall be paid no later than on the day following the demand for payment by the dismissed employee. On the dismissal day, the employer shall also provide the dismissed employee with the employee's labour book containing an entry regarding the dismissal and with a copy of an internal dismissal order.

A right to additional compensation arises if an employee has not used all of his or her holiday entitlement. According to Ukrainian law, an employee has the right to at least 24 calendar days of holiday during each working year. The duration of the holiday entitlement may be increased by the employer. The right to holiday arises after the employee has worked for six months. During each successive working year, this holiday right is renewed once the new working year begins. If the full holiday entitlement is not used during the year, then the unused days of holiday are added to the holiday entitlement for the next year. Compensation for unused days of holiday must be paid if the employee is dismissed, and in such a case, the amount paid is pro rated based on the employee's average salary. In addition, an employee may demand payment for any unused holiday days that were carried forward that the employee did not take.

The average monthly salary of an employee is calculated on the basis of the sum of all salaries paid to the employee during the 12 months before dismissal. The amount of compensation for unused holiday should, therefore, be calculated as follows: the sum of all monthly salaries paid during the 12 months before dismissal divided by the number of calendar days during these 12 months, with this amount multiplied by the remaining unused days of holiday.

Conclusion

The above review demonstrates that Ukrainian labour law is a complex area that contains many ambiguous provisions and hidden pitfalls. Appointment of a person well versed in Ukrainian labour law can be helpful to avoid making costly mistakes. However, to avoid substantial fines and penalties, it is often important to seek professional legal advice when difficult employment issues arise, particularly with regard to termination of employment at the employer's initiative.

4.9

Cultural Features of Doing Business with Ukraine

Sergiy Maslichenko, President, Ukrainian Centre for Economic and Legal Analysis (UCELA)

Introduction

To do business in Ukraine, as in other former Soviet Union countries, one should be aware of the cultural, or institutional in a broad sense, peculiarities of the country. Since the fall of the socialist system in 1990, old institutions that provided a certain economic and social stability in society have lost their authority, however new market-oriented structures have been slow to take root in the economic environment of the former Soviet Union countries. Whereas by the late 1990s many elements of a market-based formal framework had been established, their implementation was often weak. The enforcement of new laws and regulations has been constrained by the presence of old, informal institutions – strong bureaucracy, weak respect for the law, informal networking and other socio-cultural factors which were historically rooted in the behaviour of Soviet society. As a result, the economic efficiency gains, respect for the law, and contract enforcement, which are imperative for Western business practice, seem not to be as important in Ukraine as the cultural tradition and informal network.

Historical and institutional background

The behavioural patterns of Ukrainians, as of Slavs in general, underlines the importance of moral factors in society. Pecuniary factors have always been secondary motives for Slavs in contrast to the paramount importance of moral, spiritual and political stimuli. For centuries, the Slavonic genotype has absorbed such features as collectivism, the desire for equal rights and dependence on the state, or community, which contrasts with the individualism, competitive pragmatism and profit-maximization characteristics of Western (mostly Anglo-Saxon) countries related to the protestant ethic and the capitalist spirit. Thus, the Ukrainian, and the Slavonic in general, socio-cultural type has a weak motivation for private property and strongly relies on external power (independent of the individual), be it the Tsar or the Communist state, which is unsurprising given the lack of a democratic tradition. At the same time, the significance of the state in Slavic values has not been reflected in corresponding norms and stimuli because of the poor enforcement mechanism of bureaucratic rules and sanctions. As a result, most of the administrative, judicial, moral and economic norms are entangled and non-coordinated. In this respect, the traditions of state power, the vertical political and economic dependence of individuals, and bureaucratic dictatorship have to be gradually replaced by the freedom and independence of economic agents, with a strong democratic state and civil society.

In light of the foregoing, historical traditions, culture and social norms have a great impact on economic outcomes and must be taken into account when conducting business in Ukraine. Western economic strategies and organizational concepts can be transferred only to a limited extent, and the approach to doing business in Ukraine will differ from those in developed countries.

Most economists underestimate the strength and depth of politico-economic interrelations between the state and businesses, inherited since the 'perestroika' period. One should realize that an improper business environment had already begun evolving slowly in the 1970s, and then grew rapidly in the 1980s, with the introduction of Gorbachev's perestroika reforms. Some market mechanisms such as entrepreneurship, decentralization of decision making, and self-financing at some state-owned enterprises (SOEs) etc were present in the socialist system. As a result, this mixture of 'socialistic' and 'capitalistic' behaviour has been a feature retained for a period of years.

Apart from that, the socially planned economy formed informal institutions based on market norms that have been used to compensate deficits, imbalances and other barriers to normal economic activity. State enterprises used market relations unsupported by legal rules. Hidden and semi-hidden markets complemented compulsory state plans. A variety of market contracts were based on illegal relations and reflected only the short-term interests of economic agents. Entrepreneurs had become skilled at evading government regulations, turning the inefficiencies in these regulations to their own advantage, and operating in the area between the legal and illegal worlds. As a result, the illegal character of market transactions has been gradually rooted in the consciousness of most entrepreneurs in Ukraine.

By contrast, Poland, Hungary and the Czech Republic, which are often compared with Ukraine, were geographically and historically part of Central Europe, with long commercial, legal and institutional ties with Western countries. Besides, they were part of the Communist bloc for only about 40 years, and a significant element of their population remembered the non-communist past. Entrepreneurial behaviour was initially embedded in their socio-political environment, which was reflected by the significant share of retail trade and service in their economies. In the late 1980s they undertook crucial political changes and market reforms, which stood them in good stead, so that they were relatively well prepared by the early 1990s.

Corporate governance in today's Ukraine

Ukraine's privatization has not led to a good corporate governance system. This is generally because too many vestiges of the old socialist system remain. As a rule, Ukrainian companies continue under the same management, with the same compensation schemes as they had under state ownership. Management still believes that its ties to state-owned enterprises, and the ability to generate sales from them, are critical. Despite falling sales and financial difficulties, firms continue to do business primarily with the same partners with which they worked under the Soviet system, often without even a marketing department or business plan. And finally, firms continue with the same product mix and the same quality standards as before privatization. Thus, as measured by the amount of restructuring that is occurring, it appears that corporate governance is not having a substantial impact in Ukraine.

Good corporate governance is crucial for Ukrainian enterprises to attract capital. They often lack the necessary capital to modernize their production facilities, restructure their operations and expand into new areas. Attraction of both the potential sources of capital – creditors and strategic investors – is highly problematic. Foreign direct investment is miserable and home capital is waiting in offshore companies for a better political, legal and general business environment in Ukraine.

Given the fact that Ukraine has a monopolistic industrial structure and needs to take steps to restructure and downsize most state enterprises before privatization, the Ukrainian government has not been able to carry out noticeable changes at such enterprises. New amendments to the Law of Ukraine 'On the Restoration of Solvency of a

Debtor or Declaring It Bankrupt' were adopted in June 1999. It was believed that professional bankruptcy trustees would develop rational restructuring plans and break enterprises into smaller ones to attract strategic investors. The involvement of bankruptcy trustees was supposed to 'depoliticize' the role of the branch ministries and the State Property Fund of Ukraine. However, the new bankruptcy rules were widely used by oligarchs for hostile takeovers of some valuable SOEs' assets – until in 2001 the new Law 'On Moratorium on Forced Sale of Assets' banned the bankruptcy of enterprises with 25 per cent state ownership.

As a result, financial-industrial groups (FIGs) emerged in Ukraine as a network of entrepreneurs, politicians, local authorities and criminals. As each firm began to alter existing economic networks by subcontracting with other firms, distrust and isolation grew among network members. The fragmentation of socio-economic relations among them and the lack of public institutions to coordinate them became fertile grounds to take highly risky, semi-legal steps to acquire needed financing and survive. Unable to acquire needed financing from the government, some SOEs allied themselves with groups of local entrepreneurs or criminals. Together they constructed an elaborate network of new private firms (both domestic and offshore) to channel cash flows from a poorly monitored state enterprise to these private firms (usually consumers or suppliers).

Legal infrastructure

Corporate governance law in today's Ukraine remains unsatisfactory. The country still relies on laws from the Soviet era or laws adopted shortly after independence, namely the Civil Code of 1963 (a new Civil Code was enforced only on 1 January 2004), the Law 'On Economic Associations' of 1991, and the Law 'On Enterprises', also adopted in 1991. Although considerable progress has been achieved in 2002–03 by the newly elected Ukrainian parliament, new corporate law principles have not been enforced yet.

Ukraine's core problem today is less lack of decent laws than lack of the infrastructure and political will to enforce them. Trust in the law remains low and reliable enforcement by the state's legal institutions cannot be guaranteed.

Ukraine's legal system, based on civil law principles, impedes effective law enforcement. For example, the courts respect only documentary evidence, which is rarely available given limited discovery and managers' skills in covering their tracks. Moreover, a shareholder who sues a major company will usually lose at trial and first-level appeal, because of home-court bias and judicial corruption. A shareholder with a strong case has a chance of getting an honest decision on further appeal, but that will take years.

Besides, the government's own behaviour reinforced disrespect for rules. Managers had to cheat on their taxes, bribe tax and custom inspectors, and avoid legal cash transactions to survive. The government didn't pay its own bills to companies that provided it with goods and services.

Contract enforcement

Failure to honour contracts is one of the most widespread complaints about the local business climate in Ukraine.

Historical and cultural factors undermine the rule of law, including protection for parties who have suffered losses from breach of contract. During the Soviet era, all legal entities were owned by the state and contract-based relations among legal entities reflected this fact. Central planners required enterprises to enter into certain contracts, and the government played a role in enforcing the terms of the bargain. The view was fostered that contracts were no longer binding in the event of 'changed circumstances'. This legacy still thrives in Ukraine, and government interference in contracts still occurs (Seeger and Patton, 2000).

Parties entering into contracts in Ukraine often find that problems arise at the earliest stages because of the difficulty of confirming information about the other party to the contract. This difficulty in performing pre-contract 'due diligence' makes it difficult to lay the proper foundation for a contract. In part, this is due to an absence of public registries. For example, there is no real property registry of title. There is also no registry of bankruptcy cases in Ukraine.

Courts

The laws are vague, often contradictory, and the courts do not have a body of precedent to guide their decisions. The lack of precedent results not just from the fact that most laws are newly passed, but also from the lack of a system for publishing court decisions. This gives judges wide latitude, which opens up greater possibilities for bribes and other forms of influence.

The courts are slow and many judges are not experienced in resolving complex commercial law matters. Salaries for judges in Ukraine are extremely low; thus, good judges often leave the judiciary, and those who remain expect to supplement their official salaries by taking bribes. Many courts also suffer from poor facilities – including crumbling buildings, poor telephone, copying and other equipment, and minimal law libraries. A further problem is that judges are closely tied to local regions, which makes them more susceptible to bribes and local influence. The problem is further complicated by the legacy of the Soviet era when the courts were operated as direct instruments of state power. Judges routinely receive telephone calls from government officials directing the outcome of a case.

Finally, access to the judicial system is hindered by high-cost barriers. For example, the filing fee in an arbitration court, 5 per cent of the damages sought, was a significant deterrent to going to the courts until 2000 when a new law decreased the filing fee to 1 per cent.

Enforcement of judgements

Execution of judgements is also a problem in Ukraine. Only a third of all judgements have been executed in Ukraine. According to the current Law 'On Enforcement', courts must transfer judgements to the State Enforcement Service for execution. However, losing litigants are frequently able to hide their assets, either before or after judgement. Enforcement Service activity is hampered by low pay, no public respect for court decisions, no enforcement mechanism (eg it cannot subpoena someone to ask where assets are hidden), and a cash economy. Judgements that fail to result in recovery provide no remedy and, indeed, discourage even pursuing a judicial recovery process.

Tax policy

The most important regulatory obstacle to doing business in Ukraine is Ukrainian tax policy. Ukrainian tax law is amazingly complex. According to Ukraine's State Tax Administration, about 1,496 legal documents regulate the current tax system in Ukraine. This includes 459 laws, 410 Cabinet of Ministers resolutions, 401 orders and other documents of different ministries and state departments. Moreover, they are often ambiguous, poorly drafted, internally inconsistent, and inconsistent with other laws. The nominal tax rates are not so high, but apply to a measure of 'income' that grossly overstates actual income. Actual taxes can easily exceed 100 per cent of profits. In addition, tax inspectors and tax police have broad discretion to seize a company's bank account and other assets to pay taxes. Companies can appeal, but will be out of business long before the appeal is heard. Tax inspections have become a political weapon, deployed by the government against businesses that don't support the incumbents.

As a result, the confiscatory tax policy produces miserable revenues, because almost no one pays taxes. Instead, everyone hides income and bribes the tax authority to reduce the tax burden. Falsified accounting books impede strong public capital markets. Companies that cannot report income honestly to tax inspectors also cannot report honestly to investors. Investors therefore cannot use a company's financial statements to check on management honesty and skill. Hidden transactions also preclude using the courts to enforce contracts. If the true contract between two companies involves a large quantity of goods at a high price, while the nominal contract (prepared for the tax inspectors) specifies a small quantity at a much lower price, and one party defaults, the other can hardly go to court to enforce the true deal.

Conclusion

Political, cultural and other non-economic factors have a greater impact on business activity in Ukraine than they have in Western economies where economic causality plays a more significant role. The difference between a transitional economy and a stable developed one is that the former is undergoing systematic changes of socio-economic relations and, for this reason, political and socio-cultural factors significantly outweigh economic causality.

In this respect, one should be conscious of the socio-cultural background of the country when trying to do business in the Ukrainian transitional economy which might be hampered by socio-cultural inertia with regard to the market paradigm. Western economic strategies can only be transferred to a limited extent and the approach to economic and institutional transformations observed in Ukraine will differ from those in developed ones. Thus, new business initiatives should be built in such a way as to exploit existing social and cultural norms rather than copying existing Western capitalist institutions.

Reference

Seeger, Charles, Patton, Hugh (2000) Background for Financial Markets Development in Ukraine, Final Draft, Financial Market International, Inc.

4.10

Ukraine – A New European Destination for International Business?

Munk, Andersen & Feilberg

Introduction

There are many reasons why EU-based companies should be interested in Ukraine. The two most important reasons are the unique possibilities for cost reductions in its direct production and the growing market potential in Ukraine.

On the other hand, there are a number of barriers or reasons why a foreign company would choose not to enter Ukraine for the time being. The main reason is the extensive corruption in Ukraine or rather the perceived corruption in the country, as well as low transparency in the business environment. Doing business in Ukraine is not an easy task, but neither is doing business in any other foreign country – Ukraine may give your company a better annual result but it will not make your life easier or the management of operations simpler.

Since 1994 quite a lot of foreign companies have entered the Ukrainian market and more and more companies are looking into the possibilities – Ukraine is becoming the new 'hot spot' in Europe. There are two main reasons for entering Ukraine: companies are either searching for new market possibilities, or they are searching for factors of production, ie labour, raw material, land, special competencies etc. Only very few companies are aiming at both elements, ie producing in Ukraine in order to service the local market, but these types of companies are likely to increase their number in the coming years as the Ukrainian economy is expanding.

Ukraine as a market

Ukraine is one of the fastest-growing economies in Europe. For 2003 the country expects a GDP growth at some 7 per cent. And as opposed to the general belief, far from all 48 million Ukrainians are poor. Actually the middle class is living well and its size is growing. It may come as a surprise that Kyiv is placed among the top 20 of the most expensive cities in Europe (www.mercerhr.com). Rule of thumb estimations says that out of almost 50 million inhabitants, 5 million have the same purchasing power as the EU average and 500,000 are what one would consider extremely or very rich.

A clear sign of the positive development and the growing purchasing power is the explosion of supermarkets and mega stores, which have been built or planned within the past few years. The supermarkets are not only an indication of a general rising purchasing power, but they will also contribute to the professionalization and growth in the local industry. The supermarkets are demanding products of specific standards and uniformity, packed and delivered just-in-time. In many ways, the development in Ukraine and the booming sectors are exactly the same as in Poland five years ago. All the new investments that are taking place in Ukraine in these years, aiming at servicing the Ukrainian population, will bring along a huge demand in the business-to-business (B2B) sector for machinery, electronic components, building materials etc. In these new investment projects, the price is not as important as in many other purchase decisions because the investments are made in high-end state-of-the-art products.

One should be aware that Ukraine is a society based on contacts and especially personal loyalty. It may therefore take some time to get a strong foothold in the market but the business relation will likely last longer than in most other countries. Patience and commitment are therefore necessary elements when entering Ukraine. It should also be taken into consideration that there is still a lack of marketing and sales specialists in Ukraine, which has resulted in a relatively high salary level for these particular professions. It is not uncommon to give a marketing manager up to €1,000 in net salary plus performance payments, mobile phone, free company car and various other company benefits.

Ukraine as a production platform

In global competition, prices for many products are still the single most important sales argument and a way to position the product in the market. Cost reductions in the production chain have therefore become a central strategic concern for many firms. Cost-efficient production in

Ukraine enables companies to meet the steeply increasing competition on costs in Western Europe and still enjoy proximity to their main markets.

When looking at Eastern Europe from the company perspective there is one major dividing line – EU accession countries and non-accession countries (Figure 4.10.1). The dividing line determines the overall cost structure, the administrative framework, external financing opportunities etc.

Whereas economic development within the two areas has been almost identical, the development in Central Europe has been very different from the development in Eastern Europe.

If looking at the salary level in the two areas, the development is very clear. Although both areas have a relatively low salary level, the level is significantly lower in Eastern Europe than in Central Europe (Figure 4.10.2). This shift in the salary level is likewise visible when looking at the costs of skilled workers in different sectors (Figure 4.10.3).

With a highly educated population, its proximity to the EU, easy access to standard raw material and a low salary level, Ukraine has become popular as a platform for production. The production costs are among the lowest in Europe, the workforce is qualified and available,

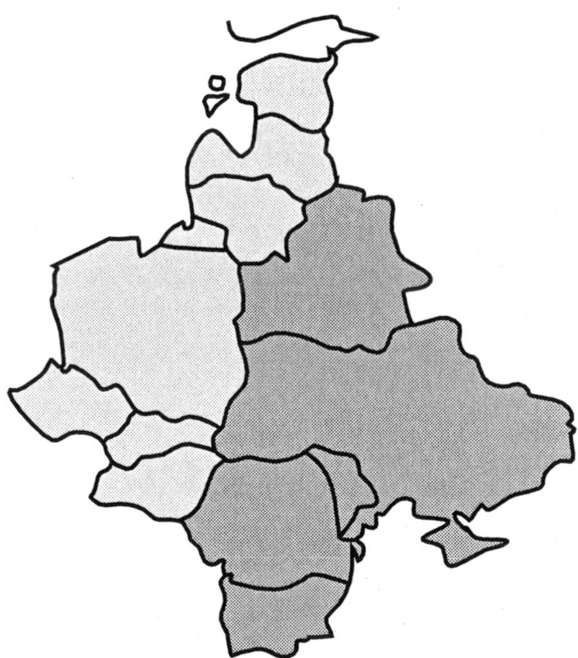

Figure 4.10.1 EU accession and non-accession countries

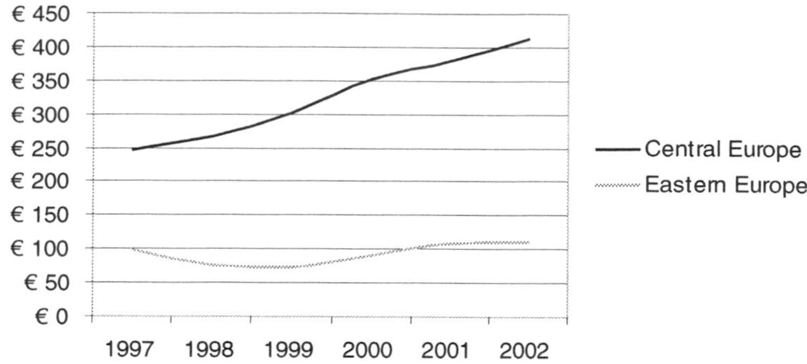

Figure 4.10.2 Salary levels in Central and Eastern Europe

the country is situated close to EU markets, the infrastructure is relatively good and the attitude is becoming more and more pro-Western as the years go by. Also, some of the sectors, such as the wood and metal sectors, are characterized by domestic prices on raw material which are lower than world market prices.

Two approaches to cost-efficient production

Basically, there are two approaches towards cost efficient production: outsource processing activities to local companies in low-cost areas or establish one's own production in low-cost areas.

The approach chosen in the end is often a question of corporate strategy, production volume, market estimates, financial abilities and management skills in the EU company. From a risk point of view the

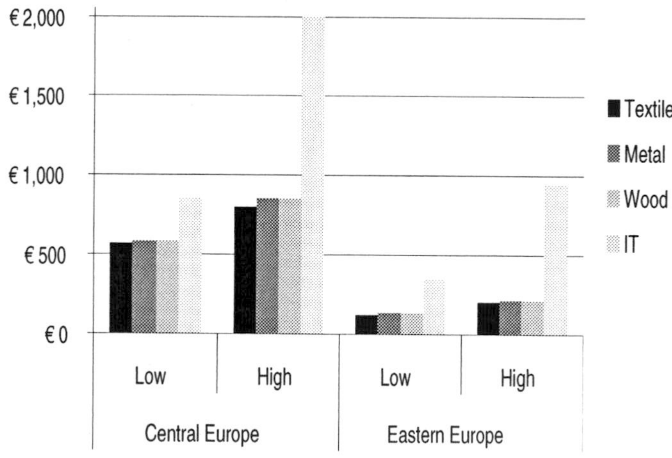

Figure 4.10.3 Net salary level in different sectors

first option puts the business idea at stake whereas the second option is mainly a financial risk. Generally speaking, it is difficult to succeed with outsourcing in Eastern Europe unless your company is experienced in this field and an organizational fit to such an approach.

Outsourcing of production activities to Ukraine

Outsourcing in EU countries is usually associated with a package of economic, technical, organizational and administrative advantages, as the business environment for the two parties involved is the same.

In Ukraine outsourcing to local companies is possible, but is only associated with low-cost structures, whereas the business conditions are completely different from what is known in Western Europe. Outsourcing to Ukrainian companies might be cheaper in monetary terms but not necessarily easier, flexible or faster.

As a minimum, the EU-based company should expect to contribute project management, technology, know-how, and in some cases even working capital or large pre-payments.

At the moment, Ukrainian companies can only contribute a well-qualified and well-educated workforce, and basic production conditions realizing the technological and professional standing of most companies.

A continuous development and professionalization of the local business community is taking place and some companies in Ukraine are now functioning very well – and also in terms of management.

Another outsourcing option is to place an order at a foreign company already established in Ukraine. By doing so the company will be able to bypass the complex local business environment but still face reduced prices.

Company establishment for production purposes in Ukraine

Because of the problem that still exists with outsourcing and owing to strategic and economic considerations, Western companies often choose to establish their own production or business unit in Ukraine. This enables them to control quality and efficiency much better, but it also puts a lot of stress on the company's management and financial capabilities. Some of the basic questions and considerations related to production establishment in Ukraine are identical from company to company and across sectors.

HOW MUCH WILL WE MINIMIZE OUR COSTS OF PRODUCTION? A LOT!

By and large, a skilled worker in the EU, on average, costs the company €25–35 per hour. The costs per hour in Ukraine are approx €1.5. If a company relocates a yearly production of 100,000 hours to Ukraine (50 people) the net savings will be close to €3 million per year – just considering the salary factor. By having this cost saving in production, the company can both lower its sales prices and increase its profit margin. Furthermore, some input factors such as steel and wood are cheaper in Ukraine than on the world market.

HOW IS EFFICIENCY IN UKRAINE? AS HIGH AS IN THE EU!
Efficiency is rarely a question of individual workers but often a question of management, organization and applied technology. Experience shows that efficiency may be as high as on the 'old' production platform and that it takes approximately three months to reach that level after production has been started. BUT, if production in Europe is not efficient it will certainly not become more efficient by moving to Ukraine. The key to efficiency is in the company itself and its ability to transfer production knowledge to the new production platform.

HOW LONG WILL IT TAKE TO GET PRODUCTION STARTED? SIX MONTHS!
This depends very much on the size and scope of the production. As a rule of thumb it takes less than six months from the time the decision is taken until the production is running. If the investment mode is a 'greenfield' investment and not a 'brownfield' investment, the establishment period naturally takes longer.

WILL RELOCATION MEAN THAT WE HAVE TO CLOSE DOWN OUR ACTIVITIES IN THE EU? NO, NOT NECESSARILY!
Internationalization and the IT revolution have made it possible to place the various company functions exactly where it gives the best pay-back. Development, procurement, administration, production and sales do not necessarily have to be located in the same place or even in the same country. Relocation will typically result in a downsizing of production capacity in the EU and in an upgrade of the existing development, marketing and sales activities. A relocation of production will imply that some jobs are lost while new jobs and functions are established – the real problem lies in the fact that the new functions can rarely be fulfilled by those who fulfilled the relocated functions.

Corruption and the mafia in Ukraine – myths and realities

The advantages are obvious but what about the disadvantages? It is fair to state that the single most important obstacle for foreign investments in Ukraine is very bad and biased media coverage in the West. The Western media mostly focuses on transitional problems on the macroeconomic level or on the elderly pensioner having a hard time overcoming the new realities in Ukraine. Only very rarely do the Western media focus on the positive dynamic developments that have taken place during recent years. These developments have made the Ukrainian economy one of the fastest-growing and most dynamic economies in Europe, and have initiated an increasing professionalization and competitiveness of the local business community.

According to Transparency International, Ukraine is placed somewhere between Nigeria and Thailand in the corruption index. Perceptions of political instability and mafia activities keep away a lot of companies which, based on objective criteria, would profit from business activities in Ukraine. Political corruption, 'big corruption', the mafia, lack of democratic rights and lack of freedom of the press are often good cover-stories but they very seldom have any direct effect on the business environment faced by most companies. Moreover, these horror stories pertain primarily, if not exclusively, to businesses where big money is involved: power generation, distribution and supply, oil and gas utilization and sale, tobacco, alcohol production and the like. In the day-to-day operations of the company, the work of the local authorities and the individual civil servant's approach and attitude to his or her job are more important than the overall score on an index. My experience is that the level of corruption faced by the company to a large extent depends on the company and its management and not just on the local administration – it takes two to tango!

Unfortunately, many foreign companies are entering Ukraine with a conviction that the local administration is useless and unstructured, and that rules and regulations are something not to be taken seriously. The realities are quite the opposite. The local administration might be inefficient and difficult to understand, but they are indeed very structured and organized. The local administration works on the basis of a 'zero-tolerance' principle, which means that everything should be exactly as stipulated in the regulations. In other words, there is no room for negotiation and the company can be sure that they will eventually be controlled.

On the more concrete level and from the macro perspective there are several rules and regulations that are not based on any legal grounds but have nevertheless become an administrative practice in Ukraine. Such administrative practices, not founded in law and with a large economic impact, almost invite companies to try alternative ways and thereby run the risk of corruption. Problems with VAT reimbursement, refusal to take a profit tax report with losses stated and the like constitute such administrative practices.

Corruption is based on a separation between the right to determine the basic regulations affecting operations of companies, and the right to the profit generated by these companies affected by the regulations. Corruption, bribery, kickbacks etc are illegal activities in Ukraine and something a company should strive to avoid. Not only is it morally wrong, it is simply an unprofitable business practice. Corruption is like an uneven game in a foreign playground – a game that never stops; a game that is snowballing; and a game you cannot win.

What to know about corruption in Ukraine and how to approach it

- *Corruption in Ukraine is overstated* and definitely not a precondition for doing business in the country. The problem of corruption is a myth and based more on 'stories' than on facts. The myth is not taking into consideration that most of the 'stories' have no direct impact on the operations of individual companies.
- *The authorities follow a 'zero-tolerance' principle.* The local administration might seem inefficient but they are indeed very structured and organized and will eventually check and control your company and its ability to comply with local standards. Therefore, no shortcuts should be made, as these shortcuts may force the authorities to halt your production or other business activities.
- *Approach the administration, the rules and regulations as if you were at home.* It takes a lot of time, a dedicated management and a structured approach, but it should be seen as a basic cost of doing business in Ukraine – exactly as administration and documentation are a basic cost of doing business in every other country. Despite a complicated administrative system, complex rules and strange regulations, they can all be learnt and understood, and the company can take action accordingly – it takes two to tango.
- *Corruption has a lot of definitions, a lot of faces but is always illegal.* It is always a good 'self-tester' to answer the easy question: 'What would happen if these actions were published and described in the largest newspaper in my country?'
- *Today's asset might become tomorrow's liability.* Good and friendly contacts with the local authorities are a must in Ukraine, but one should always have in mind that the 'insider' may soon become an 'outsider'.
- *Start from the very beginning.* Companies that from the very beginning have based their business activities on a 'stay legal' principle have a much easier task in avoiding corruption than companies that stumbled in the beginning.
- *Stay legal!* Corruption is snowballing and will over time cost you more than it takes to stay legal. Furthermore, the company will soon be known in the local community as a 'dirty player' and be even more exposed to the risk of corruption. A lot depends on dedication and a structured approach to the local management.

Part Five

An Introduction to Doing Business in Ukraine's Regions

5.1

An Introduction to Investing in the Regions

Alica Henson, Deputy Project Director, US–Ukraine Foundation and Brad Bunt, Director, Kilgore College Small Business Development Centre

What have investors done thus far?

With a consumer market of 49 million, a labour force of approximately 29 million, a developed infrastructure (though in need of modernization), and a geographic location on the eastern borders of Europe, Ukraine has great potential for investment. Kyiv, as the capital city, has traditionally been the target for Western business wanting to work in Ukraine. In the years since independence, Kyiv has attracted many businesses and boasts many successful examples of Western business activity. Apart from Kyiv, a few other large or well-known cities, such as L'viv, Odesa, Donetsk, Dnipropetrovsk and Kharkiv, have been the main focus of investors.

Working in these types of cities has its advantages: a bigger, more developed market with more clients, a more Westernized population, which understands Western business norms, and access to national government officials as business-related legislation has developed. However, there are significant untapped and advantageous opportunities for business in the small and medium-size cities throughout Ukraine.

Why look to the regions?

There are many reasons why the potential investor would benefit from looking at cities and towns apart from the capital city and other large or well-known cities.

Less competition

If your company is one of a few or the only Western business operating in a city, there will be less competition from other Western concerns. This has its advantages. It will be easier to get the ear of local government, which means that if you have concerns about incentives for business or business practices in the city, you will have greater access to those entities or authorities that can address the issues you raise. You will also have the opportunity to establish closer relationships with the local government and the community.

While many of the major cities in Ukraine have many companies mimicking Western-style retail and service companies, the smaller cities and remote regions have virtually no companies resembling those of the West. Most businesses are poorly run and offer little service to the customer. In almost all cities in Ukraine, there are gaps in retail businesses as well as those in the service industry. And while Ukraine is one of the largest consumer markets in the world, the country is a virtual frontier for establishing companies operating according to Western-style business practices. Customer service driven businesses will gain a large market share of any city's purchasing habits. In fact, in most larger cities, restaurants will not hire staff unless the employee has had training and worked in an establishment such as McDonald's.

Less corruption

Smaller cities have less experience, and indeed less incentive to practise corruption. The spotlight will be focused on those enterprises that have attracted foreign investment and there will be greater expectations for this endeavour to succeed. If you encounter business practices which concern you, it will be easier to approach the authorities or others in the business community to combat corruption.

Expedited and reduced-cost services

Outside the large or well-known cities, Western investors will have less need to rely on intermediaries that will increase your costs. In addition, there is reduced red tape to manoeuvre (licensing and registration, property ownership etc). Many Ukrainian cities are facing financial hardship, as enterprises or factories which were part of the Soviet command economy machinery are operating non-profitable activities or even facing closure. These cities are looking for Western investment to either rejuvenate the existing concern or find alternative business activities to provide employment for the community. You will often find a highly skilled or educated workforce that is prepared to support your initiatives.

Special economic zones

Many cities, such as Artemivsk, Slavutych, Krasnodon and the All-Transcarpathia group of cities, are exploring the worth of establishing special (free) economic zones in their communities. While this legislation is still underdeveloped, there is potential for city governments to provide some incentives to incoming businesses.

Strategic planning and management

More and more cities are adopting Western-style strategic planning and management practices in their approach to economic development. Working with these types of cities will be beneficial, as obviously it makes more sense to work with a city government which has a realistic view of its strengths, weaknesses, opportunities and threats. A city which has undergone strategic planning will have a more defined set of goals in order to achieve sustainable economic development.

Cluster approaches

There are great opportunities to work not just with one city, but with a group of cities that are geographically proximate to one another. In this way, businesses can be provided with the raw materials, processing and manufacturing services, shipping, training and retraining facilities from a number of cities. Smaller cities have fewer resources and are not in a position to realistically offer everything a business may need, especially if the goods produced are for export. But these same cities may already have good contacts with one another and would, therefore, be strong partners in a cluster. Shepetivka (Khmelnytskiy Oblast) has joined several surrounding cities to collaborate on economic development initiatives.

Technical assistance focus

In the years since independence, the US Agency for International Development (USAID) and other donors have targeted more technical assistance at the local level. This means that there are a greater number of cities throughout the country that have had the benefit of learning about economic development issues and business planning, thus making them a more prepared partner for a Western business.

Underserved market niches

While most larger cities enjoy a highly developed retail/service and manufacturing economy, the smaller cities suffer from lack of services.

According to the World Bank, while the services sector grew annually by 5.9 per cent in 2001, it fell by 56 per cent in 2002. This lack of services offered has created a large niche in many sectors of the economy. Some cities have completed a SWOT (strengths, weaknesses, opportunities, threats) analysis of their local economy identifying these deficiencies. Before any investment has been made into any local economy of Ukraine, your company may be able to obtain this information and your business plan can coincide with this analysis. You may also want to conduct your own market analysis of the current needs of a particular city or region, but it is safe to say that there is great opportunity across the entire country.

Emerging niche economies for Ukraine

Ukraine has advantages over other countries in several areas, both as producer and as consumer. As mentioned above, many small and medium-size cities in Ukraine have an underdeveloped service sector. As producers, Ukrainian cities are able to compete in the following areas: software development, food processing, textiles (both raw material and finished goods). The highly skilled labour force, combined with lower costs of production, make these industries highly attractive. In addition, Ukraine has some of the world's most arable land, earning the reputation as the 'Breadbasket of Europe' as 25 per cent of grain produced in the Soviet Union came from Ukraine, as well as 20 per cent of dairy and meat output.

Labour force

Unlike other developing countries, Ukraine is an attractive country for investment owing to its highly educated, highly skilled labour force and low wages. The labour force of Ukraine is made up of 32 per cent industry, 24 per cent agriculture and 44 per cent services. Major industries of Ukraine include coal, electric power, ferrous and non-ferrous metals, machinery and transport equipment, chemicals, and food processing. While many of its younger citizens have migrated to the larger cities in search of job opportunities and growth, the smaller cities and regions still have many qualified workers occupying stagnant plants and manufacturing facilities. These highly educated and skilled workers are capable of high production given the opportunity of retraining their existing skills base and upgrading their industrial equipment. In these smaller regions and cities, wages are generally lower than those of Mexico and China. Given this situation, the possibilities for Western companies to invest profitably in Ukraine are high.

What resources exist to facilitate your search?

The second part of this chapter will provide more information for the investor who is looking for business opportunities outside of Kyiv and the larger cities. There are several sources which can facilitate the preliminary search for a target city or company.

Technical assistance initiatives

Western governments and international organizations fund initiatives that assist in the promotion of democratic and free market principles. The US Agency for International Development (USAID) finances the US–Ukraine Foundation's Community Partnerships Project for Local Government Training and Education. Since 1997, this project has assisted in the development of local government in Ukraine by providing training in local government practices. Specifically, the project established five Regional Training Centres in L'viv, Cherkasy, Kherson, Kharkiv and Donetsk. To date, seminars have been conducted on a wide variety of topics related to local government reform, including economic development. City government officials from over 500 towns and cities have participated in these seminars, making the CPP RTCs a unique source of information on the more progressive and proactive local governments in the country. US government-supported Peace Corps volunteers in cities throughout Ukraine can also be a good source of information once a potential city or business has been identified. These volunteers can have extensive business backgrounds and have spent up to two years or more in their posts and can therefore be a valuable source of on-the-ground input from a Western perspective.

Western embassies

The US and other embassies should be in a position to provide you with information on problematic individuals or companies. The US Department of Commerce issues a bulletin, BISNIS, on investment opportunities in the CIS. This site also provides information on business etiquette.

City resources

It is useful to look at city property funds in cities themselves. This source can provide the investor with information about city-owned businesses or properties that are for sale. There are a number of opportunities to buy an unfinished construction site for minimal funds and finish up the building at low cost and more quickly than the government can. Also, if you identify a certain property or business that is not privately owned, the local property fund should provide you with details of which level of government has ownership.

In addition, many cities are developing their own Web sites. The English may be lacking, but you can easily see that progress is being made. More cities are learning about the benefits of marketing themselves to a wider audience.

Business incubators

A number of cities have opened business incubators, which are basically resource centres where enterprises seeking investment capital or just an improvement in management capabilities can come to get assistance. While many of these centres were initially set up with the help of various international assistance programmes, city officials and small to medium business owners have begun to view such facilities as critical to the viable growth of local enterprises. One of the primary goals of the business incubators has been to prepare certain enterprises, in some cases those of strategic economic importance to the local economy, for a variety of joint ventures and the ability to attract foreign capital.

Since 1997, the Business Incubator Program, implemented by the International Technology Research Institute of Loyola College (Baltimore, Maryland) and funded by USAID, has facilitated the establishment of several business incubators throughout Ukraine and is an ongoing resource for their development (www.stcu.kiev.ua).

Chambers of Commerce

Be careful of the name, as often these chambers are the old Soviet types. More progressive cities will often have a restructured or newly created chamber of commerce in which local entrepreneurs work together to solve problems facing business development and to network. Getting in touch with a local chamber can provide you with information about potential businesses for sale and can find you potential business partners.

The American Chamber of Commerce in Ukraine, based in Kyiv, has years of experience in working with American and Ukrainian businesses and is a good source of information for newly entering businesses.

Business support systems

Many Ukrainian cities are evaluating the need for business support systems for their existing and newly created enterprises. In fact, many cities have begun to establish some type of business support centre. While many of these centres lack uniformity, they do give some guidance to startup and existing companies. Many times the centre will be located in the City Hall or Unemployment Centre in each city. The USAID-funded Community Partnerships Project has offered training in many regions of Ukraine on establishing a business support system designed closely on the US version of the Small Business Development Center (SBDC). These centres generally offer advice on beginning your business and aid in the creation of a business plan. More advanced services would include marketing, accounting, import–export assistance, advanced business training and efficient manufacturing assistance. The city of Romny, in Sumy Oblast, was the first to establish such a centre, with Kirovske (Donetsk Oblast) and Zhmerynka (Vinnitsya Oblast) following suite, and many other cities have shown an interest in creating such a model. Contact the person responsible for economic development in the city you are selecting for investment and this person should be able to direct you to the capabilities and services offered.

How your company can invest in Ukraine

The Ukrainian government has taken a series of positive steps on improving the investment climate in the country.

Foreign investment activity is regulated by the Law of Ukraine 'On the Regime of Foreign Investments,' adopted on 19 March 1996, No. 93/96-BP. According to this newly adopted law, foreign investment includes all kinds of assets invested by foreigners into the investment objective.

Foreign investments can be made in the form of:

- hard currency;
- Ukrainian currency, in case of re-investment into the objects of primary investment, or into any other investment objective according to the Law of Ukraine subject to profit tax paid;
- any movable and real estate;
- securities in hard currency;
- monetary claims in hard currency, which are guaranteed by the first-rate banks;
- rights of intellectual property whose value in currency is estimated in accordance with the laws of the country-investor and confirmed by expert evaluations in Ukraine, including copyright, useful models, industrial patterns, trademarks etc;
- rights to do business, including the rights to explore natural resources granted by law or contracts whose value in hard currency

is estimated according to the legal procedures of the country-investor or international trade practice;

- any other assets according to the Law of Ukraine.

Foreign investors have the right to invest in the following forms:

- having shares with the Ukrainian partners in newly established joint ventures or purchasing segments of operating Ukrainian enterprises;
- setting up enterprises with 100 per cent foreign capital or purchasing entire operating enterprises;
- purchasing real estate and movable property that is not illegal in Ukrainian law;
- purchasing individually or in partnership with Ukrainian companies or physical persons rights to use land or to acquire concessions to explore natural resources on the territory of Ukraine;
- on an agreement basis for production cooperation and joint production without setting up a new company if these agreements anticipate foreign investments in Ukraine.

A foreign company with foreign investment is a legal entity of any organization and legal form set up according to the legislation of Ukraine on the condition that a paid-up share of foreign investments in its statuary fund is not less than 10 per cent.

As prescribed by the Law of Ukraine 'On the Regime of Foreign Investments', the state guarantees protection of foreign investments against changes in the legislation, forced exploration, illegal actions of government bodies and their officials, compensation and recovering damages. The state also provides guarantees in case of termination of investment activity, repatriation of profits and other incomes entailed from investment activity.

Foreign investments are registered by the Government of Autonomous Republic of the Crimea, regional, Kyiv and Sevastopol City State Administrations within three working days from the date when the investment was actually paid according to the procedures assigned by the Cabinet of Ministers of Ukraine.

According to the Resolution of the Cabinet of Ministers of Ukraine No. 112 (30 January 1997), 'On Approval of the Regulations on the Procedures for State Registration of Contracts on Joint Investment Activity with the Participation of Foreign Investors', agreements (contracts) on production cooperation, joint production without setting up a new entity signed by Ukrainian companies with foreign investors in conformity with Ukrainian legislation are subject to state registration as well.

Enterprises with foreign investments enjoy some customs privileges. The assets imported as an investment are exempt from customs duties (Para 18, Chapter 4; Para 24, Chapter 5).

All enterprises with foreign investments pay taxes according to the Law of Ukraine.

5.2

Investment Rating of the Ukrainian Regions

Markiyan Dacyshyn and Pavlo Vdovych, The Ukrainian Economic Think Tank 'Institute for Reform' (www.ipa.net.ua)

The largest European country (with a territory of 603,700 sq km), Ukraine offers a variety of regional perspectives for doing business. Eastern Ukraine is well known for its strong industrial sector, which includes coal mining, metallurgy and machine-building industries, as well as chemistry and petroleum refinery. Central and southern regions are strong in crop growing and food processing. Western Ukrainian economies are focused on light industry, trade, food and wood processing and transportation. Recreational resources are concentrated along the Black Sea coast, especially on the Crimean Peninsula, and in the Carpathian Mountains, which covers five western regions. Kyiv City is the financial centre of the economy, backed up by a number of strong regional banking centres: Dnipropetrovsk, Kharkiv, L'viv and Doneck.

It is worth noting that the investment climate of the Ukrainian regions varies throughout the country. In part this is for historical reasons – some industrial territories were targeted at the military complex, while some agrarian territories (formerly subsidized by the state) failed to develop within the market economy. However, the other group of reasons is generated today both at the central and local level. Unfortunately, Ukraine still employs the 'up–down' approach in regional policy, which limits a region's ability to influence local economic development and to develop a regional investment policy. One may often hear from the local authority accusations about the central bodies' restrictive policy: '*the centre pressures every regional initiative*'. Additionally, a negative impact on the regional investment climate is caused by the investment legislation, which is said to be unstable and contradictory in Ukraine.

Although a number of investment risks are generated at the national level, there are examples of positive experiences of investors in the regional markets. Moreover, some companies have moved their offices and production facilities from one region to another, considering the local investment climate of the new location better than the previous. Statistical data on foreign direct investment (FDI) verifies the differentiation of the investment climate throughout the country (see Figure 5.2.1). FDI in Kyiv City equals USD705 per resident, while the same figure for Chernivci oblast is about USD20. Yet, the interest of foreign investors in industries – namely food processing and trade – that are represented in every regional economy resulted in competition among the regions for investments.

In 1999 the Ukrainian Think Tank 'Institute for Reform' commenced regular rating of the regional investment climate. The Regional Investment Rating report is a unique source of up-to-date information on developments at the regional level in Ukraine. Considering both official statistical data and expert survey results, the most recent report offers comprehensive analysis of a region's performance in 2002.[1] The Businesses and Authorities Survey, covering about 400 experts in the field of investment, highlights the progress made by most of the regions since 2000. Region-by-region assessments provide information on the economies' key areas, making this semi-annual publication essential reading for investors, policy-makers and researchers.[2]

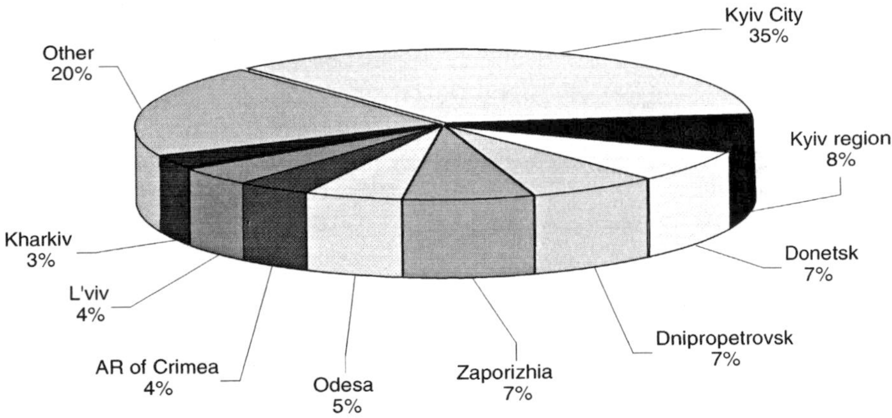

Figure 5.2.1 Foreign direct investments into Ukrainian regions, as of 1 January 2003

[1] For the Ratings update please visit www.ipa.net.ua

[2] For more details please feel free to contact Markiyan Dacyshyn on +38 044 239 23 15 or via e-mail: invest@ir.org.ua

Moreover, during 2002–03, the Institute for Reform, in cooperation with 13 regions of Ukraine, implemented the *Information for Investments Project* aimed at designing an effective investment policy at the local level. Over 40 workshops for public servants and a series of method learning materials dedicated to practical aspects of regional investment policy were prepared and implemented as part of the project. The need for a high-quality informational resource about Ukraine's regions led us to develop an Internet portal *'Invest in Ukraine'*, which is available at www.ipa.net.ua.

Investment rating of the regions

The City of Kyiv, with indexes twice as high, became the leader of the 2002 Investment Rating of the Ukrainian Regions, developed by the Institute for Reform (see Figure 5.2.3). The capital also has advantage in all categories of indexes especially in the financial sector category (see Table 5.2.1). That is why the prognosis for the capital's leadership in the rating table during the immediate future is undoubted.

The next three positions in the rating table are occupied by the industrial regions: Donetsk, Kharkiv and Dnipropetrovsk. Another trio of leaders, which was not able this time to close the gap with the front-runners, was made up of Odesa, Zaporizhia and L'viv oblasts. It should be noted that every year the advantage of Kyiv City is diminishing. Moreover, in 2002 the regions of Odesa and Kharkiv demonstrated the highest economic growth rates in the country.

In 2002 Dnipropetrovsk region fell to fourth position because of a decline in the region's positions in the economy and infrastructure development categories, while Donetsk region improved its performance to second place, which coincided with the growth of the political weight of the region on the national scale. Kharkiv region, whose third place in 2001 was quite a sensation, strengthened its position in 2002. It should be mentioned that changes in the positions of top seven regions were caused by quite different, even seasonal factors and the gap between neighbouring regions is rather relative.

The stability of the regions' leaders group in the rating table is determined, first of all, by historically conditioned factors of regional development such as industrial, transport and other infrastructure. The structure of the composite rating score of the regions' leaders is shown in Figure 5.2.4.

A so-called *'runners-up'* group is formed by seven regions this time: Poltava, Kyiv, Mykolaiv, Vinnytsia, Lugansk and Zakarpattia regions and Republic of Crimea. Their composite scores are a certain distance from the leaders, but they still differ from the rest of the regions. It is necessary to note that this time Mykolaiv and Vinnytsia regions reached their maxima in annual ratings (10th and 12th positions respectively).

Figure 5.2.2 Regions of Ukraine

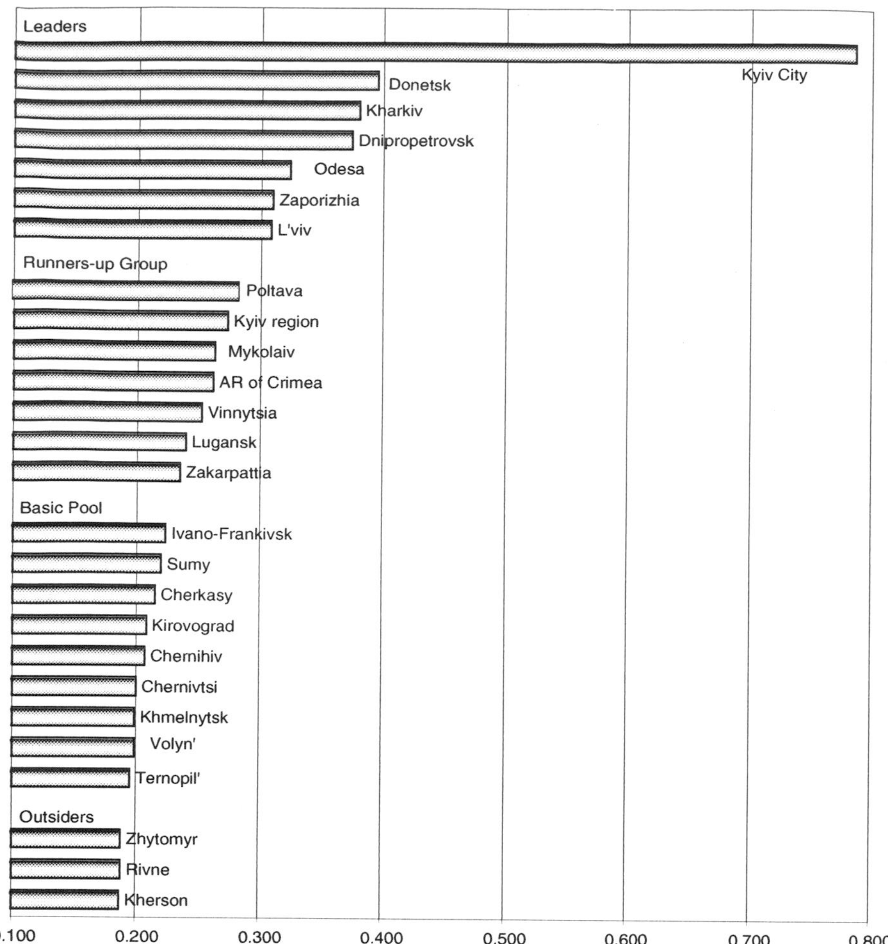

Figure 5.2.3 2002 Investment rating of the Ukrainian regions

The regions of the *basic pool* are characterized by a dense disposition of rating scores, and that makes stunning rises and falls possible. Consequently, Sumy region went up five positions in one year (from 21st in 2001 to 16th in 2002), while Kherson region lost six positions and found itself at the bottom of the rating table. It is still a fact that for the majority of regions in the lower part of the rating table, upward movement is limited owing to the weakness of their infrastructure.

Assessment of regions' attractiveness according to the results for 2002 was based on five categories of indexes: economic development of a region (1), market infrastructure (2), financial sector (3), human resources (4) and private enterprises and local authorities (5). Altogether 67 statistical indexes were analysed. A detailed description of the methodology is given at www.ir.org.ua.

Table 5.2.1 Components of the 2002 investment rating of the Ukrainian regions

	Composite Rating Score Breakdown										Composite Rating Score	Rank	
	Economic Development (25%)		Market Infrastructure (22%)		Financial Sector (25%)		Human Resources (13%)		Businesses and Local Authorities (15%)				
	score	*rank*	*score*	*rank*	*score*	*rank*	*score*	*rank*	*score*	*rank*			
AR of Crimea	0.269	15.0	0.225	11.0	0.165	8.0	0.452	6.0	0.300	6	0.262	11	AR of Crimea
Vinnytsia	0.256	17.0	0.269	7.0	0.108	19.0	0.445	9.0	0.243	15	0.253	12	Vinnytsia
Volyn'	0.272	13.0	0.161	19.0	0.046	26.0	0.439	10.0	0.142	23	0.198	22	Volyn'
Dnipropetrovsk	0.399	5.0	0.402	4.0	0.280	2.0	0.473	4.0	0.277	11	0.373	4	Dnipropetrovsk
Donetsk	0.409	2.0	0.574	2.0	0.177	7.0	0.473	3.0	0.289	8	0.395	2	Donetsk
Zhytomyr	0.239	20.0	0.161	18.0	0.099	24.0	0.381	19.0	0.092	26	0.188	24	Zhytomyr
Zakarpattia	0.271	14.0	0.204	15.0	0.093	25.0	0.429	12.0	0.245	14	0.235	14	Zakarpattia
Zaporizhia	0.408	3.0	0.258	8.0	0.198	5.0	0.435	11.0	0.249	13	0.310	6	Zaporizhia
Ivano-Frankivsk	0.244	19.0	0.222	12.0	0.115	16.0	0.423	13.0	0.148	21	0.222	15	Ivano-Frankivsk
Kyiv region	0.355	8.0	0.149	21.0	0.161	10.0	0.475	2.0	0.302	4	0.273	9	Kyiv region
Kirovograd	0.210	23.0	0.151	20.0	0.112	17.0	0.352	23.0	0.290	7	0.208	18	Kirovograd
Lugansk	0.248	18.0	0.255	9.0	0.148	13.0	0.348	26.0	0.209	16	0.240	13	Lugansk
L'viv	0.310	9.0	0.352	5.0	0.160	11.0	0.467	5.0	0.281	9	0.309	7	L'viv
Mykolaiv	0.284	12.0	0.170	17.0	0.227	3.0	0.394	15.0	0.279	10	0.263	10	Mykolaiv
Odesa	0.374	6.0	0.273	6.0	0.184	6.0	0.448	8.0	0.388	3	0.324	5	Odesa
Poltava	0.361	7.0	0.233	10.0	0.155	12.0	0.390	16.0	0.301	5	0.283	8	Poltava
Rivne	0.232	22.0	0.118	25.0	0.108	20.0	0.387	18.0	0.153	20	0.188	25	Rivne
Sumy	0.295	11.0	0.140	23.0	0.099	23.0	0.361	21.0	0.256	12	0.219	16	Sumy
Ternopil'	0.183	26.0	0.217	13.0	0.110	18.0	0.348	25.0	0.145	22	0.194	23	Ternopil'
Kharkiv	0.401	4.0	0.410	3.0	0.216	4.0	0.451	7.0	0.426	2	0.379	3	Kharkiv
Kherson	0.200	24.0	0.076	26.0	0.162	9.0	0.369	20.0	0.192	18	0.186	26	Kherson
Khmelnytsk	0.189	25.0	0.194	16.0	0.104	21.0	0.407	14.0	0.159	19	0.199	21	Khmelnytsk
Cherkasy	0.258	16.0	0.143	22.0	0.136	14.0	0.390	17.0	0.199	17	0.215	17	Cherkasy
Chernivtsi	0.239	21.0	0.208	14.0	0.099	22.0	0.350	24.0	0.116	25	0.199	20	Chernivtsi
Chernihiv	0.296	10.0	0.139	24.0	0.123	15.0	0.355	22.0	0.136	24	0.206	19	Chernihiv
Kyiv City	0.728	1.0	0.640	1.0	0.921	1.0	0.853	1.0	0.696	1	0.787	1	Kyiv City

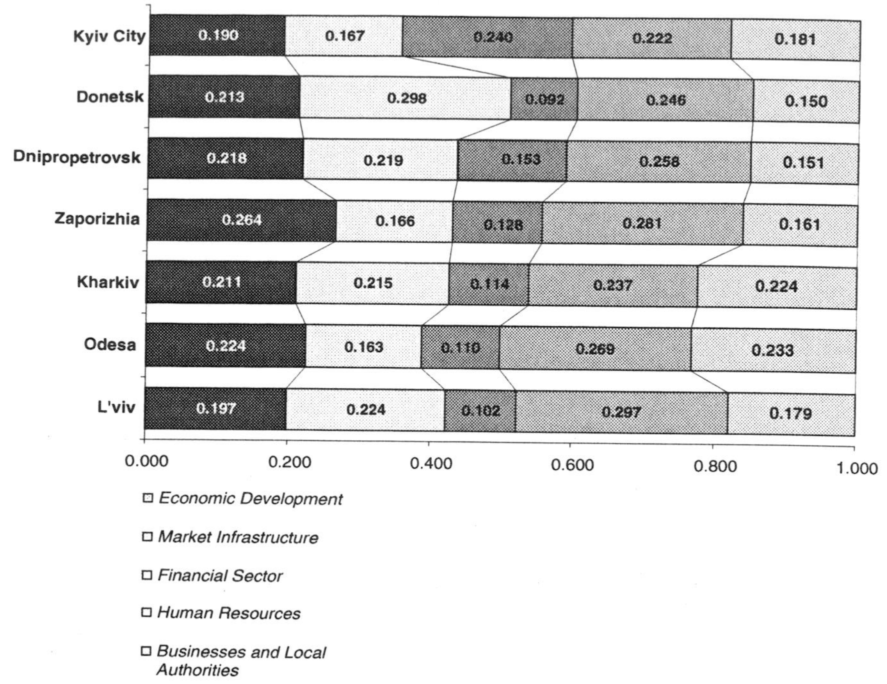

Figure 5.2.4 Composite rating score breakdown for the top-7 regions

Dynamic rating of the regions

Considering regional economies' performance, it is rational not only to evaluate the current level of their development but also to analyse the trends of changes in the major economic indexes. Such an estimate allows better-grounded assumptions to be made about the current and prospective economic situation in a region. Since 2001 the Institute for Reform has conducted such a comparative analysis. On the basis of 20 key economic indexes the Dynamic Rating of the Ukrainian regions for 2002 is composed (see Figure 5.2.5). The score table shows that there is gradual economic growth in all Ukrainian regions. It permeated even the outsider regions, whose growth rates are higher than those of the frontrunners. In 2002 the leaders in the Dynamic Rating are the following regions: Odesa, Kharkiv and Ternopil.

The leading position of Odesa region resulted from the growth of investment and exports as well as from the growth of innovations in the local enterprises. The high position of Kharkiv region is explained by a considerable decrease in salary arrears. The rating of Ternopil region grew because of high export trends and also because of a decrease in salary arrears.

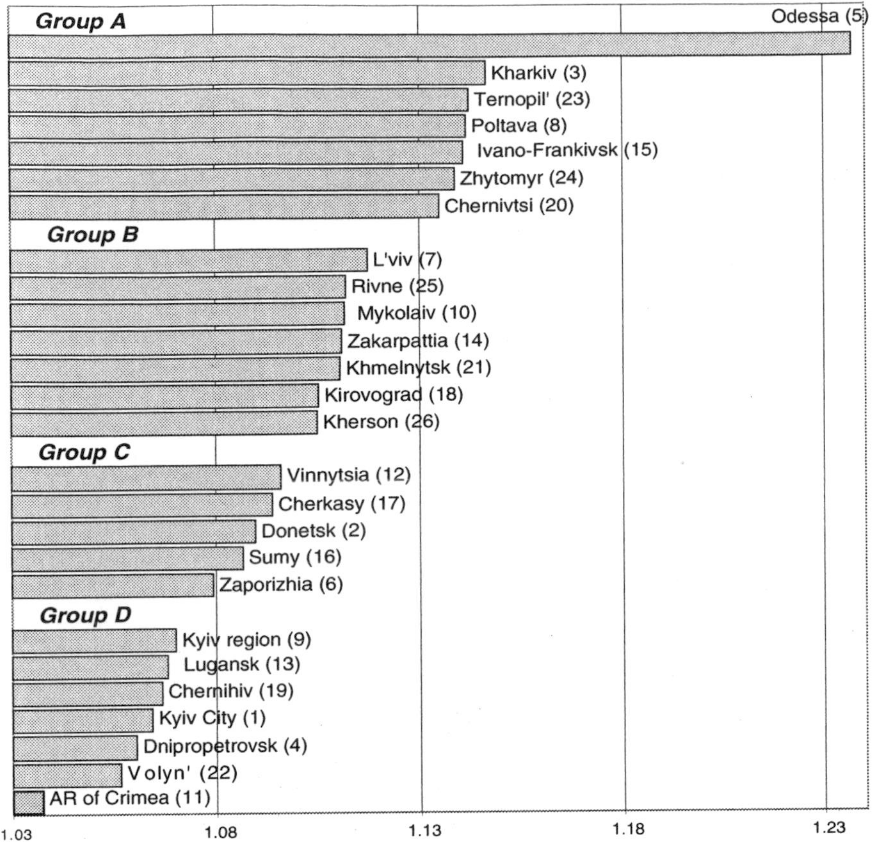

Figure 5.2.5 2002 Dynamic rating of the Ukrainian regions (region's rank in the Investment Rating is indicated in the brackets)

The leaders of the Investment Rating – Kyiv City, Donetsk and Dnipropetrovsk regions – are ranked in the lower part of the Dynamic Rating table (23rd, 17th and 24th positions respectively). Let us note that low 'dynamic' positions for the industrial regions have already become a kind of tradition. In 2001 Kyiv City and Donetsk region occupied 21st and 24th positions respectively. This can be explained by the so-called 'scale factor'. It is hard to maintain significant economic growth indexes given the scale of business activity in these regions.

The geographic concentration of the Dynamic Rating leaders reflects the high pace of economic development of the western and southern Ukrainian regions. However, it should be mentioned that growth during one period does not guarantee continuation of the tendency.

5.3

Expert Assessments of the Regional Investment Climate

Markiyan Dacyshyn and Pavlo Vdovych, The Ukrainian Economic Think Tank 'Institute for Reform' (www.ipa.net.ua)

During March–May 2003, Institute for Reform conducted a survey of business representatives and state employees in order to discover their perceptions of the investment process at the regional level in Ukraine. There were 328 heads of economic subdivisions of regional/local authorities from 10 regions, and 58 top managers of companies operating in different Ukrainian regions.

Investment climate in 2002

The majority of the businessmen questioned do not believe that there have been fundamental changes in the Ukrainian investment climate. The percentage of those who consider 2002 positively exceed those who express a negative opinion by only a very small margin. However, the spokesmen for the local authorities have a much more positive view of 2003's results. Evidently, the causes of this difference are in sources of information. For businessmen it is their own experience, for officials – official statistical data which shows improvement of the basic macroeconomic indexes in 2002.

At the same time, businessmen note the dynamism of positive tendencies in the development of the national economy. Managing director of the investment bank *Foyil Securities New Europe* Gregory Grushko affirms that 'in Ukraine 2002 is equal to Russia in 1995. But in 2004 our economy will be on the level of Russia in 2000.'

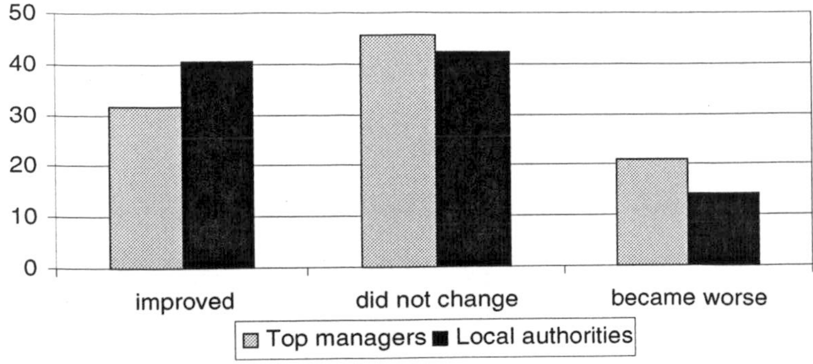

Figure 5.3.1 Respondents' answers to the question: 'How in your opinion did the investment climate in Ukraine change?'

Among events that influenced the Ukrainian investment climate in 2002, the majority of respondents pointed to the fact of Financial Action Task Force (FATF) sanctions being applied to Ukraine (over 50 per cent of those questioned). Less perceptible was the influence of the Kolchuga scandal and parliamentary crises (30 per cent each), and the appointment of Mr Yanukovych as prime minister (28 per cent). Interestingly, only 20 per cent of respondents think that elections to parliament significantly influenced the investment climate in Ukraine.

In the respondents' judgements concerning the importance of factors which are generated at the level of central authorities, first place is confidently taken by associated factors: 'intervention of authorities in business' and 'corruption of state officials'. These factors are thought to be the key ones by 60 per cent of those questioned. Slightly less than half the respondents pointed to the 'significant importance' of transparency of authorities' actions and the same number consider this

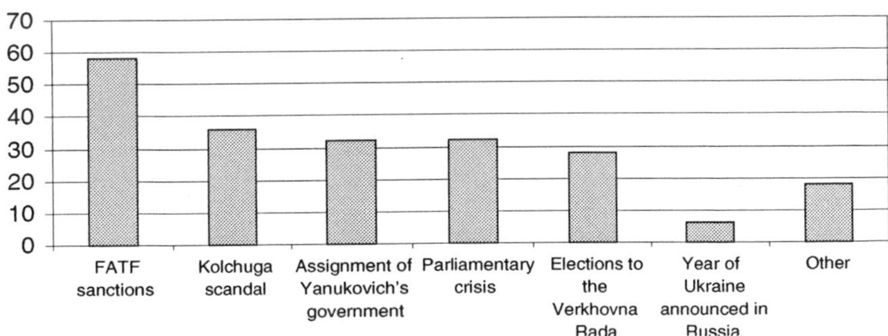

Figure 5.3.2 Respondents' answers to the question: 'Which facts had a significant impact on the investment climate in Ukraine in 2002?'

factor to be simply 'important'. One-third of those questioned said that the key factor remains 'a measure of interpenetration of authority and business'.

A somewhat different picture is observed concerning such factors as 'authorities' support in attracting investments' and 'creation of preferential conditions for investors'. These are considered crucial by only one-fifth of businessmen. Simultaneously, 50–60 per cent of respondents regard them as factors that have an insignificant influence on the Ukrainian investment environment. Thus business representatives acknowledge the considerable influence of the central authorities but question the effectiveness of their arrangements aimed at improvement of the investment climate in Ukraine. At the same time the network development head of the Ukrainian bank *Ukrsotsbank*, Oleg Blozovskyi, indicates that 'authority cannot totally turn away from business. Moreover, investors are interested in meeting with the local authority and finding out about its vision of the investment process.'

It is typical that most of the officials questioned consider 'personal meeting with investor' to be the most effective instrument of investment policy.

Regions

To discover the most attractive territories for investors we asked businessmen to name the regions they would consider first if they had the possibility of expanding their business in 2003.

Donetsk turned out to be the most popular region (31 per cent of respondents). Among the reasons for this choice were: lobbying for regional interests at the governmental level, favourable market conditions and the support of local authorities. Other leaders are Kyiv City and Dnipropetrovsk region (29 and 26 per cent respectively). Businessmen give approximately the same arguments in favour of these regions: improvement of the economic infrastructure and favourable market conditions. The latter factor is decisive for those who would expand into the L'viv (22 per cent), Kharkiv (21 per cent) and Odesa (19 per cent) regions. It should be added that respondents noticed an improvement in the crime situation in the industrial regions – Donetsk, Zaporizhzhia and Kharkiv regions.

The chairman of the *VABank*, the Ukrainian bank with foreign investment, Yurij Blaschuk, shares his plans: 'I would be very cautious when choosing certain regions on the basis of the population income growth criterion or the growth of enterprises' profitability. In the first instance I look at the economic potential and the export possibilities of regional enterprises.'

If we consider only one criterion of investment climate, namely the support of local authorities, which, as we have already said, businesses believe is very important, the situation is as follows: businessmen feel that the highest level of support is to be found in Kyiv City and the Zaporizhzhia, Donetsk, L'viv and Odesa regions.

Let us note that the most popular region in which managers would like to conduct their business causes the greatest fear in other respondents. Fifteen per cent of those questioned 'would not advise running a business in Donetsk region, even to their competitor'. An identical pattern appears for some other regions, specifically Odesa (9 per cent would never start their business there). We can assume that this difference is determined by the different investment strategies of enterprises. The same region appears to be attractive from the point of view of favourable market conditions, high demand and developed infrastructure, but from the point of view of the level of competition, high salaries, and the lack of cheap objects in which to invest it is not that attractive. Unfavourable conditions for business were also recognized in the Zakarpattia and Lugansk regions and Crimea (this fact was recognized by 9–11 per cent of those questioned).

On the other hand, the results of questioning the local authorities allow us to make a few interesting deductions about the peculiarities of investment policy at a local level. To begin with, local authorities are not inclined to search for the specific competitive advantages of a region, thinking that the main risks for investing are generated at the national level. Secondly, the majority of them believe that their basic competitors are Kyiv City and industrial giants. Seeing such considerably stronger

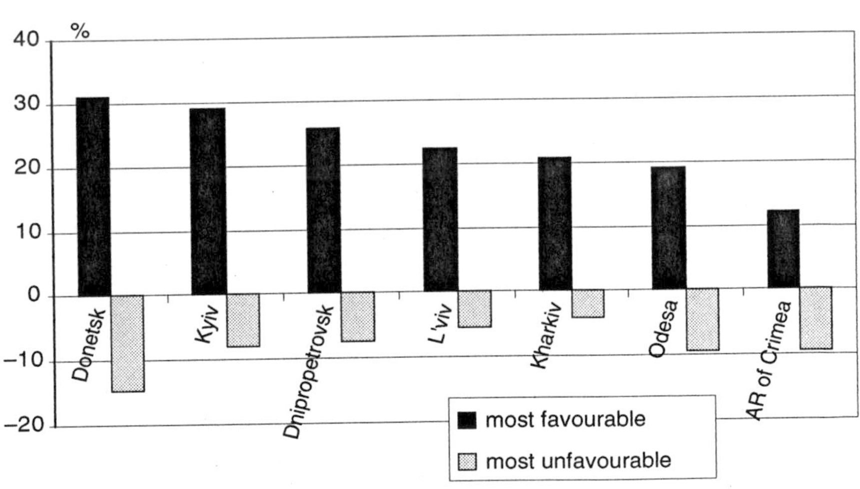

Figure 5.3.3 Distribution of answers on the question about the investment climate in Ukraine in 2002

'rivals' in competition for investment resources enables local authorities to justify the low level of investment activity 'within their jurisdiction'.

Forecasts

About 24 per cent of business respondents believe that the investment climate in Ukraine will improve in 2003. However, two-thirds of the managers questioned say that nothing will change significantly. Meanwhile the local authorities express optimism. About 53 per cent of them believe that things will be better.

Many of the local authorities and businessmen accept the assertion that 'until the presidential elections in 2004 the investment climate in Ukraine will not change significantly' (48 and 56 per cent respectively). The managing director of *The Bleyzer Foundation*, Victor Gekker, thinks that 'for a majority of state employees and businessmen, their expectations of changes after presidential elections are only a justification of their own indolence. We can and should work today and always.' Director of the investment bank *Dragon Capital* Dmytro Tarabakin agrees that the dependence of the economy on politics in Ukraine is gradually diminishing. He characterized the situation using a local saying: 'a dog barks but the caravan goes on'.

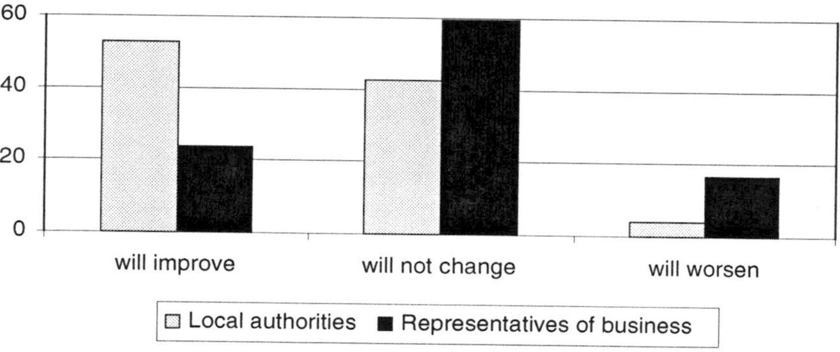

Figure 5.3.4 Respondents' answer to the question: 'Which of the following changes in the investment climate in Ukraine are most likely to happen in 2003?'

Acknowledgements: We express gratitude for assessments of the regional investment climate to the top management of the following companies: Baring Vostok Capital Partners, BC Toms, Cargill, Dragon Capital, Foyil Securities New Europe, Music Radio, Pickard & Co, Raiffeisen Investment Ukraine, Raiffeisen Bank, The Bleyzer Foundation, Western NIS Enterprise Fund, Bank 'Big Energy', VABank, European Business Association, Investment Company 'Art Capita', Investment Company 'Kinto', Kyiv-Mohyla Business School, Ukrsibbank, Ukrsotsbank, Chamber of Commerce and Industry of Zakarpattia region, Chamber of Commerce and Industry of Zaporizhia region, Chamber of Commerce and Industry of Lugansk region, Chamber of Commerce and Industry of L'viv region, Chamber of Commerce and Industry of Chernigiv region.

We are also grateful to those respondents who prefer their participation to remain confidential.

5.4

FDI Trends at the Regional Level in Ukraine

Markiyan Dacyshyn and Pavlo Vdovych, The Ukrainian Economic Think Tank 'Institute for Reform' (www.ipa.net.ua)

According to the Economist Intelligence Unit, foreign direct investment (FDI) worldwide dropped by 22 per cent recently (from USD745.5 billion in 2001 to USD580.3 billion in 2002). This shortfall was most noticeable in the developed countries and in Latin America. In the meantime, the inflow of FDI to the economies of Central and Eastern Europe (CEE) grew from USD29.2 billion to USD34.4 billion in 2002. This fact confirms the thesis that international companies still retain their interest in post-socialist economies.

At the same time, the economic consequences of European Union enlargement in May 2004 will negatively affect the investment attractiveness of the CEE economies. Such a situation stems from the fact that since the foreign investment boom (1996–98), these countries have lost some of their competitiveness factors owing to the growth of competition on the domestic markets, slowing dynamics of consumer markets, growth of labour force costs and reinforcement of regulatory demands. Thus investors will look out for the possibility of transferring their activities into countries offering more favourable conditions. Consequently, Ukraine has a chance to attract some of the FDI flows that will leave the economies of its Western neighbours. Such developments become even more probable if we take a look at the UNCTAD (United Nations Conference on Trade and Development) prognoses for FDI growth in the next five years. In 2003, global FDI is expected to reach USD655 billion.

Although political events such as the parliamentary elections and the Kolchuga scandal were significant for Ukraine in 2002, the annual inflow of FDI last year reached a record of over USD1 billion (Figure 5.4.1). Moreover, the positive trend in FDI accelerated in the first half of 2003. Consequently, cumulative FDI in Ukraine reached about USD6 billion. A sound signal for the investor community that the investment climate in Ukraine is improving is the €40 million greenfield investment project of the German company *Leoni AG*, which has begun construction of a wiring system factory for General Motors in western Ukraine.

Additionally, recent demand for Ukrainian Eurobonds proved that international investors consider Ukraine a potential market for doing business. Experts from the leading rating agencies were responsive to this course of events in Ukraine. Fitch agency in particular, pointing to the successes of the Ukrainian economy during the past year, made a higher assessment of government commitments, raising the rating index to B+. Anders Aslund, a well-known economist at the Carnegie Endowment, reckons that the key role in this belongs to reforms, which have reduced the administrative impact to a level that allows the economy to develop in accordance with free market laws.

However, there are a number of risks still in place. Therefore, the majority of investors are looking for support from state authorities before announcing intentions to invest in Ukraine. Some businesses (such as the German *Metro Cash & Carry*) even managed to have an audience with President Leonid Kuchma. The good news is that the authorities, especially at the local level, are becoming aware of the role of investors in regional development.

At the same time, more cautious experts believe that the policy '*doors are closed in the daytime, windows are opened at night*' will preserve the structure of major investors in Ukraine until 2005. They are (1) multinational corporations, which can afford to take losses while waiting for consumer market growth, (2) funds of direct investment, which still have not lost hope of making profits in Ukraine, and (3) Russian companies, for which Ukrainian risks are familiar and they know how to eliminate them. Under such a scenario, experts say,

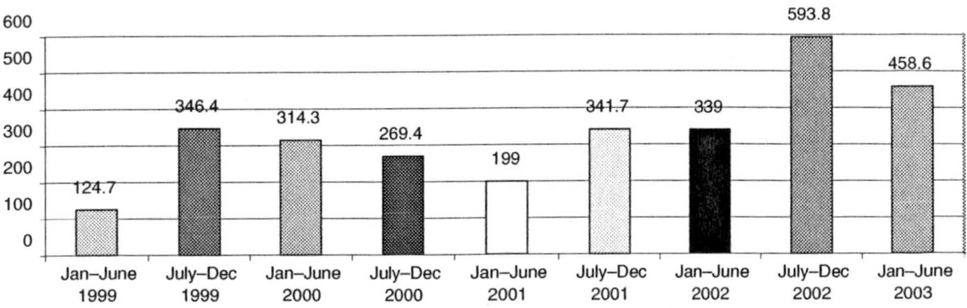

Figure 5.4.1 Net FDI inflow into Ukraine, USD million

annual FDI to Ukraine during the next two years will barely exceed USD1.5–2 billion.

Geographical disproportion in the investment climate is proved by the fact that 80 per cent of all FDI was invested in enterprises situated in eight regions and Kyiv City (see Figure 5.4.2). Concentration of foreign investment shows that investors pay attention to the infrastructure and economic development of certain regions.

During 2002, the net FDI increase in Kyiv City totalled USD307 million while in Cherkasy region this index decreased by USD3.1 million. A net increase in FDI higher than USD30 million was observed only in six regions (excluding Kyiv City): Odesa, Lviv, Zaporizhia, Dnipropetrovsk and Doneck regions and the Republic of Crimea.

The geographic origin of the majority of foreign investors looks as follows: USA (USD898 million; 16.9 per cent of total), Cyprus (USD602.6 million; 11.3 per cent), Great Britain (USD510.5 million; 9.6 per cent), the Netherlands (USD398.7 million; 7.5 per cent), British Virgin Islands (USD337 million; 6.3 per cent), Russia (USD322.6 million; 6.0 per cent).

Domestic trade and the food processing industry remain the most attractive sectors for investors (USD854.8 million and USD852.3 million respectively). The Ukrainian machine-building sector (USD469.6 million) and finance and banking (USD433.3 million) grew last year, but still attracted less FDI.

Change as a percentage, unless indicated

	1999	2000	2001	2002
GDP	99.6	106.0	109.1	104.8
Industrial production	104.3	112.9	114.2	107.0
Agriculture production	93.0	109.2	110.2	101.9
Capital investment	100.4	111.2	117.2	108.9
Foreign direct investment as of end of period, bn USD	3.25	3.87	4.41	5.33
Retail turnover	92.9	106.9	112.6	115.0
Consumer Price Index, %	119.2	125.8	106.1	99.1

Ukraine

Capital – KYIV
National currency – HRYVNIA (UAH)

Find out more information about Ukraine at www.ipa.net.ua

Territory – 603.7 thousand sq km. Ukraine is the largest European country.
Administrative-territorial system: Ukraine incorporates Autonomous Republic of Crimea, 24 regions (oblasts), cities of Kyiv and Sevastopol, and also 490 regions, 453 cities, 887 towns and 28,612 villages.
Population (as of April 2003) – 47,879 million; urban – 67.4%, rural – 32.6%.
Population of the capital – 2,622.7 thousand (Kyiv is the 9th largest European city by population).
Average density of population – 79.7 persons per sq km.
National composition (in 2001): Ukrainians – 77.8%, Russians – 17.3%, other nations – 4.9%.
Gender distribution (in 2000): men – 46.3%, women – 53.7%.
Most attractive sectors for foreign investments are: food processing (15.7% of overall FDI volume), wholesale and mediation in trade (15.6%), machine building (8.5%), financial services (8.0%) and transport (7.6%).

Figure 5.4.2 Key macroeconomic indexes

5.5

Investment Profiles of Some Prominent Ukrainian Regions

Markiyan Dacyshyn, Yuriy Grygorenko and Pavlo Vdovych, The Ukrainian Economic Think Tank 'Institute for Reform' (www.ipa.net.ua)

This chapter contains information about the regions which are the Institute for Reform's partners within the 'Information for Investments' Project.

Odesa region

Odesa region, owing to its economic growth rate, has taken the lead in the Dynamic Rating of the Ukrainian regions. This is even more impressive given the unusually high economic development rates, which are usually low for the developed regions of Ukraine. In October 2002 the Euro region 'Lower Danube', which also includes Odesa oblast, was acknowledged as the best among the Euro regions.

Currently an attractive profile for the region is being created, yet without effort on behalf of the region itself. This is due to the Odesa-region-based oil terminal 'Southern' which is attached to the oil pipeline 'Odesa-Brody'. At this time it is not yet clear which way the oil will go (it may as well be delivered the other way around), but it goes without saying that such a powerful facility has had a positive impact on the region's economic indexes.

Odesa region

Investment Rating – 2002:
position 5 (score – 0.324)

Previous Ratings:	2001 – position 5
	2000 – position 7
	1999 – position 6
Dynamic Rating:	2002 – position 1
	2001 – position 13

Web site: www.odessa.gov.ua
Population: 2,448,000 (5.1 per cent of Ukraine's population), urban – 65.9 per cent, rural – 34.1 per cent.
Unemployment rate: 1.4 per cent (Ukraine's average is 3.8 per cent)
Average monthly wages: UAH379.36 (Ukraine's average UAH376.38)
Regional GDP (2001): UAH9.5 bn (5.2 per cent of total GDP)
Regional GDP per capita (2001): UAH3.8 thousand (Ukraine's average: UAH3.8 thousand)
Export: $1,478.7 million (7.6 per cent of total Ukrainian exports)
Import: $809.9 million (7.1 per cent of total Ukrainian imports)
FDI as of 1 Jan. 2003: $289.3 million (5.4 per cent of total FDI in Ukraine)
Net FDI inflow in 2002: $53.6 million (6.8 per cent of total FDI inflow in Ukraine)

Partial ratings in groups of indexes (2002)

Group of indexes	Score	Place
Economic development	0.374	6
Market infrastructure	0.273	6
Financial infrastructure	0.184	6
Human resources	0.448	8
Business enterprises and authorities	0.388	3

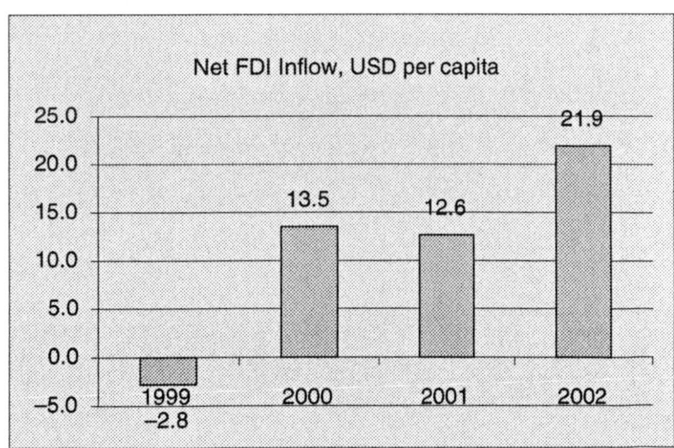

Figure 5.5.1 Odesa region

Economic development

Demonstrating high development rates are the 'heavyweights' of the Odesa regional economy: trade, food catering and service businesses. Industrial trade outputs rose 7.6 per cent to close at UAH4.4 million. Positive dynamics in the industrial sector continued into the first quarter (+18.1 per cent).

The region's foreign trade turnover (merchandise and services) in the first quarter of 2003 amounted to USD575.4 million, rising 19.2 per cent compared to the same period of the previous year. At the same time exports rose by 17.3 per cent and imports by 21.7 per cent, to close at USD329.6 million and USD245.8 million respectively.

In the TOP 100 ranking of 'Invest Gazeta' a great many companies from Odesa are represented. Odesa port plant occupies 21st position for amount of exports (USD122 million) and 80th for imports (USD21.7 million). Odesa NPZ, which belongs to the company 'Lukoil', is placed 87th for the scope of its exports (USD34 million). Moreover, Odesa Cognac Plant holds 7th place among enterprises in the alcohol sector for its level of GDP. The port 'Pivdenny' occupies 40th place for level of income.

The region's economic situation is determined predominantly by its transport infrastructure. Transportation outputs processed at the seaports of Odesa oblast in 2002 rose 17.8 per cent compared to the previous year and amounted to 74.8 million tons. Transit goods outputs rose 7.5 per cent compared to the previous year and closed at 39.4 per cent of the total commodity turnover.

Investments

As of the beginning of 2003, the region's investment widened to a record USD289.3 million in direct foreign investments. The increase in investment in 2002 was USD53.6 million. Foreign investments in Odesa oblast averaged USD118 per capita, which is a little higher than the overall Ukrainian average. As of 1 April 2003, foreign direct investments brought the total for the year to USD299.9 million. Between January and March 2003 enterprises of the region received USD10 million in direct investments.

Odesa continues with the implementation of a large-scale project: construction of the USD35 million transfer complex for liquefied natural gas. The project is implemented by the Close Corporation 'Synthes Oil', the US corporation 'Chevron' and the Kazakh joint venture 'TengizShevrOil'.

Leaders in direct investment in the region are the British Virgin Islands with USD65.7 million, the US with USD50.1 million, Cyprus with USD29.9 million, the UK with USD22.7 million etc.

The most attractive areas for foreign investors are trade and catering (23.2 per cent), transportation (18.6 per cent), petroleum refining (15.3 per cent), food industry (11 per cent) and real estate (7.8 per cent).

The issue of attracting investments into Odesa municipality is dogged by the city's notorious 'credit history'. A municipal loan borrowed by Odesa City Council back in 1997 has not yet been repaid. It is for this reason that the European Bank for Reconstruction and Development (EBRD) refused to allocate a credit to Odesa City Council, which the latter planned to use for reconstruction of the municipal heat supply system.

Special modes for investments

As of 1 January 2003, in the network of investment project implementation, actually assimilated investments amounted to USD8,516.2 thousand or 17.1 per cent of the total investment inflow. At the same time USD5,662.3 thousand worth of investments were assimilated in 2002, which amounts to 34.2 per cent of the total investment inflow in 2001. A Special Economic Zone (SEZ) has functioned in the region for a mere two years so far, which does not allow any particular conclusions as to the effectiveness of SEZ status or any significant outcomes at this point.

Project implementation of radio-electronic equipment production and container terminal construction was launched on the territory of SEZ 'Porto-Franko' in 2002. The construction budgets of these projects amount to USD19.4976 million, the share of foreign investments being 34.5 per cent (USD6.7 million).

Three projects have been implemented on the territory of SEZ 'Reni' in 2002: 'Complex for loading, conservation and unloading of petroleum gases' (Limited Partnership 'Laguna–Reni'), 'Reconstruction of the currently operating coal-tar pitch reloading complex in Reni Port'

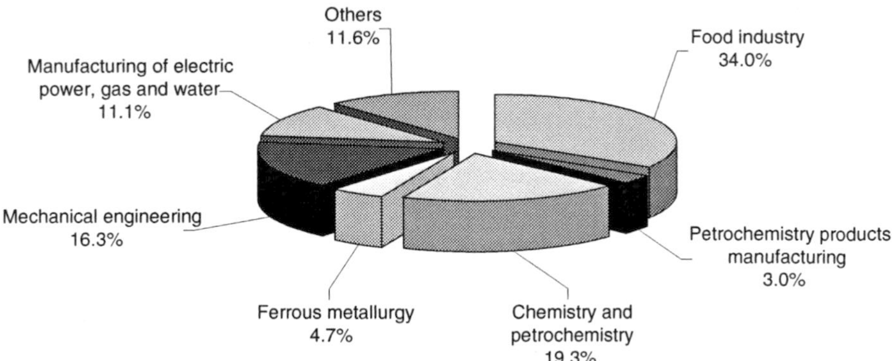

Figure 5.5.2 Industrial production in Odesa region in 2002

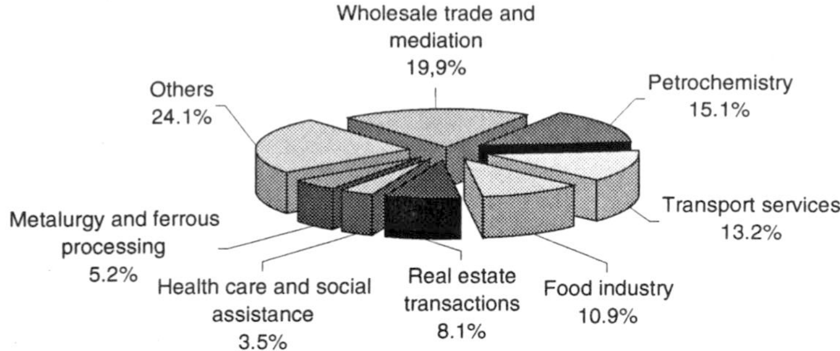

Figure 5.5.3 Industry structure of foreign direct investments in Odesa region in 2002

(State Enterprise 'Ukrchem'), and 'Grain transhipment and mixed fodder production complex' (Limited Partnership 'Reni–Line').

Zaporizhya region

Structural export diversification, ie increase of output supply of a high refining level and high-technology products, has become one of the region's major achievements in recent years. According to the World Bank, Zaporizhya region occupies quite a high place in terms of basic figures for scientific and technological development. This prerequisite is a good foundation for reorienting priorities in the area of international cooperation, switching from export of raw materials to export of integrated high-technology products and innovative technology.

Zaporizhya region, being No. 6 in the 2002 Investment Rating, is a member of the leading group and has not relinquished its position since 2001. The region occupies 19th position in the Dynamic Rating (2001 – 12th position).

Economic development

Practically all the major industrial realms are concentrated in the region. Leading roles are taken by the power industry, metal manufacture, the engineering industry, metalworking and the chemical industry. Industrial production in the first quarter of 2003 rose to UAH4.3 billion or 15.5 per cent compared to the 2002 index. The region, ranking third in overall industrial production outputs, is Ukraine's leader in the same index per capita. The most significant contribution to the efficiency of the industrial complex was made by metal manufacture and metalworking enterprises (their share of total industrial production output is 43.7 per cent).

Zaporizhya region

Investment Rating – 2002:
position 6 (score – 0.310)

Previous Ratings: 2001 – position 6
2000 – position 5
1999 – position 8
Dynamic Rating: 2002 – position 19
2001 – position 12

Web site: www.oda.zp.ua
Population: 1,907,000 (4 per cent of Ukraine's population), urban – 75.7 per cent, rural – 24.3 per cent
Unemployment rate: 3.4 per cent (Ukraine's average is 3.8 per cent)
Average monthly wages: UAH444.97 (Ukraine's average UAH376.38)
Regional GDP (2001): UAH7.9 billion (4.3 per cent of total GDP)
Regional GDP per capita (2001): UAH4.1 thousand (Ukraine's average: UAH3.8 thousand)
Export: $1392 million (7.2 per cent of total Ukrainian exports)
Import: $500 million (4.4 per cent of total Ukrainian imports)
FDI as of 1 Jan. 2003: $362 million (6.8 per cent of total FDI in Ukraine)
Net FDI inflow in 2002: $55 million (7.0 per cent of total FDI inflow in Ukraine)

Partial ratings in groups of indexes (2002)

Group of indexes	Score	Place
Economic development	0.408	3
Market infrastructure	0.258	8
Financial infrastructure	0.198	5
Human resources	0.435	11
Business enterprises and authorities	0.249	13

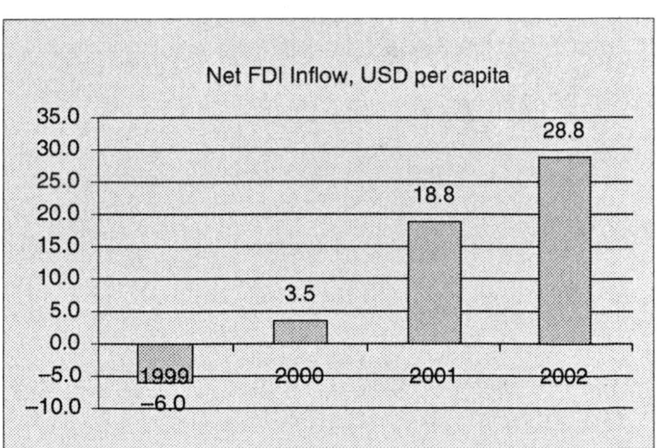

Figure 5.5.4 Zaporizhya region

The powerful industrial potential of the region is proved by the high positions of some enterprises. 'Zaporizhstal' is present in the TOP 100 ranking of 'Invest Gazeta' in all nominations and occupies fourth position for level of capitalization (UAH726 million) and of exports (USD460 million). 'Zaporizhyaoblenergo' is fifth for level of capitalization (UAH40 million) while in 2001 it was only in 48th place. Zaporizhya plant for ferroalloys occupies 34th position for amount of exports (USD92 million). The enterprise 'Motor-Sich' is present in all five nominations of the ranking, with its highest result for level of income – 21st position (UAH108.6 million).

There are more than 160 large industrial enterprises in the region. The region's metal manufacturers are represented by such internationally known enterprises of ferrous and non-ferrous metallurgy as 'Zaporizhstal', 'Dniprospecstal', 'Zaporizhya Aluminium Industrial Complex' (the only aluminium manufacturer in Ukraine), 'Titanic and Magnesium Industrial Complex' (the only titanic manufacturer in Ukraine) etc.

Another well-known joint venture, 'AutoZAZ-DAEWOO', whose cooperation with Daewoo corporation turned out to be unsuccessful, launched the assembly of leading European car brands, ie Mercedes and Opel.

With 2000 hectares of arable land, Zaporizhya is a region of considerable agricultural capacity. The region's farming industry has been making profits for three successive years now. The level of profitability here in 2001 was 12.8 per cent (third position in Ukraine), in 2002 it was 7.9 per cent (fourth position), Ukraine's average for 2002 being 1.9 per cent. Within the past two years more than 70 per cent of the agricultural enterprises in the region have been making net profits.

Foreign trade turnover in the first quarter of 2003 widened to USD474.5 million (5.2 per cent of Ukraine's foreign trade turnover). The region occupies fourth position in exports and ninth in imports (7.3 and 2.9 per cent of Ukraine's overall capacity respectively). At the same time, exports of goods rose to USD350.1 million (73.8 per cent of total turnover) and imports amounted to USD124.4 million (26.2 per cent). The positive balance of foreign trade amounted to USD225.7 million.

Investments

As of 1 April 2003, the total amount of foreign investments into the region's economy widened to USD386.64 million, of which USD377.22 million are direct investments. Taking into account variations in currency exchange rates (USD1.74 million), the net increase of foreign investments in the first quarter of 2003 was USD11.42 million. The amount of direct foreign investment per capita is USD173.3 (third in Ukraine), which is higher than Ukraine's average.

Among Zaporizhya region's enterprises that work with foreign capital the most successful are Close Corporation 'IVECO – Motor-Sich', the co-founder of which is the Italian company 'IVECO' (amount of investments – USD8.1 million), Public Corporation 'Beer and non-alcoholic industrial complex "Slavutich"' (investments of the Swedish company BBH – USD20 million), and Close Corporation 'Zaporizhya Iron Ore Industrial Complex' (USD20.6 million worth of investments by the Slovak firm 'MINERFIN').

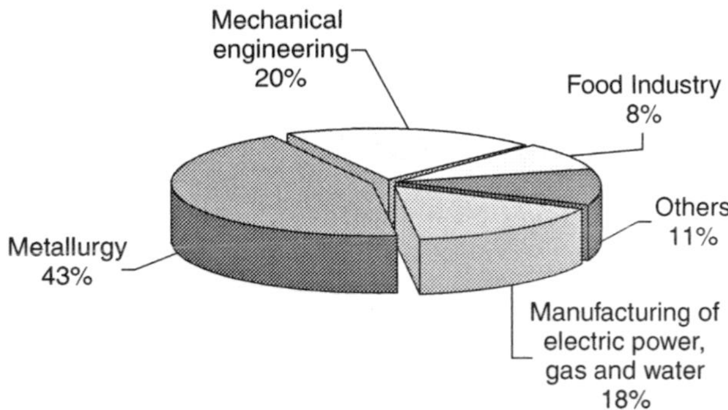

Figure 5.5.5 Industrial production in Zaporizhya region in January–October 2002

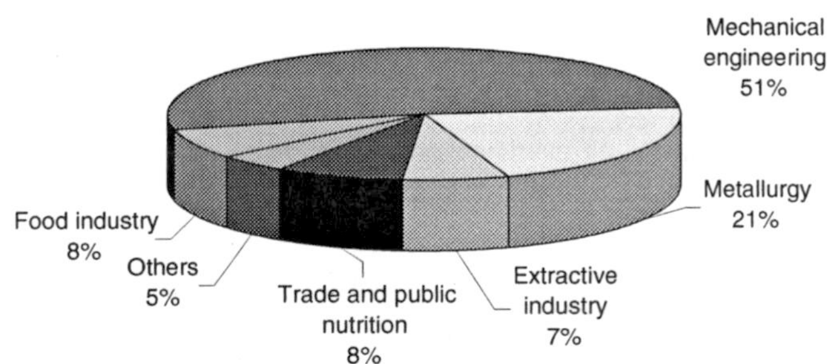

Figure 5.5.6 Industry structure of FDI in Zaporizhya region in January–October 2002

L'viv region

L'viv region is the only representative of western Ukraine among the leaders of the Investment Rating. Throughout 2001–02 the region remained firmly fixed at position 7 of the rating list. In the Dynamic Rating the region climbed to position 8, up from 16th in 2001.

L'viv region

Investment Rating – 2002:
position 7 (score – 0.309)

Previous Ratings:	2001 – position 7
	2000 – position 6
	1999 – position 4
Dynamic Rating:	2002 – position 8
	2001 – position 16

Web site: www.loda.gov.ua
Population: 2,611,000
(5.4 per cent of Ukraine's population),
urban – 60 per cent, rural – 40 per cent.
Unemployment rate: 4.1 per cent
(Ukraine's average is 3.8 per cent)
Average monthly wages: UAH339.31
(Ukraine's average UAH376.38)
Regional GDP (2001): UAH7.3 billion
(4 per cent of total GDP)
Regional GDP per capita (2001): UAH2.768
thousand (Ukraine's average: UAH3.8 thousand)
Export: $473.9 million (2.4 per cent of total
Ukrainian exports)
Import: $528.7 million (4.6 per cent of total
Ukrainian imports)
FDI as of 1 Jan. 2003: $220.3 million
(4.1 per cent of total FDI in Ukraine)
Net FDI inflow in 2002: $60.6 million
(7.7 per cent of total FDI inflow in Ukraine)

Partial ratings in groups of indexes (2002)

Group of indexes	Score	Place
Economic development	0.310	9
Market infrastructure	0.352	5
Financial infrastructure	0.160	11
Human resources	0.467	5
Business enterprises and authorities	0.281	9

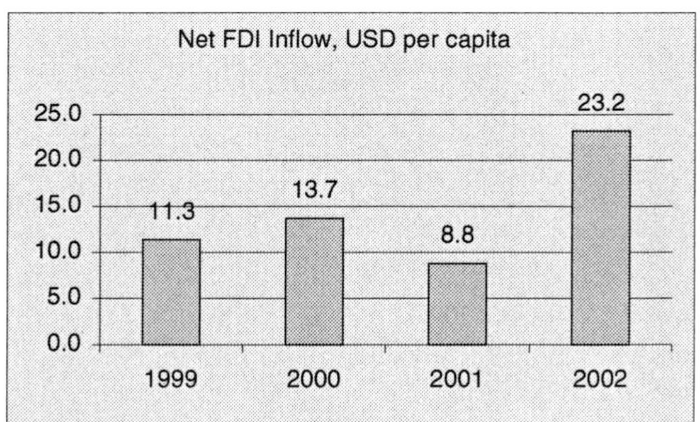

Figure 5.5.7 L'viv region

Border region status is one of the reasons for the increase in investment inflow. EU enlargement strengthens trans-boundary co-operation. One of the region's biggest partners is Poland. A bright example to illustrate bilateral cooperation is the work of 'Credit-Bank' (Ukraine) and its Polish investor Kredyt Bank SA. With Polish experience and powerful investments the Bank is pursuing an aggressive policy of extending its presence in the market for banking services.

The year 2002 was marked by a conflict in which the Regional Tax Administration was involved. The local State Tax Administration hurled accusations against two companies with foreign capital: 'Credit Bank (Ukraine)' and 'Orlan Trans'. Multiple actions at law failed to substantiate STA's accusations, but this episode turned out to have been perniciously impressive from the point of view of current and potential investors.

Economic development

In 2002 the region's industrial enterprises ended the year with USD5,498.2 million worth of output and an increase of 13.5 per cent in industrial capacity. During January 2003, the industrial enterprises of the region manufactured UAH1,416.2 million worth of output (USD267.21 million). The region's share of the overall industrial output capacity of the country is 3 per cent, ie ninth position among Ukrainian regions. Among well-known enterprises of the region are Close Corporation 'Svitoch', Petroleum Refinery 'Galychyna', 'Zhydachiv Pulp and Paper Mill', Public Corporation 'L'viv Bus Factory' and others.

In the TOP 100 ranking of 'Invest Gazeta', the L'viv company 'Himotex' occupies third place for amount of imports (USD391 million). The confectionery factory 'Svitoch' holds 46th position for amount of imports (USD33 million) and 88th position for level of income (UAH22 million).

One-fifth of the region's output is manufactured by the agricultural complex. As of 2001, the gross output of the farming industry rose 14.3 per cent.

Such strategic tasks as mobilization of funds received from taxes, fees, and other official payments are being fulfilled by the region. Mobilization of tax funds into the consolidated budget as of 1 January 2003 amounted to UAH1,707.4 million or 107.3 per cent of the volume of tax funds forecast in the current year.

Foreign investments

FDI in the region's economy as of 1 January 2003 was USD220.3 million or 4.1 per cent of Ukraine's total FDI. Investments from 99 countries were channelled into 990 enterprises of the region. L'viv region is in seventh place among the regions in terms of total investment volume.

In 2002, the volume of foreign investment jumped to USD60.6 million, which is six times more than the record of the previous year. The region has occupied third place following the city of Kyiv and Dnipropetrovsk region in terms of investment volumes attracted during 2002. The most significant investing partners of the region are Poland – with USD50.0 million worth of investments or 22.7 per cent of the total investment flow, Switzerland – USD26.6 million (12.1 per cent), the UK – USD21.0 million (9.5 per cent), Germany – USD16.0 million (7.3 per cent) and the USA – 15.9 million (7.2 per cent). The total amount of investments in the region as of 1 April 2003 was USD231 million in FDI or 4.1 per cent of the total FDI index in Ukraine. L'viv region occupies fifth place in terms of foreign investment flow during the first quarter of 2003.

One of the most important events was the Leoni AG (Germany) project to construct a wiring manufacturing factory to satisfy the needs of the world's leading car manufacturers.

Special investment modes

There are two Special Economic Zones in L'viv region: SEZ 'Yavoriv' and SEZ 'Kurortopolis Truskavets'. The total estimated price of approved investment projects is USD251.5 million.

A total of USD53million in investments was obtained by the region, of which USD23 million are foreign investments. The fact that it is a border region results in Poland being the region's biggest investor.

One of the outcomes of SEZ is a decline in unemployment in Yavoriv district from 15.4 per cent in 1999 to 4.6 per cent in 2002 and in the city of Truskavets from 5.4 per cent to 2.8 per cent. The total output of Special Economic Zones in 2002 was UAH167 million, of which UAH41 million

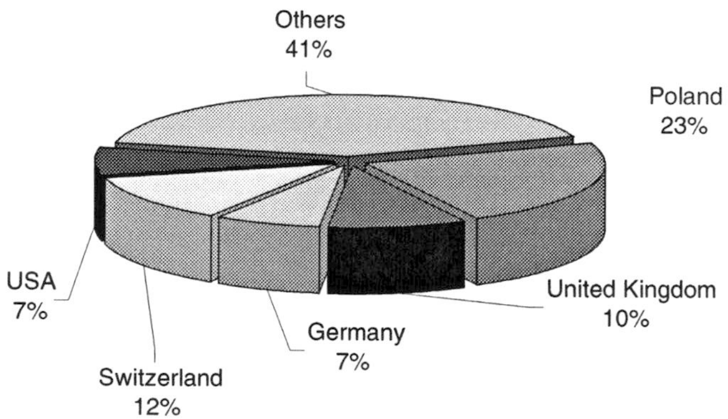

Figure 5.5.8 FDI in L'viv region in 2002

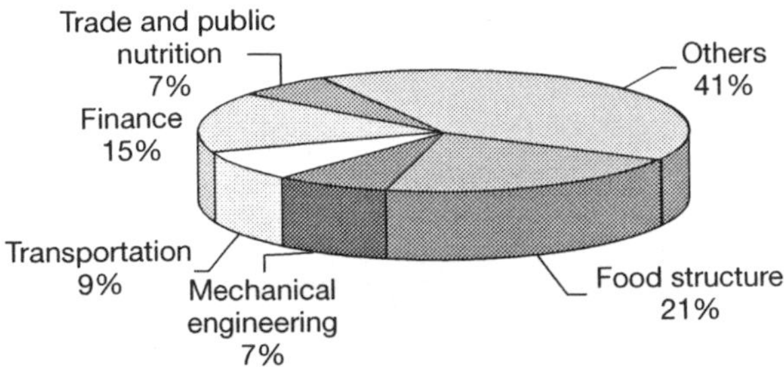

Figure 5.5.9 Industry structure of FDI in L'viv region in 2002

was goods for export (25 per cent). Furthermore, 90 per cent of the project is oriented to producing manufacture that will take the place of imported goods.

Poltava region

According to the results for 2002, Poltava region won eighth place. As a leader of the 'runners-up group', Poltava region drew level with L'viv and Zaporizhya regions, with a fair chance of leaving them behind in the next period. After all, in terms of economic development rate, the region is far ahead of its closest competitors: in Dynamic Rating Poltava region occupies an honourable fourth position, which is not typical of the upper positions in Investment Rating.

One of the last year's major events was the settlement of a conflict between the biggest Ukraine-based joint venture in the oil and gas production industry – Poltava Gas and Oil Company (British JP Kenny Exploration & Production Company) and the State Property Fund of Ukraine. The ultimate ruling was made in favour of the British investor, allowing it to acquire majority ownership. Recently, JP Kenny Exploration & Production purchased the government's shareholding, taking full control of Poltava Gas and Oil Company.

Economic development

The increase in production of the regional industrial enterprises over 2002 amounted to 37.7 per cent, which amounts to UAH8.3 billion. Positive trends in consumer goods production still continue and have risen 13.3 per cent compared to 2001, totalling UAH1.6 billion.

The region's transportation complex (apart from pipeline transportation) carried 21.0 million tons of cargo in 2002, which is 24.9 per cent more than in 2001. Gross agricultural output in all categories rose

Poltava region

Investment Rating – 2002:
position 8 (score – 0.283)

Previous Ratings: 2001 – position 10
2000 – position 10
1999 – position 10
Dynamic Rating: 2002 – position 4
2001 – position 25

Web site: www.obladmin.poltava.ua
Population: 1,609,000 (3.4 per cent of Ukraine's population), urban – 58.9 per cent, rural – 41.1 per cent.
Unemployment rate: 5 per cent (Ukraine's average is 3.8 per cent)
Average monthly wages: UAH353.7 (Ukraine's average is UAH376.38)
Regional GDP (2001): UAH6.6 bn (3.6 per cent of total GDP)
Regional GDP per capita (2001): UAH4.043 thousand (Ukraine's average: UAH3.8 thousand)
Export: $877.8 million (4.5 per cent of total Ukrainian exports)
Import: $192 million (1.7 per cent of total Ukrainian imports)
FDI as of 1 Jan. 2003: $155.9 million (2.9 per cent of total FDI in Ukraine)
Net FDI inflow for 2002: $6.3 million (0.8 per cent of total FDI inflow in Ukraine)

Partial ratings in groups of indexes (2002)

Group of indexes	Score	Place
Economic development	0.361	7
Market infrastructure	0.233	10
Financial infrastructure	0.155	12
Human resources	0.390	16
Business enterprises and authorities	0.301	5

Net FDI Inflow, USD per capita

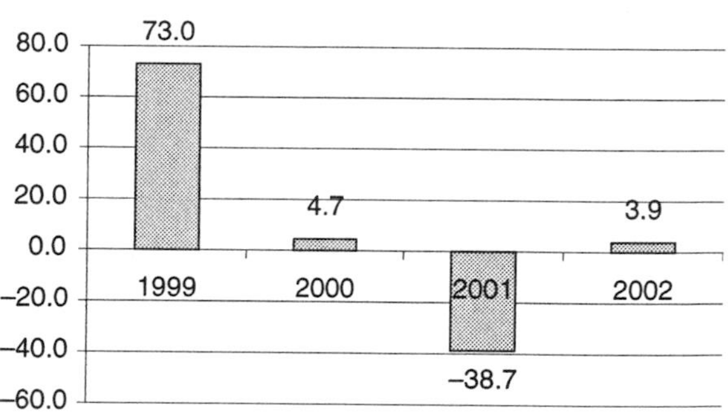

Figure 5.5.10 Poltava region

8.6 per cent (according to 2002's true market value) compared with the same period of the previous year.

In the TOP 100 ranking of 'Invest Gazeta' the companies of Poltava region occupy quite high places. The company 'Ukrtatnafta' occupies a high 13th position for amount of income for the year 2003 – UAH195.5 million. 'Poltava GOK' is in 20th place for scope of exports (USD127 million) and in 61st place for level of GDP (USD874 million), while 'Poltavaoblenergo' is in 85th position for level of GDP.

The volume of foreign trade over 2002 amounted to USD1,058.8 million (a 27.8 per cent increase). Export volumes rose 30.5 per cent, import volumes 21.1 per cent, and amounted to USD773.60 million and USD285.16 million respectively. The positive balance of foreign merchandise trade equals USD488.4 million against USD357.4 million in 2001. The biggest amounts of products and services were purchased by non-residents from the UK, the Russian Federation, Italy, Austria, Slovakia and Poland. The largest merchandise and service export inflow was to Russia, Germany, the US, Italy, Sweden and France.

Foreign investments

Over the first quarter of 2003, foreign direct investments into the region rose USD36.93 thousand. Ultimately the total FDI volume of Poltava region enterprises as of 1 April 2003 amounted to USD153.27 million or USD97 per capita.

The largest amounts were invested by Russia – USD104.2 million (68 per cent of FDI in the region). Poltava region has accordingly accumulated almost half the Russian investments in Ukraine. The rest of the investments came from non-residents of Cyprus – USD10.1 million (6.6 per cent), the Netherlands – USD9.7 million (6.3 per cent), the US – USD9.6 million (6.2 per cent), and Canada – USD4.6 million (3.0 per cent).

The most popular areas among investors are petroleum refineries (USD106.5 million of investments and 70 per cent of the total amount of investments), enterprises engaged in the food industry and the processing of agricultural produce (USD17.3 million, 11 per cent), enterprises engaged in the extractive industry (USD10.8 million; 7 per cent), and enterprises engaged in wholesale and intermediary trade (USD4.6 million, 3 per cent).

Among enterprises with foreign investments that successfully operate in the region are Kremenchug Car Assembly Plant Ltd (assembly of components and aggregates, spare parts production), JT International Ukraine Tobacco Factory, D-Star Corporation (production of diamond stone-work tools), Agrosula Close Corporation (production and processing of agricultural produce), Poltava Oil and Gas Company and Poltavcondyter Confectionery.

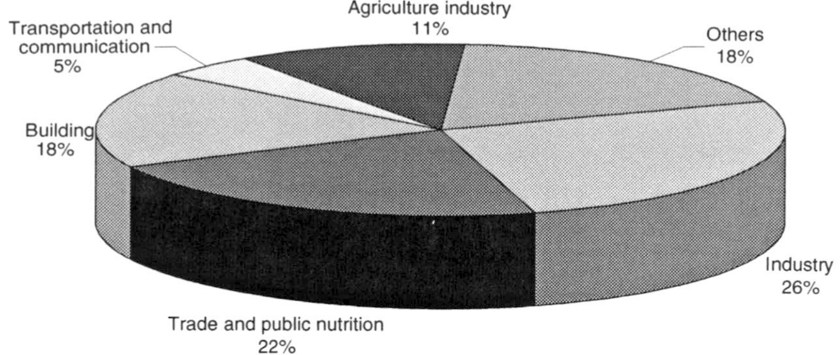

Figure 5.5.11 Industrial production structure of small enterprises in Poltava region in 2002

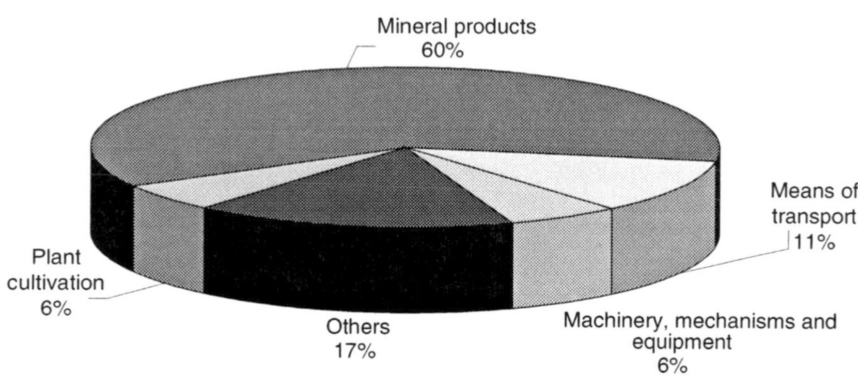

Figure 5.5.12 Poltava region exports in January–September 2002

Autonomous Republic of Crimea

The economy of the peninsular is less renowned than the Crimea's recreational capacity. However renowned, it is not being used in full, although 3–4 million holidaymakers do contribute to the region's economic confidence. The Crimea's Minister of Economy reckons that the Crimea must become a 'resort for the wealthy'. Yet although the level of prices for Crimean services even at this point is compatible with that of Bulgaria and Turkey, the service quality being way behind.

According to the results of the 2002 Investment Rating of Ukrainian regions, Crimea ranked 11, dropping from 8th position (2001). This happened because of an index decline in infrastructure and human resource development, which can be explained by the seasonal nature

AR Crimea

Investment Rating – 2002:
position 11 (score – 0.262)

Previous Ratings: 2001 – position 8
2000 – position 8
1999 – position 7
Dynamic Rating: 2002 – position 26
2001 – position 9

Web site: www.crimea-portal.gov.ua
Population: 2,018,400
(5 per cent of Ukraine's population),
urban – 62.7 per cent, rural – 37.3 per cent.
Unemployment rate: 2.3 per cent
(Ukraine's average is 3.8 per cent)
Average monthly wages: UAH358.46
(Ukraine's average UAH376.38)
Regional GDP (2001): UAH5.4 billion
(3 per cent of total GDP)
Regional GDP per capita (2001):
UAH2.691 thousand
(Ukraine's average: UAH3.8 thousand)
Export: $414 million
(2.1 per cent of total Ukrainian exports)
Import: $161.4 million
(1.4 per cent of total Ukrainian imports)
FDI as of 1 Jan. 2003: $209.6 million
(3.9 per cent of total FDI in Ukraine)
Net FDI inflow in 2002: $31.2 million
(4 per cent of total FDI inflow in Ukraine)

Partial ratings in groups of indexes (2002)

Group of indexes	Score	Place
Economic development	0.269	15
Market infrastructure	0.225	11
Financial infrastructure	0.165	8
Human resources	0.452	6
Business enterprises and authorities	0.300	6

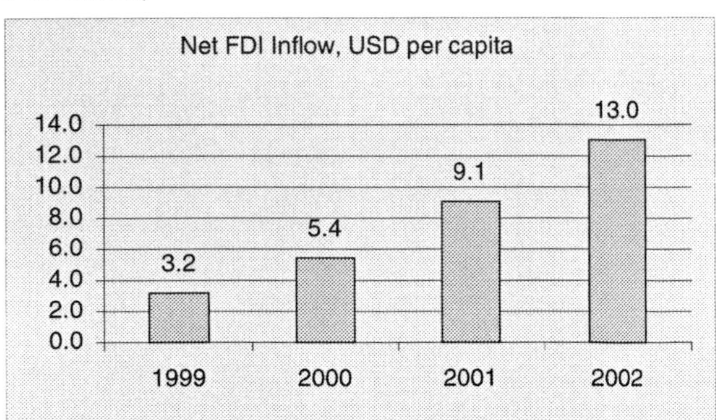

Figure 5.5.13 AR Crimea

of economic development. But for Crimea's economic development index and corresponding 15th place, the majority of group indexes position the Crimea among the top 10 regions.

Economic development

In terms of economic structure Crimea can be referred to as an agricultural and industrial region, yet one of Ukraine's most powerful southern regions. Thus, in the account of regional GDP weight, Crimea was the second among southern regions in 2000. The Republic's GDP structure looks like this: industry – 19.8 per cent, agriculture – 19.8 per cent, transport and communications – 14.2 per cent.

Region's industrial annual output in 2002 was UAH2,505.4 million. Located in Crimea are the biggest chemical enterprises which have a monopoly (more than 90 per cent of market share) both in Ukraine and in the CIS: State Stock Company 'Titan' and 'Crimean Soda Factory'. They are also the region's biggest exporters. These industry giants (however geographically separated from seaside resorts) somewhat overshadow the Crimea's recreational profile.

In the TOP 100 ranking of 'Invest Gazeta' the company 'Krymenergo' occupies ninth position for level of capitalization (UAH352 million). The company 'Chornomornaftogaz' is 29th for level of income – UAH63 million. The company 'Soyuz-Viktan' holds 69th position for amount of exports (USD42 million).

The trend of increasing retail turnover secured in the field of commerce was successfully strengthened by a record UAH1,524.4 million in 2002, ie a 28 per cent increase compared to 2001. According to these indexes the Republic is the second in Ukraine. With good indexes of agricultural development, Crimea is famous for its trademarks 'Masandra' and 'Soyuz-Victan'.

Investments

Crimea, ranking 8, is among the top 10 regions that are most active in obtaining new investments. As of 1 April 2003, USD204.3 million was invested in Crimea's economy. Fifty per cent of this amount was invested in the recreational complex. Investments in Crimea's economy in 2002 amounted to USD31.2 million, almost doubling the amount of the previous year. The overall share of direct foreign investments is 3.9 per cent.

Hiking and tourist resources as well as a particular recreational infrastructure provide opportunities to develop extreme kinds of tourism.

Special modes for investment

Several Special Economic Zones and Territories for Priority Development (TPD) have been functioning in Crimea since 2000. Crimea's TPD are 'Velyka Yalta', 'Alushta', 'Sudak', 'Feodisia', 'Sivash' (cities of Krasnoperekopsk, Armiansk and Krasnoperekopsk districts), 'Kertch' and 'Eastern Crimea'. The localization of these 'special territories' leads to the conclusion that these sites are on the threshold of an investing boom, which is partly hindered by the season-based economic activity of these territories.

Forty-nine investment projects with a total value of USD275.7 million were approved as of 5 May 2003. The special territory-based enterprises received USD83.4 million in investments (30 per cent of the total value of investment projects). Practically USD30.9 million in investments was obtained in 2002.

In terms of the number and value of approved projects, the leaders are the TPDs of 'Velyka Yalta', 'Sivash' and 'Alushta'. Twenty-nine projects with a total value of USD180.1 million were approved at the territories for priority development (ie 68 per cent of the overall project value at the Republic's TPDs and SEZ 'Crimea Port'). The TPDs of 'Kertch', 'Eastern Crimea', 'Feodosia' and 'Sudak' are resort oriented. TPD 'Kertch' is focused on the fishing and transport industries, TPD 'Sivash' on agriculture and the chemical industry. Among the largest investment projects are the reconstruction of the hotel complex 'Oreanda' – USD31.1 million; productive capacity reconstruction and technological improvement at SSC 'Titan' – USD25.5 million; construction and maintenance of the resort and recreational complex 'Almond Grove' – USD20 million.

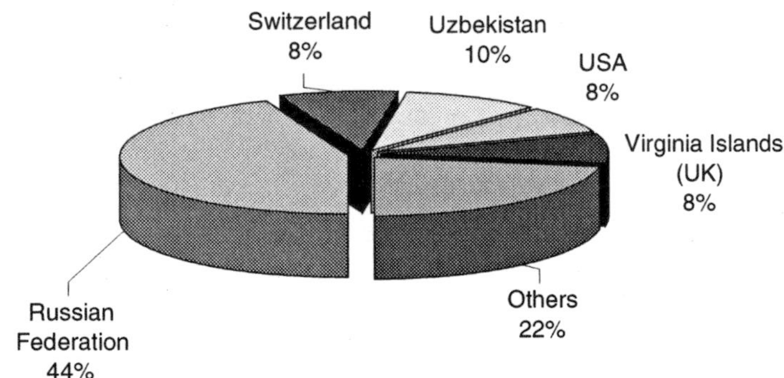

Figure 5.5.14 Foreign direct investments in Crimea region in 2002

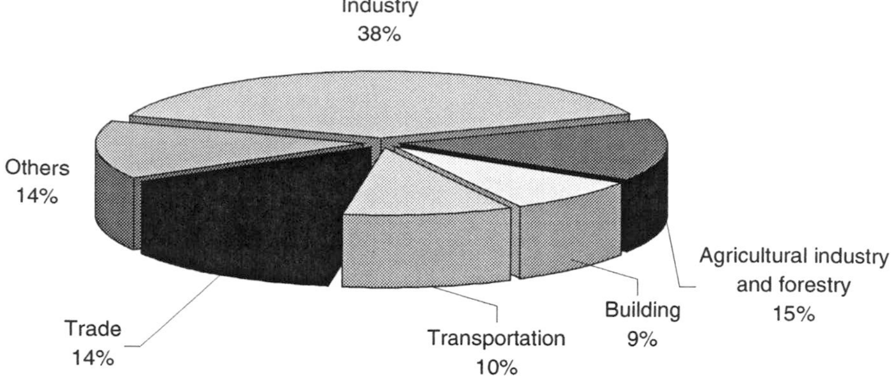

Figure 5.5.15 Industrial and services production in Crimea region in 2002

Vinnycya region

The region has lately demonstrated positive trends in Investment Rating: in 2001–02 the region managed to climb from position 15 to position 12 (in 2002), ie the region's highest record in the annual ratings. The region has also improved its standing in the records in terms of the 'infrastructure development' and 'human resources' index. In Dynamic Rating the region ranks 15th, up from 19th in 2001. However, the ratio of the rating score and FDI level shows that the region is not utilizing its current potential to the full.

The region's geographical location, however favourable, is not being fully exploited: 202 kilometres of the Ukraine–Moldova frontier and borders with seven regions of Ukraine are sufficiently favourable conditions for the region's economic development.

The territory of the region hosts the strategic oil pipelines 'Druzhba' and 'Urengoy–Pomary–Uzhgorod'. In addition, the region is intersected by the Ukrainian autobahn Kyiv–Odesa, which is likely to be reconstructed and so create opportunities for concomitant infrastructure development of the region. In the future the region will also host transport corridors: Lisbon–Neapol–Budapest–Kyiv and Warsaw–Odesa.

Economic development

The region's economic development in 2002 entailed a 4 per cent increase in industrial output, a 20.3 per cent increase in wages, and a decline in unemployment. In terms of increase in industrial output the region ranked 18th in Ukraine.

Vinnycya region

Investment Rating – 2002:
position 12 (score – 0.253)

Previous Ratings: 2001 – position 15
2000 – position 19
1999 – position 20
Dynamic Rating: 2002 – position 15
2001 – position 19

Web site: www.vin.gov.ua
Population: 1,754,000 (3.7 per cent of Ukraine's population), urban – 46.6 per cent, rural – 53.4 per cent.
Unemployment rate: 4.4 per cent (Ukraine's average is 3.8 per cent)
Average monthly wages: UAH265.36 (Ukraine's average UAH376.38)
Regional GDP (2001): UAH5 billion (2.7 per cent of total GDP)
Regional GDP per capita (2001): UAH2.812 thousand (Ukraine's average: UAH3.8 thousand)
Export: $252.3 million (1.3 per cent of total Ukrainian exports)
Import: $151 million (1.3 per cent of total Ukrainian imports)
FDI as of 1 Jan. 2003: $38.4 million (0.7 per cent of total FDI in Ukraine)
Net FDI inflow in 2002: $11 million (1.4 per cent of total FDI inflow in Ukraine)

Partial ratings in groups of indexes (2002)

Group of indexes	Score	Place
Economic development	0.256	17
Market infrastructure	0.269	7
Financial infrastructure	0.108	19
Human resources	0.445	9
Business enterprises and authorities	0.243	15

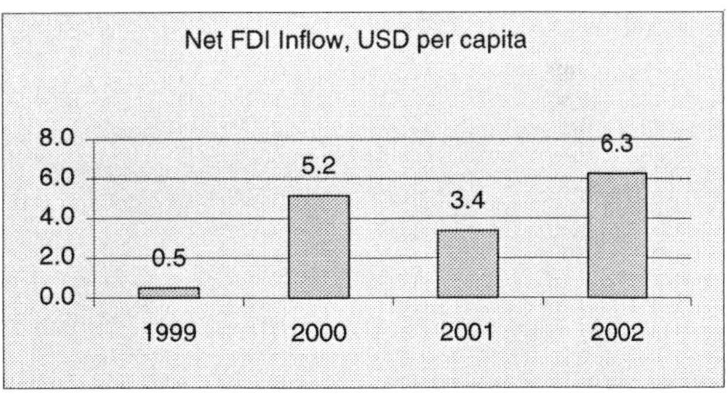

Figure 5.5.16 Vinnycya region

The company 'Enzym' (in the town of Ladyzhyn, Vinnycya region) occupies 74th position for level of income (UAH26 million) in the TOP 100 ranking of 'Invest Gazeta'.

The food industry, with 52 per cent of the overall industrial output capacity, demonstrates the highest growth rate. The region has a distinct agricultural orientation and thus hosts a lot of reprocessing facilities. With over 30 sugar-refineries, the region is shaping the country's 'sugar image'. Economic results for the year were positively influenced by the progress in the agricultural complex, where specific crops of grain rose 8.5 per cent and sugar-beet 8.3 per cent.

'Nemiroff' company is considered to be one of the region's most active business structures. The outcome of the company's aggressive marketing policy both in home and foreign markets was that current international recognition of the trademark is greater than that of Ukraine as a country.

Investments

Foreign investors have directly invested USD38.4 million in the economy of the region as of 1 January 2003. The amount of investment per capita is USD21.6.

Investments were received from 28 countries. The highest amounts were invested by Austria – USD14 million (36.5 per cent of total amount), Czech Republic – USD6.6 million (17.3 per cent), the United Kingdom – USD3 million (7.9 per cent), and Spain – USD2.5 million (6.4 per cent).

The highest amounts of investments – USD29.8 million (77.6 per cent) – was channelled into the processing industry, USD18.8 million (49.0 per cent) into the food industry and reprocessing of agricultural

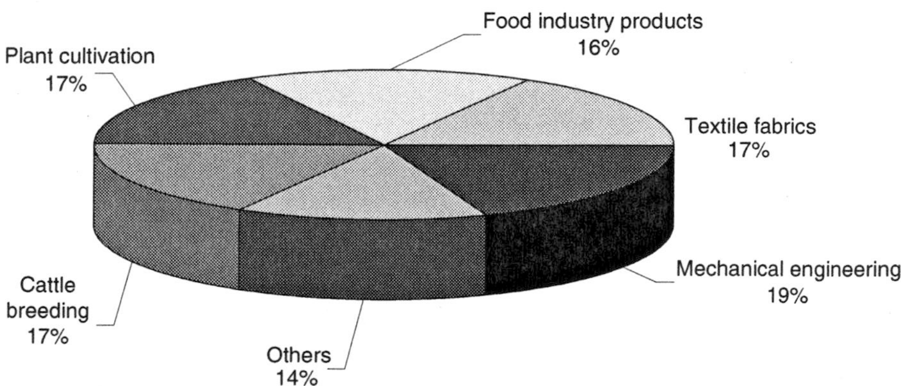

Figure 5.5.17 Vinnycya region exports in 2002

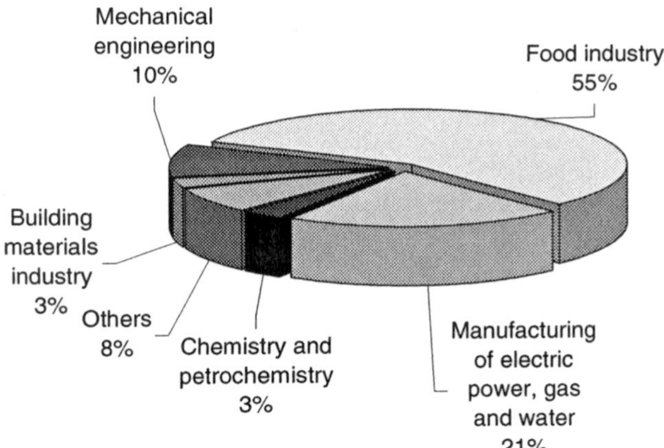

Figure 5.5.18 Industrial production in Vinnycya region in 2002

produce, USD9.3 million (24.1 per cent) into the chemical industry and USD0.6 million (1.6 per cent) into light industry.

The highest investments were obtained by 'Akvaplast' Ltd (City of Nemiriv – plastic products manufacture), 'Podillya-OBST' enterprise – reprocessing of agricultural produce and production of foodstuffs, and Public Corporation 'Vinnicya Confectionery' – production of confectionery.

Lugansk region

Lugansk, being the most eastern region, is called the 'dawn' of Ukraine. The region was ranked 13th in the Investment Rating (12th in 2001). The region's economic capacity, although quite substantial, is not yet being used in full. The region has become the zone of interest of more powerful neighbours (usually Donetsk). With these economic giants in the background, the region's indexes and records do not look so optimistic. In spite of powerful metal, coal and chemical enterprises functioning in the region, there is a problem with small depressed cities and territories that mostly specialize in one sort of activity, usually coal mining. Unfortunately, it is the human resource development index that consistently ranks the region among the outsiders. The region has occupied 21st position in the Dynamic Rating (2001 – 10th), which is evidence of the negative 'sustainability' of the social and economical development of the region.

Bordering on Russia's underdeveloped territories, the region does not have much advantage in terms of geographical location, while the existing transport connections are not so significant a factor for investment attractiveness.

Lugansk region

Investment Rating – 2002:
position 13 (score – 0.240)

Previous Ratings: 2001 – position 12
2000 – position 12
1999 – position 11
Dynamic Rating: 2002 – position 21
2001 – position 10

Web site: www.oda.lg.ua
Population: 2,507,000 (5.2 per cent of Ukraine's population), urban – 86.1 per cent, rural – 13.9 per cent.
Unemployment rate: 3.3 per cent (Ukraine's average is 3.8 per cent)
Average monthly wages: UAH393.32 (Ukraine's average UAH376.38)
Regional GDP (2001): UAH7.4 billion (4.1 per cent of total GDP)
Regional GDP per capita (2001): UAH2.9 thousand (Ukraine's average: UAH3.8 thousand)
Export: $1,427 million (7.4 per cent of total Ukrainian exports)
Import: $199 million (1.8 per cent of total Ukrainian imports)
FDI as of 1 Jan. 2003: $51.6 million (1.0 per cent of total FDI in Ukraine)
Net FDI inflow in 2002: $12.3 million (1.6 per cent of total FDI inflow in Ukraine)

Partial ratings in groups of indexes (2002)

Group of indexes	Score	Place
Economic development	0.248	18
Market infrastructure	0.225	9
Financial infrastructure	0.148	13
Human resources	0.348	26
Business enterprises and authorities	0.209	16

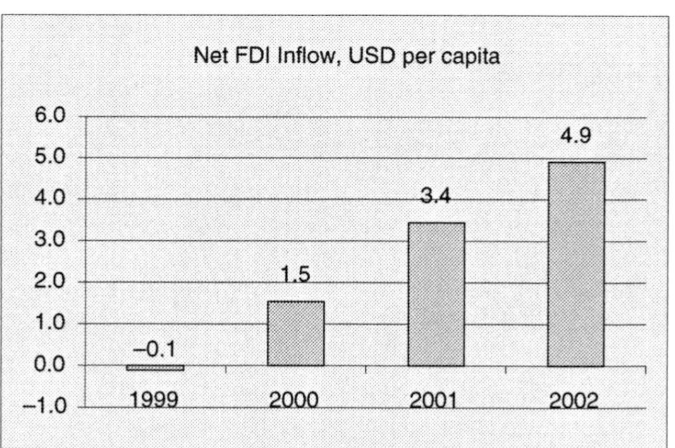

Figure 5.5.19 Lugansk region

Economic development

The output of industrial enterprises in 2002 was UAH13.3 billion, which is 104.2 per cent of the periods prior to 2001. In terms of industrial output rate, Lugansk region is ahead of regions that are similar in terms of industrial capacity, such as Zaporizhya region, and is not far behind Kharkiv, Donetsk and Dnipropetrovsk regions. The share of Lugansk region in the volume of overall industrial output has increased to 7.5 per cent from 6.4 per cent in 2001.

In the TOP 100 ranking of 'Invest Gazeta', the company 'Luganskoblenergo' occupies 19th place for level of capitalization. Severodonetsk chemical enterprise 'Azot' is listed in the ranking under four nominations (profit, income, export, import), with the highest position in import – USD36 million (42nd place).

According to the results for 2002, 51 per cent of enterprises in the region received a total of UAH641.5 million in profits. Economic growth created a basis for active incomes to the budgets of all levels, totalling UAH1.7 billion in 2002.

The region mostly specializes in light industry despite a 10 per cent decline in output in 2002 (because of low competitive capacity in competition with the cheap and low quality produce of Turkey, Poland and China).

Investments

The major sources of fixed capital investments are traditionally the own funds of enterprises and organizations (about 70 per cent). The amount of adapted capital investments in 2002 is UAH1.5 billion, of which 86 per cent are fixed capital investments.

During the first quarter of 2003, foreign investors invested USD3.3 million and the total capital of non-residents equalled USD55.1 million. In 2002 the amount of foreign money invested in the region was USD12.3 million, which is 9 per cent higher compared to 2001. The 2002 index of FDI per capita is USD20. The current level of foreign investments is not sufficient for the region's high capacity and even with territories for priority development taken into account, there is not much that can be done to improve the situation.

Special modes for investment

The region introduced a special investment mode on the territories for priority development, which now include nine cities and districts. Since that time the region's economy has obtained USD31.7 million worth of investments, including USD3.5 million in 2002 and USD0.2 million in the first quarter of 2003.

Domestic capital (92.7 per cent) is the major source of investments, with foreign investments making up the remaining 7.3 per cent; 2,330 jobs were created and 10,589 others preserved in the course of implementation of the investment project. The amount of inflow to the budgets of all levels as well as dues and fees received by various funds-in-trust was 2.8 times higher than the total amount of concessions.

The largest investment projects implemented under the special investing mode is 'Organization of Pollution-free Fuel Production' in the city of Sverdlovsk by Close Corporation 'Tenneco' (construction budget – USD10 million) and 'Geological Research of Makeyevka Condensate Pool' by 'KUB-GAS' Ltd (construction budget – USD5.2 million).

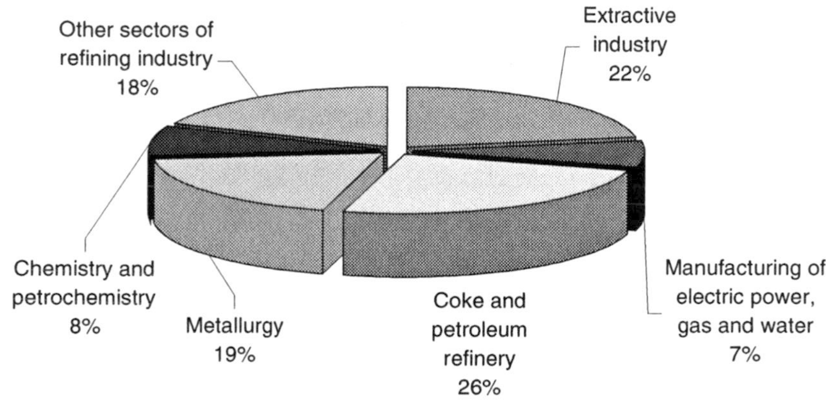

Figure 5.5.20 Industrial production in Lugansk region in 2002

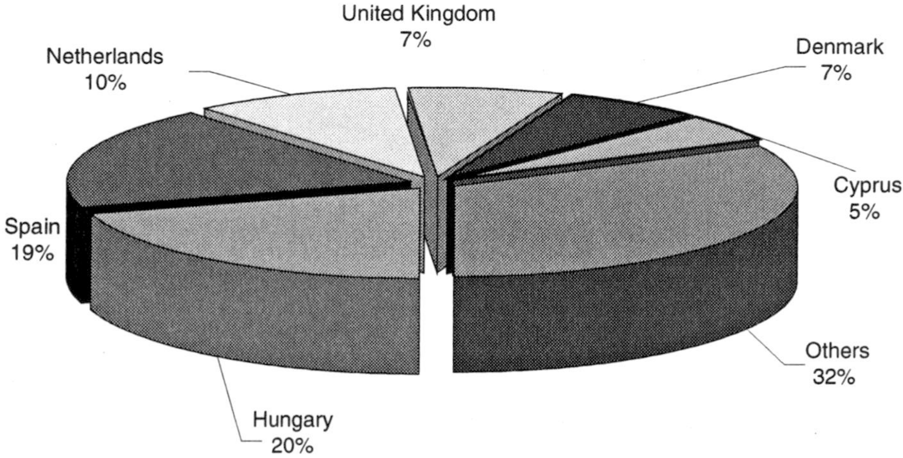

Figure 5.5.21 Foreign direct investments in Lugansk region in 2002

5.6

Ukraine's Dominant Financial-Industrial Groups

Sergiy Maslichenko, President, Ukrainian Centre for Economic and Legal Analysis (UCELA)

Introduction

Upon independence, Ukraine inherited a huge public enterprise sector, with enterprises of all sizes spanning the full range of economic activities. Privatization in Ukraine began in earnest only in 1995 and picked up considerably in 2000. Results have been uneven, both in terms of the volume of successful privatizations and the scope of enterprise restructuring that it has encouraged. Throughout this period, problems in enforcement of shareholders' and creditors' rights have led to a corporate governance model oriented towards strategic investors and financial-industrial groups (FIGs). A number of financial-industrial groups have emerged as a result of highly politicized privatization when powerful politicians and businessmen got control of enterprises and then used their influence to limit competition, to obtain favourable finance from the government, and in other ways to alter the game in their favour.

FIGs have arisen in an environment where property rights are not well established and contract enforcement is problematic. In principle, FIGs provide a mechanism by which finance providers can undertake monitoring, enforce payment systems, and enforce contracts without the need to go to court.

Moreover, in the absence of developed capital markets, finance generated internally to the group can also be used for investment. Indeed, in Ukraine the actual role of external finance is less clear than in developed countries because of the weaknesses in investor protection, rules of law, enforcement and transparency. Here, internal finance is more important and business groups play a crucial role: a group, by channelling resources between its firms, relaxes the financial liquidity constraint at the firm level. This mechanism is enhanced if the group contains a bank, as is often the case.

However, FIGs engender conflicts of interests, and thus facilitate rent-seeking behaviour and corruption. The composition of the directors' boards of these groups, for example, reflects less commercial principles and more a system of personal affiliation. There is extensive cross-ownership of shares across FIGs, creating a complex web of interlocking directorates with unclear lines of authority. In addition, these groups have established a system for the provision and allocation of internally provided credit to control the activities of members, rather than rely on other (external) sources of credit that would serve an important due diligence and financial control function. It is also fairly common practice for FIGs to have access to the management of state shareholdings through trust management arrangements.

Privatization experience in Ukraine

One of the major factors that contributed to the FIGs' evolvement was the nature of the privatization process in Ukraine. Compared with other transition countries, Ukraine has lagged behind in privatization. In 1992–94 a significant number of large enterprises were privatized by lease-buyouts, at very low prices, to the employees and managers. During 1995–98, the government embarked on a mass privatization programme, under which a total of 9,240 LMEs (about 50 per cent of the total) were privatized[1] through auctions for privatization certificates[2] (Elborgh-Woytek and Lewis, 2002). An estimated 35 per cent of Ukraine's citizens have become shareholders through the mass privatization programme (PWC, 1998).

This complex and highly politicized process achieved some results. By 1997, the EBRD (1998) estimated the share of the private sector in Ukraine to be around 55 per cent, up from 10 per cent in 1991 and only 30 per cent at the start of mass privatization in 1994. By the end of 1997, just over 40,000 (about 90 per cent of the total) small-scale enterprises and 11,591 (65 per cent of the total) LMEs had been privatized (Estrin and Rosevear, 1999). However, the enterprises that were privatized through certificate privatization were large in number, but

[1] Definition of 'privatized' has been accepted to mean that 70 per cent or more of a company's shares are owned by the private sector.

[2] Each Ukrainian citizen received one non-tradable and indivisible certificate free of charge.

often small in value.

In 1998, the Ukrainian government moved to case-by-case privatization and shifted its emphasis to the maximization of state revenue through cash privatization of LMEs via tenders and stock exchanges, while remaining reluctant to offer significant shares of attractive enterprises. During 1998–99 the State Property Fund of Ukraine (SPFU) offered for tender both blocking (25 per cent + 1) and majority (50 per cent + 1) stakes in large enterprises. Among the biggest sales were 44 per cent of the holding company 'Ukrnaftoproduct' (UAH15.2 million), 15 per cent of the JSC 'Alchevsk metallurgical plant' (UAH11.75 million), and 81 per cent of the JSC 'Lutsk Car Plant' (UAH10.8 million).

In 2000–02 the Ukrainian government proceeded with 'individual approach' privatization of monopolies and strategic enterprises under the new Privatization Programme for 2000–02 adopted by parliament. As a result, during this period 298 LMEs were privatized and UAH4,783.62 million (about USD887 million, 73.5 per cent of total privatization receipts since 1992) was transferred to the state budget as privatization revenues. The largest enterprises that were privatized during 2000–02 included six electricity distribution companies (UAH865.7 million), 30 per cent of the JSC 'Mykolayiv aluminium plant' (UAH547.2 million), 68.1 per cent of the JSC 'Zaporizhia aluminium plant' (UAH380.6 million), 76 per cent of the JSC 'Khartsyzk pipe plant' (UAH126 million), 4 per cent of the JSC 'Zaporizhstal' (UAH91.1 million), 81.6 per cent of the automobile plant 'AvtoZAZ' (UAH54.2 million) and 67 per cent of the JSC 'Lysychansk Refinery' (UAH53.1 million).

According to the SPFU 'Privatization Programme for 2003–08' (not adopted by parliament), privatization in Ukraine is to be completed by 2008. Apart from the large-scale enterprises not privatized during recent years (the state telecommunication monopoly 'Ukrtelecom', 12 electricity distribution companies, the state iron-mining monopoly 'Ukrrudprom' etc), the SPFU intends to privatize large state enterprises (about 1,000) that were previously prohibited for privatization owing to their strategic and security importance for Ukraine's economy. These sectors include the military complex, aircraft, coalmines, railways, shipbuilding, the electricity complex (both power generation and distribution), oil and gas enterprises, and the state monopoly 'Khlib Ukrainy' (Bread of Ukraine).

Apart from the large-scale nature of privatization, FIGs have emerged as a result of Ukraine's industry features inherited from the former Soviet Union. The industry of today's Ukraine has been formed by the allocation of productive capacities according to the Soviet government's plans and the distribution of natural resources. Ukraine has inherited high-concentrated primary industry mostly in the east and light industry in the west. Moreover, eastern Ukraine was divided into regions of specialization – metallurgy, coalmines, iron ore mines etc, which were attached to certain administrative districts. As a result, such allocation of natural resources and capital has predetermined the concentrated type of Ukrainian industry. Being based in a certain administrative region and exercising close business and political contacts with local authorities, the majority of Ukraine's FIGs have emerged initially at regional level.

Dominant financial-industrial groups

It should be noted that there is considerable difficulty in documenting both direct and indirect control in Ukraine's financial-industrial groups. Groups often use cross-ownership and pyramiding mechanisms when a firm is controlled by another firm, which in turn may be controlled by a third entity, and so on. Besides, insider ownership is often hidden in offshore companies where the actual holders of control are difficult to identify. Financial-industrial groups have also strong business interrelations with each other that complicate their analysis. However, a certain pattern of dominant FIGs in Ukraine has been plotted having used both official (SPFU publications) and unofficial (business surveys, periodicals, articles) information.

Most analysts suggest that the following FIGs dominate in Ukraine (as for the middle of 2003):

- Donetsk Business Group;
- 'Interpipe' Business Group;
- 'Privat' Business Group;
- 'Consortium Metallurgy' Business Group;
- Russian 'Alfa Group'.

Donetsk Business Group

The largest and the most powerful financial-industrial group in Ukraine is the Donetsk business group (DBG) with an annual turnover of USD4–5 billion (Table 5.6.1).[3] It operates mostly in Donetsk oblast, which is located in south-eastern Ukraine and has a population of 5.2 million people (10.4 per cent of the overall population), producing about 20 per cent of Ukraine's industrial output. Metallurgy dominates

---

[3] For comparison, in 2001 the GDP of Ukraine was about USD37.6 billion, the revenues of the State Budget were USD10 billion.

Table 5.6.1 Donetsk Business Group

Approximate turnover	$4–5 billion
Region of activity	Donetsk, Lugansk, Zaporizhia, Dnipropetrovsk oblasts
Industry	Metallurgy, coal mining, coke production, gas and electricity distribution, machine building
Largest enterprises	Azovstal metallurgical plant, Enakievo metallurgical plant, Avdiivka coke plant, Zaporizhia coke plant ('SCM'), Alchevsk metallurgical plant, Alchevsk coke plant, Khartsyzsk pipe plant, machine building company 'Azovmash' ('ISD')
Key owners	Rinat Akhmetov, Sergey Taruta

the region, with 80 metallurgical companies producing half of the region's industrial output and exporting to 50 countries. Donetsk Business Group consists of the vertically integrated companies (VICs) that comprise the production chain 'coal–coke–cast iron–steel'.

Although there are, in fact, two huge business corporations that operate in Donetsk oblast, 'System Capital Management' (SCM) and 'Industrialnyi Soyuz Donbassa' (ISD) (Industrial Union of Donbass), both companies jointly own some large enterprises and coordinate their activity in the region.

The main features of Donetsk Business Group are as follows. DBG's industry profile is metallurgy, the energy sector, and machine building. Such specialization has been caused by its historically formed industry location in the former USSR with a concentration of metallurgical plants inside the Donbass coal basin.

DBG recognizes the importance of international standards of doing business and tries to follow them. For example, 'SCM' initiated several tenders to attract international consulting companies (AT Kearney, Deloitte & Touche, Ernst & Young, KPMG and PricewaterhouseCoopers) and employed top managers from the Big 4. 'ISD' has a good business reputation with Western banks and implements the European Commission tender for gas supply to Ukrainian energy companies. 'ISD' also participated in the privatization of the large Polish metallurgical plant 'Huty Stali Czestochowa'.

DBG has built a positive reputation by not participating in the widespread privatization scandals. As a result, until recently DBG has been perceived by society as a regional business group that operates in the Donetsk oblast and does not participate in political processes at the national level. However, last year appointments of Donetsk oblast representatives to the Ukrainian Cabinet of Ministers strengthened DBG's political power at national level.

'Interpipe' Business Group

Dnipropetrovsk oblast is the second-largest industrial region, producing about 15 per cent of Ukraine's industrial output. There are two dominant financial-industrial groups in the region – the 'Interpipe' Group and the 'Privat' Group.

The main features of 'Interpipe' Group are as follows (Table 5.6.2). 'Interpipe' Group is the largest producer of pipes in Ukraine. Its monopoly on the production of large-diameter pipes, which are mostly consumed by the Russian oil and gas industry, allows the Group to gain extra profits from the export of pipes.

'Interpipe' Group is building business in a transparent way in order to raise external finance and expand its foreign trade. The Group's close business contacts with Russian partners, in particular with 'Alfa Group', allow them to attract highly qualified top managers from Russia. For example, the former chief executive of 'Interpipe' Group, Evgeniy Bernshtam, and other senior managers were previously employed by 'Alfa Bank'.

'Interpipe' Group has significant political influence in Ukraine through its strong positions in the mass media. It controls a nation-wide newspaper '*Fakty*' and three TV channels (ICTV, STB and 'Novyi Canal').

'Privat' Business Group

Another financial-industrial group that operates in the Dnipropetrovsk oblast is the 'Privat' Group, which is based on the large Ukrainian bank 'PrivatBank'. The Group owns the majority of enterprises in the iron ore industry of Ukraine. Analysts suggest that it controls the majority of iron ore mining and processing companies (Gornoobogatitelnye kompanii – GOKs)[4] and two ferroalloy plants.

Table 5.6.2 'Interprip' Business Group

Approximate turnover	$3–4 billion
Region of activity	Dnipropropetrovsk, Lugansk, Donetsk, Sumy oblasts
Industry	Metallurgy (mainly pipe production), coal mining, ferroalloy production
Largest enterprises	Nizhnedneprovskiy pipe plant, Novomoskovkiy pipe plant, Nikopolskiy pipe plant, Dneprovskiy pipe plant, Alchevskiy metallurgical plant (together with 'ISD'), Nikopolskiy ferroalloy plant
Key owners	Victor Pinchuk

[4] Ukraine's proven reserves of iron ore are 20 per cent of the world total.

The main features of 'Privat' Group are as follows (Table 5.6.3). The Group owns Ukrainian companies through offshore firms, which makes its ownership structure very complicated. 'PrivatBank' *de jure* owns neither production companies nor offshore firms; however, it controls them, as it is the financial centre of the Group. The Bank also registers the shares of controlled privatized enterprises.

By appointing loyal managers at the controlled production companies, the Group benefits from control over financial and material flows of privatized enterprises, transferring these through affiliated suppliers and consumers as well as using processing contracts.

The closed and complicated system of ownership allows the ultimate owners of the Group to avoid responsibility in regard to the performance of privatized enterprises. There is evidence that owners of privatized companies have refused to fulfil investment obligations imposed on them by privatization contracts of SPFU. As the owners are typically offshore companies, it is difficult to enforce financial obligations on them. Besides, offshore owners contribute to increased capital flows abroad.

Another important peculiarity of 'Privat' Group is the profit-stripping exercised by the Group's affiliated firms (suppliers and consumers) that makes privatized enterprises unprofitable. For example, in 2002 Dnipropetrovsk Metallurgical Plant had losses of USD9 million; 'Ordzhenikidze GOK' significantly decreased its profits, whereas its production output rose 16.8 per cent.

'Consortium Metallurgy' Business Group

Until 2002 'Consortium Metallurgy' was the fourth-largest financial-industrial group in Ukraine, owning assets of USD800 million and having a USD400 million turnover and USD80 million profit annually ('Zerkalo Nedeli') (Table 5.6.4).

The Head of the Group, Konstantin Grigorishin, played a significant role in Ukraine's energy sector. He headed Boards of Directors at

Table 5.6.3 'Privat' Business Group

Approximate turnover	US$1 billion
Region of activity	Dnipropetrovsk, Zaporizhia, Lugansk oblasts
Industry	Iron ore, ferroalloy, oil production, refineries
Largest enterprises	Marganets GOK, Ordzhenikidze GOK, 'Suhaya Balka' GOK, 'Yuznyi' GOK, Dnipropetrovsk metallurgical plant, Zaporizhia ferroalloy plant, Stakhanov ferroalloy plant, refinery 'Naftohimik Prykarpatya'
Key owners	Igor Kolomoyskiy

Table 5.6.4 'Consortium Metallurgy' Business Group

Approximate turnover	$0.4 billion
Region of activity	Majority of oblasts
Industry	Electrical energy distribution, metallurgy
Largest enterprises	Sumyoblenergo, Prikarpattyaoblenergo, Chernigivoblenergo, Poltavaoblenergo, Lvivoblenergo, Ternopiloblenergo, Zaporizhiaoblenergo, metallurgical plant 'Dneprospetsstal' (until 2002), Zaporizhia and Stakhanov Ferroalloy Plants (until 2002)
Key owners	Konstantin Grigorishin

Sumyoblenergo, Lvivoblenergo and Zaporizhe Ferroalloy Plant and was a Board member of the Metallurgical Plant 'Dneprospetsstal' and other companies. Moreover, through offshore companies he personally owned about 58 per cent of 'Dneprospetsstal' ('Investgazeta').

Mr Grigorishin has built part of his business in partnership with other Ukrainian financial-industrial groups. In particular, in 1998 the Ukrainian government delegated the governance of Zaporizhe Ferroalloy Plant, Kirovogradoblenergo, Ternopiloblenergo and Khersonoblenergo to the 'Ukrainian Credit Bank',[5] owned by the Group of G Surkis and V Medvedchuk. Apart from that, both Groups controlled Sumyoblenergo, Prikarpattyaoblenergo, Chernigovoblenergo, Poltavaoblenergo and Lvivoblenergo.

However, in 2002, after a series of political scandals, some enterprises owned by K Grigorishin (Sumyoblenergo, Lvivoblenergo, etc) were sold to other FIGs. Kirovogradoblenergo was sold to a Slovak company, which already owned 51 per cent of its shares. Stakhanov Ferroalloy Plant and Zaporizhe Ferroalloy Plant (48 per cent of shares) were sold to 'Privat' Group (see above).

Other Ukrainian FIGs

There are some other business groups in Ukraine that own a few large enterprises and operate mostly at regional level. One of them is the business group affiliated with the Ukrainian Bank 'Finance and Credit' and owned by Konstantin Zhevago (a member of the Ukrainian parliament). In 1998, two offshore companies of this Group bought 35 per cent of Odessaoblenergo and 35 per cent of Luganskoblenergo shares (the largest energy distribution companies in Ukraine).

[5] 'Ukrainian Credit Bank' already owned 25 per cent of Zaporizhe Ferroalloy Plant shares.

However, in 2000–01 the Group lost control of these enterprises and had to sell them. The 'Finance and Credit' Group owns the iron ore mining and processing plant 'Poltavskiy GOK', which is the largest exporter of iron ore in Ukraine. However, in 2002 the Group lost full control of the plant when the SPFU sold its blocking shares to another company ('Investgazeta').

The Kharkov business group 'Ukrsibbank', headed by Alexander Yaroslavskiy, owns 25 per cent of 'Ukrainian Aluminium' and also controls the Nikolaev Clay Plant. This Group is also in the process of building a new aluminium plant in Zaporizhia oblast (together with 'Russian Aluminium'). 'Ukrsibbank' owns 12 per cent of the shares of the iron ore mining and processing plant 'Severnyi GOK' and intends to buy another 36 per cent of its shares. At present (2003), 'Ukrsibbank' manages 50 per cent of the state-owned shares of 'Severnyi GOK'. It also owns some shares of the largest telecommunication company, 'Kievstar GSM'.

Russian 'Alfa Group'

The biggest and the most influential Russian business group that operates in Ukraine is 'Alfa Group'. In 1995 the investment company 'Alfa Capital Ukraine' was established to participate in privatization and to strengthen contacts with Ukrainian business groups.

At present (2003), 'Alfa Group' owns the oil-processing company 'Lisichansk NPZ'[6] (through Tumen Oil Company 'TNK'), pharmaceutical companies 'Galichpharm' and 'Zdorovye', a telecommunications company, 'Golden Telecom', and 40 per cent of another telecommunication company, 'Kyivstar GSM'. It also manages shares of the oil processing company 'Naftohimik Prikarpattya' and has jobber contracts with 918 petrol stations in Ukraine ('TNK').

Apart from that, 'Alfa Group' is a large investor in the power generation companies 'Centrenergo' and 'Dneprenergo' and in the chemical and agricultural industries of Ukraine.

The financial centre of the Group is 'Alfa Bank-Ukraine' which has established strong business contacts with a number of Ukraine's strategic enterprises such as the state oil and gas monopoly 'Neftegaz Ukrainy', the machine-building plant 'Sumskoe NPO im. Frunze', the metallurgical plant 'Dneprospetsstal' etc.

[6] Lisichansk Refinery (JSC LiNOS) is one of the biggest refineries in the former Soviet Union and Europe, with a planned capacity of 23.5 million tons a year.

Conclusion

Financial-industrial groups represent the key corporate governance structure in today's Ukrainian economy. Although, in general, FIGs hinder efficiency gains and facilitate rent-seeking behaviour, they provide an effective mechanism by which finance providers can undertake monitoring, enforce payment systems and enforce contracts. By channelling resources between their firms, FIGs relax the financial liquidity constraints at the firm level and decrease the overall transaction costs of doing business.

Apart from that, FIGs have sufficient resources for expanding their activity on international product and financial markets or for representing their interests against the antidumping campaigns initiated recently by some countries. The large capital and strong political influence of Ukrainian FIGs can guarantee profits for Western investors dealing with these groups. At the same time, there is a political risk of investment losses as Ukrainian FIGs are highly dependent on an informal network and sometimes operate in a non-transparent way. However, Ukrainian groups are moving their businesses towards Western standards and can be potential partners for Western companies doing business with Ukraine.

References

Elborgh-Woytek, Katrin and Lewis, Mark (2002) Privatization in Ukraine: challenges of assessment and coverage in Fund conditionality, Policy Discussion Paper, IMF

Estrin, Saul and Rosevear, Adam (1999) Enterprise performance and corporate governance in Ukraine, *Journal of Comparative Economics*, **27**, pp. 442–458

European Bank for Reconstruction and Development (1999) Transition Report 1999, London.

Investgazeta (1999–2003), Ukrainian newspaper, available at http://www.investgazeta.net

USAID, PricewaterhouseCoopers (1998) Final Report: Ukraine Mass Privatization Project

Zerkalo Nedeli (1999–2003), Ukrainian newspaper, available at http://www.zerkalo-nedeli.com

Part Six

Appendices

Appendix 1

Contributor Contact Details

American Chamber of Commerce
42–44 Shovkovychna Vul
LL1 Floor
Kyiv 01601
Ukraine
Tel: +380 44 490 5800
Contact: Jorge Zukoski, President
Email: jzukoski@amcham.ua
Contact: Oksana Panchuk, Dep-Director
Email: opanchuk@amcham.ua
Web: www.amcham.kiev.ua

BC Toms & Co
London office
64 London Wall
London
EC2M 5TP
UK
Tel: +44 (0) 207 638 7711
Fax: +44 (0) 207 382 9360
Contact: BC Toms, Iness Krasnokutskaya
Email: bt@bctoms.com
Web: www.bctoms.net

Kyiv office
18/1 Prorizna Street, Office 1
Kyiv 01034
Ukraine
Tel: +380 44 228 1000/490 6000
Fax: +380 44 228 6508
Email: kyiv@bctoms.net
Contact: BC Toms, Taras Dumych, Svitlana Kheda
Web: www.bctoms.net

Institute for Reform
14-B Dimitrova Street
03150 Kyiv
Ukraine
Tel: +380 44 220 5151
Fax: +380 44 246 6525
Contact: Markiyan Dacyshyn
Email: marko@ir.org.ua
Web: www.ir.org.ua

International Finance Corporation (IFC)
3rd Floor
4 Bohomoltsya Street
Kyiv 01024
Ukraine
Tel: +380 44 253 0539
Contact: Roman Zyla
Email: Rzyla@ifc.org
Contact: Bohdan Senchuk
Email: bsenchuk@ifc.org
Web: www.ifc.org

Investment Company 'ITT-invest'
30 Fizkultury Street,
Kyiv, Ukraine, 03150
Tel. +380 44 2466841, +380 44 2466842
Fax +380 44 2272112
Contact: Mr Vladimir Piddubniy
Email: vi@itt-invest.kiev.ua
Email: office@itt-invest.kiev.ua
Web: www.itt-invest.kiev.ua

KPMG
11, Mykhailivska Street
01001 Kyiv, Ukraine
Tel: +380 44 490 5507
Fax: +380 44 490 55 08
Contact: Mason Tokarz, Managing Partner
E-mail: MTokarz@kpmg.kiev.ua
Contact: Rob Shantz, Tax & Legal director
Email: rshantz@kpmg.kiev.ua

Mykhaylo Kuzmin
Energobank
9/9 Lyuteranska Str.
Ukraine 01001
Tel: +380 44 201 6935
Fax: +380 44 228 3954
Email: kuzmin@energobank.com.ua

Dr David Marples
11719 Edinboro Road
Edmonton
Alberta
Canada T6G 1Z9
Tel (home): +1 780 439 9912
Tel (office): +1 780 905 8859
Email: David.Marples@ualberta.ca

Miratech Software
41 Nauki Ave
Kyiv 03028
Ukraine
Tel: +380 44 206 4090
Fax: +380 44 206 4091
Contact: Nikolay Royenko, President
Email: info@miratech-software.com
Web: www.miratech-software.com

Munk Andersen & Feilberg
JM Moerks Gade 1
DK-8000 Aarhus C
Denmark
Tel: +45 70 22 8455/86 18 2507
Contact: Christian B Christensen, Partner
Email: cbc@mafcon.dk
Contact: Bo Eske Nyhus, Partner
Email: ben@mafcon.dk
Web: www.mafcon.dk

Raiffeisen Bank
40, Vorovskogo Street
01054 Kyiv
Ukraine
Tel: +380 44 490 0545/00
Contact: Margarita Drobot, Public Relations & Marketing
Email: margarita.drobot@rbu-kiev.raiffeisen.at
Web: www.raiffeisenbank.com

Softjourn Inc
39270 Paseo Padre Pkwy
Suite 251
Fremont
CA 94538
USA
Tel: +1 510 744 1528
Contact: Ms Emmy Gengler, CEO
Email: emmy.gengler@softjourn.com

TECHINVEST
16/15 Vyborzka Street
Kyiv 03056
Ukraine
Tel: +380 44 461 8882
Fax: +380 44 461 8883
Contact: Ihor Semenov, Investment Manager
Email: is@techinvest.com.ua
Web: www.techinvest.com.ua

Marat Terterov
C/o GMB Publishing Ltd
120 Pentonville Road
London N1 9JN
UK
Tel: +44 7931 383 336
Email: m-terterov@ftnetwork.com

UCELA
8, 40A, Bratyslavska St
02166 Kyiv
Ukraine
Tel: +380 44 518 8423
Tel: +380 50 358 5003
Contact: Sergiy Maslichenko
Email: maslichenko@yahoo.co.uk

Ukrainian Mobile Communications (UMC)
Tel: +380 50 110 3106
Contact: Andriy Hunder, PR Manager
Email: hunder@umc.com.ua
Web: www.umc.ua

US–Ukraine Foundation
Community Partnerships Project
733 15th Street, NW, Suite 1026
Washington, DC 20005
Tel: + 380 44 290 7912/290 6563
Web: www.usukraine.org

Index

References in *italic* indicate figures or tables

Index of Advertisers